THE LAND OF THE VEDA

THE

LAND OF THE VEDA:

INDIA BRIEFLY DESCRIBED

IN SOME OF ITS ASPECTS,
PHYSICAL, SOCIAL, INTELLECTUAL AND MORAL

BY THE

REV. PETER PERCIVAL

GYAN

Published by

Gyan Publishing House
5, Ansari Road
Daryaganj, New Delhi-110002
Phone: 011-47034999, 9811692060
E-mail: books@gyanbooks.com

Distribution Network
gyanbooks.com
India, USA, Canada, UK, Australia, France

ISBN: 978-81-212-8200-0 (PB)
First Published, 1854

2nd Impression 2023

Printed at: Gyan Press, Delhi.

THE LAND OF THE VEDA
Author: PETER PERCIVAL

THE LAND OF THE VEDA.

BISHOP'S COLLEGE, CALCUTTA.

THE

LAND OF THE VEDA:

INDIA BRIEFLY DESCRIBED

IN SOME OF ITS ASPECTS,

PHYSICAL, SOCIAL, INTELLECTUAL AND MORAL;

INCLUDING THE SUBSTANCE OF

A Course of Lectures

DELIVERED AT

ST. AUGUSTINE'S MISSIONARY COLLEGE, CANTERBURY.

BY THE

REV. PETER PERCIVAL.

LONDON:

GEORGE BELL, 186, FLEET STREET.

1854.

PREFACE.

A WORD relative to the origin of this little volume may not be out of place.

His present directors, the Committee of the Society for the Propagation of the Gospel in Foreign Parts, thinking that the writer's past experience in missionary work among the Hindus,—a work in which he has spent the greater part of his life,—might prove beneficial to the missionary students of the College of St. Augustine, decided that he should for some months take up his residence in that institution. He accordingly became an inmate of the College, and remained through Michaelmas Term, 1852, during which period, besides communicating instruction in the rudiments of the Sanscrit—the Sacred language of the Hindus—to a select class, he delivered a series of Lectures on India and its Evangelization, in the College Hall. They were attended, not only by the authorities and students of the institution, but by ladies and gentlemen from the neighbourhood. Several of those who heard the Lectures, as well as other friends who have seen the manuscript, have expressed opinions favourable to their publication. Under these circumstances, the writer was induced to prepare the present work for the press.

It is not professed that the volume contains much that is new or original on the subjects of which it treats, nor does it lay any claim to literary merit. It must be regarded only as a brief sketch of the subjects it comprehends. The object of the work is to supply information respecting India, its people, and their condition, in such a form and to such an extent as may, it is hoped, contribute to awaken interest where little may have been felt, and to produce among the friends of missions in the Church of England a deeper sympathy and greater effort in behalf of the Hindus and other Eastern nations, whose intellectual and moral improvement demands from the Church of Christ greater earnestness and self-sacrifice. The volume will, no doubt, prove acceptable to those clergy who are endeavouring to promote the missions of the Church.

It is distinctly to be understood that the authorities connected with the College of St. Augustine are in no degree responsible for the sentiments contained in this volume. Neither before nor after delivery were the Lectures which form its substratum subjected to their remark or criticism, and therefore the writer alone must be held accountable for the opinions expressed. It is the more necessary that this be borne in mind, because the present volume, though it includes the substance of the addresses delivered at St. Augustine's, contains additional matter, and the arrangement is altogether new.

Some of his readers, aware that the leading Protestant Missionary Institutions of Great Britain, Germany, and the United States of America have numerous agents in the field under review, may wonder that the writer has made so little reference in the following pages to the state of Missions generally; and possibly his old friends and fellow-labourers may think the omission unworthy of one who knows how much of Catholic feeling prevails among Christian missionaries in India and Ceylon. When, however, it is recollected that the Lectures were prepared for delivery in the Hall of a Missionary College belonging to the Church of England, and that the present volume is designed chiefly for that communion, it will be felt that the proper course to be pursued, under the circumstances, was the one adopted. Those who may desire general information relative to the results of missionary labour in India, may find it in a valuable article contained in one of the numbers of the Calcutta Review, which has been published in a separate form in England.

In the preparation of this volume, the writer has been materially aided by various valuable works, which have been written by different authors, on the country and people to which it relates, and particularly by the numerous articles contained in the able Review already mentioned. Colebrooke's Essays, Elphinstone's History of India, Dr. Duff's India, Hough's Christianity in India, Sir Emerson Tennent's Christianity in Ceylon, Phillips's Missionary Vade Mecum, and other valuable sources of information, have been carefully consulted.

The Lithographic Prints and the Engravings have been prepared by the first artists, and it is hoped they will prove satisfactory to those who have encouraged the publication of the work.

Care has been taken to make the Map as complete as possible. It is arranged so as to be useful as a language map, and also for reference to the missionary stations of the Church of England. The proposed lines of railways are also indicated, and the distances by sea to places connected with steam navigation.

I have to acknowledge my obligations to the Society for the Propagation of the Gospel in Foreign Parts, and also to the Church Missionary Society, for the use of several engravings which give additional value to the book; and also to Richard Clarke, Esq., the Secretary of the Royal Asiatic Society, for access not only to the library of that body, but to his own private collection of valuable books on India; and also for the use of models, &c., which, by means of photography, have been made subservient to the illustration of the volume.

Feeling, as he does, his inability to treat adequately the important subjects now offered to the public, the writer would indulge a hope that his readers, bearing in mind that this is his first attempt at authorship in his own language, will kindly restrain the severities of criticism.

LONDON, *August* 15, 1854.

CONTENTS.

CHAPTER I.

CHAPTER II.

CHAPTER III.

CHAPTER IV.

CHAPTER V.

CHAPTER VI.

CHAPTER VII.

CHAPTER VIII.

CHAPTER IX.

CHAPTER X.

CHAPTER XI.

CHAPTER XII.

CHAPTER XIII.

CHAPTER XIV.

CHAPTER XV.

CHAPTER XVI.

CHAPTER XVII.

CHAPTER XVIII.

CHAPTER XIX.

CHAPTER XX.

THE

LAND OF THE VEDA.

CHAPTER I.

INTRODUCTORY REMARKS.—INDIA DEFINED.—ITS SCENERY, FERTILITY, PRODUCTIONS.—COMMERCE WITH ARABIA, PERSIA, EGYPT, PHŒNICIA, GREECE, ROME, CONSTANTINOPLE, BAGDAD, VENICE, LISBON, AND HOLLAND.—THE ENGLISH—THEIR CONQUESTS IN INDIA, ADVANTAGES AND RESPONSIBILITIES.

THE Land of the Veda, a designation which is intended to comprehend the continent of India, is certainly one of the most interesting portions of the world. In respect to area and population it is but little inferior to Europe; and since it includes within its boundaries the characteristics both of the tropical and temperate zones, it possesses greater natural resources. Indeed, its diversified physical features, climates and capabilities, constitute it an epitome of the globe. In a commercial point of view no country, whether of ancient or modern times, can be compared to it in importance; and as it is the largest territory that has ever been placed under a foreign sceptre, so it is unquestionably the most valuable appendage of the British Empire.

Under other aspects bearing on the history of the human race, India presents to us features not less remarkable. Its primitive manners; its original civilization; its refined languages; its civil and religious institutions; its mythological and legendary traditions; its dramatic and heroic poems; its magnificent temples and numerous architectural monuments; as well as other matters, pertaining to the social and religious condition of man, are of deep interest. It can hardly be said that we know the history of mankind, while unacquainted with the condition of the Hindus; a people, in number equal to a sixth portion of the inhabitants of our planet; and who have brought down to our own times the language, literature, and institutions that their ancestors possessed when Moses was a student in the sister-country, Egypt.

There are yet other aspects under which the Land of the Veda may be viewed, that to those who are likely to take an interest in this volume, will not be less impressive. Whilst fully participating with the statesman, the philosopher, and the political economist, in the sentiments they may indulge in regard to the importance of India as a source of national aggrandisement, and as a sphere for commercial enterprise, and philosophical research into subjects of an archæological nature, the enlightened philanthropist cannot overlook the moral wants of the country, nor the claims its population has on the sympathies and efforts of the Christian Church. True it is that her territorial possessions in India are of vast importance to the British nation; and equally so that the social, literary, and scientific concernments of the Hindus are deeply interesting to the scholar; but it is also true that, notwithstanding the manifold features of attractiveness the prospect wears in these respects, the people of India, generally, are greatly debased: they are the victims of religious error, and enslaved by an ancestral faith and social institutions of the most degrading character. Under these circumstances the Christian, be his station what it may, will not be satisfied merely because the secular objects connected with our paternal and beneficent rule are secured to the country; he will extend his regards further, and seek the spiritual interests, and consequently the evangelization of its inhabitants, as the most important object to be achieved. Whilst blinding ignorance and brutalizing superstition enslave their deluded votaries, and foul and cruel rites pollute and disgrace that fair country, he cannot cease to strive for the diffusion among the people of the "saving health," designed, as he believes, for all nations.

The matter of Christian duty may be placed in another light. If it be admitted—and it is thought that history, sacred and profane, alike compel the admission—that "true religion is not only the source and measure of national prosperity, but the very end of national existence," it may be consistently assumed that patriotism will combine with Christian sentiment in the attempt to promote its extension at home and throughout the empire. And since, in the course of providence, India, with its population of more than one hundred and fifty millions, has been placed under the rule of a Christian government, it can scarcely be doubted for what end this enlarged empire has been vouchsafed in view of the principle just enunciated, and the necessities of those who are brought within the sphere of our influence.

As regards the connexion that subsists between this country and India, the history of the past may be added to the motives which principle supplies, to urge on the attention of the British Church the promulgation of Christianity among its inhabitants. It has been stated as a fact of history, "that whatever city, or nation, has, in the lapse of past ages, held in its hands the keys of Indian commerce and Indian influence, that city or nation has, for the time being, stood forth in the van of the civilized world as the richest and most flourishing." If this position cannot be gainsaid, then surely it behoves Britain to weigh well the conditions under which she now possesses the advantages her connexion with India confers: for on her fidelity in the fulfilment of those conditions must depend the continuance of the favours she enjoys. No one who believes in the divine inspiration of the Sacred Scriptures will question the truth of this sentiment: it is, in part at least, for its enforcement that the present work is offered to the Christian public.

There can be no doubt that one great reason why so little is attempted in certain quarters for the conversion of India, is the lack of information respecting its condition, and its claims on Christian sympathy. There appears no ground to believe that where right views of duty are entertained by the earnest Christian, any reluctance in its performance will be shown when self-sacrifice and aid are required. It is fair to conclude that, if it can be proved that a beneficent act is demanded under circumstances authorizing the belief that good can thereby be accomplished, few will withhold their aid if it be within their power to afford it. In the course of the following pages it will be made to appear, I think, that in India there is not only an urgent necessity for the ameliorating doctrines of Christianity, but facilities for their promulgation of the most encouraging kind; so that the command that enjoins duty in this behalf, proportioned to opportunity, must be felt to be binding. The information concerning the condition of the Hindus, and the progress of the Gospel among them, now offered for consideration, may, it is hoped, induce a more active and enlarged charity, and thereby augment the means which the Church employs for their intellectual and moral regeneration.

In furtherance of the object attempted in this little volume, it is thought that a few pages may be devoted to the physical characteristics of the country, its boundaries, extent, scenery, productions, and other kindred matters, which require to be known in order to a correct estimate of our Indian Empire, and its inhabitants. Such information must however be supplied in the briefest possible way, and ought to be regarded, like the work itself, as a mere epitome of the subject to which it relates.

With a view to facilitate an acquaintance with India physically and geographically, a map has been attached to this volume, whose outline it may be convenient to trace.

India may be defined by the Himalaya, the rivers Indus and Brahmaputra, and the sea. It consists of a large triangular peninsula, with the sea on the east and west. To the north is a vast alluvial plain, which stretches to the foot of the Himalaya mountains. The triangular and elevated region, of which the eastern and western ghauts with the Vindya mountains form the outline, may possibly have been an island at some remote period, before the alluvial deposits formed the valleys through which the Indus and the Ganges now flow. From the remote north to Cape Comorin the length of India is about 1,900 miles; and from the Indus to the Brahmaputra it is at least 1,500 miles. The mountain barrier to the north, which in some of its peaks rises to a height of 27,000 feet above the sea, is impenetrable except at its eastern and western extremities. At those extremities openings exist through which the two mighty rivers, which bound India east and west, flow. The Indus runs through the Punjaub, Scinde, and the adjacent provinces, conveying to the Arabian Sea 80,000 cubit feet of water per second. The plain of the Ganges, extending in an easterly direction, is remarkable for its magnitude and fertility; it is 1,200 miles in length and 600 miles in breadth. This magnificent territory within its ample sweep sustains a population nearly twice as numerous as is to be found in the whole of North and South America. On the southern limit of the Gangetic plain may be traced the Vindya chain of mountains, to the south of which are several large rivers as the Godavery, the Nerbudda, the Tapty, the Cauvery, &c. The Vindya mountains, with the ghauts on the east and west of the peninsula, bound the diamond-form country called the Deckan, and containing the countries of Mysore, Hyderabad, Berar, and the Mahratta territories.

India Proper may be said to comprise, on the west, Cashmere, the Punjaub, and Scinde, a separating and unmitigated central desert; on the east, the plain of the Ganges; and on the south, the Deckan.

A continent like India, possessing such a diversity of physical feature, including the loftiest mountains on the globe as well as majestic rivers, cannot fail to be distinguished in its scenery. The Himalaya range presents magnificent mountains, clothed to the very summit with gigantic rhododendrons and numerous other flowering trees that diffuse the most extraordinary radiance, glowing with tints of the finest brilliance and beauty. Amid the ghauts of Southern India, where the scenery is proverbially grand, the hills and slopes are densely crowded with primeval forests of the most valuable timber. In my journeys in the south, I have often passed through natural scenery that riveted me to the spot, and compelled the tribute of silent admiration. Where lofty mountains looming in the distance, rising many thousand feet above the surrounding plains, rugged and diversified heights clothed with the richest vegetation, gentle slopes terminating in the rural beauty of woodland heights, grassy plains skirted by variegated and wild jungle, amid the music of distant cascades, mountain torrents, gushing streams, and gentle rivulets—where such attributes of nature combine to form the scenes that surround the traveller, it cannot be that he can remain unimpassioned. In India nature is invested with the most charming aspects: the qualities of beauty and magnificence are blended in their finest combinations; these everywhere, amid mountain scenery, meet the eye, affect the fancy, and fire the imagination. The Himalaya, the prince of hills, with its lofty peaks surpassing the clouds and towering in the pure fields of ether, is the most majestic feature of our globe. In less lofty regions towards the south, the expanding valleys, the green heights, the stately forests, the flowers, the mountain streams, the birds, the insects, as I have passed along have often affected my sensibilities in the most delightful manner, and raised the mind to the far more glorious though invisible Being who originated them.

The rivers of India add to the beauty and grandeur of its scenery, and also enrich its soil. The sacred Ganges, venerated from generation to generation, and still the theme of pilgrims and devout travellers, in its sublime descent from the everlasting hills, spreads life and beauty throughout the length and breadth of the wide sweeping valleys that receive its fertilizing streams. The reports which travellers have given of the beauty of India are not to be regarded as fancy pictures, exaggerated statements, wherein descriptive power has thrown over scenes comparatively tame a brilliant colouring, in order to magnify common objects into the marvellous. The physical features of that vast country are in point of grandeur and beauty equal to the finest regions in the world; description, however vivid, can but inadequately paint the splendid reality.

With the exception of the great desert lying between the table-land and the plain of the Indus, the soil possesses an inexhaustible fertility. In the plains are found all the productions of the tropics, and on the hills all the productions of the temperate zone; and beyond these, in the lofty range of the Himalayas, arctic productions everywhere meet the eye. Far from possessing a homogeneous character, either in soil or climate, India is diversified by all the characteristics incident to the tropical, temperate, and arctic regions, and consequently yields every diversity of wealth. In its physical aspects and capabilities, India may with truth be regarded as an epitome of the entire habitable globe. The diversities of climate arising in other countries from their relative distance from the equator, are here realized by the varied altitudes of the earth's surface; consequently, the tropical regions of India yield the grain, the vegetables, the fruits, and the flowers of Europe, as well as those peculiar to hot countries. Such is the fertility of the soil, that in some parts of the country it yields several crops in the year; and not only supplies the wants of the inhabitants, but permits the exportation of its products, on a large scale. Much of the cultivation is regulated by the periodical rains; and when these are not available artificial irrigation supplies their deficiency. The rivers, the tanks and wells are used for this purpose. The sides of the hills in the Himalayas and in the ghauts are brought into cultivation, as well as the plains and the flat alluvial deposits; they are arranged in successive terraces, and watered by the mountain streams diverted for that purpose into the cultivated plots. To promote vegetation by artificial irrigation much is done by the natives themselves, in the formation of canals from the rivers, as in some parts of Egypt, by forming immense reservoirs, and also by digging wells. The Government, too, has executed immense works in various provinces, whereby the periodical rains are distributed for the irrigation of extensive tracts, that, but for these artificial provisions, would be partially, if not altogether, unproductive.

After what has been said of the fertility of the soil and the diversities of the climate by which India is characterised, it is almost unnecessary to enumerate its varied productions. Whatever Providence has provided in other parts of the world for the comfort of human life, may here be found in profusion. Articles of food of every kind are abundant and cheap. The staple food in the upper provinces of India are wheat and barley, which in that region may be produced in any quantity, and are procurable in the bazars. In the high lands of the Mysore, above the ghauts, the people generally feed on various kinds of small grain, regarded by them as much more nutritious than rice, which forms the principal aliment in Bengal and the maritime provinces of Southern India. The chief articles of diet, wheat, barley, maize, rice, and a great variety of vegetables and fruits, are, as the different provinces favour their respective production, found in abundance.

Sugar-cane may be produced in any part of India, and it is said to attain maturity in half the time it requires in the West Indies. This product is not only used for sugar, of which immense quantities are exported to western countries and to Australia, but a coarse kind is cultivated and sold as a vegetable. Sugar is also manufactured from the juice of the palmyra and date-trees; I have heard of the juice of cocoa-nut palm, too, being used for the same purpose.

Cotton is extensively cultivated, and enormous quantities are consumed by the inhabitants. It being used not only for the various purposes to which it is applied by Europeans, but also in place of flax, wool, and other raw materials, the quantity required in India is in greater proportion than in Europe and America. The cultivation for home consumption is, of course, large, but nothing in comparison of what it might be, if facilities were afforded for its conveyance to the coast. Several varieties are produced in Bengal, the Upper Provinces, Bombay, and the Deckan. Under favouring circumstances, it is believed that India would not only supply its own population with the article, but also the greater part of Europe. It may be hoped that the report of Mr. Mackay, the cotton commissioner, who has presented for the consideration of the Manchester-men a vast amount of valuable information, may lead to greater encouragement in behalf of the culture of this invaluable product.

Tobacco is cultivated extensively, and large quantities are consumed. India is said to rival every other country in its growth of opium. The revenue derived from the exportation of this deleterious article is immense. The mode in which the revenue is raised from opium in the Bengal territories, and the position which the East India Company occupies with respect to it, are points which have excited considerable attention among those who are anxious to promote our political morality.

Silk is generally supposed to have been imported into India from China; yet there is every reason to conclude that it is indigenous to the former. Several articles of dress made from this material, as is proved by very ancien records, have been always worn by the Hindus; and the cultivation of the mulberry is as ancient as the growth of rice.

Though we may not attempt an enumeration of all the articles India produces, a few may be added to the above-mentioned. Its timber, suited both for cabinet and building purposes, is equally varied and valuable;—teak, sal, sisu, satin-wood, ebony, rose-wood, sandal-wood; palms of every description, as the palmyra, the cocoa-nut, the areca, the date, the sago, and the wonderful talipot—whose magnificent leaf is large enough for an ample canopy,—and other trees far too numerous to include in this brief reference to the productions of the soil. The banyan-tree may not, however, be omitted. This extraordinary production is found in almost every part of India and Ceylon. I know one of immense extent, that consists of a combination of separate trunks of great size, each being a dependent shoot growing perpendicularly from an upper arm, and taking root, thus becoming at once an auxiliary and daughter-tree among the innumerable sister-stems around it. From the margin of this

sylvan temple I entered through an opening like one of the arches of a cathedral, and passed under the shade of its overhanging foliage, as if the path had been leading through a forest. This wonderful specimen of vegetation, like many of the kind which I have seen, was consecrated to purposes of idolatry, and contained a rude stone, smeared with oil or clarified butter, as the venerated object of worship.

The spices of India include some of our most valuable

dietetics, as pepper, cinnamon, nutmegs, and ginger. Well known and most valuable aromatics are found on the wildest hills, and yield some of the most costly of the scented oils; camphor, cassia, aloes, and other ingredients of the Materia Medica; as also useful resins, gums, and varnishes, are among the productions of this wonderful country. Of the Indian Flora we cannot speak, except by way of reference to the variety and beauty of both wild and cultivated specimens. The forests and jungles afford to the botanist a rich exhibition, in the endlessly diversified objects that crowd on the attention. The giant creepers are very remarkable, frequently forming graceful festoons from the branches of the lofty denizens of the forest. The oleander and the *gloriosa superba* grow wild in the open country. The beautiful lotus, so rich in its tints and delicate in structure, is a most elegant flower, not only remarkable as one of the frequent objects referred to by the Hindu poet, but as the floating shrine of a popular divinity.

The fruits of India are numerous, and many of them used in abundance even by the poorest. The delicious mangoe and the wholesome banana, are common in every part of the country. Oranges, limes, citrons, pine-apples, figs, custard apples, and grapes, are easily raised. On the high lands in the peninsula and in the Mysore country, the peach, the apricot, the nectarine, apples, pears, and strawberries, are among the luxuries that serve to remind the European, amid the peculiarities of an Eastern clime, of the land of his nativity. On the Shevroy Hills, not distant more than eighty miles from the Eastern sea, I was informed by a gentleman resident there, that he had seen eighteen varieties of fruit, European and tropical, on the table at the same dessert.

To enumerate the animals found in India would be to repeat the names of all the tribes in Natural History. The elephant,[1] the rhinoceros, the bison, the wild buffalo,

[1] In the course of my missionary tours I have often met with elephants in the jungles and open plains, but when they have been in

tigers,[1] chetas, leopards, panthers, bears, wild hogs, hyenas, wolves, and jackals abound. Game of every description exists in all parts of the country. Monkeys in great variety are seen

herds I have never felt the least fear, they being considered quite harmless when found in company. The natives, however, generally manifest great reluctance to proceed when it is apprehended that these formidable creatures may be in the way. On more than one occasion, I have been unable to induce my native companions to venture onwards, and once I was obliged to take up my lodging in a tree, being several miles from the nearest house. The elephant that has been deserted by the herd is an exceedingly vicious and most dangerous animal. When travelling on foot in company with several natives in a dense jungle, there being only a narrow path sufficient for one person to walk in, one of these isolated elephants suddenly rushed out upon us and caused no little consternation, as may be imagined. Each person took to flight, and escaped into the trees. While I was there, where I was obliged to wait a long time, a couple of bears came into my vicinity and were quarrelling for some time. Only a few days before, a postal runner had been killed by an elephant, most likely the one that I encountered.

A very remarkable circumstance occurred not many years back, at an elephant hunt, in the district of Coimbatore, one of the provinces of Southern India. On enclosing a number of elephants in a ring fence, it was discovered that one of them bore marks of having been tamed. On the word of command being given, the animal obeyed, and, as in obedience to one of the initiated, she knelt down, he mounted her and rode out of the herd. About three weeks afterwards she gave birth to a young one, which was of a light pink or fawn colour, called by the natives a *white elephant.* Knowing that a white elephant is held in great esteem by the Burmese, the Government of India directed the animal to be sent to the King of Ava. The absence of the colouring matter in the skin and eye produced the albino species of elephant here noticed.

[1] I have heard of instances of the Bengal tiger leaping on board a boat and carrying off one of the men. Two missionary brethren on one occasion saw an interesting rencounter between a tiger and an alligator, on the margin of a stream in the Sunderbunds below Calcutta. The alligator was lying partially out of the water with his head on the mud, as is their wont, and the tiger, after eyeing him for some time, sprang from the bank, a considerable height above the stream, upon the alligator, and after a severe struggle captured him, and carrying him as a cat would carry a rat, bore away his victim into the jungle.

I saw the skin of a tiger at Bancoora, in Bengal, that had destroyed as many as eleven persons.

in the open country as well as in the jungles, and are often attached to the temples even in cities. In Madras they are numerous, where they may be seen on the towers of the temples and also on the tops of private dwellings, often proving exceedingly troublesome to the inmates from their mischievous habits. They do not hesitate entering a house through a window or door, and sometimes they carry away not only articles of food, but even trinkets; I know an instance of one of these troublesome creatures carrying off a gentleman's gold watch. Porcupines, ichneumons, armadillos, iguanas, and lizards of every form, are very numerous. The serpent[1] tribe and other reptiles, some of which are venomous and even deadly in their bite, may be seen almost daily. Not unfrequently are these seen in human dwellings, and many natives lose their lives from their bite. Alligators abound in some of the rivers and lagoons. I have seen scores in the course of an evening's walk in East Ceylon.[2] Birds of every description may be seen among the branches of trees, floating in the air, and in attendance at the homesteads of the inhabitants. Some of them are distinguished for the extreme richness of their plumage. In the maritime provinces and in the Mysore are found innumerable specimens of the feathered tribes, many of them singularly beautiful, but these are

[1] A friend of mine in North Ceylon, when out in the jungle, fell in with a boa constrictor coiled round a deer which it had killed, and was in the act of preparing it for deglutition. The gentleman discharged his piece at the monster and killed it; I saw the skin.

[2] The back-water, the lagoons, and canals connected therewith, frequently abound with alligators. In my journeys I have often, on fording sheets of water by night, driven off those monsters by splashing the water with a staff, carrying a torch, and have seen them plunging about in every direction. I have heard of numerous persons being devoured by these animals. Like the tiger, when once they have tasted human flesh they are ever on the alert to obtain it. I have heard that when a wedding party was passing along on a back-water on the western coast of India, one of these brutes raised its head out of the water and seized the side of the shallow boat, when one of the party fell overboard, and the alligator disappeared with the bride.

greatly surpassed by the superb and brilliant specimens to be met with in that treasure-house, the Himalayas. In some of my journeys I have seen ten or a dozen peacocks in a single tree. Flocks of parrots are frequently seen. Vultures, falcons, and kites are very common. Fish abound in all the rivers and tanks; and on all the shores of the peninsula salt-water fish may be had in abundance. Poultry may be obtained in every part of the country at moderate prices. Horses are easily procured. The Arab, the Persian horse, the Pegu or Acheen pony, and latterly horses have been imported from Australia, as they have long been, (though not in large numbers,) from the Cape of Good Hope. The European and native gentry have splendid saddle and draught horses.

The giant forests of useful trees, such as the teak, the sal, the oak; the topes of cocoa-nut and Palmyra palms, and the endless variety of vegetable productions that solicit appropriation at the hands of man, are associated with other kinds of natural wealth, which may here be specified. India is not only furnished with a rich supply of useful articles above ground, but enriched likewise beneath the surface. Fields of coal, beds of copper, lead, and iron, invite attention, and promise their valuable help so soon as the arts and manufactures of the country shall apply mechanical power.

Pearls are among the precious things which the deep brings forth. The pearl fishery in the Bay of Condatchy some years ago yielded in one season about 40,000*l.* sterling. Ivory is exported from India and Ceylon to England. Precious stones are among the minerals of that wonderful country. Diamonds, the largest and most valuable in the world, have come from the mines of India; and now at length we are informed that gold has been discovered in Taprobane. Thus we realize the language of Milton in the British possessions of the East, which in ancient times

> "Shower'd o'er her kings barbaric pearl and gold."

The resources of India are almost boundless; her natural

products and her textile fabrics are equally celebrated for richness and magnificence. Her raw material, so varied and valuable, has from time immemorial been worked up into the finest articles of dress. Her machines constructed for manufacturing purposes, and her tools and implements for agricultural uses, are of the simplest possible kind; and whilst they serve as memorials of an ancient civilization, demonstrate the skill and intelligence of those who have produced, by means of such appliances, effects so wonderful. The elegance and perfection of her manufactures have from the remotest times challenged the admiration, and invited the intercourse of civilized nations. Egypt, Persia, and Arabia, in the earliest periods of the world derived their luxuries from this extraordinary country. Some of her manufactures are, notwithstanding the advancement made in machinery, still unequalled. In the delicacy, fineness, and transparency of texture therein displayed, the muslins of Dacca defy the imitation of Manchester manufacturers. They are doubtless the finest instances to be found in the world of the production of a difficult effect by means apparently quite inadequate. The shawls of Cashmere are wonderful. The carpets of Mirzapore and some of the silk fabrics manufactured in Bengal are among the most valuable products of the kind brought to market.

A country so vast, possessing such diversities of climate and so many articles of luxury, could not fail to attract the attention of ancient as well as modern nations. The Arabian peninsula and Persia were favourably situated for Indian commerce, and we are informed by history that their navigators availed themselves at a very early period of the benefits which its merchandise offered to their enterprise. The Phœnicians, not content to receive the luxuries of the East by the long route established along the desert of Arabia through Petra and Palmyra, prepared a fleet on the Red Sea, and established a direct communication between ancient Tyre and India. Alexandria subsequently became the emporium of the same trade, and transmitted to Greece and other countries of the Mediterranean the precious products of India. Arrian, the biographer of Alexander, informs us that the fleet placed under the command of Nearchus "was equipped for the specific purpose of opening the direct intercourse between India and Alexandria." When, after the lapse of ages, Alexandria fell into the hands of the Romans, it continued to maintain its commercial importance, and long enjoyed the advantages which the wealth of India conferred on it.

The commercial intercourse that was carried on with India by the merchants of Imperial Rome, is alluded to in one of Pliny's Letters, wherein he complains that such was the taste for the luxuries of the East, that Indian commerce had emptied Italy of its gold. In accordance with the fact here stated I may remark, that a short time ago, when in Tinnevelly, I saw several gold coins belonging to the period of the Emperors, bearing the images of Julius Cæsar, Caligula, and Tiberius; these coins had been discovered in one of the rivers of western India. The images and the superscriptions were beautifully perfect. In other parts of India, and in Ceylon also, especially in the neighbourhood of the pearl banks, Greek and Roman coins have frequently been found: from the progress made in the numismatics of India considerable light is now being shed on its history. As the commercial capital of the Roman empire, Alexandria was equally distinguished by its architectural monuments, opulence, splendour, and population. The valuable productions of India and other eastern countries were the source of its grandeur.

When the empire of the Cæsars was superseded by the fanatical followers of the warrior-prophet of Arabia, and the crescent took the place of the eagle, Bagdad became the commercial capital of the Mohammedan conquerors. These indomitable warriors subdued the realms of Imperial Rome, and possessed themselves of the commerce long enjoyed by its citizens from the Mediterranean Sea to the remotest parts of India. When in the course of political changes the Mohammedan empire was broken up and became enfeebled by division, the commerce of the East partook of the same character, and Alexandria resumed somewhat of its former consequence. The same traffic revived the cities of Syria, and gave new importance to Constantinople. The revival of commerce in these more northern regions arose from the opening up of the route lying through the countries stretching from the Black Sea to the Indus and the Oxus. Concurrently with the progress of eastern commerce in any of these directions, it is remarkable that the same undeviating result attended it; wealth, luxury, splendour, were its certain consequents.

In the course of events, as civilization advanced westward, the jewels, the spices, and the precious fabrics of India, were in demand there also. The taste for these luxuries infused the spirit of improvement into the various arts of social life, and impelled to activity and enterprise those who had hitherto been content to exist on the necessaries of life. Industry was stimulated, and commerce was promoted, because production was the only means of supplying the wants which a growing refinement had created. From the new wants thus excited in Western Europe, there arose a necessity for some more direct communication with the source whence luxuries could be obtained. Hence arose the commercial states of Italy: the cities of Venice and Genoa became the emporia into which the wealth of India and other Eastern commerce flowed; and so long as those cities retained its advantages, they far exceeded all others in their almost unbounded prosperity.

Down to the end of the fifteenth century, the articles which formed the material of Eastern commerce were conveyed, at least in a great part of the route, by overland arrangements; the Red Sea and the Euphrates being made subservient to their transit. Eventually, however, as the art of navigation progressed, Henry of Portugal, whose skill was well fitted for the age in which he lived, discovered the way to India round the Cape of Good Hope, and a new stimulus was given to the trade carried on with India. In 1498 Vasco de Gama made the voyage round Africa, and arrived at Calicut, on the western coast of India. The Portuguese "proposed nothing less than to become immediately the first commercial and maritime power in the world." A bull from "God's Vicegerent" conferred on the Portuguese monarch the proud title of "Lord of the Navigation, Conquests, and Trade of Ethiopia, Arabia, Persia, and India." Thus Portugal attained the envied preeminence then sought, of becoming the chief among commercial states, and because she had possessed herself of the trade of India and other eastern countries.

Her distinction was, however, of short duration, for very soon the industrious and persevering sons of Holland followed in her wake, and for a while shared and eventually superseded the Portuguese both in commercial enterprise and political influence in the eastern seas: the trade of India was transferred from Lisbon to Amsterdam.

It was, however, reserved for England to improve the splendid trade with India, and to confer on its inhabitants the benefit which her free institutions and reformed faith so well fit her to convey. The long and peaceful reign of Elizabeth favoured the growth and extension of her maritime power. Various attempts were made to reach the prize of Indian commerce by some new passage by the north-west, and also the north-east; but all failed. They attempted to seize the dazzling object by the difficult and dangerous navigation by way of Cape Horn. All these efforts had one object—the Indian trade. "The tide of maritime adventure," says the historian of British India, "which these splendid voyages were so calculated to swell, flowed naturally towards India, by reason of its fancied opulence, and the prevailing passion for the commodities of the East. The impatience of our countrymen had already engaged thrice in a circuitous traffic with that part of the globe. They sailed to the eastern shores of the Mediterranean Sea, where they found cargoes of Indian goods conveyed overland; and a mercantile company, denominated the Levant Company, was instituted, according to the policy of the age, to secure to the nation the advantages of so important a commerce." The capture of some of the Portuguese merchant-vessels richly laden with spices, calicos, silks, gold, pearls, porcelain, ebony, &c., "inflamed the imagination of the merchants, and stimulated the impatience of the English generally to be engaged in so opulent a commerce."

In 1599 Elizabeth was petitioned to grant permission to certain parties to engage in the trade with India by the Cape of Good Hope. A royal charter was accordingly granted in 1600, and in May the following year the first fleet of the East India Company sailed for India direct by the southern cape of Africa. And as we now see, not only did the trade of India fall into the hands of the English, but the vast territory also, whose products formed its staple articles. And as time has advanced, England, possessed of the advantages which the wealth of India confers, has gradually risen in wealth and power, till she has acquired a position the most exalted ever attained by any civilized nation. London, the emporium of her trade, now sits undisputably as the queen among the cities of the nations. But that this proud position may not be forfeited, and her national glory diminished, it behoves her to understand the conditions on which she has been put in trust with the mighty interests now in her keeping; else, like Venice, and Lisbon, and Amsterdam, and the commercial cities of antiquity, she too must give place to some other power in the course of commercial and political revolution. It may be hoped that her fidelity in the discharge of her high duty will continue to her the stewardship now subsisting in relation to India.

We have been so long accustomed to view as among the necessaries of life many of the luxuries which eastern commerce has conferred, that we forget their source. Even many of the articles, especially fabrics, that once came from the East are now regarded as home products; silks, cottons, in imitation of Indian manufactures, are now made at home, but the raw material is still foreign. What, if tea, coffee, sugar, and spices were no longer to be obtained? It is impossible for us to estimate the influence which these articles of eastern commerce have had on the national and domestic habits of western countries. It needs not much effort of the imagination to trace the advantages we derive from India. There is not a person in the land, however humble his condition, who has not daily evidence thereof. The food, the raiment, the luxuries enjoyed by the millions of Britain, serve to remind us of the source whence they come, and may well enhance our admiration of that providence that has not only conferred them upon us, but given us the empire of those wealth-creating regions whence so many of them come. A due consideration of these important facts may not only contribute to augment our admiration and our gratitude, but also lead to a more practical evincement of our sense of indebtedness to the nation that has for so many ages poured forth its stores for the enrichment of Europe. May we not hope to convey, in return for material benefits bestowed upon us so abundantly, something of a higher value? For the splendour, the luxury, the opulence that everywhere meet the eye, and for the conveniences and comforts that await us in the course of every day life, serving to remind us of the debt we owe to distant and unknown tribes, we have it in our power to convey a boon of inestimable value—"the word of truth, the gospel of salvation."

However interesting it might prove to narrate the events connected with eastern conquest, that issued in the establishment of the formal routine of a European government on the soil of India, it may not be attempted in these pages. The subjection of the millions of such a vast country, and the expulsion of other Europeans from its shores by a mere handful of British, are, however, among the most extraordinary phenomena of history. The events, civil and military, that have taken place within the last two hundred and fifty years are truly wonderful. That a few foreigners whose home, till modern science shortened the distance by opening the so-called overland route, was some fifteen thousand miles from our shores, should be able to exercise government, preserve peace, administer justice, and regulate the multiplied relationships, internal and external, of so many tribes and people, speaking different languages and entertaining diversified forms of religious belief, may well be regarded as the most astonishing phenomenon that the human mind was ever called to contemplate. That something like forty thousand British should occupy such a relation as we do to a whole continent of diversified nations, and consolidate so many mighty states into one powerful empire, may well excite surprise, and induce the belief that some grand design is thereby destined to be accomplished in the counsels of Heaven.

Whilst the statesman, the politician, the merchant, and the philosopher may each, from his own point of view, behold much of transcendent interest in the past and present as regards India, the devout reader of the Bible discovers a far higher interest that requires his practical attention. He cannot but feel that Divine Providence, in placing in her hands such a power as that which Britain now possesses in India, has designs beyond those which political rule and commercial prosperity confer. True it is that England derives from her connexion with India aggrandisement, wealth, luxury, and splendour; but in return for these it is her duty to convey privileges of a loftier character, riches of a more durable nature. Favoured as she is beyond all the nations of the earth by her central position, her political eminence, and her commercial greatness, with unbounded facilities for communicating whatever she may enjoy to the various tribes of mankind, and blessed above all with the light and life of Revelation, it cannot be conceived that her relations with India, where she rules *one-fifth* of the population of the globe, are only those of a secular nature. Men of wealth, of learning, and of power, may, in pursuing their ends, overlook all but that which pertains to these possessions, and they may be excused if they affect to contemn the objects sought by the Missionary of the Cross, and denounce as visionary all attempts to overcome the prejudices of the Hindus, their ancestral faith, their social institutions; but Christian believers, who take their measures of duty from the inspired volume, must nevertheless aim at the conversion and salvation of the millions of India. They believe that "the kingdoms of the world shall become the kingdoms of God and of his Christ." And they are taught to look for such results, not as produced by miracle, whilst the Church is supine and indifferent, but as the effects of those moral causes with which she is entrusted. As "opportunity" offers, the Christian is to "do good unto all men." The mercies of the Everlasting Covenant, which are to be extended to all the kindreds of the nations, are not to be monopolized by a slothful and self-indulgent indifference to the condition, the danger, and destitution of those whose spiritual interest the Church can advance. India, whose greatness and whose value to us are so apparent, is open to "the messengers of the churches." Facilities for the promotion of Christianity are as great there as in England. There may be difficulties—all but insuperable—in some parts of the world in the way of the Church; but in our Indian empire there are none, except those which error and superstition present; against which the truth of God is commissioned to be made known, and the promised grace of God prayerfully sought. A door, great and effectual, has there been opened to the Church, into which she may enter and take possession of the land in the name of her immortal King. Everything invites to action: "Over the whole of that region of moral darkness, stable and uncontrollable power presides, and that is, the power of a Christian monarchy. There Christian governors legislate, Christian judges and magistrates decree justice, and Christian captains, wielding the sword of power, guarantee security of person and of property. How are we to interpret the *final cause* of such a state of things?" We cannot do better than conclude this chapter in the words of the venerable and revered Daniel Wilson, the Metropolitan of India.

"What can exceed the inviting prospect which India presents? The fields white for the harvest, and awaiting the hand of the reaper! Nations bursting the intellectual sleep of thirty centuries! Superstitions no longer in the giant strength of youth, but doting to their fall! Britain, placed at the head of the most extensive empire ever consigned to a Western sceptre: that is, the only great power of Europe professing the Protestant faith entrusted with the thronging nations of Asia, whom she alone could teach! A paternal government, employing every year of tranquillity in elevating and blessing the people, unexpectedly thrown upon its protection! No devastating plague, as in Egypt; no intestine wars; no despotic heathen or Mohammedan dominion, prowling for its prey: but legislation going forth with her laws; science lighting her lamp; education scattering the seeds of knowledge; commerce widening her means of intercourse; the British power ever ready to throw her ægis around the pious and discreet missionary.

"Oh! where are the first propagators and professors of Christianity? Where are our martyrs and reformers? Where are the ingenuous, devoted, pious sons of our universities? Where are our younger devoted clergy? Are they studying their ease? Are they resolved on a ministry tame, ordinary, agreeable to the flesh? Are they drivelling after minute literature, poetry, fame? Do they shrink from that toil and labour which, as Augustine says, OUR COMMANDER, (Noster Imperator,) accounts most blessed? Let us unite in removing misconceptions; let us join in appealing to societies; let us write to particular friends and public bodies; let us afford correct and intelligible information; let us send specific and individual invitations; and let us pray 'the LORD of the HARVEST,' that He would 'SEND FORTH MORE LABOURERS INTO HIS HARVEST.'"

CHAPTER II.

INDIA—ITS EARLY HISTORY OBSCURE.—MOHAMMEDAN CONQUESTS.—BRITISH SUPREMACY.—INHABITANTS DIVERSIFIED.—ABORIGINES AND HINDUS.—HINDUS, THEIR IMMIGRATION AND PECULIARITIES.—POPULATION, EXTENT, AND DISTRIBUTION.—FURTHER PARTICULARS RESPECTING THE ABORIGINES—HOW THEY DIFFER FROM THE HINDUS.—SUPPOSED ORIGIN OF THE HINDUS.—CASTE, ITS ORIGINAL CHARACTER—ITS SUB DIVISIONS—HOW IT IMPEDES CHRISTIANITY.

THE history of India does not fall within the scope of this work; not even can it be attempted to trace the brief outline of those political events which relate to its progress either in ancient or modern times. The origin of the Hindu nation is involved in mystery, and the events connected with the early dynasties, states, and kingdoms, are but very obscurely indicated in the records of the country. From the national epics something may be inferred regarding the early struggles of a solar and lunar race of kings, but up to the time of Alexander, who invaded India, we have little more than fabulous and mythological data for our guides. Considerable obscurity rests on the history of the Hindus even after the invasion of Alexander; of late, however, as already intimated, some light has been cast on this period by the progress made in the deciphering of ancient coins discovered in various parts of the country. Eventually Mohammedan conquerors overran the provinces of India, and the vast territory was for centuries subject to their despotic sway. The events connected with this period may be seen in the valuable history of India by the Honourable Mountstuart Elphinstone.

It may be stated succinctly, that what the history of the

world was between the earliest settlement of nations to the advent of the Messiah—a series of revolutions, of strifes, of violence, and of bloodshed—till the world found repose in the universal peace of the Roman empire, such was the history of India for three thousand years, when it was emancipated from anarchy and misrule by the conquests of Britain; and now it is blest with tranquillity, and enjoys the advantages of a mild, beneficent, and stable government. The following description from an eloquent author, the Reverend Doctor Duff, is as correct as it is graphic, and may be taken as an epitome of the state of India for many ages:—"At one time divided into a thousand petty states, scowling defiance at each other; here the parricide basely usurping the father's throne; and there the fratricide rescuing the lawful crown from his brother. At another time, split up and parcelled into groups of confederacies, cemented by the bond of indomitable hate, and leaving the retaliation of fell revenge as a legacy to children's children. After ages had rolled their course, in the tenth century of the Christian era, our eyes are turned away from the interior to the far distant north. There the horizon is seen thickening with lurid clouds, that roll their dense masses along the troubled atmosphere. Suddenly the tempest bursts; and one barbarian conqueror issues forth after another. At length the greatest and mightiest of them all, from the hyperborean regions of Tartary, from the gorges of the Indian Caucasus, descends upon the plains of poor unhappy India, proclaiming himself the scourge of God and the terror of men. His path is like the red lightning's course. And speedily he blasts the flower of India's chivalry, and smites into the dust her lordly confederacies. Her villages, and cities, and temples, and palaces, lie smoking in their ruins. Through fields of carnage and rivers of blood, he hastens to prop the sceptre of a universal but transient dominion. All India is made profusely to bleed; and, ere her old wounds are healed, all India is made to bleed afresh. In swift and destructive succession, new imperial dynasties spring up out of the blood and ashes of the old."

Such was the disastrous career of devastating armies, and such the disastrous effects, till the long oppressed tribes of that now peaceful land were freed by the progress of British enterprise. In the course of God's overruling providence, our embassies, our sieges, and our battles, have issued in the subjugation of those who, by their misrule, had so long afflicted the unhappy country in which we now behold the uniform administration of equitable law. As in the times anterior to the advent of the Saviour, the Roman armies prepared the way for the messengers of mercy who were commissioned to publish peace by Jesus Christ, so in these latter days the armies of Britain have in India prepared the way for the introduction of those heaven-derived doctrines which are now gradually diffusing light, and life, and happiness among the emancipated nations that compose our Indian empire.

Being, then, in a position such as that we have attained, it becomes us to survey the extent of the responsibility involved in so weighty a trust. India, that immense territory, with all its resources and its teeming millions, whilst it enhances our power and augments our wealth, entails responsibilities. And that the brightest gem in the crown of our gracious and beloved Queen may never be removed, it behoves us to consider well the condition attached to its position there. Heaven designs Britain to convey to her Indian subjects those hallowed privileges which have been assured to her by a gracious Providence, through a long and arduous struggle, in which the constancy of her confessors, the blood of her martyrs, and the patience of her saints, have been conspicuous. To transfer these holy and heaven-born advantages to those whom she now rules, is the work that more than aught beside will assuredly enhance the glory of Britain. The treasures of the Gospel will be an ample return for the diamonds, and the pearls, and the rubies, wherewith India has enriched us. Assuming, then, as we feel it right to do, that Britain has a solemn and important mission to discharge in regard to the millions placed under her rule in our Eastern empire, it will be natural to inquire into their condition, their wants, and the means at our disposal for their amelioration: on the due consideration of these concernments must depend the strength of our sympathy, and the vigour of our efforts in the work of India's evangelization.

In discussing the subject now before us—the origin and social condition of the inhabitants of India—we have to do with a subject of extreme difficulty, and chiefly because the population is not homogeneous, but diversified in origin, in habit, as well as in religious sentiment and practice. Though the greater part of the inhabitants of India consists of Hindus, or followers of the Brahmanical system of religion, yet in the inaccessible heights among the hills of the country there are scattered tribes amounting to some millions, in a condition of barbarism equalled only among the savages who people the isles of the Pacific. And besides the Hindus and these mountain tribes, there are dispersed abroad in every province at least ten millions of the followers of the false prophet of Arabia. These notices will be sufficient to show that in India there are diversified inhabitants, whose several characteristics need to be considered in order to a due estimate of the condition of our fellow-subjects in that part of the world. It may be convenient here to state, that it is the Brahmanized portion of the population, as forming by far the largest part, that the present volume is designed mainly to present: not that the other races will be overlooked. The Brahmanized or Hindu population is of *Caucasian* origin; it sprang from Central Asia, the parent seat of population, of knowledge, of languages, and of arts. When it entered India, bringing its own language, of which the Sanscrit is the most polished type, it found an aboriginal race in possession of the country. The period of this immigration cannot be ascertained. Assuming that it was anterior to the composition of the Vedas, which are supposed to have been written about the time of the Exodus of the Israelites from Egypt, it would seem that its date was very remote. Speaking of those Brahmanists who entered India and civilized the aborigines, Professor Wilson says:—"That they had extended themselves from a more northern site, or that they were a northern race, is rendered probable from the peculiar expression used on more than one occasion, in soliciting long life, when the worshipper asks for a hundred winters,—a boon not likely to be desired by the natives of a warm climate. They appear also to have been a fair-complexioned people, at least comparatively so, and foreign invaders of India, as it is said that Indra divided the fields among his white-complexioned friends after destroying the indigenous barbarians."

The Hindu invaders brought with them an Indo-Germanic language, closely allied with those of Europe; they subjugated the aborigines they found in the country; and throughout India established municipal institutions. It would further appear that the Hindus did not advance rapidly towards the south, as Manu describes the inhabitants lying south of the twenty-second degree of latitude, as being "barbarians living in forests, and speaking an unknown tongue."

Lieutenant-General Briggs, F.R.S., in a lecture on the aboriginal races of India, has recorded some valuable deductions, and appended thereunto some statistics regarding population, which I shall, for the elucidation of the general subject here transcribe:—

He says,

"The points I desire to establish are—

1. That the Hindus entered India from a foreign country, and that they found it pre-occupied by inhabitants.
2. That by slow degrees they possessed themselves of the whole of the soil, reducing to serfage those they could retain upon it.
3. That they brought with them the Sanscrit language, a tongue different from that of the Aborigines.
4. That they introduced into the country municipal institutions.
5. That the Aborigines differ in every respect from the Hindus.
6. Lastly, that the Aborigines throughout India are derived from one common source.

"In dealing with this subject, I beg to call your attention to the fact, that we have before us a vast field to explore; that India, according to Campbell's statistics, occupies an area exceeding that of Europe, if we exclude Russia, Norway, and Sweden; and that its population, as compared with the same part of Europe, does not fall very far short of it.

	Acres.	Population.
Punjaub	83,006	8,000,000
Saugor	17,543	2,143,599
Bengal	225,103	41,094,325
North-Western Provinces	85,571	23,800,549
Madras	144,889	16,339,426
Bombay and Scinde	120,065	10,485,017
	676,177	101,862,916
Allied States	690,261	52,941,263
	1,366,438	154,804,179

	Acres.	Population.
Europe	2,793,000	227,700,000
Russia, Sweden, Norway	1,758,700	60,518,000
	1,034,300	167,182,000

"In India, as in Europe, there are great national divisions of dialects, each of which extends over a population of several millions."

"Manu, the Hindu legislator, makes specific reference to the race subdued by the supervening and conquering class. The relation they were doomed to occupy is clearly pointed out. In the tenth chapter of his Institutes, it is ordained that,—

> 'Their abode must be out of towns.
> Their sole property is to consist of dogs and asses.
> Their clothes should be those left by the dead.
> Their ornaments rusty iron.
> They must roam from place to place.
> No respectable person must hold intercourse with them.
> They are to perform the office of executioner on all criminals condemned to death by the King.
> For this duty they may retain the bedding, the clothes, and the ornaments of those executed.'"

This race, thus reduced to an abject condition by the Brahmanical conquerors, had, prior to their subjugation, extended themselves throughout India; and there are conclusive proofs of their having attained to a high condition of civilization, so as to form large communities, to establish kingdoms, and besides cultivating the soil, to carry on extensive commerce. Some of their works of art, as castles, excavations, and other monumental ruins, still exist. They must have settled in India at the time of the dispersion, when the germ of the various nations east and west sprang from the patriarchal seat of the human family; the more adventurous possibly subsisting mainly by the chase, whilst the milder and less courageous gave themselves up to the arts of social life.

"In every part of India, where the soil has not yet been reclaimed, are found relics of the abnormal race more or less barbarous; while throughout the land, from Ceylon to Cashmere, they are met with in a state of slavery, consistent with the edicts of the Hindu law." In Bengal and in the South, whether emancipated or in slavery, they live apart from their Hindu neighbours, filling the lowest offices, and possessing no property but dogs and asses. In this condition, however, they perform important services, for which their moral virtues fit them. In the duties of rural police, and in conveying treasure to the offices of revenue in the chief towns, they are singularly faithful. Their general and accurate knowledge of all around them makes them clever in detecting criminals, and in the discharge of this duty they generally disregard family ties, and rarely screen their own relations.

They are singularly expert in the capture of animals. They are excellent guides, and truthful protectors of the traveller within their respective districts. They can track game by their footmarks, and with equal accuracy they trace robbers by the prints made by their bare feet. They are now in appearance, in habit, and occupation what they were when described by Herodotus. The men wear no clothing except what decency enjoins. "The women wear a cloth a yard wide, and from six to twelve yards in length, wrapped round the waist, carried over the left shoulder, and sometimes covering the back part of the head. It is then brought under the right arm, crosses the body, and is tucked in in front, having a very graceful appearance."

The following distinctive features existing between the Aborigines and the Hindus, pointed out by Lieutenant-General Briggs, will prove instructive, being well arranged for the elucidation of this interesting subject :—

"They differ from the Hindus, inasmuch as the Hindus—

1. Are divided into castes.
   The Aborigines have no such distinctions.
2. Hindu widows are forbidden to marry.
   The widows of the Aborigines not only do so, but usually with the younger brother of the late husband,—a practice they follow in common with the Scythian tribes.
3. The Hindus venerate the cow, and abstain from eating beef.
   The Aborigines feed alike on all flesh.
4. The Hindus abstain from the use of fermented liquors.
   The Aborigines drink to excess; and conceive no ceremony, civil or religious, complete without.
5. The Hindus eat of food prepared only by those of their own caste.
   The Aborigines partake of food prepared by any one.
6. The Hindus abhor the spilling of blood.
   The Aborigines conceive no religious or domestic ceremony complete without the spilling of blood and offering up a live victim.
7. The Hindus have a Brahmanical priesthood.
   The Aborigines do not venerate Brahmans. Their own priests [who are self-created] are respected according to their mode of life and their skill in magic and sorcery, in divining future events, and in curing diseases: these are the qualifications which authorize their employment in slaying sacrificial victims, and in distributing them.
8. The Hindus burn their dead.
   The Aborigines bury their dead, and with them their arms, sometimes their cattle, as among the Scythians. On such occasions a victim ought to be sacrificed, to atone for the sins of the deceased.
9. The Hindu civil institutions are all municipal.
   The Aboriginal institutions are all patriarchal.
10. The Hindus have their courts of justice composed of equals.
    The Aborigines have theirs composed of heads of tribes or of families, and chosen for life.
11. The Hindus brought with them [more than three thousand years ago] the art of writing and music.
    The Aborigines are not only illiterate, but it is forbidden for the Hindus to teach them."

This epitome of the peculiar customs of both races, together with the comparison of their physiognomy, establishes beyond doubt their dissimilarity in every respect.

The Aborigine is not more distinguished in his other habits than he is in his moral virtues from the Hindus. The man of the ancient race scorns an untruth; and seldom denies the commission even of a crime that he may have perpetrated, though it lead to death. He is true to his promise, hospitable and faithful to his guest, devoted to his superiors, and is always ready to sacrifice his own life in the service of his chief. He is reckless of danger, and knows no fear. At the same time he is by profession a robber, levying black mail on all from whom he can obtain it, under the plea of his ancient right to the soil, of which more civilized men have deprived him."

It may be well here to state that the religious peculiarities of the Aborigines, which are very remarkable, will require a distinct notice, and they are reserved for review in the subsequent pages of this volume.

The Hindus, the Brahmanized inhabitants of the country, are foreign in their origin. Their civilization, which at a very remote period had attained to great advancement, is not unlike that which prevailed contemporaneously in Persia, Assyria, and Egypt. Whether these countries had any remote connexion does not appear, nor is it possible to trace the origin and early history of the Brahmanical race. The rich alluvial lands of the Nile, the Euphrates, and the Ganges seem to have originated powerful nations, that attained to a high degree of refinement at a period long anterior to the time when Western civilization took its rise from the Greeks.

There seems no reason to doubt that the Brahmanized race was, prior to its settlement in India, associated together in some country west of the Indus, and exterior to the range of the Himalayas. Sir William Jones was of opinion that the Brahmanized race came from Irân, or Central Asia. Klaproth brings them from the Caucasian Mountains; Schlegel from the borders of the Caspian Sea; and Vans Kennedy from the plains of the Euphrates.

The Sanscrit, or sacred language of the Brahmans, is cognate with the Zand, the language of ancient Media; and with the Palhavi, that of ancient Persia, bordering on Mesopotamia. The Hindus fix their Holy Land and their Paradise in the north, in which they speak of gods and ancient sages as residing. One of the places of pilgrimage, the Manusarovar, or Lake of Intelligence, is beyond the Himalayas; and the river Brahmaputra, (Son of Brahma,) takes its rise beyond that range. The Punyabhumi, or Holy Land of Manu, is a small district lying between the rivers Drishadonto and Sarasvati. On the banks of the river Savasvati, Vyása, the compiler of the Vedas, is said to have lived. It is now impossible to say what the state of the Hindu religion and sacred literature was when the Brahmans entered India. There is, however, abundant evidence to show that their religion has undergone considerable change, and proofs are furnished by the Sacred Sanscrit of progressive refinement. The sacred books were written at different and remote periods.

Speculations on such points do not enter into the design of these pages; and, therefore, waving their consideration, it will be convenient here to give some account of the Hindus —the people of India whose condition and peculiarities it is the design of this little work briefly to delineate.

The most remarkable feature of the Hindu race is the division of society into four classes or castes[1]—the sacerdotal, the military, the industrial, and the servile. This peculiarity of Hindu society demands a special consideration, not merely as defended on the ground of its divine origin, but because, as a fundamental principle of Hindu polity, it exercises the most baneful influence on the people of India, and more than any other operates as a barrier to the spread of Christianity among them.

Caste, unlike the distinctions of rank in European com-

[1] The word *caste* is derived from Portuguese; *casta*, a breed. The Hindus use the word "jati," *birth*, and sometimes "varna," *colour*, the latter word possibly having reference to their comparatively light complexion.

munities, is not contingent on the advantage which learning, wealth, and station may give, but on descent from a particular class; it is founded upon supposed birth purity, or impurity, and in the way it is viewed by the natives of India, operates as a religious institution, as a civil distinction. This system, in the code of Hindu law, attributed to Manu, the son of Brahma, the Hindu legislator and saint, a work which is supposed to have been written about nine centuries before the Christian era, is stated to be of divine origin. The four classes are said to have sprung respectively from the head, the shoulder, the breast, and the feet of Brahma. In the Bhagava Gita, Krishna is made to say, "Mankind was created by me of four kinds, distinct in their principles and in their duties." We are informed that at the same time that these genera, or classes, or castes were produced in the manner to be described, there proceeded from the mouth of Brahma, in finished and completed form, the four Vedas for the instruction of mankind. Of these the Brahmans were constituted the sole depositaries, the sole interpreters, the sole teachers. To all the rest of their fellow-creatures they were to give out such portions and fragments, and in such manner and mode as they might deem most expedient. Hence the emanation from the mouth of Brahma of the first or sacerdotal caste, whence they derived their name Brahmans, became emblematical of their future function or office, as the sole divinely appointed preceptors of the human race. From Brahma's arm or shoulder, the protecting member of the body, proceeded the Kshattrya, or military caste; the source of emanation being emblematical of their future office, which is to wield martial weapons for the protection of their fellows against internal violence and external aggression. From Brahma's breast, the seat of life, originated the Vaisya, or class of productive capitalists, whether pastoral, agricultural, or mercantile; the source of their origin being emblematical of their future function, which is to raise or provide for themselves and the rest, all the necessaries, comforts, and luxuries which serve to support or exhilarate human life. From Brahma's foot, the member of inferiority or degradation, sprung the Sudra, or servile class, placed on the base of society; the source of their production being emblematical of their future calling, which is to perform for the other castes all manner of menial duties, either as serfs, or manual cultivators of the soil, domestic attendants, artisans, and artificers of every description as connected with the reputable grades of the community.

From this brief account of the assumed origin of caste, it will be seen that the Hindus represent the institution as coeval with creation; yet from evidence to be found in some of their sacred books, it would appear that the formation even of the first four orders was gradual, and that there was a time when all mankind acknowledged themselves as one race. Though the Vedas recognise the division of mankind into four distinct classes, they nevertheless separate the first three from the last by a large space, assigning to the former classes peculiar excellency. Birth in any of the first three is held to be a peculiar privilege, and as the reward of anterior virtue. The Sudra, on the contrary, is represented as low and ignoble, and unentitled to the secular and religious prerogatives of the superior castes. Whatever pretensions the Brahman may claim for himself and the other members of the first three orders, there can be no doubt entertained by those who examine the Hindu writings for themselves, that caste was gradually formed, and the Brahmans in course of time established the supremacy of their own order, and assumed its prerogatives as those of a primeval distinction ordained by God himself.

From the statement of the origin and designation of the four castes or classes as already given, we see their duties. It is permitted in seasons of calamity to modify the functions of the castes as laid down in one of the sacred books. A Brahman may then follow the occupation of the Kshattrya or a Vaisya; these latter may interchange occupations, but never adopt those of the Sudra. But ordinarily each caste has its peculiar laws and institutions, its duties and its professions, and these may not be infringed or violated without inflicting consequences fatal to caste altogether. The man who infringes the rules of caste is degraded, sinks beneath his birth-rank, and in fact becomes, in every sense of the term, an outcast. The loss of caste may be regarded as little less than civil death. Till by a *lex loci*[1] recently passed by the Governor-General in council, a man who had forfeited his caste could not inherit, could not contract engagements, or give evidence in a court of justice, and was excluded from all the intercourse of private life as well as from those which belong to a citizen. If any one violates his caste he cannot be admitted into his father's house; his nearest relatives must not communicate with him; he is deprived of all the consolations of religion in this life, and all the hope of happiness in the next. So it is evident that caste is not the effect of circumstances, but in the Hindu system an essential and unchangeable ordinance.

The civil disabilities incident to the forfeiture of caste, according to Hindu prescription, as has just been stated, have lately been removed. It is now enacted that no penal consequences shall follow a change in religious profession. Some of the early converts to Christianity had literally to suffer the loss of all things that they might win Christ. I knew a devoted man in Calcutta who forfeited a large property by becoming a Christian.

To show the real nature of caste it may be necessary to

[1] Lex Loci Act, passed April 11th, 1850:—"So much of any law or usage now in force within the territories subject to the government of the East India Company as inflicts on any person forfeiture of rights, or property, or may be held in any way to impair or affect any right of inheritance, by reason of his or her renouncing, or having been excluded from the communion of any religion, or being deprived of caste, shall cease to be enforced as law in the Courts of the East India Company, and in the Courts established by Royal Charter within the said territories."

select a few quotations from the Hindu sage Manu. He says, "Since the Brahman sprang from the most excellent part, since he was the first-born, and since he possesses the Veda, he is by right the chief of this whole creation." His prerogatives are further announced by the same authority:— "Neither shall the King slay a Brahman, though convicted of all possible crimes." "A King, though dying of want, must not receive any tax from a Brahman learned in the Vedas." "Whatever exists in the universe is all in effect, *though not in form*, the wealth of the Brahman; since the Brahman is entitled to it all by his primogeniture and eminence of birth."

Preternatural endowments are conferred on the Brahman by Initiation, which, performed when he is six years old, constitutes him *Dwija*, (twice-born,) because the rite of taking the sacred and symbolic thread is believed to be accompanied by the privilege of *regeneration*. He is hence regarded as a terrestrial deity, an incarnation of virtue, receives the salutation which is made by raising and joining the hands above the head; and also that which requires the reverential prostration of the worshipper, who receives from his divinely-constituted priest the benediction. If a Sudra bow before a Brahman, his sins enter the fire which lodges in the Brahman's hand, and they are consumed. Few among the Hindus but have heard the following original exposition of a Brahman's relation to the universe:—

> "All the universe is subject to the gods;
> The gods are influenced by incantations;
> Incantations are in the keeping of the Brahmans;
> The Brahmans therefore are our gods."

The Brahmans were not satisfied with the dignity attaching to priesthood. They took the title of *earthly gods*, and arrogated to themselves divine honours. They assumed more than the sovereign pontiff of the Romish Church, who, as a royal priest, holds the keys of heaven and earth by election and appointment. The Brahman assumes, as the offspring of

Brahma's mouth, the powers and privileges of a pope by virtue of his birth. His person and property are declared sacred, his word immutable and infallible, and his powers unlimited.

The question is sometimes put, as to whether the Brahmans, the priestly order, all engage in the performance of sacred functions. Far otherwise; they may be found connected with every profession. They are in the army, in trade, and they engage in agricultural pursuits. Thousands subsist by begging, or at any rate they subsist on alms. Great numbers occupy, among the wealthy, the office of domestic priest; and in the double capacity of confessor and secretary, they prescribe religious duties, aid in the performance of ceremonies, and engage in the lighter parts of secular business, such as letter-writing and accounts. In this capacity they are greatly reverenced. It is nevertheless certain, that the education which the English have promoted among all classes, has tended to weaken the veneration formerly entertained for the Brahmanical order. The extension of English literature and science has a tendency to create an independence of thought and action that is unfriendly to the prerogatives of the Brahman; yet he maintains his position. He entertains a high notion of the dignity of his order; and this, in some degree, imparts ease and weight to his manners. "The consciousness of being first in whatever society he may be thrown, and the feeling of perfect security from insult or impertinence, gives him a bearing which conduces to promote his influence over the masses; and especially as they are trained from infancy to reverence his character."

The Kshattrya are scarcely to be distinguished as a distinct class. The Rajpoots, those sons of kings, as the name imports, profess to be the pure military class; perhaps they are.

The Vaisyas are not now distinguishable from the fourth class, the Sudras; and it is generally affirmed that in the present *iron age* the only castes existing are the first, the Brahman, and the last, the Sudra. The agricultural class in the south of India and Ceylon declare themselves to be of the Vaisya caste, and not unfrequently do they give expression to the sense of superiority which accompanies the profession.

That the servile class was subject to the greatest degradation, may be seen from certain passages in Manu, that relate to it :—" A man of the servile class, whether bought or unbought, a Brahman may compel to perform servile duty; because such a man was created by the Self-existent for the purpose of serving Brahmans." They could not possess property, nor were they permitted instruction. " Let not a Brahman give advice to a Sudra, nor what remains from his table, nor clarified butter, nor spiritual counsel, nor the knowledge for the expiation of sin." Any attempt furtively made for the attainment of religious knowledge, was to be punished with the severest infliction.

Besides the caste-tribes who are subject to the social rules peculiar to the Hindus, who constitute the mass of the inhabitants of India, there are, as before indicated in the paragraphs on the Aborigines, numerous *non-caste* and degraded people, known as Chandálas in the north, as Pariars[1] in the south. These, as well as the scattered tribes of the hills, are descendants of the aboriginal settlers, who peopled India in the remote periods anterior to the Brahmanical invasion.

In order fully to comprehend the social condition of the Hindus, it is needful to offer a few more observations on the distinctions of caste. There are numerous *subdivisions* of the servile class, the Sudra. Whilst the Brahmanical caste has maintained its unity through all time, the Sudra has been broken up into numerous varieties, who hold no social intercourse with each other. And in the south of India a further distinction, denominated *right-hand* and *left-hand* castes, has, perhaps in comparatively modern times, obtained. The animosities and strifes incident to this artificial state of things,

[1] The Pariars are employed as tomtom beaters, and are therefore called by that name from Pari, a Tamil word signifying *tomtom* or *drum*.

frequently causes serious disturbance; and the authorities are sometimes obliged to interfere for the restoration of order. It may be interesting to some of my readers to be informed, that the *right-hand* division includes numerous classes among the landlords and cultivators of the soil, as well as the washermen, barbers, potters, &c.; whilst the *left-hand* division consists of artisans, &c. From these facts it may be seen, that caste is not now what it was in the days of Manu, the Hindu legislator, who propounded its original constitution.

It is also equally evident from what has been adduced on this difficult and perplexing system, that far from being, what is frequently imagined, a social distinction confined to four classes, it is in reality a system involving immense diversity, there being upwards of forty castes, each of which is, for all social purposes, a distinct and separate order, and possesses as complete an individuality, as that which divides the Englishman and the Patagonian.

It may easily be inferred that caste proves to be one of the greatest obstacles to the progress of the Gospel in India. No Missionary can long be practically ignorant of the baneful effects it produces in those parts of the country where it has been in any degree tolerated among the members of the Christian Church. The fundamental principles with which it sets out; the manner in which it is enforced by the sanction of future rewards and punishments; and, as may be gathered from the preceding pages, the restrictions thrown around it in social intercourse; may serve to show that it is with the Hindu not a mere civil, but a religious distinction. "On the scale of caste, wealth, talents, industry, and moral character, confer no elevation; and the absence of these imposes no degradation. It is ceremonial pollution alone which destroys it. This may be conveyed to a person of high caste, through the sight, the taste, or the touch, of one of an inferior grade. Such an institution, therefore, can never be called *a mere civil distinction;* for whatever it may have been in its origin, it is now adopted as an essential part of the Hindu religion." Its spirit may be inferred from the fact, that a man must perish with hunger rather than take food from a *non*-caste person. Even the water of the Ganges may not be received from one of an inferior caste. No moral delinquency, however, leads to the loss of caste. In case of forfeiture a heavy fine may restore it, as some of the decrees of the Hindus in Bengal have shown.

The origin of the system of caste is involved in mystery, like almost all subjects connected with the ancient people of whose social polity it has been so long a fundamental principle. Whilst it may be admitted that distinctions of trade or occupation had much to do in the origin of caste, which was most probably gradual in its development, the position of the Brahmanical order as the first in caste would seem to indicate, that they were once a dominant class, and content, perhaps, when overcome by a conquering and military class, to take a moral and religious control, whilst the Kshattriya, or military order, became first in civil rank. Be the origin what it may, it is certain that the spirit of this national distinction can only be accounted for on the selfish principles which take their rise in the depravity of our fallen nature, of which pride is one of the most prominent and easily besetting.

The political ascendancy of the Mohammedans and other foreigners in India, and the diffusion of superior education among the wealthy and influential classes of the natives, have no doubt tended to diminish Brahmanical influence; but the sacerdotal class still enjoy a large share of reverence; and the principle of caste among the various subdivisions it has undergone, maintains its influence as much as ever it did. Though the Kshattriya have lost their importance, and the Vaisya no longer exist, yet the *twice-born* occupy the position they did when the Hindu legislator composed the code that assigns them their prerogative. Experience abundantly proves that all who are attached to the religious institutions of the country pay the greatest deference to the spiritual relation which the Brahman is supposed to hold to its privileges.

The prevalence of the baneful system is most remarkably evinced too in the total prohibition of intermarriage, and of the interchange of hospitalities between the several castes. In the present day the restrictions of caste are chiefly maintained in these two particulars. It is remarkable how rigid the Hindus are, in regard to the question of caste, in all that relates to marriage contracts and convivial intercourse. Where the best possible feeling may prevail among members of the different classes, and considerable intercourse in the common affairs of business almost daily take place, the most scrupulous care will be observed lest the usages of caste should be violated, and especially when a question of marriage or the rites of hospitality may be concerned.

And even among those educated and intelligent natives, who are members of the Christian Church, whose general sentiments on the abstract question of caste concur with those of the European, there will be found an indisposition, to say the least, to depart from the ordinary usages of the Hindu system in regard to questions of marriage and hospitality: their actions, though defended on other grounds, are quite in character with the caste feeling of their less enlightened countrymen. Such evince a repugnance to descend in the social scale, similar to that met with among families of rank in Europe; and they defend it, not on the ground of principle, but sentiment. This seems to show that caste has had a dissocializing influence that separates family from family quite as great as that which severs the European from the Negro. This class of persons—the educated and Christian observers of caste—in such matters defend their conduct on the principle of a civil distinction; and although they profess to have repudiated the doctrines of caste as held by the Hindus, they maintain that they are at liberty to choose their own society in all respects.

The agents of the Leipsig Missionary Society, who are

labouring in Southern India, permit the observance of caste in the members of the Christian Church somewhat on the principle just mentioned. These Missionaries defend the position they have taken against all other Protestant ministers, on the plea that caste is "apparently a rather natural distinction of race and occupation," that in the "course of development" was "stamped with a higher authority," being "based on a religious ground." In a conversation I had with one of the gentlemen connected with this Mission at Tranquebar, he expressed the opinion that caste was a thing with which the pastor of a Christian flock had no more to do than with their costume or domestic habits, unless its usages contravened the principles and amenities of the Gospel; against which teaching and discipline were to be directed as against any other evil tendencies of our fallen nature. In retaining caste-observing persons in the Church, they urge that, "the Kingdom of God is not meat and drink, but righteousness, and peace, and joy in the Holy Ghost."

Among the members of the Native Church in some parts of India caste distinction was for many years tolerated; but on a closer and more careful consideration of its evil tendency, the Right Reverend the Bishop of Calcutta, so long ago as 1834, expressed the strongest opinions on the unchristian principle of caste; and those opinions he has uniformly endeavoured to enforce. Within the last few years the subject has been taken up by the Clergy and Missionary agents generally, and numerous documents have been carefully prepared in the three Presidencies of India, for the purpose of expressing opinions on the question; and for the establishment of some joint action for the suppression of caste prejudices and practices among the members of the Christian Church. It may be necessary to state that in many places the evil of caste was so rife, that some Christians not only refused to receive a brother Christian into their houses, but also excluded Native Catechists because of a lower, or *non*-caste, class; and also refused to drink promiscuously with those of a lower caste from the same cup at the celebration of the Lord's Supper.

It is now generally agreed among the Missionaries that whilst the native converts may be left to their own discretion in matters of food and costume, and the selection of their friends, they shall not be tolerated in their refusal to receive into their houses a brother Christian,—especially a Catechist or Preacher,—to eat with him, to listen to his instructions, to join with him in prayer, or to receive the Lord's Supper from a native minister, on account of caste. They regard it as "utterly inconsistent to recognise caste distinctions in that body of which Christ is the head, and where all are members one of another."

The subject of caste has occupied more space than its importance would seem at first sight to demand. When, however, its mischievous features and its manifold evils are seen and fully understood, and especially as they have hindered the progress of the Gospel, the reader will not regret that care has been taken to set the subject in its true light. Claiming, as caste distinction does, the prerogative of a divine and original institution; and being in theory and practice one of the greatest hindrances to the advancement of the Hindus in industry and social happiness; and also one of the most decided obstacles to the progress of Christianity in India, it is highly satisfactory that the bishops and clergy, and the missionaries of different denominations in the Presidencies, have agreed to lift up their united testimony against it, and to use every effort to preserve the Church of Christ from its baneful influence.

Four or five years ago several admirable essays were written in India on the subject of caste in competition for a prize. Thus concurrently with the full consideration of the question as bearing on the character of the Christian Church, the subject was generally discussed in its principles and in its effects. An able essay appeared on the subject in the *Calcutta Review*, in which the writer, after discussing the subject of caste in its development, its principles, and its various modifications, proceeds to show in various ways how inimical the institution is to society. He proves that the institution of caste exercises a baneful influence on the development of the human mind; that the moral evils are not less conspicuous, involving self-esteem often where virtue and real excellence are wanting, and as extinguishing sympathy and fellow-feeling among its adherents, some being puffed up, others depressed, and all morally deteriorated; and since it has a tendency to retard the advancement of the mind, and to hinder its progress in science and in the arts of social life, the Essayist considers that it is one of the sorest evils that can affect society. This writer thus forcibly speaks of this great evil:—

"The principal cause of India's humiliation is caste. It is this unnatural institution, which, by detaching man from man, trade from trade, mechanic from mechanic, tribe from tribe, puts an end to unity and strength in the nation. A people divided and subdivided like the Hindus can never make head against any power that deserves the name. The Mohammedan conquest was the natural result of such national weakness."

The effects of English education are manifestly against the continuance of the evils of caste, as may be gathered from the sentiments expressed by a native essayist, whose production on the subject obtained a prize on the occasion before alluded to. Babu Shashi Chandra Datta says: "Though not myself a Christian, in marshalling arguments against the institution of caste, I cannot well overlook the doctrines of that beautiful revelation, which makes no distinction but between the virtuous and the vicious,—recognises no uncleanness but that of the heart, and invites the poorest and the proudest to one common heaven. The heaven of the Hindus, like their earth, is made for the Brahmans alone; and, before the soul can wing its flight thither, it must, as a general rule, have passed its Brahmanical birth. But the religion of the Gospel inculcates doctrines of a different character. Is thy soul athirst for God? Dost thou pant after Him as the hart panteth after the water-brooks? Have the words of the law been a lamp unto thy feet, and a light unto thy path? If so, be of good cheer, whoever thou art—it matters not whether Jew or Gentile—the gates of heaven shall open to let thee in. Christianity everywhere recognises the equality of mankind."

This earnest writer, urging his countrymen to action, says further: "Let all, then, gird up their loins, who profess to reverence reason, and aspire for intellectual freedom; let us do it under a conviction that no power on earth can help us if we do not help ourselves. The British Government has done much to allay our sufferings, and elevate our national character. It may yet do more, for much remains undone. But all the laws that ever were created will not render a vicious, ignorant, and superstitious people, intelligent, virtuous, and happy. The deadly upas, whose noxious exhalations have made us what we are, must first be uprooted, ere we can reasonably expect to reap any solid advantages from even the most enlightened administration on the face of the earth."

The ancient Egyptians had a classification of the population, which has sometimes been compared to Hindu caste; but it was of human appointment. European nations have their distinctions of rank and station, but they are the accompaniments of virtue, or of wealth, or of learning; these differ essentially, therefore, from the selfish and dissocializing caste institution of India, which claims an origin coeval with creation, a divine ordination, and defends a system the most monstrous, oppressive, and degrading, under sanctions at once religious, moral, and political. A system so injurious to all classes must be abandoned ere India can rise to the freedom and dignity of a great nation.[1]

[1] Several documents relating to caste, from Bishop Heber, Bishop Wilson, and others, are placed in an Appendix.

CHAPTER III.

LANGUAGES—THE SANSCRIT, THE PRACRIT, THE ABORIGINAL.—THE EXCELLENCY OF THE SANSCRIT.—PROFESSOR WILSON'S VIEWS OF ITS IMPORTANCE TO PUBLIC MEN IN INDIA.—ITS VALUE TO THE CHRISTIAN TEACHER.—SOME NOTICES OF ITS ALPHABET AND CAPABILITIES.

THE subject of language, like most other topics relating to India, is one of peculiar interest. The languages spoken are numerous, and most of them highly cultivated and refined. Indeed the tribes of India are more divided into nations or families by their languages than by their religions; in the latter, as in their literature, they may be regarded as one. The languages are not merely diversified as dialects proceedings from one radical source,—though to some extent this is the case,—but different in origin, in structure, and in idiom. Although many distinguished orientalists have laboured hard to elucidate the subjects of Indian philology and literature, the origin of the existing languages and a great amount of ancient learning still remains in obscurity. There are numerous books of which little is known but the names; even the sacred Vedas, those earliest and most extraordinary fountains of the Hindu theology and religion, are but partially investigated.

Leaving matters of an extraneous nature, and of comparatively little importance as regards the design of this little work, it will be the object of the few paragraphs devoted to this subject, to present in a condensed form some general information relating to the languages and literature of the Hindus. More specific and extended information is to be found in numerous works published by learned men, most of which are accessible to the student in this country.

The most remarkable points connected with languages may easily be stated. The Brahmans have one sacred language, called by way of eminence *Sanscrit*, the perfected, as distinguished from certain dialects denominated Pracrit, the vulgar language: hence we have the Sanscrit, the Bengali, the Hindi, the Panjabi, the Guzeratta, the Mahratta, the Ureya, the Pali and other languages, all linked together in one family. Besides this family there is also the Tamil in the south of India, which in basis, structure, and expression, is wholly independent of Sanscrit and its derivatives. This language is remarkably sweet, as one of its names, Tamil, imports; and it is connected by strong affinity with the dialects of the barbarous tribes who are scattered about on the mountains and almost inaccessible forests of the Peninsula. It has however received a large infusion of Sanscrit terms on theological, philosophical, and philological subjects. These bear the same relation to its radical structure that Latin terms bear to the English language. The Brahmans as they advanced into the country imparted their civilization and their religion to those who spoke the dialects of this aboriginal tongue, and along with these, the terms expressive of their ideas on such subjects.

It would appear, therefore, that prior to the invasion of India by the Sanscrit-speaking Brahmanized conquerors, one common language prevailed throughout the country, which eventually issued in the polished *Tamil*, in a region remote from the seats of Brahmanical power. There are not wanting indications in this language of its having been cultivated in imitation of the refined Sanscrit; and it may be imagined that the learned among the Aborigines were impelled to effort as well by opposition as by rivalry. The fact that the Tamil has been mainly cultivated by the secular class, is not only apparent in the authors who have written on it, but has become proverbial. "The Brahman in Tamil, and the cultivator in Sanscrit, are respectively deficient." The other languages of the South—the Telugu, the Canarese, and the Malayalim—have a near affinity to the Tamil, but have received larger contributions from the Sanscrit, and they have adopted the Sanscrit alphabet; whereas the Tamil has retained the Aboriginal imperfect character with the addition of a few, a very few, Sanscrit symbols. The purest Tamil works are almost entirely free from any admixture of Sanscrit, and the language may be spoken without a word from the Brahmanized vehicle of thought. Most of the languages spoken further north, such as the Oreya, Bengali, and Hindi, though partaking largely of Sanscrit, and indeed almost composed of it, have evidently a substratum of original tongues. In some it is greater than in others. The Bengali is the most closely allied with Sanscrit; nine-tenths of that language being purely classical. It may be looked upon practically as the same speech, divested of the whole mass of grammatical finesse, in a dress simple and unpretending. "The skeleton, nay even the body, with all its members, remains as entire as ever; but the numerous folds of dress, the drapery, so to speak, thrown around it by the subtilties of nouns, and the vagaries of verbs, have departed for ever one and all, as by the touch of the enchanter's wand." The Bengali language, perhaps the best example of the Pracrit division, is far less vigorous in structure than the Tamil. The idiom differs little from English, and the abundance of its particles enfeebles the expression as they affect the quality of terseness so characteristic of the Tamil. There is a structural power in the latter language analogous to that of a mechanical arrangement, that gives it great force and precision.

It may be presumed that the Sanscrit grammar grew by degrees or was engrafted on the original Pracrit language. Little doubt can be entertained as to the Sanscrit being originally a simple dialect, as all other languages have been in the outset. Its declensions and conjugations are on a regular model, its alphabet is perfect, its flow and rhythm are beautifully modulated; it has words of one syllable, we may say of one letter,—and so has the Tamil,—expressive of quality, and actions, and of most natural objects, of the powers of the understanding, the passions and affections of the mind. As distinguished from the Pracrit, the rude, the inelegant spoken dialect current among the illiterate vulgar, the Sanscrit is a highly elegant and polished tongue, capable of expressing with precision, force, and beauty, every movement of the human will, and every exercise of human thought. In the facility of forming compound terms, in the endless diversity and easy formation of derivatives, in flexibility, sententiousness and other valuable qualities, it is considered unrivalled even by the classical Greek of the West. Such is the judgment of the most competent European scholars.

Within this sacred enclosure, this divine language, as the Brahmans call it, all philosophy, all religion and science are deposited and preserved from the desecration of the vulgar. The *twice*-born, the divine Brahmans, the terrestrial divinities as they denominate themselves, consigning the transactions of civil and military life to kings and military chiefs, retained the legislative and administrative in their own hands. They exercised absolute dominion over all minds by their dogmas and ritual; the former impalpable, extravagant, esoteric, mystic; the latter, exoteric, gross, tedious, yet imposing:—the former offered gratifying employment for the thoughtful and reflective; the latter pastime and licentiousness for the ignorant, sensual, and thoughtless. These facts serve to infer the opinion that from the beginning Sanscrit was made an instrument by a dominant priesthood for promoting their own aggrandizement. For this purpose, by a sort of hieroglyphical device it was adopted, and by a careful process made as artificial, concise, and difficult as it was possible to make it; it was perfected, wrought, Sanscritized, and thus elevated to a position above its substratum the Pracrit, which left in the vulgar, unwritten, not reduced to grammar, never taught, would, in its downward course, by the converse of the process to which the Sanscrit was subjected, become barbarous and rude. The greater the divergence by the double process of refinement and vulgarity, and the better would the Sanscrit be fitted to serve the ends of the Brahmanical order: it may be assumed that Sanscrit was wrought to its present state for the express purpose of rendering its stores inaccessible to all but the privileged class. In a lower degree the same principle was exhibited when I first became acquainted with the learned among the Hindus even in matters pertaining to philology. The first copy of the Tamil grammar, known as Nannul, then not in print, which I obtained, was furnished to me as a special favour, and the party who lent me the book was afraid of the fact—traitorous as he conceived it—being known in his neighbourhood. In the south to this day, the Sanscrit is called Grentham, from the word *grantha*, a book, indicating, as it would seem, the fact that originally that tongue was the only book language.

That Sanscrit was once a spoken language, at least among the patrician class, cannot, I think, be doubted; and that it was called by its present name because of its fitness to become the vehicle of literary, scientific, and religious communication, and as such underwent those gradual changes which issued in its perfected character, I think is easily inferred. This inference is the more legitimate, from the fact that the compositions originating at different and distant periods are in point of style and refinement similar to those which mark the different periods of Latin authorship. That a language so remarkable in all its features could be invented, seems to be at variance with the testimony of all history. The two terms, Pracrit, vulgar, Sanscrit, perfect, in the absence of history, seem in themselves to indicate the process by which the latter rose above the other.

The classical literature of India affords by its allusion to the state of society, some insight into usage in remote times, and in the absence of history may be applied to valuable purposes in elucidating this and similarly obscure subjects. In one of the early dramas, written before the Christian era, we have in the speech of the various personages introduced the distinction of language under consideration exemplified. Kings and nobles communicate in the Sanscrit,—refined speech; whilst the inferior characters in the piece speak the Pracrit,—the vulgar tongue.

The position assigned to the perfected language of India with reference to things sacred and scientific, accords with that which the mystic symbols of Egypt attained. The ancient Egyptians, however, advanced another step beyond the sister country in the farther east: they had three distinct classes of writing; viz. the *hieroglyphic*, a sacred sculptural character, which was the original and monumental method; the *hieratic*, which is an abbreviated method used by the scribes and priests in literary pursuits, in current use 1500 B.C.; and the *demotic*, styled by the Greeks enchorial, used generally after the Persian Conquest, which took place 525 B.C., and is a more expeditious way of writing. Thus St. Clement of Alexandria, in the year A.D. 194, says, "Those who among the Egyptians receive instruction, learn first that species of Egyptian writing which is termed *epistolographic*, *i.e.* our demotic; they next learn the hieratic, or sacerdotal; and lastly the hieroglyphic, or sacred."

The Sanscrit language was cultivated anciently in that part of India called by the Brahmans Punya Bhumi, the Holy Land. This included the north-western part of India and the regions of the Gangetic Valley. The Troy, the Athens, the Olympus of Indian classical story, must be sought there. Though now no longer spoken except by a few (the learned), it is held in the highest veneration by all the natives of India. Learned and unlearned hold it in equal veneration, and speak of it as the language of the celestials. Its alphabet, said to be of divine origin, is called *Deva Nagari*, the writing of the gods.

European scholars, who have become acquainted with its merits, are not behind the Hindus in their appreciation of its excellences. Halhed says, "As a language it is very copious and nervous, and far exceeds the Greek and Arabic in the regularity of its etymology." Sir William Jones's enraptured mind thus embodied its impressions: "It is a language of wonderful structure; more perfect than the Greek, more copious than the Latin, and more exquisitely refined than either." Talboys applies to Sanscrit the praise bestowed on Greek by Gibbon. "It is," says he, "a musical and prolific language, that gives a soul to the objects of sense, and a body to the abstractions of philosophy." The greatest Sanscrit scholar of the age, Professor Wilson, says, "The music of Sanscrit composition must ever be inadequately represented by any other tongue." German testimony, not to be overlooked on a subject like the present, says, "The Sanscrit, as a written language, has been raised to the highest pinnacle of perfection." This is more than echoed by France. One of its distinguished literati, by way of expressing his admiration of its intrinsic superiority, adopts the sentiment of the Hindus, and says that "it is the celebrated dialect perhaps spoken by the gods of Homer; and if not, worthy to be so."

These are not the enthusiastic eulogies of men who spoke on insufficient data, or incapable of judging from the knowledge of facts. Such may entertain exaggerated notions of unexplored regions, and overrate and magnify the value of their subject. The estimate put on the language by dispassionate, clear-headed men, giving a calm judgment, in terms such as we have produced, may well authorize the natives of India entertaining the highest opinion of this incomparable vehicle of human thought. Professor Heeren, in his profound researches into the antiquities of India, has recorded an estimate of the language that may be a fitting corroboration of this part of our subject. His testimony is as follows:—"It would indeed be difficult," he remarks, "to instance another language exhibiting so just a proportion between the vowels and the consonants, in which it is not exceeded by the Spanish. It admits the employment of rhyme, without, however, being fettered by its restrictions; and possesses a poetic prose richly embellished. It has, moreover, reached a high degree of scientific cultivation; and presents us with an abundance of technical terms to express the most abstract ideas. Altogether, admitting that its claims upon our admiration have been enthusiastically overrated, yet it is hardly possible to avoid considering it as one of the richest, most harmonious, and refined languages in the world."

It were superfluous, after these testimonies, to add anything by way of further eulogy on the language itself. The fact that it is the repository of all things connected with Hindu philosophy and religion, and as such venerated by all ranks of men throughout India, may be sufficient to prove how important it is that all who have aught to do with the Hindu mind, whether in matters civil or sacred, should acquire a knowledge of this wonderful tongue. Of the importance of an acquaintance with Sanscrit on the part of any agency that either the Church or the State may employ in promoting the improvements of the social and religious condition of the Hindus, it may not be irrelevant to quote in this place a very high testimony. The passages now to be introduced are valuable, not merely as they bear on the question before us, but as more or less elucidating, at least by remark and suggestion, other topics connected with the relations in which we as a nation stand to the millions of India.

Professor Wilson observes, "It were superfluous in the present day to offer any observation upon the value and interest of Sanscrit literature. The principles of etymological affinity have been placed upon secure grounds, and the history of languages, and through these the history of man, has received novel and important elucidation. Nor is this the only service which it has rendered to general literature. The history of philosophy and science is also largely indebted to it; and in the civil and religious codes which it has laid open to our knowledge, and in the mythological and legendary traditions, and the dramatic and heroic poems, which it offers to our curiosity, it presents a series of new, interesting, and instructive pictures of society, in which the features of a highly artificial but original civilization are singularly blended with the characteristics of primitive manners and archaic institutions. The history of mankind can be but imperfectly appreciated without some acquaintance with the literature of the Hindus.

"It is, however, to the educated youth, whose manhood is to be spent in India, and who is there destined to discharge high duties, and sustain heavy responsibilities; who is to regulate the affairs of civilized government over millions of subject Hindus, and to make that government a blessing, not a curse to India,—a glory, not a shame to Britain; it is to him that the study of Sanscrit commends itself by considerations of peculiarity and importance.

"A careful examination of the various dialects which are spoken in different parts of India is yet to be effected; but enough is known to admit of their being distinguished as belonging to two great families, that of India Proper and that of the Dekan. Of the former, the numbers are, so far as we are familiar with them, recognised as Sanscrit. They have undergone great changes, have simplified their grammatical structure, have suffered in a greater or less degree admixture and adulteration from foreign words. They probably also comprehend a small portion of a primitive, unpolished, and scanty speech, the relics of a period prior to civilization; but in the names of things of the most ordinary observation, in terms for the functions of life, as well as the relations of society, as much as in those words which are the offspring of civilization, and which spring from science, philosophy, law and religion, they are almost wholly dependent upon Sanscrit, a knowledge of which consequently places the members of this family, Bengali, Hindi, Panjabi, Guzriati, Marhatta and others, almost without effort within the power of any to whom it may become a duty to acquire either or all of them.

"In the south of India the case is somewhat different. Cultivated languages of local origin are there met with, largely supplied with words which are not of Sanscrit origin. There, however, as in the north, the introduction of Sanscrit was a precursor of civilization, and deeply impressed it with its own peculiarities. The spoken language was one cultivated in intimation and rivalry, and but partially aspired to an independent literature. The principal compositions in Tamil, Telugu, Canara, and Maliyalam, are translations or paraphrases of Sanscrit works, and largely borrow the phrascology of their originals. And hence so large a proportion of the language of education and of society is Sanscrit, that a knowledge of it is absolutely essential to a correct understanding of the spoken dialects of the Peninsula.

"There is however a higher point of view, from which the advantages to the servants of the East India Company in India of a knowledge of Sanscrit are to be contemplated, than the aid it is calculated to afford them in their executive functions. It will not only enable them to understand the uttered words of those with whom they hold official intercourse,—it will not only teach them to interpret the language of representation or complaint, or to express the decrees of justice, or the commands of power,—it will enable them to understand the people, and to be understood by them. The popular prejudices of the Hindus, their daily observances, their occupations, their amusements, their domestic and social relations, their local legends, their national traditions, their mythological fables, their metaphysical abstractions, their religious worship, all spring from, and are perpetuated by the Sanscrit language. To know a people these things must be known."

The able reasoning contained in this extract none can gainsay or reject. If to the civilian in his intercourse with the Hindu in matters civil and judicial the knowledge referred to be important, where all is connected with administrative officiality, and political power, how much more important must such an advantage be to one who has to do with things sacred, where no power but that of moral influence can avail to command attention. If he would attain to a self-affected acquaintance with Hindu philosophy and Hindu faith, or deal intelligently and to any good purpose with the present race of sophists, who draw from its hidden recesses all their armoury of thought, argument, and objection, the Christian teacher must acquire a competent knowledge of Sanscrit. If it be important to command the respect of the powerful Brahmanical and other educated leaders of public sentiments, men whose esteem would be a passport to public confidence,—if the teacher of a foreign and antagonistic faith would draw his information from the fountain head without fear of mistake or danger of being worsted in argument, by the sophistry, bad faith, or ignorance of his opponents, he must address himself vigorously to this arduous and important undertaking.

Some urge that there is nothing worthy of pursuit in the stores of Hindu literature. Granted that, in one sense, there may not be much of a theological, historic, ethical, or scientific nature that can contribute to the improvement of the Biblical student; yet in relation to the faith, the conduct, the destiny of millions of India, there is something that ought to be known. There is in the records of Hindu faith and practice that which commands the veneration of a sixth portion of mankind. Whatever it may be, whether valuable or valueless, it ought to be comprehended and set forth in its true bearing on the destinies of its votaries. Error, gross error, even on some of the physical sciences, abound in the works of Sanscrit literature, and the discovery of this, and its exhibition, more than aught else, is calculated to weaken the resources of the enemy to be combated. The extravagances of mythology serve to heighten, by contrast, the truth, the rational, the truthful narratives of the Bible. As affecting vernacular languages, it contains the terms employed in theological dogmas, metaphysical abstractions, as well as those in which the teachings of inspired truths are to be conveyed. By an acquaintance with the sources of Hindu sentiment, the foreigner acquires, not terms only, he becomes acquainted with the national mode of thinking, and soon his mind acquires the habit of viewing things through a medium that is intelligible in regard to the objects of his solicitude. His mind acquires new moulds of thought; in phraseology, in manner, in recondite expression, he becomes natural to the native mind, and able, therefore, to move its sympathies.

It must be evident to any who are interested to give the matter consideration, that however well qualified a man may be by natural talent, literary, scientific, and theological attainment, acquired through the media of western languages, those qualifications can no otherwise advantage the cause of Christianity in India than as they are made appreciable by those to whom he is sent. He must not only possess the requisite qualifications, but their possession must be apparent. He must not merely appear well acquainted with his own side of the question, but with that of his antagonist; otherwise the Hindu has the sagacity to know, that at any rate his antagonist has not been able to see his system as it is seen by himself. The Hindus—I write from long acquaintance with the native character, and much intercourse with the learned among them—will not listen respectfully to a man who is ignorant of their system, except to contemn him as a partisan, who, if he knew the views of his antagonist, might possibly be inclined to embrace them. The Christian must know the errors of Hinduism, and be able to set them forth in their own shape. He must not only know Christianity, but be competent to present its truths in a comprehensible form. An acute people, like the Hindus, will not abandon an ancestral faith, the faith of many centuries, at the bidding of a foreigner. They must be convinced ere they are converted. It affects not the case to refer the spiritual effects sought, to the power of the Holy Spirit, since he ordinarily employs the truth as the instrument of enlightenment and conviction; hence the presence of the teacher in the realms of paganism: "How shall they hear without a preacher?"

Though but little can be said in this brief sketch on the structure of the Sanscrit language, a few sentences may be added by way of elucidating some of its characteristic peculiarities. Beginning then with the alphabet, which contains forty-seven letters, *i.e.* thirty-three consonants and fourteen vowels: the aspirated and unaspirated are distinguished and classed according to the organ chiefly concerned in their articulation. In point of completeness and perfection, it is generally admitted that nothing can be produced superior to the Sanscrit alphabet, as an arrangement for conveying all sounds with correct utterance. The alphabet is syllabic. The first letter, *a*, in Sanscrit, as indeed in the Tamil family of languages, is inherent in every consonant. In the Tamil, it is worthy of remark, the perfect consonant is characterised as a living *body*, each having a definite and independent form, instinct with the vowel, which is considered as its animating *soul*. Hence the beautiful distich, "As among letters the vowel is essential to sound, so in all worlds the Eternal God is chief;" intimating the fact that a pure consonant cannot, of itself, be sounded. The vowel being inherent in the consonant, which, for the sake of expressing its fourteen modifications, assumes as many forms by symbolic alterations; it follows, that except as an initial, the vowel is not used. In the Tamil language the vowel ought never to appear, except at the commencement of a sentence. The value of the vowels being fixed as the laws of nature, and having two sorts of signs, one for the short and the other for the long, there needs be no hesitation in determining quantity, none relative to sound. One vowel never follows another in the arrangement of words in a sentence; that is, it is never permitted that the sequence shall appear, and to obviate this they change for euphonic expression into a longer vowel, or into a cognate consonant. Hence the fertility in producing compound terms in endless combination and variety. The noun has two cases in addition to those found in Latin and Greek; viz. the *instrumental* and *locative*. The verbs of the Sanscrit language are the most intricate and complex possible. The roots or stems do not amount to more than two thousand, which are, for the most part, but one syllable; but by means of prepositions affixed, these assume immense modifications, in form and sense; and so increase into what grammarians call an ocean of words. Its poetic capabilities are endless. There is such a flexibility in the language that the same composition, variously analysed by grammatical rule, may have two, sometimes three, different meanings. There is a poem that may be read either as the history of Rama, or that of Yuddhistira: two distinct stories are told in the same words. The Tamil is equally flexible in the hands of an ingenious and skilful composer. Some months ago I saw a poetic eulogium prepared for a public occasion, which was read in a public assembly, under three aspects: one reading presented an ascription of praise to Siva, another to a deceased benefactor, whose charities were on the occasion more particularly alluded to, and the third was an encomium on the gentleman who presided at the meeting.

CHAPTER IV.

HINDU LITERATURE, SACRED—THE VEDA, THE UPANGA, THE VEDANGA, THE DHARMASHASTRA, THE PURANA :—HEROIC POEMS—THE NATIONAL EPICS, THE DRAMA, &C.—SCIENTIFIC AND OTHER WORKS—ASTRONOMY, GEOMETRY, ARITHMETIC, AND ALGEBRA—LOGIC, GRAMMAR, RHETORIC.

THE opinions we have produced, and the brief account given of the sacred language of the Hindus, will prepare for further communications on the subjects contained in this remarkable depository. So far as quantity is concerned, the voluminousness of the literature contained in the Sanscrit language, leaves nothing to be desired, but the quality is capable of varied appreciation. In the attempt to comprehend the general character of Hindu literature, little trouble needs be given to that contained in the various languages of the country ; for, although in some of them there are independent treatises on different subjects, yet the major part of their literature will consist of versions from the sacred language ; and when it is otherwise, the works are tinged with a colouring derived from the ancient source of Hindu civilization, religion, and literature. It follows, therefore, that to understand the literary and scientific productions contained in the sacred language, may suffice to give us a tolerably correct, as well as adequate, conception of the whole.

In the brief notices it is here proposed to give of the literature of the Hindus, it may be convenient to furnish, in the first place, some account of those original writings, which are generally deemed sacred and canonical. Afterwards a few specimens may be presented from the dramatic and heroic poets.

The sacred writings of the Hindus are denominated Shastras, or ordinances, as the word imports. The word *Shas*, from which the term is derived, signifies to govern, and its application in this case implies divine origin and authority.

The following enumeration of Hindu sacred literature is in accordance with that of the best native authorities:—

I. The four VEDAS, the Rik, Yajush, Sáma, and Atharva.

The four UPAVEDAS or Sub-Vedas, the Ayush, Dhanush, Ghandharva, and Artha, sometimes called Sthápathyá.

II. The VEDANGA or Six ANGAS, or bodies of learning, treatises subsidiary to the Vedas; comprehending *Shikská* rules for reciting the Vedas, and particularly as regards the accents and tones to be observed; *Kalpa*, treating of the ritual of the Vedas, and containing a detail of religious acts and ceremonies; *Vyákarana*, treating of grammar; *Nirukta*, commentary on the form of glosses; *Chandas*, or dissertation on metres; *Jyotish*, explanatory of astronomy and astrology. These works, as well as the Vedas, are regarded as proceeding from the breath of God. Their object is to instruct the Brahmans in the study and comprehension of the Vedas.

III. The UPANGAS, or inferior bodies of learning,—the *Mimánsá*, comprehending theology; *Nyáya*, logic; *Dharma-shástra*, institutes of law; *Puránas*, or legendary and instructive treatises, eighteen in number.

The sacred Veda consists of two parts, the first called *Sanhitá*, which is a collection of sacred hymns, prayers and invocations. To each Veda is attached the Bráhmana, a work of more modern date than the Veda itself. This Bráhmana consists chiefly of preceptive and argumentative matter relating to ceremonies, duties, and opinions. The hymns contained in these sacred writings are addressed to the elements of nature, or the regents, or deities who are supposed to preside over these elements. Professor Wilson, speaking of the character of the worship inculcated in the Vedas, says:—"The prevailing character of the ritual of the Vedas, is the worship of the personified elements; of Agni, fire; Indra, or the firmament;

Váyu, the air; Varuna, the water; of Aditya, the sun; Soma, the moon; and other elementary and planetary personages. It is also true, that the worship of the Vedas is for the most part domestic worship, consisting of prayers and oblations offered in their own houses, not in temples, by individuals for individual good, and addressed to unreal presences, not to real types. In a word, the religion of the Vedas was not idolatry."

It is probable that the compiler of the Vedas flourished at a period of from thirteen to fifteen hundred years before the Christian era: his name was *Vyása.*

Omitting further particulars respecting the second department of the sacred books, the VEDANGA, already sufficiently indicated in the above paragraph, it is now proposed to offer a few words explanatory of the third class, the UPANGAS.

The UPANGAS, though an inferior body of literature, have at the present day more influence on the faith and practice of the Hindus than the superior treatises. There is on the part of the Brahmans and other learned nations, a constant reference to the fountain head authority, the Vedas, which are spoken of with the profoundest veneration; but in practice, and as regards the sentiments they entertain on religious subjects, they may be said to be obsolete. It is, indeed, questionable whether the objects most venerated by the modern Hindus are even mentioned in the Vedas. The simple ritual of the Vedas has long been abandoned, and a system professedly based upon them of a more elaborate character has been devised.

The first of the Upángas is that of the MIMÁNSÁ, which resolves itself into two branches, the practical and the philosophical. One is called *Púrva Mimánsá, i.e.* the *Anterior Mimánsá;* its founder was Jaimini. It treats of the "Way of Works," the philosophy of religious ceremonies and observances which are here set forth as accordant with the orthodox Hindu notions of the present day. The *Uttara Mimánsá, i.e.* the *Posterior Mimánsá,* which claims Vyása and Badaráyan as its founders; it discusses the "Way of Wisdom," setting forth a pantheistic psychology, denying the existence of matter—the apparent development being attributed to *Máya* or delusion—resolving the physical and intellectual universe into the supreme spirit, the sole self-existent being. These subjects of difficult speculation are discussed in a class of works called *Upanishad,* which the Brahmans would have it believed are portions or abstracts of the Vedas. The system of philosophy is therefore called by them Vedanta, a term signifying the scope, or purport of the Vedas. One of the greatest commentators on the Vedanta, is Sankaráchryá, the author of the Saiva Form of Modern Hinduism.

Under the head of Upanga, the *Nyáya* philosophy of the Hindus is classed. The word *Nyáya* signifies reasoning, discrimination, logic. The system of dialectics, included in this division of literature, is not unlike that of the Aristotelian school. Gautama is said to have been its author. The metaphysics of logic exhibited in this system have not so much to do with the art of reasoning, as with "the discrimination and realization of the identity of the soul with the supreme spirit, and its non-essential connexion with the resolvable corporeal forms in which it is now resident." As a system it is admitted to be most wonderful in its terminology. This branch of Hindu philosophy, variously modified and disseminated, has had a great influence on the Hindu mind. It seems to have created a fondness for matters of contemplation and metaphysical inquiry even among the lower orders. The ordinary native of India, I think, differs greatly from the European in some of these peculiarities of his intellectual character and tendency.

"Under the head of DHARMASHASTRA, the Hindus place all their authorized works on law and jurisprudence, personal, domestic and public, civil and sacred. Every act of human life, connected with every individual man, and every relation of society, they profess to regulate by Divine institutions."

Of the principal work on jurisprudence, known as the

code of Manu, written about nine hundred years before our era, Sir William Jones, its translator, thus speaks:—"The work contains abundance of curious matter, extremely interesting to speculative lawyers and antiquaries, with many beauties which cannot be pointed out, and many blemishes which cannot be justified or palliated. It is a system of despotism and priestcraft, both indeed limited by law, but artfully conspiring to give mutual support, though with mutual checks. It is filled with strange conceits in metaphysics and natural philosophy, with idle superstitions, and with a scheme of theology most obscurely figurative, and consequently liable to dangerous misconception; it abounds with minute and childish formalities, with ceremonies generally absurd, and often ridiculous; the punishments are partial and fanciful; for some crimes dreadfully cruel; for others, reprehensibly light; and the very morals, though rigid enough on the whole, are, in one or two instances (as in the case of light oaths and of pious perjury), unaccountably relaxed."

The next division of sacred literature is called the *Upangas*,—the PURANAS, the antiquities, the great sources of Hindu instruction and amusement. They are eighteen in number. These works are very voluminous, amounting, it is said, to 1,600,000 lines of sacred verse. Though they profess to be very ancient, the oldest is not anterior to the eighth or ninth century of our era, and some are not more than three or four hundred years old.

The subjects of the Puranas are: 1, primary creation or cosmogony; 2, secondary creation, or the destruction and renovation of worlds, including chronology; 3, genealogy of gods and patriarchs; 4, reigns of the Manus, or periods called Manwantara;[1] 5, history, or such particulars as have been

[1] A Manwantara in the Hindu system is a period of time otherwise called a day of Brahma. It is the period of the reign of Manu, the legislator and saint, the son or personification of Brahma himself, the creator and progenitor of the human race. The name is however now generic, and in every *Kalpa* or interval from creation to creation, there

preserved of the Solar and Lunar races, and of their descendants till modern times. Though these are the subjects they contain, they have no such arrangement as that indicated.

The Vishnu Purana has been translated into English by that profound Sanscrit scholar, Professor Wilson. In that work a question is put by Maitreya to Paráśara, the father of Vyása, by whom the Purana is said to be narrated. In that question, which I shall give at length, we have a general view furnished of the contents of this class of books. "I am now desirous, O thou who art profound in piety, to hear from thee how this world was, and how in future it will be? What is its substance, O Brahman, and whence proceeded animate and inanimate things? into what has it been resolved, and into what will its dissolution again occur? How were the elements manifested? whence proceeded the gods and other beings? What are the situation and extent of the oceans and the mountains, the earth, the sun, and the planets? What are the families of the gods and others, the Manus, the periods called the Manwantaras, those termed Kalpas, and their subdivisions, and the four ages: the histories, O great Muni, of the gods, the sages, and kings, and how the Vedas were divided into branches (or schools) after they had been arranged by Vyása? the duties of the Brahmans, and the other tribes, as well as of those who pass through the different orders of life? All these things I wish to hear from you, O grandson of Vshistha. Incline thy thoughts benevolently towards me, that I may, through thy favour, be

are fourteen successive Manus presiding over the Universe for the period of a Manwantara, respectively; in the present creation there have been six Manus. The period of a Manwantara is equal to seventy-one ages of the gods, or 306,720,000 years of mortals, or with its Sandhi or interval of universal deluge, 308,448,000 years. Fourteen Manwantaras constitute a Kalpa; the general period of creation and destruction, 4,320,000,000 years; each Manwantara is governed by its distinct Manu, and is provided with its own *Indra*, and minor deities; according to *Hindu* Cosmogony there have been innumerable *Manwantaras* since the first creation of the world.

informed of all I desire to know." The sage, after performing his devotions, commences his disquisitions for the instruction of his pupil. He enters upon subjects physical and metaphysical of the most abstruse character, in the true style of the Vedantic theorists, who were then such as we find them in their native land at the present time.

It is needless to add that this class of writings, the Puranas, teaches nothing that is fitted to elevate and purify the mind. On the great subjects which relate to God and to man—the dependence of the latter on the former, the provisions of mercy, their application to the fallen and depraved condition of humanity, the rule of Heaven, and the destinies of our race—these voluminous records furnish no satisfactory light.

It may be interesting to have a more extended notice of the national epic writings of the Hindus. The most remarkable are the Ramayana and the Mahabharat, written respectively by Valmiki and Vyása. To these works is also ascribed a divine origin. Rich as the Hindu literature unquestionably is in epic poetry, the Ramayana and Mahabharat eclipse all other writings of this class. These are the Iliad and the Odyssey of the Hindus, and, like the poems of the Ionian bard, outshine all the rest. The great object of these extraordinary productions of human genius and industry, is to rehearse the achievements of Vishnu, the second person in the Hindu Triad, who is represented in the Ramayana as incarnate in the person of Rama; and in the Mahabharat as incarnate in the person of Krishna. Both, however, abound with digressions, or interlocutory conversations, put into the mouths of the gods, sages, and heroes introduced into the scenes the books describe. Of these the most remarkable is the Bhagavat Gita,—an episode of the Mahabharat, in the form of a dialogue between the god Krishna and his favourite votary, the hero Arjun. The subjects of this episode are intended to enunciate the metaphysical abstractions, and theological doctrines of Pantheism. It has been pronounced one of the most singular expositions of the semi-mythological, and half-philosophical Pantheism of the Brahmans in existence.

It must be understood that the literary productions enumerated are not by any means the only works of the Hindu writers,—these are the great shastras, the divine and authentic records of faith and practice. There are, besides these, countless productions in the Sanscrit, and in the different dialects of the north and of the south, original and derived, whose authority, although not divine, is nevertheless, held in the highest veneration. The Hindu writings are altogether so large and voluminous, that the most persevering, the most industrious and learned of the Brahmans, could never read a hundredth part of them.

It may be to the curious a matter of some interest to see a comparison instituted, as regards size, between some of the principal Hindu writings and the well-known works current in Europe. The Æneid contains about twelve thousand lines, and the Iliad about twice that number; whereas the Ramayana contains one hundred thousand. The Mahabharat extends to four hundred thousand. The four Vedas form eleven huge folios. The puranas, which are but a portion of the class to which they belong, extend probably to more than two millions of lines.

Though the literary productions of the Hindus are so voluminous, and as they say of divine origin, they possess little that is of value either as regards philosophy or religion. On some matters of physical science they contain assertions that are demonstrably false. This is not however to be wondered at, since European nations long after the age of the best writers of India entertained but very imperfect and even erroneous opinions on matters of physical science. The Hindu philosophers, like those of all nations in early times, overlooked the true principle of philosophizing—reasoning from ascertained facts. On psychological subjects the Hindus have written laborious treatises, but they contain no legitimate inductive reasoning, and hence they do not avail for the elucidation of the subject, nor can they be applied to the purposes of scientific investigation: they consist of nothing but sheer dogmata. On matter and spirit, on body and mind, substance and form, nature and accident, they havê written ingeniously, but nothing worthy the name of science has been produced. There is subtlety of the most extraordinary character, and sophistry, but no sound and rational eduction of the true principles and constitution of things, either physical or intellectual. Where the light of European science has not shed its enlivening beams on the darkness of the Hindu mind, we find now the same condition as that which the literary works of antiquity imply. The native mind delights to luxuriate in ideal speculation, and it ignores the sober induction which apprehended phenomena authorize. The Hindu is too fond of the transcendental to see any beauty in the truth that meets him in the plain paths of created wisdom. It is not wonderful that under such circumstances the Hindu literature and religion should produce nothing but "a nation of sophists, sceptics, and licentious idolaters." 'Man by wisdom knew not God' has its corresponding truth in relation to himself; for the same veil that hides God from man, veils man in regard to himself.

Considering the antiquity of the Hindu nation, the influence it has exerted on others, even on the great empire of China in respect to the Buddhism it transmitted to that vast country, the influence it had in relation to the commerce of the West, from the earliest ages of Phœnicia and Egypt, it is a most remarkable fact that its literature contains no history. We may gather more information respecting India from Greek and Chinese writers, than from its own annals. Its kings, its military chiefs, its statesmen, its philosophers, and its poets, have found no one to inscribe their glorious achievements on the page of history. Its poets have emblazoned the mighty deeds of illustrious heroes, but when they flourished, and where they reigned, we cannot ascertain. European scholarship and industry have endeavoured to extract from the pages of fabulous and uncertain narration, historic information; but after all there is little more than conjecture in the profoundest researches. The early history of this most interesting country lies hid in the deepest obscurity.

Sanscrit literature contains no geographical or statistical science. Extravagant myths make up its cosmogony. On the subjects of natural history and mechanical science the books of the Hindus teach nothing. Medical science is very limited, and much as it was in the earliest ages. On anatomy they have nothing worthy the name. Musical treatises exist, but no progress has been made in this branch of the fine arts since the days of Kalidas. On the subjects of architecture and painting there are also certain works, and some on the former branch of art merit the consideration of the student.

Although the Hindu writers are deficient in works of scientific value, and present but little of utility in practical knowledge, it cannot be denied that they, at least many of them, were keen observers and deep thinkers, but they surveyed nature rather for purposes of poetry than for the ascertainment of philosophical principles. Metaphysical abstractions, ingenious theories, and not experimental inquiries or rigid induction, were the subjects they most loved and cultivated. The display of their own skill and ingenuity was too much the object they sought. They cared little for truth on any subject. Their works are characterised by brilliance, acuteness, ingenuity, and great beauty of composition. There being an utter want of the practical and useful, the works of the Hindu writers do not affect or improve the heart. The study of them needs caution. Their tendency is to bewilder. Great care is needed lest the perusal and study of many of them should lower the tone of the mind or mar the moral sense. In this respect they are the same in their effects as similar works to be met with in Europe. And the same may be said of intercourse with minds that are wholly under the influence of such literature and the tastes it induces. The influence of character is felt in intercourse with the natives of India, and much strength of moral principle, and great caution alone can preserve, amid the deteriorating and plastic influences around, the high and pure sentiments that inspire the upright bearing of the Christian and the gentleman.

Though the Hindus abound in works of a metaphysical and psychological character, they have absolutely nothing of value on the subject of intellectual science. The attempt to deduce from the operations of the mind itself any of its principles and faculties is never made, and because of this utter want of analysis nothing is ascertained, no step is taken in the right direction. In some of the writings on this branch of knowledge the most strange assertions are made, and theories the most impalpable are propounded or rather averred that one fails to find the correspondents of in nature. The intercourse of the European with men of acute minds affords frequent opportunities of hearing much on such subjects that is deplorable. Adherence to ancient theories and the utterance of antiquated dogmas are reposed in with implicit confidence, though at variance with such attributes of mind as may be recognised by the acts of consciousness. Among the educated classes who have prosecuted their studies in English literature and science there is gradually being formed a more correct appreciation of such speculations. I know several Natives who have given great attention to the subject of intellectual science, and who have prosecuted their studies so far as to induce the composition of essays on this branch of knowledge, both in the English and Native languages.

The ethical writers in Sanscrit are but few. The Panchatantra, which is the basis of the Hitopadésh, seems to be the only original treatise. In the numerous works on various subjects, excellent rules suited to every relation of life may be found ; but the theory of Hinduism, as we have seen, has a direct tendency to neutralize them. Expediency is indeed in most matters the ultimate principle to which conduct is referred in matters of morality. Some of the Tamil writers on ethical subjects are, it is believed, superior to those in Sanscrit.

From what has been advanced in the preceding paragraphs it might be inferred that nothing of value is to be found among the Sanscrit writers, were we to dismiss the subject without further detail; some notice must therefore here be introduced of such productions as are esteemed by European scholars as worthy of regard.

Primitive treatises on the Science of Astronomy, as well as the continued calculation of eclipses, and the preparation of calendars by Hindus, indicate some knowledge of the position, size, orbits and revolutions of the chief planets. When the stores of Hindu literature were first discovered and made known to Europe, and the extravagant assertions some of the Hindu astronomers have made on the subject of chronology were brought to light, there was an amazing alacrity manifested by infidels to seize on these statements for the purpose of disparaging the Mosaic account of the creation. But subsequent inquiry into the claims of the Hindu chronology, conducted on rigidly inductive principles, and on the data of the Hindu Shastras themselves, though proving the antiquity of their observations, has proved irrefragably the utter groundlessness of their supposed cycles. The works hitherto examined do not furnish sufficient data to determine some matters still under discussion, especially those relating to the claims of very remote antiquity. There is, however, abundant evidence to show that the Hindus had made great progress in this science before it was known in Greece. In this and kindred sciences the Brahmans of ancient India exhibited extraordinary ability and industry.

In those branches of science arguing deep reflective power, such as the abstruse branches of mathematics, the Hindu mind has shown its greatest capacity. In algebra, in mathematics, in geometry, mensuration, and trigonometry, they must have made great progress at a very early period, as some of their treatises on these subjects are regarded by competent judges as of a superior character. The system of arithmetical notation by ten ciphers, now in universal use, was bequeathed to western countries by the Hindus. In all probability it came to us through the Arabians.

In the department of logic the Hindu mind is framed for distinction, and numerous works on this subject are found among their writings, not only in the Sanscrit, but in the vernacular languages. They are subtle dialecticians, and it is therefore wise in the Christian teacher, who is not well acquainted with this science, to avoid those who are forward to contend with him on any nice point of subtle disquisition. If the preacher and defender of a new faith seems unskilled in the art of defence, the Hindu is apt to conclude that his own feeble intellect is but a poor guarantee for the character of his belief. It must be confessed, however, that in the Hindu system of logic, and in its application to questions of ratiocination, there is a great tendency to take illustration for proofs, and idle quibbles for sound reasoning. Indeed it may be assumed that the striking illustration their ingenuity has produced in support of their theories of spiritual and materialistic pantheism, has greatly tended to beguile the mind into acquiescence in their conclusions. When just reasoning, based on the analysis and phenomena of nature, man, and his moral relations, shall take the place of the far fetched analogies in which they are prone to indulge, the Hindu mind may escape the meshes of sophistry, and enter into the safe and rational field of true philosophy.

It has been said that in the code of Hindu law, a system of jurisprudence that dates as far back as about nine centuries before the Christian era, the department of criminal jurisdiction is very defective. Along with a great deal of practical wisdom, there is much obvious folly and inconsistency; indicating great ignorance or unconcern about social rights and practical jurisprudence. The false notions entertained about rank and caste blinded the mind, and perverted the judgment; so that any just and impartial standard on the real merit and demerit of moral action was out of the question. It is so now. It is difficult for the exclusive and the proud to arrive at the full conviction and acquiescence of the truth that all men are on an equality; that the principles of equity are like the light, pure and universal, not one thing in the palace and another in the lowly hut, but one in application to the principles of action, whosoever the actor may be. I have heard the flexible and dangerous expedient of doing evil that good may come defended with much subtlety by men of great ability and learning, and apparently with the full persuasion that they were in the right. Their reasonings, or rather sophistry, and their writings, very often transform vices into virtues and virtues into vices.

On the subject of grammar, rhetoric, and poetry, the Hindus possess admirable treatises both in Sanscrit and in the vernaculars. Grammatical rules of the most exquisite structure, comprising within the most sententious brevity wonderfully comprehensive matter, are a distinguishing peculiarity in their philology. Their short, obscure, and technical sentences are happily compared in one of the Tamil grammars to the retina of the human eye, which, although one of the smallest of superficies, is capable of receiving and containing the multiform and varied objects of a boundless prospect, the countless beauties of nature's expanded panorama. There is much in their rhetorical works that would not be applicable to similar treatises in the West; yet to the student who wishes to acquire facility and effectiveness in address, they are invaluable. It is not necessary to say that poetry of every kind, some of it of the most remarkable character, abounds both in the learned Sanscrit and in the other languages.

CHAPTER V.

HINDU LITERATURE CONTINUED.—SOME ACCOUNT OF THE HEROIC POEMS RAMAYANA AND MAHABHARAT.—THE HINDU DRAMA, MEGHADUTA, THE CLOUD MESSENGER.—SACANTOLA, THE FATAL RING.—THE NALODAYA.—HEEREN'S OPINION OF HINDU AND GERMANIC POETRY.

THE great national epics, the Ramayana and the Mahabharat, have been referred to as the most invaluable productions in the Sanscrit language. I shall here, with as much brevity as possible, present some notices of their contents. A glance at the first two books of the gigantic Ramayana will suffice to give an insight into the whole work, and serve also as a specimen of the numerous productions which, in imitation thereof, have been written in the Sanscrit, and also in the vernaculars. The subject of the Ramayana is the victory of the divine hero Rama over Ravana, prince of the Rakshas, or evil genii. It is not an allegorical representation of good triumphing over evil, but a real epic. Rama was no doubt a historic person. The Rakshas had obtained supremacy over the benevolent deities, and could not be overcome because they retained a promise of invulnerability. In this emergency the gods invoke the aid of Vishnu, and pray him to become incarnate for Ravana's subjugation. Vishnu complies, and becomes incarnate in four brothers. The chief hero is therefore a god-man; he overcomes Ravana, and puts him to death, and returns to his celestial mansions with his subjects. This is the principal matter of this most popular poem, and it is treated in a manner so rich and copious as to merit comparison with the most splendid productions of the muse.

Rama appeared as the son of Dasaratha, a wise and pious prince who dwelt at Ayodya. The description of the royal city is one of the most striking pieces of composition. This city, the modern Oude, is said to have been founded by Manu, the first sovereign who ruled over mankind. Its streets, well arranged, were refreshed by ceaseless streams of water; its walls, variously ornamented, resembled the chequered surface of a chess-board. It was filled with merchants, dramatists, elephants, horses, and chariots. The clouds of fragrant incense darkened the sun at noon-day, but the glowing radiance of the resplendent diamonds and jewels that adorned the persons of the ladies, relieved the gloom. The city was decorated with precious stones, filled with riches, furnished with abundance of provisions, adorned with magnificent temples, whose towers, like the gods, dwelt in the heavens,—such was their height—palaces, whose lofty summits were in perpetual conflict with the clouds,—baths, and gardens. The air was embalmed with incense, with the perfume of flowers, and the fragrance of sacrificial offerings. It was inhabited by the twin-born, the regenerate, profoundly instructed in the Vedas, endowed with every good quality, full of sincerity, zeal, and compassion, and like the venerated sages.

Then comes an episode. The King, who was engaged in the efficacious sacrifice of a horse, was instructed to secure, in order to its success, the marriage of his daughter Shanta with an ascetic who dwelt in the solitudes of a forest. He was enticed by a company of maidens who assumed the guise of sages to abandon his ascetic life, and he became the husband of Shanta. Vishnu becomes incarnate. The gods beseech Brahma to engage on their behalf against Ravana. Vishnu then arrives on an eagle dazzling in splendour like the sun on a cloud. Vishnu promises an incarnation of eleven thousand years for the destruction of Ravana. Eventually the four brothers were born. A sage, aware that none but Rama the son of Dasaratha could overcome the evil genii that prevented the sacrifice he wished to perform, is introduced to the aged monarch. He obtains a promise of being accepted in his petition. He requests the aid and company of Rama. The father is distressed at this, and cannot imagine that the beloved strippling can cope with demons in conflict. The sage, witnessing his reluctance, becomes incensed, at which the earth quaked, and amazement seized the gods. He prevails: the King kisses his sons Rama and Lakshman, and confides them to Visva Mitra the sage. A shower of odoriferous flowers intimates the approbation of heaven, and a choir of celestial choristers celebrates the event with songs of joy. The journey affords the poet a new and exuberant subject. Rama obtains from Visva Mitra weapons, as Achilles did from Thetis. The weapons, however, are of a different description; they are ever ready at his call on pronouncing a formula; they become personified, and converse with their master. The Ganga is reached, and described as descending from the Himalaya to purify the world and to replenish the ocean. Rama's marriage is described. He is introduced to Sita's father, and accepted. He had promised that whosoever could bend a certain bow he had, should be favoured with the hand of Sita. It is brought on an eight-wheeled car by the united efforts of eight hundred men. Rama breaks it. Sita is obtained, and her sister becomes the wife of Lakshman. They return to Ayodya. Eventually the expedition against Ravana is undertaken in consequence of his having carried off Sita. Hanuman, a Simian hero, obtains an interview with her, and delivers a message. The sea between the Indian Peninsula and Lankra (Ceylon) is filled up by mountains uptorn by Hanuman the leader of marshalled monkeys, and a bridge is thus constructed. The army passes over, and besieges the fortress of Ravana. The description of the conflicts between the armies of Rama and Ravana is the most graphic and exciting, minute in detail, and crowded with everything that renders war terrible. Ravana is overthrown. Sita is recovered. She is subjected to the ordeal of fire at

Romisseram to prove her innocence. Brahma and his attendant celestials appear, and he pronounces his benediction on them. Dasaratha the father arrives, and they all proceed in company to Ayodya, where Rama places his brother Lakshman on the throne, and ascends to heaven. Such in part is the scheme of this wonderful poem.

The other great epic, known as the Mahabharat, is a work of great ability. It is considered by competent judges one of the richest specimens of epic poetry that any age or nation has produced, and eminently distinguished for majesty of style. It is highly venerated by the Hindus of every sect, and is at once the most popular and voluminous of their writings. Its comprehensiveness is proverbial in Bengal, as appears in the proverb, "Apart from the Bharat, what narratives are there?" The varied style of this epic, and the number of subjects therein discussed, would lead us to suppose that the hypothesis once entertained, but now abandoned, respecting the Iliad and Odyssey, might be more successfully tested in regard to the Mahabharat. The immense extent of the poem precludes the possibility of its being the work of one author. Yet, according to the compiler, we have but a fragment of what was recited before the assembly of the gods.

"The subject of the poem is the struggle that took place between the Pandus and Kurus for regal supremacy: the former are the sons of the old blind king, Dhritarashtra, and are one hundred in number: the Pandus are five, Yudhisthira, Bhima, Arjuna, and the twin brothers Nakula, and Sahadeva, the Castor and Pollux of Oriental mythology. The first of these, Yudhisthira, is the Agamemnon of his day; he claims emphatically to be the 'King of men,' and performs a sacrifice in proof of his claims to universal dominion: at the same time his right, if allowed, must have more resembled the feudal authority of a powerful chief over others of lesser note, than the paramount sway of a mighty sovereign. Bhima and Arjuna are the heroes of the fight. The former is of a somewhat Achillean temperament, and the latter, like Ulysses, bends a famous bow, and accomplishes the feat of shooting five arrows in succession through a mark which swings round in the air at the famous passage of arms, for the hand of the beautiful Draupadi; whilst out of the large number of kings assembled to tilt for the prize, not one is found who can even string the bow. These two personages are still quoted as those in whom all heroic qualities are united, and it is not unworthy of remark, that though we repeatedly meet with the name of Yudhisthira amongst Hindus, we have more rarely seen a living Nakula and Sahadeva, whilst Bhima and Arjuna, curtailed of their fair proportions, occur to our eye at every turn. The sons of Pandu, after the completion of their education, run the gauntlet through a series of practices directed against their lives by the malice of Duryodhana and his brothers, and at length fall victims to a passion so fatal to every age and country—that of gaming. Yudhisthira loses everything, from his palace and his wealth to his personal liberty and that of his friends: these are all restored by the interference of the king; but on trying the venturous game a second time, and again losing, he is doomed, under a previously made condition, to undergo banishment in the woods for a period of twelve years."

"The poem is now protracted by a long series of episodes, some evidently of later date, without making any real progress in the epic; four cantos are taken up with the battles between the two parties, in which the aid of deities and supernatural weapons give the victory to one party or the other, alternately, in the same manner as we read in the Iliad. At length the great obstacle to the final catastrophe is removed by the death of Duryodhana, who is killed in single fight by Bhima, and we should naturally have expected the poem to have terminated with this event. Instead of this we are conducted through another series of episodes till we attain the mark on which the Hindu vision would seem ever to be fixed—the disunion of the soul and body, and the final rewards of the virtuous."

"The remaining books of the Mahabharat, although more or less episodical, are in better keeping with the story. They are also short and hasten to the catastrophe." It were tedious to go through all the parts. We may select one or two leading events. "The seventeenth book, called the 'Maha-prastanika,' or special exodus, witnesses the abdication of his hardly won throne by Yudhisthira, and the departure of himself, his brothers, and Draupadi, to the Himalaya, on their way to the holy mountain Meru. As they proceed the influence of former evil deeds proves fatal, and each in succession drops down dead by the way-side; Yudhisthira, and a dog that had followed them from Hastinapura, are the only survivors. Indra comes to convey the prince to *Swarga* (Paradise): but Yudhisthira refuses to go unless,

> Admitted to that equal sky,
> His faithful dog shall bear him company.

Indra complies."

The eighteenth book, the Swargarohana, introduces Yudhisthira in his bodily form to heaven; to his great dismay he finds there Duryodhana and the other sons of Dhritarashtra, but sees none of his other friends, or Draupadi; he demands to know where they are, and refuses to stay even in *Swarga*, without them. A messenger conveys him through terrible shades, where he encounters all sorts of disgusting and terrific objects. He essays to return, but is arrested by voices imploring his stay, as already his presence had alleviated the tortures of the place. He is overcome, and resolves rather to share the fate of his friends in hell than abide with their enemies in heaven. Here he is brought into the extreme of trial. The gods assemble and applaud his virtue. All the horrors that had beset his path vanish; and his friends and kindred are carried along with him to *Swarga*, where they again become the celestial personages they were originally, before they became incarnate for a season to aid Vishnu in relieving the world from the tyranny of those evil beings who were oppressing the virtuous and propagating impiety."

This short account thus presents the main features of the work. As in the Ramayana, Vishnu, the preserver of the world, appears for its relief from the oppression of evil genii in the person of Ràma; so in the Mahabharat he appears for the same benevolent purpose in the person of Krishna. The popularity of these two divinities, Ràma and Krishna, are thus accounted for. The remarkable episode known as the Bhagavat Gita, contains, as before observed, much on the religious philosophy of the Hindus that is peculiarly interesting. In this work Krishna, who instructs his disciple Arjuna, appears as an incarnation of God. The doctrines of this work are those of pantheism and mysticism.

The brief account we are giving of Sanscrit literature would be defective, without some reference to the bards of a later age than those of the Epics. In the last century before our era, one of the Hindu kings, named Vicramaditya, was distinguished as a patron of learning; his eight poets, with himself, are known in Hindu literature as the nine gems. Of the nine, Kalidas was incontrovertibly the most distinguished. He raised the Indian drama to the highest pitch of perfection. He has been termed the Hindu Shakespeare; and certainly not without some reason. Our own great master suffers naught by the association. Though he did not certainly possess the master mind of Shakespeare, he possessed his gentle fancy, his simple heart, and his delicate sensibilities. I shall supply a few examples from this writer, who united most successfully the glow of eastern imagery with manliness of expression. The first drama to be noticed is called Meghaduta, the cloud-messenger.

The subject is simple and ingenious: a Yaksha, a divinity of an inferior order, an attendant upon the god of riches, Kuvera, and one of a class which as it appears from the poem, is characterised by a benevolent spirit, a gentle temper, and an affectionate disposition, has incurred the displeasure of his sovereign, and has been condemned by him to a twelve-months' exile from his home. In the solitary but sacred forest in which he spends the period of his banishment, the Yaksha's most earnest care is to find an opportunity of conveying intelligence and consolation to his wife; and in the wildness of his grief, he fancies he discovers a friendly messenger in a cloud—one of those noble masses of vapour which seem almost instinct with life as they traverse an Indian sky in the commencement of a monsoon, moving forward in solemn progression from the equatorial ocean towards the Himalayas. In the spirit of this bold, but not unnatural personification, the Yaksha addresses the cloud, and entrusts to it the message he yearns to despatch to the absent object of his attachment. He describes the direction in which the cloud is to travel—one marked out for it by the laws of the universe—and takes this opportunity of alluding to the most important scenes of Hindu mythology and tradition, not with the dulness of prosaic detail, but with that true poetic pencil which, by a few happy touches, brings the subject of the description vividly before the mind's eye. Arrived at the end of the journey, the condition of his beloved wife—the object of the exile's anticipations—is detailed; and it is dwelt on with equal delicacy and truth: and the poem terminates with the message which is intended to assuage her grief and animate her hopes. The whole of this part of the composition is distinguished by the graceful expression of natural and amiable feelings, and cannot fail to leave a favourable impression of the national character; whilst the merely descriptive portion introduces the student to a variety of local and mythological information of great value, with which it becomes necessary to familiarize himself, and which, should he ever find himself in India, he will contemplate with additional interest and pleasure, from his previous acquaintance with the verses of Kalidasa.

The Yaksha having described the regions over which the cloud is to pass, conducting him as it were to his journey's end, imagines that he beholds his absent wife:—

"I view her now! long weeping swells her eyes,
And those dear lips are dried by parting sighs;
Sad on her hand her pallid cheek declines,
And half unseen, through veiling tresses shines,
As when a darkling night the moon enshrouds,
A few faint rays break straggling through the clouds.
Now at thy sight I mark fresh sorrows flow,
And sacred sacrifice augments her woe;
I mark her now with fancy's aid retrace
This wasted figure, and this haggard face.
Now from her favourite bird she seeks relief,
And tells the tuneful Sárika her grief;
Mourns o'er the feather'd prisoner's kindred fate,
And fondly questions of its absent mate.
In vain the lute for harmony is strung,
And round the robe-neglected shoulder slung;
And faltering accents strive to catch in vain
Our race's old commemorative strain;
The faltering tear that from reflection springs
Bedews incessantly the silvery strings,
Recurring woe still pressing on the heart,
The skilful hand forgets its grateful art,
And idly wandering strikes no measured tone,
But makes a sad wild warbling of its own."

Space obliges me to curtail my reference to this incomparable poem within this brief extract. The entire work, with others, may be seen in the volumes of the Hindu Drama, which the accomplished scholar, Professor Wilson, has prepared for English admirers of this species of composition.

The Hindu drama is not only ancient, but stamped with features of originality. The productions of the most gifted authors do not exceed about sixty, of which only nine have assumed an English dress. The best dramatic compositions are written in Sanscrit. One of the peculiarities of the pieces is the absence of everything of a tragical character: the natives of India are averse to such scenes. This feature of the

Hindu mind is practically evinced too in its instinctive dislike to anything severe even in religious teaching. Allusions to painful catastrophes, the inflictions of providence, or even an inauspicious word or sentence, especially in the conclusion of an address or epistle, could not fail to tax painfully the sensibilities of the Hindu.

The next distinguished dramatic writer is Bhavabhuti. He differs in many features from his unequalled rival. "Kalidas excels in the softer kinds of description. Love, newborn love, is the passion he most delights to portray. Haunts of repose and meditation, sequestered groves and flowery banks, fanned by odorous winds, and watered by purling rivulets, where the hum of bees and the notes of birds proclaim the never-dying spring, are the spots he is wont to frequent. Wood nymphs crowned with stars, and sylvan deities with wings of gold, are the companions with whom he delights to associate. Not so with Bhavabhuti. He describes nature in her magnificence. Cloud-capped mountains, and blasting heaths, the hoarse murmur of his native stream, and the gloomy grandeur of his native forests, midnight incantations—

> ——— Calling shades, and beckoning shadows dire,
> And airy tongues that syllable men's names,

are his favourite subjects. The battle field and the charnel-house have for him peculiar attractions."

Sacantola, or the fatal ring, by Kalidas, is considered his masterpiece. It is a natac of the mytho-pastoral class, and was acted at the beginning of summer, as appears from the sweet song of the actress in the prologue.

"Mark how the soft blossoms of the *Nag-cessar* are lightly kissed by the breeze." "Mark how the damsels delicately place behind their ears the flowers of the *Srisha.*"

"The story is simple. It is this:—Menaca, a goddess of the lower heaven, had entrusted to a devout hermit, who spent his life in the depth of a forest, the care of her only daughter, Sacantola, so called from a compound word that has a reference to the fact that, till found by Kanwa, she was brought up by birds. There the sovereign of the country arrives, by accident, on a hunting excursion. Himself unseen, he observes Sacantola and her two companions, Anusya and Prijamvada, watering their plants, and is immediately captivated. He dismisses his attendants, and enters into conversation with the damsels. The heart of Sacantola is soon won, and she confesses it. The king on this discovers himself, and she becomes his wife. He is almost immediately summoned to his court, parts from Sacantola with many expressions of regret, promises to send for her within three days, and leaves a ring in token of remembrance. In the meantime a Brahman of the name of Durvasas comes to the residence of the hermit, when his two daughters are at a little distance, and Sacantola is overtaken with sleep. The Brahman finding no one to receive him, pours forth a malediction in the following words: 'He, on whom thou art meditating, on whom alone thy heart is now fixed, while thou neglectest a pure gem of devotion, who demands hospitality, shall forget thee when thou seest him next, as a man restored to sobriety forgets the words he uttered in a state of intoxication.' Anusya and Prijamvada overhear his words, and, in love for their sleeping companion, hasten to appease his anger. The Brahman says that his words cannot be recalled, but that the spell would be dissolved when the king should look upon his ring. In prospect of an interesting event, her foster-father, who was absent at the time of her marriage, resolves to send her to the palace of her lord. Her friends instruct her to produce the ring, should she not be immediately recognised. Arrived at her destination, she is discovered by the king and finds that the ring is lost. In this extremity she asks the protection of the king's priest, which is granted. On her way to his house, a body of light in a female shape descends from the heavens, and having caught her hastily in its bosom, disappears. The king regards this as the work of sorcery, and dismisses the whole thing from his mind. After a time a poor fisherman is brought up in custody of the officers of police, for having in his possession a ring of value. This proves to be the ring that Dushmanta gave to Sacantola, as she took up water to pour on her head; and was found in the bowels of a fish. With it he recovers his memory. Struck with horror at his past conduct, he clothes himself in vestments of penitence. The seasons lose their charms. The songs of his favourite Queen Hansamati delight him no more. Whilst thus afflicted he is summoned by Indra, the god of the firmament, to subdue a race of giants who defied his prowess. He is conveyed to the celestial regions by the Matali, Indra's charioteer, and acquits himself gloriously in this divine service. On his descent he lights on the mountain of Hemacuti, where Casyappa, father of the immortals, and Aditi, his consort, reside in seclusion. Here he meets his wife and his son, and perfect happiness succeeds.

"When Kanwa parts with Sacantola he breaks out in the following strain:—'Hear, O ye trees of this hallowed forest; ye trees in which the sylvan goddesses have their abode, hear and proclaim that Sacantola is going to the palace of her wedded lord; she who drank not, though thirsty, before you were watered; she who cropped not, through affection for you, one of your fresh leaves, though she would have been pleased with ornaments for her locks; she whose chief delight was in the season when your branches are spangled with flowers.'"

"Sacantola weeps at parting, and after she had disengaged herself from a gentle fawn that clung to her skirts, was thus addressed by Kanwa:—'Thy tears, my child, ill suit the occasion: we shall meet again—be firm: see the direct road before thee, and follow it. When the big tear lurks beneath thy beautiful eyelashes, let thy resolution check the first effort to disengage itself. In thy passage over this earth, where the paths are now high, now low, and the true path seldom distinguished, the traces of thy feet must needs be unequal, but virtue will press thee right onward.

"The aerial journey of Dushmanta in Indra's car is considered one of the finest specimens in dramatic writers. Our space permits not our joining him in the ascent. One or two specimens must conclude this reference to the Hindu Drama. The following is an expressive simile:—

"My body moves onward, but my restless heart runs back to her like a light flag borne on a staff against the wind, and fluttering in an opposite direction."

A swan, a very favourite bird among the Hindus, and often referred to by their writers for its beauty and grace, is described in the following lines:—

> "Behold awhile the beauties of the lake,
> Where on its slender stem the lotus trembles
> Brush'd by the passing swan, as on he sails,
> Singing his passion."

The appearance of a shadow in water is attempted to be expressed in the following lines:—

> "There, where the Pandu and the Sindhu wind,
> The towers and temples, pinnacles and gates,
> And spires of Padmavati, like a city,
> Precipitated from the skies, appears
> Inverted in the translucent wave."

Dramatic entertainments, being intended to exhibit characters and feelings, and to present the natural indications of passion, poems to be seen and heard, may well serve to indicate the feelings and character of a people among whom they are produced; and in this way they may illustrate a vast variety of topics. It is, in fact, the case with all Hindu writings. They are so replete with reference to the social, the mythological, the philosophical notions of their race, that they serve to illustrate their social, their religious, and their national characteristics. The literature is such as the Hindus would produce, and the Hindus exhibit the general characteristics their literature would tend to enstamp upon them. Hence, among others, a strong motive for the study of their national writings to those who have much to do with their interests, either sacred or civil.

I cannot resist the temptation of giving some account of another work of the distinguished author already named, Kalidas. The book to which I refer is known by the name of *Nalodaya Emergence*, from Calamity. It is the story of a king of the name of Nala. His kingdom was called Nishadha. He married, under very romantic circumstances, the beautiful and accomplished Damyanti. The poet, when speaking of her personal charms, says, that when Brahma created her, he despised the ordinary elements of our own planet, and formed her from materials taken from the concave surface of the moon, and thus left a scar which is still apparent. The royal personage who espoused this unequalled beauty, under the promptings of demoniacal influence, lost his kingdom by gaming. Accompanied by his afflicted queen he retires from the kingdom he had forfeited. Reduced to the greatest extremities he ultimately abandons his wife, not from want of attachment, so much as from his inability to witness inevitable sufferings. After various adventures and afflictions they are reunited, and by strange events he recovers his kingdom, and dies, full of honours, in a good old age. Kalidas has exhausted his poetic genius in the mode of constructing this poem, which contains many wonderful specimens of alliteration. The late Dr. Yates, an eminent Oriental scholar, whom I had the honour to know as a friend, and in some sort a fellow-labourer, says of the composition of *Nalodoya:* " Kalidas has in this work ornamented his subject with pearls drawn from the very deepest recesses of the sea of Oriental learning."

I will select a few specimens from Dr. Yates' translation :—

> " His army was a ship, his foes a sea,
> And arrows were the waves—while he on board,
> In triumph sailing through those dashing waves,
> The port of safety reach'd."

Damyanti, bewailing her lost husband, exclaims:—

"Long as my soul within this body dwells,
So long in it will Nala not reside,
As glowing fire within the heated iron?"

The following is a striking passage:—

"And now the sun had set with crimson tinge;
The lotus red had lost its glowing hue,
From which it was apparent to the eye
The sun had been a most notorious thief:
The colour of his beams the fact discloses.
But soon he lost his most unlawful gain,
And suffer'd for the sly nefarious deed:
The darkness thicken'd round his path—to show
That loss of glory is the fruit of sin."

The subjoined quotations may be regarded as evincing the tendency of Hinduism to neutralize the force of natural conscience; on the one hand, referring events to divine decree, and on the other, to satanic influence. This reference of events, that proceed on many occasions from deliberate choice, is sometimes made the ground of palliating crime; and the subterfuge may often be met with in one's intercourse with the people. This tendency is not, however, confined to the Hindu philosophy—it is exemplified in western countries, and seems to be natural to the human family. Our own immortal bard has very felicitously expressed the pitiable shifts of those who would attribute their evil practices to aught but themselves. "When we are sick," he says, "often the effect of our own behaviour, we make guilty of our disorders, the sun, the moon, and the stars; as if we were felonious by necessity, fools by heavenly compulsion, knaves, thieves, and traitors by spherical predominance; drunkards, liars, and adulterers, by an enforced obedience of planetary influence, and all that we are evil in, by divine thrusting on."

So Nala's unnatural abandonment of Damyanta is expressed as follows:—

"His heart reproach'd him for the cruel deed,
His only consolation was in fate—
That so it happens in an evil hour
The strongest foes he had subdued before,
But now by Kali, moral evil conquer'd."

Apostrophising her selfish and traitorous husband, Damyanti says—

"Shall I impute it to the want of love?
Ah! no! be far from thee all treachery!
I know that some malignant power unseen
Has led thee to commit this foolish act,
And therefore from my heart forgive thee all."

These examples must suffice as specimens of Sanscrit writers. They will, I am inclined to think, produce a favourable impression, and together with what has been advanced on the language, and other branches of literature, induce the conviction that the Hindus, early enjoying, as they unquestionably did, the advantages which refined language and literature impart, must have attained to a high standard of civilization at a period long anterior to the Christian era. One or two general remarks may close the notices required in elucidation of the Sanscrit language and its literature.

The Ramayana and the Mahabharat determine the character of the Indian epos, and to a certain degree the whole range of the national poetry. This being the case, the poetry of the Vernaculars, indeed almost all the literature of the Vernaculars, bears a relation to those two great epics, and other original Sanscrit works, exactly the same as Latin literature bears to Greek. The Iliad and Odyssey of Homer reappear in Latin authors. A parallel might be run between the authors in Greek and Latin, Sanscrit and the Vernaculars. The latter are echoes, many of them faint indeed, of the voice that speaks in the sacred tongue.

The theories of the Hindus on physical and religious subjects give a character to their entire literature. The doctrine of Pantheism invests all nature, animate, and inanimate, human and divine, with a community of being; and hence the facility with which a human personage becomes super-human or infra-human. Those who were wont to figure on earth as heroes, in the embattled-field, or as sages in the solitude of forests, appear in the abodes of Paradise. Divinities, known as the inhabitants of celestial mansions, appear as men; and the ever-playful fancy of the Hindu disposes of them as he pleases in endlessly varied places, and in equally diversified offices and relationships. They assume any shape and animate any object. Hanuman leads his monkeys; Yamvent is the king of bears; and Garud is the prince of eagles. In Greek poetry, gods are subordinate actors, affecting the destiny of human beings; in Hindu poetry they become the principals.

It has therefore been suggested that the Hindu epic and the sacred poetry of the English and German writers are possessed of some resemblance. Heeren has a bold thought on this point. In reading Milton myself I have often been struck with the remarkable coincidence there is between his sentiments, his imagery and his machinery, and those of some of the Hindu writers. Had he lived at a later period one could not have resisted the conviction that he had borrowed from the Hindu. Heeren says, "May we not be allowed to conjecture that during a separation of some thousand years, admitting the connexion between the Anglo-German and Hindu nations, they have mutually preserved that sentiment of the divine and heavenly, which afterwards burst forth in their respective epic writers at the same time with the rise of their national poetry? And may we not suppose that Vyása and Klopstock, Vamiki and Milton, though far removed from each other by the longest intervals of space and time, were nevertheless animated by the same spirit?" Had he been a Hindu he might have supposed these poets the same person, appearing at successive periods.

CHAPTER VI.

LANGUAGES:—URDU—ABORIGINAL—THE TAMIL, ITS CHARACTERISTICS AND MERITS; ITS PROSE AND POETIC DIALECTS—TAMIL LITERATURE—SPECIMENS FROM AVVEYAR, TIRUVALUVAR, AND KABILAR,—JESUIT AUTHORS—THEIR WORKS—PRESENT STATE OF LITERATURE IN INDIA—NATIVE, ROMISH, AND PROTESTANT—BIBLE TRANSLATION—LITURGICAL VERSIONS—GENERAL LITERATURE—CHEERING PROSPECTS.

As the subject of language is one of considerable interest and importance in regard to the Anglo-Indian empire, I have endeavoured to elucidate it, as far as possible, in the Map attached to this volume. By a reference to the map and its language-key, the reader may at once ascertain the territorial limits within which the nineteen languages are vernacular.

In regard to the sixth language in the enumeration, the Urdu, it may be as well to state that it is not an original Hindu language, but one that has sprung from the Mohammedan conquest. It bears very much the same relation as the English to the events of history. As the English language was formed by an admixture of Anglo-Saxon and Norman-French, so the Urdu, often called Hindostanee, was formed of several dialects, after the invasion of the country by the Mohammedans. The account of the origin of the Urdu is given as follows:—

When Akbar succeeded to the throne of Delhi, A.D. 1555, various races, Hindu and Mussulman, presented themselves in the royal city. They differed in language and dialect; but when they came to live and traffic together, one language, termed Urdu, became definitely fixed. The word Urdu signifies camp, and serves to indicate the origin of this comparatively new language, which consists of Persian and Arabic, brought in by the invaders, and Hindi, one of the cognates of the Sacred Sanscrit.

Having completed the brief notices it was judged fit to offer on the subject of the Hindu sacred language and its literature, it is now intended to add some further information relative to the other family of languages already referred to.

That the religion and literature, as well as the political constitution, of the South of India, were derived from the north, the earliest seat of the Hindu empire, as well as of the arts and sciences,—and that the southern peninsula was before that period a vast, uncultivated forest, inhabited by small and insulated tribes, speaking a jargon which hardly furnished them with terms expressive of their immediate and natural wants,—there is scarcely any doubt. While in this state, a sage named Agastya appears to have conveyed thither the first colony of Brahmans, and other classes, from the north, and with them the Hindu religion and literature, in form the same as at the present day. He is believed to have been the inventor of the letters now in use in the Tamil, and the first who refined the southern language, the Tamil, on the principles of the Sanscrit cultivated in the north.

Whether, prior to the introduction of the Sanscrit, and the establishment of the Brahmanized race, there were more than one language common to India generally, we have not at present the means of deciding. Sufficient information we have to establish the fact of an affinity between the Tamil language spoken in the south of India, and some of the dialects spoken by the semi-barbarous tribes of the hills; and I have been informed by those competent to give information on the subject, that there is a striking similarity between this family of language and the Scythian tongues. It may be hoped that the inquiries of Orientalists will be pushed forward on this and kindred subjects, and through their successful efforts we may hope that much light may eventually be cast on a subject that is at present confessedly obscure.

We may fairly regard the Tamil language as the highest and most finished example of that family of Indian tongues that have no connexion whatever with Sanscrit, excepting that which is purely adventitious. It may be worthy of remark that the word Tamil (sweet) is applied to the language in regard to the predominance of that quality in its expression. It is certainly, when well spoken, one of the sweetest of human tongues. The language is also called Ten Molji (Southern speech), to distinguish it from Sanscrit, which is called Vada Molji (Northern speech), in evident allusion to the region of its special cultivation. The term Dravida is also used to designate the Tamil language. Sanscrit writers use this word for the Coromandel coast, lying between Madras, or thereabouts, and Cape Comorin. Dravida was the name of a descendant of a degraded Kshattriya. Five Dravida are mentioned—Dravira, Kernata, Gujjeratta, Maharashtra, and Telanga.

The Tamil language is spoken from the region lying a little north of Madras, down to Nagercoil, close to Cape Comorin, in the region below the Ghats, and also throughout the northern and eastern provinces of Ceylon. The Tamil speaking population amounts to many millions.

The alphabet consists of eighteen consonants and twelve vowels, besides several Sanscrit consonants that have been introduced along with the words in which they occur. The consonants are transformed or modified, to indicate the occurrence of the vowel that may be present; and hence each consonant assumes as many modifications as there are vowels.

The Tamil grammarians attribute the origin of the different letters to different deities: the twelve vowels to Brahma; *ka* and *inga*, to Siva; *cha*, *nya*, to Vishnu, &c. Certain letters are supposed to be appropriated to certain castes. To Brahmans are assigned the letters that Brahma,

Siva, Vishnu, and Supramanya originated. To kings are dedicated the letters originated by Indra, the sun, and moon. Yama, the king of the dead, and Plutus, give letters to merchants. Neptune originates two letters for agriculturists. The other castes are entitled to all except the vowels. In the construction of verse, attention must be paid to the peculiarities here specified. Reference must also be had to the constellations in the composition of the invocation. As before stated, Sarasvati, the consort of Brahma, is the patroness of the fine arts, and she is therefore looked up to by all who essay to tune the lyre. Her names are numerous, and they indicate the influence her inspirations have on the success of the Muse.

The consonants are classed into hard, soft, and medial, and the vowels into long and short. The rules of Sandhi, or combination and permutation, are used as in the refined Sanscrit. The nouns are declined as in Latin, having two additional cases, instrumental and locative. The verb is not complex, yet very full and effective in its conjugations. It has a double causal form. Take, as an example, the verb *to do:* I may express in the verb, without encumbering it with more than a single additional letter, either the sense of doing a thing myself, by another, or by a third party through a second. It needs scarcely be added that the last refinement is not much in use. The second form, however, is in constant use, as the ordinary mode in which the verbs intransitive are presented in their transitive state. Thus, by an easy provision in the conjugation, the verb *to see* takes the sense of the verb *to show;* the verb *to learn* becomes the verb *to teach;* the verb *to write* becomes the verb *to copy* by another, &c.

The Tamil language is distinguished as colloquial and poetic. Thus it has a vulgar and refined aspect. The refined is used in composition by classic writers; the comments written thereon being in the ordinary style. The common spoken language is highly wrought, and generally, even by the common people, it is spoken with great propriety. The idiom or syntax of the language is widely different from that of the Indu-Germanic tongues; and for the most part the order of arrangement is the opposite of that which is followed by them. This peculiarity renders the language difficult to a foreigner for a long time. Another peculiarity of this language is, the absence of the relative pronoun. It has no articles. It possesses but few particles and prepositions. These apparent defects are, however, very effectively supplied in construction. Perhaps no language combines greater force with equal brevity; and it may be asserted that no human speech is more close and philosophic in its expression as an exponent of the mind. The sequence of things—of thought, purpose, action, and its results—is always maintained inviolate. Rank and station are provided for by the use of various pronouns, extending to several degrees of honorific expression. The language teems with words expressive of the different degrees of affinity. Where in European languages a long periphrasis would be required, Tamil presents the thing in its own single term. And this fecundity extends to all the ramifications of the family tree. If I speak of a sister I may either take a word that gives the relationship subsisting between us, or I may select one that will indicate our relative ages. Measures and divisions of time are equally minute and expressive. The language, thus specific, gives to the mind a readiness and clearness of conception, whilst its terseness and philosophic idiom afford equal means of lucid utterance. The colloquial language is called Kodun Tamil.

The poetic dialect called Shen Tamil, has its separate grammar and peculiar inflections. To read the literature of the Tamil people which is written in this refined language, it is needful to learn the grammar connected with it. This grammar, called Panjalakanam, or *Belles Lettres*, consists of five parts, as the name imports—viz. letters, words, matter, versification, and embellishment. On the importance and value of this branch of learning, the testimony of the most learned foreigner that has ever appeared in the Tamil Provinces, the learned Beschi, a distinguished Jesuit who flourished more than a century ago, may not be inappropriate in this place. In his introduction to a grammar of the poetic dialect prepared for his fraternity, he says: " Among the natives themselves very few can now be found who are masters of the higher dialect. He among them who is even acquainted with its rudiments, is regarded with respect, but should he quote their abstruse works, he is listened to with admiration; what praise then would they not bestow on a foreigner, whom they should find deeply versed in a science which they themselves consider rarely attainable? They will easily attend to one whose learning is the object of their admiration. And as this evidently may lead to the honour of religion, and promote the salvation of those about us, I am satisfied that this consideration alone, operating on zeal like yours, will excite you to the study of this dialect, notwithstanding the difficulties that attend it."

This reasoning is cogent, and in the mind of the Christian teacher, who is under proper influences, it cannot fail to produce its effect. It is a matter to be regretted that missionary institutions have not as yet any fixed standard whereby to measure the attainments of agency, and none whereby that agency can measure itself. It cannot be doubted that much, very much, valuable time and labour are lost, and consequently money misspent, and hopes disappointed, because in regard both to home and foreign acquirements, men sometimes fail to bring to the work the requisite qualifications. It may be that the Church of Christ underrates the difficulties of the undertaking it has taken up in regard to the conversion of India; and hence the adaptation of means to ends is not infrequently overlooked. This is confessedly a very important point, as affecting the success of the efforts that are made for the conversion of India to the faith of Christ.

The Tamil people have an extensive literature. Many

popular works already named or alluded to, as the Ramayana, the Mahabharat, some of the Puranas, and other productions found in the Sanscrit, have been translated, in whole or in part, into the Tamil language. Of such it is not necessary to speak particularly. The Tamil is also rich in original authorship. Its works on grammar are voluminous. Agastya, a saint before referred to, celebrated in Hindu mythology, is said to have given the first rules of grammar. He is the Cadmus of the Tamil language. He is fabled to have been born in a water-jar, to have drunk up the ocean, and to have prostrated the Vindya range of hills, and hence his name, which signifies one who fixes mountains. After his time seven distinguished writers devoted their powers to the cultivation of the grammar of the language: their works have perished. A writer of the name of Tôlcàppiyanàr (ancient author) has bequeathed the fruit of his labours to posterity; but his work is short and obscure. Pavananti, a learned devotee, has left a grammar called Nannul, which will doubtless live as long as the language: it is an incomparable work. Writings on almost every subject, commonly treated of by the Sanscrit authors, abound; but in many instances the names of those who composed them have been lost. The prince of the Tamil poets wrote an epic called Chintá-mani, which is one of the most masterly performances found in the language. In this work the power of the language and the talent of the author are equally conspicuous. This poem extends to 15,000 lines, and contains some brilliant gems. In ethical writings the Tamil has been more fortunate than the Sanscrit. The most remarkable work of this class is from the stylus of Tiruvalluvar (the Divine valluvar) a spiritual leader of the Pariah class. They call their soothsayers or spiritual guides by the name Valluvar, to which, in his case *Tiru*, divine, is added by way of expressing his superior excellence. The Kural, for that is the name of his work, contains 1,330 distiches, and is regarded by the Tamil people as a book of sacred aphorisms, from which there is no appeal. Tradition attributes to Avveyár, a name appropriated to aged matrons among the Tamil people, several works of great beauty and value, replete with lessons of wisdom, in the form of aphorisms and moral sentences. These works have never been surpassed for sententious brevity; and generally they are equally distinguished by purity of principle. Náladiyár is a beautifnl composition. It consists of 400 epigrams on moral subjects, such as truth, purity, friendship, &c. Beschi thus states the tradition attached to this work:—"One thousand poets visited the court of one of the Pandya Rajas, who, being a lover of the muses, treated them with favour, and in so doing excited the envy of the resident poets, who succeeded in prejudicing their master against the new comers, and as a consequence they fled from the danger that menaced them. Previous to his departure each poet wrote a verse on a small scroll and deposited it under his pillow. When this was made known, the king ordered the scrolls to be collected and thrown into the river, when four hundred of them were observed to ascend the stream four feet (Nàladi). The king was struck with the occurrence, ordered the scrolls to be collected, and the volume was called Naladiyar."

Of the two popular writers, Avveyár and Tiruvalluvar, it may not be considered out of place to give some account, as the fabulous stories related of them and their connexions serve at once to illustrate the character, the manners, and the sentiments of the Hindus. The above-named persons are two of seven renowned philosophers, who were the children of the same parents. The legend regarding them is as follows:—

The grandfather, a sage of the name of Vedamolji, saw a bright light descend from the heavens, and fall on the house of a low caste family, where a girl had just been born, and which he foresaw would become the wife of his own son Pérâli, a youth then twelve years of age. He forthwith informed the fraternity of Brahmans of the phenomenon, which he said was an ill omen, but concealed from them his impressions regarding his son. The twice-born informed the father of the girl that evil would befall them through his child, and it was put to him, on whom it was right it should fall, on them or on the child. He left the matter in their hands, and the holy personages resolved unanimously on the expediency of destroying the infant. Vedamolji would not consent to this decision, and an ark was therefore prepared, and the little one being deposited in it, the frail vessel was cast adrift on the bosom of the river Cauvery. The old man requested his son to ascertain if any distinguishing mark appeared on any part of the child's body; and it was found that there was a black mark on the thigh.

As the little voyager floated down the stream, it was descried by a Brahman, when performing his ablutions. He looked into the little vessel, and his eye was met by that of a smiling infant. He had no children, and he was moved to rescue this, as if sent by heaven in answer to his prayers. He adopted the child, and had her carefully educated as she grew up. Pérâli, having arrived at man's estate, went on a pilgrimage to some holy place; and in the course of his peregrinations, he met with the Brahman who had adopted the little water-nymph. The young man was distinguished by so many prepossessing qualities, that the foster-father conceived a desire to retain him as a suitable match for his adopted daughter. He became her husband, and they lived happily together, till, on her changing her dress after ablution, he accidentally espied the black mark on her person, and at once inferred her low origin. He inquired after her history, and found that her birth and origin were alike obscure. He left her. She followed him, and entreated his return; but he refused, and eventually deserted his wife. She feared to return to her father, as she regarded the Brahman, and wandered about overwhelmed with grief. A Brahman seeing her, and ascertaining the cause of her distress, took her in and placed her among his own daughters, by whom she was received as a sister. Her benefactor died and left her an equal portion of his property, with which she built a choultry for the convenience of pilgrims whom she received and entertained with water, and milk, and rice, and fruit, and indeed all, a pilgrim could desire. She also imparted to such her counsel, and elicited from them information, and gave them her own narrative. In the course of years her own husband came. They did not recognise each other, but on her relating her affecting history he perceived that in this virtuous and faithful patroness of holy pilgrims he had met his discarded wife. He was silent, indeed feigned sleep while she was narrating the events of the past. He rose early, and was departing without the accustomed salutation, on which she questioned his motive, and demanded whether he had seen aught in her conduct that was wrong, and besought forgiveness if her hospitalities had been in any respect deficient. In her gentle objurgations she remarked, "Your departure was like that of my husband." He could now no longer refrain himself, confessed his relation to her, and they became reunited. She and their children also, as they multiplied, thenceforward accompanied him in all his wanderings.

It had been engaged between them that all his injunctions must be most promptly obeyed. In the course of events, he directed her to abandon all her children to the care of Providence, and leave them in the open forest. This was a trying behest, but she nevertheless obeyed. The tender sympathies of maternal love were repressed as far as possible, and she gave each a parting kiss. Seeing her deep agony of mind each endeavoured to assuage the mother's grief by appropriate words of comfort. One said, "My Maker formed me in thy womb, nourished me, and there till birth caused me to grow; canst thou doubt his future care of me? Go, put thy trust in him and follow his ways." The second observed, "God provides even for a frog in a stone, can he do less for me? why art thou careful about me? be of good comfort, and go thy way." The third spoke as follows, "God has brought me into the world, and has appointed my destiny; can it be that he is dead? Surely he will not desert me; go, dear mother, and fear nothing on my account." The fourth observed, at parting, "Is not the egg surrounded with a hard shell? yet God vivifies the little chick within it; will he not feed it after it has broken the shell? He will also feed me; be not troubled, be cheerful, and trust in God." The fifth said, "He who has made the finest veins and channels within the trees, through which the nourishing particles of the earth circulate and cause their growth, and who has formed the smallest insects in so wonderful a manner, and sustains them; will he not do the same for me? be not, therefore, cast down, be firm, and hope in him." The sixth remarked, "Manifold and trifling are the occupations of men, but the great work of the Almighty is to create and preserve; believing this, be comforted." The seventh, at parting, thus encouraged his sorrowing mother; "God creates such different qualities in the trees and plants, that they produce sour, sweet, bitter, and various delicious fruits. He who is powerful to do this, will also provide for me: why weepest thou, dearest mother? Be cheerful and hope in him." These children were found. One was trained by a king; another by a washerman; another by a poet and philosopher; another by a climber of the palm-tree; another by a basket-maker; another by a Brahman; and the seventh by an outcast. Avveyár was educated by a poet.

This distinguished matron is said to have lived to be 240 years old, because she was in possession of some secret chemical preparation that prolongs life. Her works are most popular; she wrote five treatises, which are the first books taught in Tamil schools. The first work I propose to select quotations from is written alphabetically, *i.e.* each successive precept commences in the order of the Tamil letters, and has been not inaptly called the "golden alphabet." The following beautiful and sententious aphorisms are familiar to all who can read, and are the first moral lessons inculcated. How often have I heard them quoted by all classes, male and female, as conveying sentiments which none can reject.

Be virtuous.
Conceal not your means of doing good.
Begging is disgraceful.
Subdue anger.
Shrink not from doing good.
Having given alms, eat.
Be polite.
Speak not enviously.
Speak to good effect.
Reciprocate known friendship.
Forget not a kindness.
Do no wrong thing.
Do not speak deceitfully.
Fasting must be observed.
Desert not a friend.
Associate with the wise.
Love not gambling.
Revile not.
Act as one who is worthy.
Put away vicious acts.
Consider, then act.
Walk uprightly.
Live so as to be respected.
Do not speak much.
Listen to the wise.
Speak not angrily.
Strive to get to heaven.
Rise at daybreak.
Neglect not learning.
Say what you saw.
Build not a large house.
Protect your father and mother.
Sow in due season.
Play not with a snake.
Do not sleep long.
Avoid base actions.
Be firm in right ways.
Avoid doing injury.
What you undertake, do well.
Wander not in idleness.
Serve God.
Yield not to adversity.
Do nothing hazardous.
Do not feed on delicacies.
Aspire after eminence.
Till the ground and eat.
Be not gluttonous.
What you say, say correctly.
Desire knowledge.
Live on terms with your neighbours.

I have been obligingly favoured by my friend, the Rev. E. J. Robinson, formerly one of the members of the Wesleyan Mission in North Ceylon, with the following poetic versions of the Hindu Matron's thirty aphorisms. They are very beautiful, and will be read with equal pleasure and regret, when it is known that the English versifier is not now in circumstances where his superior talents can avail at once to benefit the Hindus by his labours, and his countrymen by continued examples from an ancient literature that, in some of its moral features, suffers nought from comparison with the best ethical writings ever brought to light. Mr. Robinson is now pursuing his ministerial labours in England.

AVVEYÁR'S THIRTY APHORISMS.

Who statedly with floral gifts attend,
Before the trunk-faced Red One's[1] footstool bend,
And sacred homage reverently pay,
True eloquence and wisdom shall acquire;
The Lotus-throned[2] shall grant what they desire;
They shall not sink in bodily decay.

If suffering worth to acts of kindness move,
Forbid the doubt your bounty will not prove
A source at last of profit and delight.
The water furnish'd to its early root,
Ere long in sweeter draughts, from loads of fruit,
The cocoa's head will gratefully requite.[3]

The valued favours the deserving gain,
Like sculptures in eternal rock remain;
Of virtue's tribute charity is sure:
But kind attentions to the worthless shown,
Who debts and duties evermore disown,
Like letters written in the wave endure.

In vain attractively the garden blooms,
When senseless grief the livelong day englooms:
In vain the spouseless maid her beauty wears.
So youth, when needy, proves a tedious stage;
And wealth is misery in feeble age,
A bitter mockery of fretful cares.

---

[1] Ganesha, or Ganapaty.

[2] Lachsmi, goddess of wealth.

[3] Only give the deserving a start or lift, and in the end he may repay you richly. The young cocoa-nut-tree needs carefully watering; but by-and-by it will maintain itself. And then, for the water you poured at its foot, it will reward you from its summit with nectar. It is well, no doubt, thus to create in our favour a fund of obligation. But from how much more noble a motive Christianity teaches us to be charitable.

It may be gathered, from this stanza, and others, that Hindus are not, as has too often been stated, incapable of ingratitude. Valluvar's "Kural," the greatest of Tamil poems, contains a section of ten stanzas expressly upon this virtue.

To love, though loved, the callous base ne'er learn:
But love for love the good and wise return;
  Their greatness through calamities remains.
The sea-shell thus a purer whiteness shows,
The fiercer the surrounding furnace glows:
  Thus seething milk its flavour all retains.

Although, in foliage richly clad, they rise,
In figure faultless, and mature in size,
  As trees no fruit except in season bear;
In any project sooner to succeed,
And gain the end before the time decreed,
  Nor toil avails, nor wealth, nor wakeful care.

Not softly yielding as the building towers,
Not gently bending when the load o'erpowers
  The strongest column will asunder fly:
So they who scorn their honour to survive,
Still bravely with their adversaries strive,
  Nor do them homage when they muster nigh.[1]

The depth and surface of the pool decide
The growth and limit of the lily's pride:
  So erudition is on study based;
So riches show accumulated worth,
By penance purchased in a previous birth;
  So character from son to sire is traced.

Happy the eyes that on the pious rest;
The ears that hear their useful words are bless'd;
  And bless'd the lips that all their virtues tell;
Supremely bless'd their character who wear,
Their friendship gain, their reputation share,
  Their sacred paths frequent, and with them dwell.

The sight alone of wicked men is ill;
Their graceless words the air with evil fill;
  With risk the lips their attributes portray;
And 'tis the height of self-inflicted wrong
To mingle with their sin-infectious throng,
  Attend their cursed steps, and with them stay.

---

[1] Frangas, *non flectes.*

The stream, propell'd to where the rice-crop grows,
Refreshes likewise as it thither flows,
The common grass that in its channel lies:
In every age, the genial rains that fall
To cheer the good, are thus enjoy'd by all,
And virtue's revenue the world supplies.

To instruments the great their glory owe;
The lofty are supported by the low;
Without assistance, rank and skill were vain.
We spurn too oft the object we should prize:
The rice, denuded, unproductive dies;
The husk we scorn preserves the living grain.

The scentless taly [1] far in bulk excels;
The tiny magul-flower more sweetly smells:
Apparent meanness proves no lack of worth.
The vasty sea, with all its vauntful roar,
E'en for ablution fits not; while ashore,
The humble spring with nectar gushes forth.

The branching trees that in the forest grow
Have no surprising excellence to show.
Assembled proudly with the learned, he
Who, lacking skill to scan the proffer'd verse,
Or seize the sense of what the rest rehearse,
Stands disconcerted, is the veriest tree.

As when the clumsy turkey, having seen
The forest peacock move with graceful mien,
Struck with the beauty of his gorgeous train,
And thinking one of kindred plume he spied,
His ugly feathers spread in strutting pride,
Poetic skill unlearned coxcombs feign.

Who aid the ingrate in their yearning zeal,
Like him who dared the poison'd tiger heal,
But raise the fallen to become their prey;
And, like the vase against the granite block,
Or freighted bark that strikes the sunken rock,
Their blind beneficence is thrown away.

---

[1] A coarse wild flower.

The noble still are in distress esteem'd;
The mean, of wealth bereft, are worthless deem'd:
  The former like a cup of gold are found,
That, fractured, its intrinsic worth retains;
The latter, like an earthen bowl, that gains
  Contempt when strew'd in fragments on the ground.

Insult not over those in self-conceit,
Whose self-restraint may end in your defeat,
  Though void they seem of wisdom, tact, and strength.
If smaller fishes dart securely by,
The heron watches with unerring eye
  The proper victim that appears at length.

No friends are they who heartlessly forsake,
As waterfowl the sun-exhausted lake,
  Their old acquaintance in the time of need:
Like lilies withering when the pond grows dry,
That, where they flourish'd, parch'd and prostrate lie,
  Who share our troubles are our friends indeed.

Say, fretful spirit, whether shall ensue,—
The visionary good we fondly view,
  Or all the just awards decreed by fate?
From Indra's tree, for fruits of blessing known,
Who gilded nuts of poison pluck, atone
  For deeds that stain'd their pre-existent state.

Drawn from the soundless deep, not four times more
The measure holds than it contain'd before.
  What futile hopes our silly sex employ!
Though wealth be gain'd, and spousal sweets abound,
No larger happiness is therefore found;
  For fate has fix'd the measure of our joy.

'Tis not in blood that genuine kindred lies,
From birth connexions that true friendships rise:
  Congenital disease may mortal prove.
Some distant mountain must the med'cine yield,
By which alone our sickness may be heal'd;
  And strangers may desponding care remove.

The dwelling with a frugal mistress bless'd,
Though all things lacking, is of all possess'd;
  For peace, content, and cleanliness are there.
The house not suited with a thrifty wife,
Or cursed with one intent on angry strife,
  Though plenty reign, is like the tiger's lair.

The learned to the erudite repair,
As seeks the gentle swan the water where
  The lovely lotus breathes its fragrance round;
But like the crow, by carrion-instinct led,
That scents the grave, and feasts upon the dead,
  The ignorant with kindred fools are found.

Disjoined by hasty wrath, the meaner kind,
Like broken stone, are never more combined:
  Remingle soon the better sort their hearts,
Like fractured gold by fusion blent again:
No longer sunder'd do the best remain
  Than water that the pointed arrow parts.

While, conscious of his fatal power to harm,
The guilty cobra hides in just alarm,
  The guileless water-snake at large appears.
And so deceivers, shunning public view,
In secret their perfidious schemes renew,
  While artless innocence no danger fears.

Though loyal hosts the king's behests obey,
The grave philosopher bears ampler sway:
  While homage meets the sage wherever known,
And every step extends his spotless fame,
The monarch's title is an empty name,
  Beyond the narrow realms that prop his throne.

To fools the words of the resentful wise,
To vicious souls the virtue they despise,
  As plantains to the stalk from which they sprung,[1]
Deserve grim-visaged Yama's dreadful name,—
But, more than all, the stubborn tyrant dame
  To those compell'd to hear her clamorous tongue.

Attrition, in its merciless delay,
May wear the precious sandal-wood away,
  But leaves its grateful fragrance all behind:
So, though calamities their coffers drain,
Triumphant o'er misfortune, kings retain
  Their royal fortitude of heart and mind.

---

[1] Having yielded one bunch of fruit, the plantain or banana-tree perishes, making room for virgin stalks, new springing from its roots. In gardens, the old stem, having served its turn, is immediately cut down.

With Lakshmi come, and vanish when she flies,
The pleasures that from constant friendship rise,
  Resources keeping pace with high desire,
The pride of beauty, dignity of birth,
And all things loved and coveted on earth:
  Then toil for wealth, and prize what you acquire.

As trees afford a cool refreshing shade,
Till by the ringing axe in ruin laid,
  To mortals shrinking from the scorching heat;
The sons of knowledge, till they cease to live,
As far as can be, good for evil give,
  And acts of kindness to their foes repeat.[1]

E. J. R.

The following extracts from the ethical work of Tiruvalluvar, the fabled brother of Avveyár, will be read with pleasure, as affording proof of the existence of the loftiest sentiments, the purest moral rules, and equal power of conception and expression: nothing certainly in the whole compass of human language can equal the force and terseness of the sententious distichs in which the author conveys the lessons of wisdom he utters.

The Kural, from which the extracts are made, consists of 108 chapters. Some portions of it were translated, several years ago, by a gentleman connected with the H. E. I. Company's Civil Service, of the name of Ellis; and recently, a translation of the same portion, and some of the subsequent chapters, has been published by the Rev. Mr. Drew of Madras. The first part of this Tamil work is on Virtue, and, like all other books of the Hindus, opens with an ascription to God. Instead of an invocation often comprised in one stanza, Tiruvalluvar devotes a chapter to the Divine Being.

[1] We are not prepared to prove that this is a leaf from the book of the Christian religion. But the concluding stanza is different in our oldest copy.

The praise of God:—

What is the fruit that human knowledge gives, if at the feet of Him who is pure Knowledge due reverence be not paid?

They who adore His sacred feet, whose grace gladdens with sudden thrill the fervent heart, high o'er the earth shall soar to endless joy.

To Him, whom no affection moves, nor hate, those constant in obedience, from all ill in this world and the next are free.

The anxious mind against corroding thought no refuge hath, save at the sacred feet of Him to whom no likeness is.

The praise of rain:—

As by abundant rain the world subsists, life's sole elixir in this fluid know.

It spreads destruction round; its genial aid again revives, restores all it destroys; such is the power of rain.

The praise of just men:—

A strict adherence to the rule professed, than do all other virtues, the devout exalteth more; this every code ordains.

As the hook restrains the elephant, so he in wisdom firm his sensual organs rules, who hopes to flourish in the soil of heaven.

Taste, light, touch, sound, and smell, if these be known, and with them all connected, of the world the whole is known.

On the power of virtue:—

What more doth profit man than virtue doth, by which felicity is given, and whence eternal bliss ensues?

No greater gain than virtue canst thou know; than virtue to forget, no greater loss.

That which in spotless purity preserves the mind is real virtue; all besides is evanescent sound.

Refer not virtue to another day; receive her now, and at thy dying hour she'll prove thy never-dying friend.

Know that is virtue which each ought to do; what each should shun is vice.

On domestic virtue:—

Domestic virtue is to him ascribed, whose care defends the pious and the poor, and aids departed souls.

Thine ancestors deceased, thy God, thy guest, thy relatives, thyself; these cherished, know of life the five great duties are fulfilled.

If love and virtue be thy constant guests domestic life is blest, and finds in them its object and reward.

He who from virtue swerves not, but her path to others shows, joined in domestic life, more merit hath than the recluse can boast.

On the virtues of a wife:—

To every household duty fitly trained, the wife should to her husband be in all a helpmate meet.

The wife maintains the glory of the house; all other glory, if she fail in this, as if it were not, is.

On the possession of children:—

Of all the world calls good, no good exists like that which virtuous offspring give; I know no other good.

Children are offspring called, and justly so: for from their parents' deeds, or good or ill, their disposition springs.

Sweet the sensation to the parent's breast his child's soft touch imparts; 'tis real bliss, which others hear of, fathers only know.

Sweet is the pipe and sweet the lute, they say,—they who have never heard their children's tongues in infant prattle lisp.

When men shall say, "By what inflictions hard in penance borne gained he this child?" the word requiteth all a father's pain.

On love:—

What bolt can love restrain? what veil conceal? One tear-drop in the eye of those thou lov'st will draw a flood from thine.

As in a barren soil a sapless tree, so flourish those in wedded bliss whose souls know not the sweets of love.

What if the body each perfection own, if in the breast, the beauty of the mind, sweet love exist not?

That breast alone contains a living soul which love inspires; void of this genial warmth 'tis bone o'erlaid with skin

On hospitality:—

To honour guests with hospitable rite, domestic life and all its various joys were given.

He who with smiles receives a virtuous guest, shall see Prosperity, with joyful mind, make his abode her home.

As that sweet flower [1] which droops its head and dies, when once its fragrant odour is inhaled, from unwonted love shrinks the guest.

---

[1] The flower alluded to is said to be so delicate, that if smelled without being touched, it withers and falls from its stalk: it may be a species of sensitive plant.

On courtesy:—

Though bounty may rejoice the heart, yet words of courtesy, which dress the face in smiles, will more avail.

The grace of fair humility, the grace of courteous words, far more adorn than do all other ornament.

Discourteous speech, when courteous may be used, is like the sickly appetite, which culls fruit immature, leaving the ripe untouched.

On gratitude:—

Though earth and heaven could in return be given, a benefit received when none was due, they would not recompense.

Small as a grain of millet though it be, large as the towering palm a benefit to grateful eyes appears.

The exalted mind no benefit esteems by mere return repaid, but by the scale of its own greatness measures each.

On equity:—

That virtue, which in all relations holds unchangeably its nature, that alone deserves the name of justice.

By justice do the just their wealth uphold, and confirmation, strong as virtue's self, bequeath their heirs.

It is the glory of the just to stand like the adjusted balance duly poised, nor swerve to either side.

On self-control:—

To intercourse with gods forbearance leads; but passion unrestrained, its victims, plunged in utter darkness, leaves.

Though self-control be excellent in all, it most befits the envied state of those that fortune smiles upon.

Though unrestrained all else, restrain thy tongue, for those degraded by licentious speech will rue their tongue's offence.

The wound may heal, though from a burning brand, and be forgotten; but the wound ne'er heals a burning tongue inflicts.

The preceding quotations may be left without remark to make their own impression. I much regret that space does not permit additional examples.

Another of the illustrious children before mentioned, whose name was Kabilar Agaval, was brought up in a Brahman's family. He was carefully educated; but when the time arrived for investing him with the sacred thread, to secure his second birth, the Brahmans refused the rite, because the youth was of low origin or non-caste parentage. His reputed parents were full of grief on account of this untoward event, but knew no remedy. Kabilar, being endued with special divine favour, went to pour out his lament before the assembled Brahmans, in a strain that demonstrated to their ingenuous minds that mere birth-rank avails not—gained their assent to his request—and was initiated into the privileges of their order: such is the legend. The following translation of Kabilar's effectual remonstrance and apology delivered before the assembly of Brahmans was kindly sent to me along with the metrical version of Avveyar's aphorisms:—

Of the world, Nanmuga's[1] grand creation,
With its secret laws, an explanation,
  And its glories, who can render?
O ye sages, did the male sex first,
Or the female, into being burst,
  Or things of the neuter gender?

Does the day or star precedence claim?
From the other which derived its name?
  Which is older, good or ill?
Which must higher, lore or wealth, be rated?
Was the ancient spacious earth created,
  Or a work that knew no will?

Are the births and castes you fondly own
The event of nature's growth alone,
  Or a scheme design'd and finish'd?
Who will live till fate shall fairly call?
Who will prematurely victims fall,
  Their appointed time diminish'd?

Will infectious evil ever die?
Why and where do all the senses fly,
  When the man that own'd them's dead?
Do ascetics some new form obtain,
Or acquire a human birth again?
  Is the soul or body fed?

[1] The four-faced Brahma.

With a ready mouth and tongue I come,
As a drum-stick this, and that a drum:
  Ye good people, all attend.
But a hundred years our life can number;
And of these we fifty lose in slumber,
  And in childhood five expend.

Then of thrice five more by youth bereft,
From the hundred we've but thirty left:
  And now joy, now grief, is rife.
What is wealth? a river overflowing.
What is youth? its crumbling bank. And growing
  Like a tree thereon, is life.

So of only one pursuit be heedful;
And from doing well, the one thing needful,
  Not a moment dare to borrow.
This first concern demands to-day,
Nor admits another hour's delay:
  Ye are fools who cry, To-morrow.

For you cannot tell what luck is near,
If to-morrow Yama[1] may appear,
  Or another day you'll gain:
Every moment Kuttuvan[2] expect:
When he comes, all worship he'll reject,
  And your richest gifts disdain.

You may argue, but you'll be denied;
With your kin he'll not be satisfied;
  All alike in death must share:
He will neither from the good man turn,
Nor the needy, nor the wicked spurn,
  Nor the man of money spare.

Not a moment will the Fierce-eyed stay,
And the body he'll not bear away,—
  With the soul alone content.
For a spirit fled, O man bereaved,
Or a carcase dead, are ye so grieved?
  Or for what do you lament?

---

[1] Yama, Death. [2] Ibid.

Do ye say ye mourn the spirit's flight?
As it ne'er before appear'd in sight,
So to-day it is not seen.
Do ye say the body stirs your grief?
Why, ye watch it still, though like a thief,
When itself has rifled been!

For ye strip it; hands and feet ye tie:
From the kindled pile the flame mounts high:
Only ashes now remain.
Ye have laved, and to your kindred go:
Does complacency or wrath o'erflow,
That ye mingle tears again?

With repeated mantras and good cheer,
Will your children keep you lingering here,
O ye Brahmans, when ye die?
To return were suppliant ghosts e'er known,
And with outstretch'd hands keen hunger own,
And their cravings satisfy?

While the Hunas,[1] Ottyas,[1] Singalese,
The Mlechas,[1] Yavanas,[1] Chinese,
With the Chonakas,[1] and others,
Have no Brahman class in all their borders
You have ranged in four exclusive orders
Whom creation meant for brothers.

It is conduct stamps the high and low.
The consorted cow and buffalo
Were a wonder to be seen.
Do your castes thus mutually repel?
Is their union thus impossible?
Has it never fruitful been?

Wheresoe'er whatever seed is sown,
It will there produce its kind alone;
So the sons by Brahmans got,
Though to Puliah[2] dames they owe their birth,
Must be counted with the gods of earth,[3]
With their fathers, must they not?

---

[1] These names are now used to signify Mohammedans, barbarians, &c. It seems impossible to determine exactly their ancient application. Probably the Arabians were called Chonakas. The Greeks were called Yavanas. The other tribes occupied countries bordering on Hindustan.

[2] Pariah, low-caste. [3] Brahmans.

Who have ever such a difference seen
As the cow and buffalo between,
  Among men of divers classes?
In the life men lead, the limbs they wear,
In their bodies, in their shape and air,
  And in mind, no rank surpasses.

When a Puliah with a Brahman's mouth
For the north forsakes his native south,
  He is there a Brahman deem'd.
When a Brahman from the north betrays
In the south a Puliah's crooked ways,
  But a Puliah he's esteem'd.

In the mire as crimson lilies grow,
So Vasishta,[1] Brahma's son, we owe
  To a lowly concubine.
A Chandaly[2] to Vasishta gave
Sattyanada, by a Puliah slave,
  Who prolong'd the noted line.

To Parásara her son, the birth
Of Vyása[3] seal'd a fish-girl's worth.
  And because all meanly born,—
In the Vedas versed, for learning famed,
With the very first of sages named,—
  Are they aught of glory shorn?

I am Kabilar, whom Athyi bore
Unto Pagavan in Caruvore;
  She a Puliah, he the sage.
And I'll tell you how we all have fared;
For by seven of us is proudly shared
  The unequal parentage.

In a place where ready springs abound,
With a lowly washer, Uppei found
  All the fostering care she needed.
Nor could Uruvei of aught complain,
Though its juice they from the palm-tree drain,
  Who her wants have kindly heeded.

---

[1] One of the seven great sages, son of the mind of Brahma.

[2] A Pariah woman, an outcast. [3] Compiler of the Vedas.

With musicians Avvey found a home;
On the mountain-side, with those who roam
  In the woods, was Vally bred.
Among Pariahs Valluvar appear'd.
In a grove Athigaman was rear'd,
  Where the bees on flowers fed.

And the Brahmans[1] I am bound to bless,
Who these richly water'd lands possess,
  For their never-failing care.
Do the breezes in their progress scorn,
Does the rain keep clear of men low-born?
  Does the earth disdain to bear?

Does the sun refuse them light and heat?
Does the jungle yield what mean men eat,
  While the fields support the high?
All alike may wealth or want inherit;
All alike may earn devotion's merit;
  And we all alike must die.

There is but one caste, one race, on earth;
Men are one in death and one in birth;
  And the God they serve is One.
Who the sayings of old time revere,
And in virtue firmly persevere,
  Are inferior to none.

Who relieve the suppliant day by day,
Who abhor to lie, or steal, or slay,
  Who the sexual sense subdue,
And who blandly speak, contemn your scorn.
O ye fools, let graces rank adorn,
  Or no good can thence accrue.

E. J. R.

Reference has been made to Beschi, a Jesuit missionary. He was not the only man of the order who became eminent, but he was certainly the best Tamil scholar of his age, not excepting the natives themselves. His voluminous works composed in Tamil, both in prose and verse, as well as his numerous translations, are held in great esteem. He com-

[1] With the exception, therefore, of Kabilar himself, all were brought up in low-caste families. The sisters are the four first mentioned.

posed an excellent Tamil grammar on the principle of the native authors. He also composed two Tamil grammars in Latin, one in the common, and the other in the poetic dialect. He compiled an excellent dictionary, with special reference to the classical authors; it is divided into four parts: the first consists of an ordinary vocabulary, with the signification attached to the words; the next is an arrangement of synonymes; the third is a rhyming dictionary; and the fourth a classical dictionary. It is altogether an invaluable compilation. The first part was made the basis of a school manual, prepared some years ago in North Ceylon, and published under the auspices of the American Board of Foreign Missions. Some idea may be formed of the diffusiveness of the language from the fact, that this school lexicon contains 58,500 words. Beschi wrote a work called "The Splendour of the Veda," the Sacred Book, the Bible; it is divided into eighteen parts, called eighteen daggers wherewith to pierce the Lutheran heresy. A kindred work is also attributed to him, called "The Splendour of Wisdom," intended as a refutation of some of the errors of the Hindu religion. He also composed a remarkable book, entitled "Instructions to Catechists," which in many respects is a valuable work. This book may be read with great advantage by any who are desirous of obtaining good, come whence it may. Another treatise, entitled "Spiritual Counsel," is attributed to Beschi; it is divided into fourteen parts, and much of its contents is very striking, from the figurative style he has adopted; it is well fitted for readers of simple minds. A tract on the disparity between time and eternity, which is said to be his, is well worth reading. His greatest work, however, is his Sacred Epic, which contains, in a highly wrought form, after the model of the Hindu epics, the chief narratives of the Bible. The scenes are laid in the Holy Land, Palestine being the territory, and Jerusalem the sacred city. The name of this poem is, "The Unfading Garland." There is a work of a somewhat comic character, called sarcastically, the Guruparamartan (Heavenly Teacher), which is said to be a burlesque on the Protestant missionaries of Tranquebar; by others it is supposed to be written against the Brahmanical and other spiritual guides of the Hindus. Beschi's name is known and venerated even among the Hindu literati. He is called Véramámunevar, The renowned heroic sage. Many extraordinary anecdotes respecting him are current among the Romanists, some of which, no doubt, are myths; but he was unquestionably a man of brilliant talent, profound erudition, and untiring industry. His labours extended over a period approaching to half a century.

Robert de Nobili was another of the Jesuit missionaries of Southern India. He entered the field at the beginning of the seventeenth century, and became an eminent Tamil scholar. He was known by the name of Tatwabodhakar, The true teacher. He translated the Romish Missal into Tamil, which is still in use, and known as "The Garland of Prayer." He wrote a work on Metaphysics, in twenty-seven books; it is called, "The Ascertainment of the Soul," and treats of the identity and individuality of the human spirit. He also composed an elaborate work on Christian Theology, which, like the former work, evinces the great talents and scholarship of the author. He was, however, inferior to Beschi in his Tamil acquirements; and, as a writer, far less happy in the purity and strength of his style.

Other Tamil works have been written by Romish missionaries, but they are comparatively of little value.

A few remarks may not be out of place, on the present influence native literature has on the Hindu mind, and the extent to which it is patronised by the public. From what has been advanced in the course of these pages, it will have become apparent that the natives of India are disposed to intellectual pursuits. In the village group, in the boat's crew, among a set of palanquin bearers, evidence of this is not wanting. Judging from what I have heard and seen among Europeans and Hindus, I should say that the latter are more disposed to entertain thoughts of the past, the future, the distant and unseen, than are the former; and I think better qualified to estimate questions of an abstract and intellectual character. The mental aptitude and sentimental tastes are not merely found among the educated few, but generally they are manifest in ordinary conversation among the natives, as any intelligent person will find in the course of travel from village to village; and they are likewise evinced in the readiness displayed in defence of dogmata, the bare conception of which involves the exercise of considerable acumen. There is no difficulty in inducing a Hindu to enter on a religious discussion.

In travelling, I have often seen an ordinary labouring man take out his knife, to which a stylus is attached, and inscribe a note on a slip of palm leaf, addressed possibly to a distant brother or friend, and conveying some information or direction respecting himself, or family, to be transmitted, perhaps, by a companion who is returning home. As the school is a part of the village system of the Hindus, the respectable portion of the male population is taught to read and write.

At the present time popular works issue from the presses of the chief cities of India and Ceylon in great numbers, and many of these presses are under the sole conduct of the natives themselves. The works published are, for the most part, extravagantly fabulous stories, told in a popular and attractive style, and calculated to enforce, as well as to illustrate, the rites of religion. This might be made very evident by extracts on the adoration of the Ganges, the worship of the sun, and other kindred acts. Selected topics from the national literature are also wrought into a popular form, and presented so as to interest the mind. Some of the dramatic personages are frequently chosen, and the incidents connected with the drama, especially those of a vicious tendency, are amplified and so prepared as to gratify the depraved and wicked fancy of abandoned minds. Romantic stories are treated so as to command admiration, as far as richness of language and description are concerned, but not unfrequently containing a vein whose tendency is essentially and grossly immoral. Even the beautiful story of Nala and Damyanti, that in the hand of India's illustrious dramatic bard is so inimitable, and free from objection as it exists in its original form, has been so interlarded with poetic license and licentiousness, that on expurgating one of its versions for the use of a select class, I was obliged to expunge upwards of five hundred out of eleven hundred stanzas. It is not meant that the Hindus are exclusive in this sort of taste; the dramatists and novelists of Europe, even of England, furnish evidence to the contrary. But the Hindu exceeds the Westerns in his utter transgression of all bounds of decency. No conception can be formed of some of the productions of the Hindus; they are grossly extravagant in the fertility of licentiousness. Gross obscenity, dark superstition, an extravagant and horrible marvellousness, with frequent references to idolatry, form the principal ingredients of that seasoning which renders the popular literature of the Hindus palatable to the taste of the public. It would be interesting to have specimens of some of the less objectionable parts of the popular literature, but our limits do not admit of them.

The press of the Romanists is not inactive. The native press of Pondicherry, a French settlement, has printed most of the minor productions of the famous Beschi, and they are widely circulated among the Romanists of Southern India and Ceylon. It is remarkable that the books published at Pondicherry should obtain such a wide circulation. Those who cannot afford to pay the price for a printed copy obtain the loan of one, and transcribe it on the palm leaf. This is not an uncommon practice among the Tamil speaking population. Common literature is multiplied in this way very much as musical compositions are in Europe. The Romanists have also a periodical literature in English, and the Vicars-apostolic occasionally publish reports of their proceedings, some of which are made subservient to the severities of their criticism and their sarcasm on the opinions, plans, and progress of the agents of Protestant institutions.

The Romanists, as well as the Hindus, in employing the press for the purpose of diffusing their literary productions, are only imitating the course long pursued by the teachers of the British and Lutheran churches. These have, from the early part of the last century, employed this important engine in the siege they have been conducting against the strongholds of the enemy. In the presidencies of India, in the principal cities of the interior, and in the northern, western, and central provinces of Ceylon, the press is daily pouring forth the means of enlightenment for the dark and deluded millions who are perishing for lack of knowledge. The first missionaries who entered the field, the venerable Ziegenbalgh and his coadjutors, employed the press for the purpose of giving greater efficiency to their labours. For more than a century it has been gradually multiplying Christian books and other useful works, that serve, in various ways, the diffusion of general knowledge and the interests of the Church. The Indo-Christian library contains numerous works of great value, on subjects of a scientific, geographic, historic and didactic nature.[1] Many of those employed in promoting the evangelization of the Hindus, have enriched the literature of Europe by their literary labours and Indian contributions on archæological, philological, scientific, philosophical, and metaphysical subjects. The Christian Church, too, has received from the pens of some of the missionaries who have laboured in India, works on the condition of its people, which, from their interesting contents, are admirably fitted to awaken its sympathies, and to stimulate its energies in behalf of the nations of that great continent.

[1] Some of these works are of a highly valuable character: the learned Sanscrit work, the Christo Sangit of Principal Mill, formerly of Bishop's College, Calcutta, a Diatesseron of the Four Gospels in heroic metre, designed for circulation among the learned Brahmans of India, may be mentioned as an example. The works of the venerable men connected with the Serampore Mission, as well as those of the profound scholar, Dr. Yates, of Calcutta, may also be named in this connexion as worthy of the highest commendation.

The progress made in Bible translation is perhaps the most remarkable feature connected with the Christian Missions of India. The piles of manuscript in varied characters, wearing marks of careful emendation, involving years of laborious thought, witness the ability, the zeal and industry of the men whom the Church has employed in the enterprise for India's conversion. These versions of the word of God, amounting, I believe, to ten in number, are so many editions of the chart of salvation, prepared to guide as many nations over the sea of life to the shores of immortality. Labours of this character are significant, too, of the views which the men engaged entertain of the means to be employed for the enlightenment of the Hindu mind, and its conversion to Christ: they evince that, in their judgment, "the word of truth, the Gospel of . . . salvation," is the instrument to be used in the work they are sent to perform. The Liturgy of the British Church, in numerous versions, also witnesses to the progress of sacred literature.

The Society for the Promotion of Christian Knowledge has, from the beginning, helped forward the cause of Christian Missions, as well by the press, as by its munificent support of other means for the conversion of India.

The British and Foreign, and the American Bible Societies, and the Religious Tract Societies of the two countries, have also contributed munificently to aid the labours of all who are engaged in the field; indeed, these invaluable Societies give effect to the intellectual labours that, but for them, must remain inoperative.

Periodical literature exists in almost all the languages employed as vehicles of Christian instruction, and this reaches thousands who cannot in any other way be made acquainted with the truths of Christianity.[1]

[1] The friends of Missions in Bombay employ colporteurs to convey to various parts of that presidency books and tracts on subjects of useful knowledge and Christian teaching, which are sold extensively among the people.

From the brief notices contained in these paragraphs of the Hindu languages and literature, sufficient has been advanced to indicate their deeply interesting character. Yet we find nothing satisfactory on those important subjects which are essential to the well-being and progress of mankind,—nothing upon which the anxious and intelligent inquirer after truth can repose amid the conflicts of life, and in the prospect of that future being which is changeless and eternal. In the voluminous records of Hindu literature we discover nothing that wears the stamp of inspiration, no divinely authenticated revelations of the will of Him with whom we have to do; nor have we anything in the way of true science, that may be made subservient to the practical purposes of life. History, as we have seen, the Hindus have not. The lights which the events of nations and individuals supply are nowhere held out, either to warn or to guide the traveller in the difficult and dangerous journey of life. Thus it follows that the Hindus need something more than what they possess, in order to their secular and spiritual, their temporal and eternal welfare.

Under the fostering care of that rule which Heaven has vouchsafed to India, in the stable government of Great Britain, it must be deeply gratifying to the enlightened Christian philanthropist, to learn that the wants of the Hindus are being gradually supplied; that true science, useful knowledge, and revealed truth, are diffusing their beneficent influences among the people: it is really so. The page of true inspiration is beginning to open to their view; and they may read, not in an obsolete and dead language, but in their own living tongues, the wonderful works of God. The gift is presented to all, without distinction of station, and by those who are the ministers—not the lords of the people. Truthful Science, delighting to call herself the handmaid of religion, is displacing the prostitute "Philosophy, falsely so called." Veritable History, recording the ways of God to man, engages the attention of those who have been perplexed by "endless genealogies." The light of the Sun of Righteousness begins to dawn on the eastern horizon; and it will shine till the perfect day. "The gods that have not made the heavens and the earth shall perish," and Jehovah shall be acknowledged to be the Most High. Meek and enlightened devotion will be substituted for formal and frivolous ceremony. The drink-offerings and oblations of blood will cease; and in the Cross of Christ will be seen the great and only Atonement. The muddy waves of the Ganges will be forsaken, for that Fountain which has been opened for sin and uncleanness. The shouts of those who are mad on their idols, will grow faint; "and there will be heard, as it were, the voice of a great multitude, and as the voice of many waters, and as the voice of mighty thunderings, saying, ALLELUIA, FOR THE LORD GOD OMNIPOTENT REIGNETH."

Day & Son Lithrs to the Queen

CHAPTER VII.

THE FINE ARTS: ARCHITECTURE—ANCIENT TREATISES, THEIR CONTENTS; HINDU ORDERS;—MUSIC: SOME OF ITS FEATURES DESCRIBED; THE VÍNA; ANCIENT AUTHORS;—PAINTING;—SCULPTURE.—MEDICINE: SKILL OF THE ANCIENTS IN CHEMISTRY, PHARMACY, AND SURGERY.—THE PROGRESS OF THE MODERN HINDUS IN MEDICAL SCIENCE.

THE illustrations of this little volume may best serve to introduce a few brief notices on Hindu architecture. The group of sacred buildings at Trivalore, and the splendid temple at Ellora, given in two of the plates which present them to the reader, may well assure us that the originators of such stupendous monuments must have attained to eminence in the fine arts. The ancient Hindus were not only acquainted with the practice of building, but possessed scientific works on the subject, some of which are still extant. Treatises on Architecture, Sculpture, &c., are called the Silpa Shastra, a name literally meaning, The science of manual art. These treatises, according to some enumerations, amounted to thirty, and as given by others, to sixty-four. The works themselves, if so many ever existed, are lost, and nothing remains but fragments, still known, however, as the authorized guides of the artist. Like every other subject in the economy of the Hindus, architecture is blended with religion, and includes various directions relating to the observances requisite, not only in the construction of sacred edifices, but in the laying out and building of villages, towns, &c. The architectural treatises still extant are in many respects of a deeply interesting character, because they not merely illustrate the art itself, but give us an insight into the character of the ancient Hindus.

Though little space can be devoted to this subject, I cannot withhold some notice of the contents of one of the works alluded to. It is given in an able essay on the architecture of the Hindus, by Rám Ráz, a native of Southern India, who prepared the document for the Royal Asiatic Society.

Speaking of the most perfect original treatise, he says, "In order that a more accurate idea may be formed of the subjects contained in this work, a particular description is given of the contents of each adhyaya (chapter) as taken from the preface." The first chapter treats of the measures used in architecture, sculpture, carpentry, &c.; the second describes the qualifications of a Silpa (artist), and gives a brief account of the five different classes of artists, said to have descended from Visva Karma (Architect of the Gods), and to have followed respectively the occupations of sculptors, joiners, braziers, jewellers and blacksmiths. The third, fourth, and fifth chapters explain the nature and qualities of the soil on which buildings should be erected—such as temples, palaces, and private dwelling-houses for the several classes of people. The sixth contains rules and directions for the construction of a gnomon, for the purpose of determining the several points of the compass. The seventh treats of the parts into which the ground-plan of the cities, towns, temples, palaces, and houses, should be divided. The eighth chapter gives a minute description of sacrifices and other devotional rites, to be performed on various occasions in the building of temples, houses, &c. The ninth chapter treats of villages and towns, and prescribes rules for the formation of streets, and the allotment of fit places for the erection of temples, and for the residence of the different classes of the people. The tenth contains a description of the different sorts of cities; the eleventh treats of the dimensions of the several sorts of edifices; the twelfth of the Garbhavinyása, or laying the foundation-stone in the centre of the intended building; the thirteenth, of *Upapithas*, or pedestals; the fourteenth, of Adhistána or basement; the fifteenth, of the several species of pillars, with their respective dimensions; the sixteenth, of *Prastáras*, or entablatures; the seventeenth, of the junction of the several parts of timber-work, with reference to their points; the eighteenth, the *Vimánas*, temples, or palaces in general: ten successive chapters, from the nineteenth to the twenty-eighth, contain descriptions of temples surmounted by pyramidal domes, consisting of from one to twelve stories, with their respective dimensions. The twenty-ninth chapter treats of *Prácáras*, or outer courts of temples; the thirtieth, of the attendant deities, and the parts respectively assigned to each within the walls of the temple; the thirty-first, of *Gópuras*, or pyramidal buildings or turrets raised over the gateways leading into the temples; the thirty-second, of *Mantapas* or porticos, or resting-places for the deity; the thirty-third, of *Sálas*, or halls; the thirty-fourth, of cities; the thirty-fifth, of private dwelling-houses; the thirty-sixth and thirty-seventh, of gates and doorways, with their dimensions; the thirty-eighth and thirty-ninth, of the palaces and their appendages; the fortieth, of princes with their titles; the forty-first, of the building of cars and other vehicles of the gods; the forty-second, of couches, cushions, and the like; the forty-third, of the thrones for the gods, and for princes; the forty-fourth, of ornamental arches; the forty-fifth, of the *Calpatára*, or the all-productive tree, which is supposed to be planted in Indra's heaven, and to supply all the wants of those who have the happiness to take shelter under it. The forty-sixth chapter treats of *Abhishécas*, or ablutionary rites, by which images are sanctified; the forty-seventh, of jewels and ornaments worn by the gods and mortals; the forty-eighth, of statues of Brahma and other deities; the forty-ninth, of the *Linga*, the emblem of Siva; the fiftieth, of seats and forms raised for the reception of images; the fifty-first, of the form of Sakti, the goddess of nature; the fifty-second and fifty-third, of the images worshipped by the *Bauddhas* and

Jainas; the fifty-fourth describes the statues of the *Yakshas*, and *Vidyadharas*, and the Choristers; the fifty-fifth, those of the saints or holy men; the fifty-sixth and fifty-seventh, those of the *Devas* or gods, with their respective vehicles; and the fifty-eighth concludes with rules for chiselling the eyes of the statue, and the ceremonies to be performed on the occasion."

These works are supposed to have been written in the south of India, and at a period subsequent to the Buddhistic schism, to which it is apparent reference is made.

It will be seen that a vast amount of extraneous matter is contained in these architectural treatises, that does not properly belong to the science. There are some curious intimations relating to the character and qualifications of architects, builders, and artificers. Their importance in the construction of buildings is indicated in the following words:—"Woe to them who dwell in a house not built according to the proportions of symmetry! In building an edifice, therefore, let all its parts, from the basement to the roof, be duly considered."

Much specific direction is contained in the treatises on the choice of ground—its nature, its form, the quality of the water, its vegetation, &c. The manner of preparing it for the erection of a temple is singular. It is to be ploughed—the plough is prescribed, as to the material, the form, the size; and even the oxen that drag it are to be selected with due reference to their age, shape of horns, &c. The maimed, the weak, the meagre, toothless, or lame, must be rejected. Those with a white spot on their legs and foreheads, with eyes resembling the petals of the lotus, are to be preferred. They are to be decorated with fillets, and the like, and their horns and hoofs with gold and silver rings. The architect, clad in fresh vestments, and adorned with chaplets of flowers, having ascertained the auspicious moment for the duty, is to draw the first furrow with due religious ceremonies. The ground is sown with Sesamum seeds, pulse, and kidney-beans, incantations are repeated, and the oxen and plough are to be presented to the Spiritual Teacher. When the crops are matured, they are to be grazed by cows for one or two nights; and thus purified, the ground is ready for the future temple. The mode adopted for ascertaining the cardinal points is striking and correct, and in principle the same as that Europeans adopt for procuring a meridian line.

It is very evident from the Essay already alluded to, that the Hindus had accurate and scientific ideas of the principles of architecture. The rules for the construction of the various parts of a building are given with great minuteness. The mouldings are twelve in number; the forms and proportions of pedestals, bases, shafts, capitals, and entablatures, are given in all their respective modifications. The height of the column is from six to ten diameters, and the intercolumniation must be accordant with the proportions of the shaft and capitals.

The Hindu column is often presented in singularly symmetrical proportion, superior in its effect to the Egyptian, and much in harmony with the orders of Greece and Rome. In some modifications of the column they excel the Grecians and Romans; for whereas the columns of the west are always round, those of the Hindus admit of every shape, quadrangular, octangular, and they are enriched frequently with elaborate sculpture. The various orders of India, like those of Greece and Rome, are remarkable for the beautiful effect of their proportions—a circumstance which gives them great advantage over the Egyptian style of architecture. The pedestals, the capitals, and the entablatures, are equally striking, as evincing the superior skill of the Hindu.

The portion of the architectural works relating to villages and towns offers some curious matter to our notice. The forms and proportions of the different kinds of villages are specified, and the width of streets, the character of the gateways, and other matters, are described with the greatest minuteness. Different names were assigned to the various kinds of villages, to characterise the disposition of their arrangements. There were those called "In every respect happy;" "The abode of happiness;" "The lotus-formed," &c.' Certain gateways are appropriated to particular divinities, whose temples must be built there, and without the walls shrines are to be placed for the guardian deities.

The directions given for the construction of temples are minute. Of the magnificent fanes that the zeal of the Hindus has raised to their divinities, some notice must be taken in another part of this work. In the same connexion it may be convenient to offer some information on the subject of the magnificent tanks of the Hindus, which, more than anything else, perhaps, in the way of artificial works, are fitted to impress the stranger.

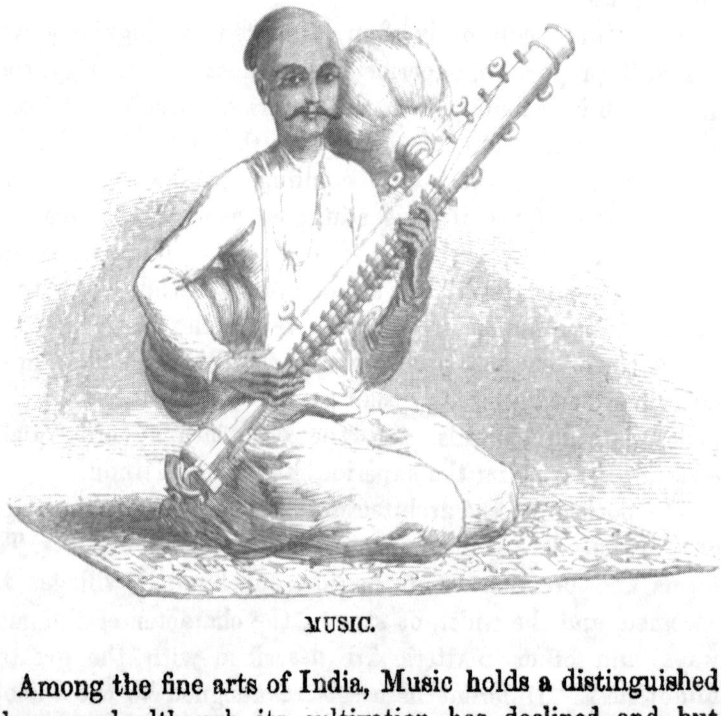

MUSIC.

Among the fine arts of India, Music holds a distinguished place; and although its cultivation has declined, and but few are now found who have attained to eminence either in the science or art of this unequalled source of recreation, refinement, and pleasure, yet no people are more susceptible of its charms than the Hindus. Reading is with them invariably, as with the Arabians and other Eastern nations, a species of *recitativo*, a sort of speaking music, delivered in dulcet though not measured tones. The recitation of lessons in a school or academy always takes this form. The man at the oar, women beating lime, the labourer engaged in irrigation, alike accompany their toil with song.

The word *sangíta*, symphony, as applied to music by the Hindus, conveys the idea of the union of *voices, instruments*, and *action*. Musical treatises accordingly treat of *gáná, vádya, nritya*, or *song, percussion*, and *dancing;* the first comprising the measures of poetry; the second, instrumental sounds; and the third, theatrical representation. The ancient dramas of the Hindu exhibited the union of these in their unequalled poetry, modulated with the accompaniments of voice, and instruments, and the attractions of appropriate scenery.

The music of the Hindus includes eighty-four modes, each supposed to have a peculiar expression, capable of moving some particular sentiment or affection. The modes take their denomination from the seasons, or from the hours of day or night. Musical composition is supposed capable of adaptation to the different periods of the day, and therefore its provisions are regulated by the hours. The ideas of the Hindus on music, as promoting the pleasures of imagination, may be inferred from the names applied by ancient authors to their musical treatises. One is called *Rágárnava*, the Sea of the Passions; another, *Rágaderpana*, the Mirror of Modes; and a third, *Sóbhavinóda*, the Delight of Assemblies; a fourth, *Sangítaderpana*, the Mirror of Song; and another, *Rágavibódha*, the Doctrine of Musical Modes. Some of these works explain the law of musical sounds, their divisions and succession, variations of scales by temperament, and the enunciation of modes; besides a minute description of the different *vínás* (lute), and the rules for playing them. This is a fretted instrument of the guitar kind, usually having seven wires or strings, and a large gourd at each end of the finger-board. Its extent is two octaves, and its invention is attributed to Náredá, the son of Brahma. There are many varieties, named according to the number of their strings.

Music, like everything else connected with India, is invested with divine attributes. From the sacred Vedas was derived the Upaveda, or subsidiary Veda of the Gandharbas, the heavenly choristers. The art was communicated to mortals by Sarasvati, the consort of Brahma. She, as before stated, is the patroness of the fine arts, the goddess of speech. Their son, an ancient lawgiver and astronomer, invented the Víná. The first inspired man, Bherat, invented the Drama.

The Hindus call the seven musical sounds comprising an octave, by the common name *Swara,* and dispose them under the following names: *Sarja, ríshabha, gándhara, madyama, panchama, dhaivata, nishada.* The first is emphatically called *Swara,* sound, as leading in the scale. Taking the *initial letters* of the above words as the exponents of the successive sounds or notes, they devised a gamut, which is called *Swaragráma,* or *Septica,* and thus express it—

Sa, ri, ga, ma, pa, dha, ni.

The notation is made in five of the sounds, by varying the length of the vowel, which, as we have seen, is inherent in every consonant or letter, and by the vowels forming the initial of the names of the other two. In this way the means of indicating notes of two different lengths are found in the gamut; other marks are used to indicate greater length. Then for the purpose of expressing the octave as above or below, the connexion and succession of notes, the process of execution, or of fingering the víná, little circles, ellipses, crescents, chains, curves, lines, straight, horizontal, or perpendicular, are employed; and the close of a strain is distinguished by a lotus flower. The notes of the major and minor scales are subject to division beyond the range of semitones, and all these tones are regarded as nymphs bearing distinct names, and their variations are effected by attendant sisters. It may be remarked that the word *Rág*, as applied to musical modes, signifies passion, and it is intended to intimate the purpose of these modes to affect the simple and combined susceptibilities of the emotions. The Hindus divide the year into six seasons, whose peculiar characteristics are provided for in the compositions appropriated to each. The religious festivals of the Hindus have also a connexion with the seasons, regulated as they are so much by astronomical phenomena; and therefore, as suggested by Sir William Jones, devotion contributed to heighten the charms of music. The day is also subject to seven divisions, morning, noon, and night, with their *trysandhya*, intervals, for the day and night. Thus the six *Rágas* of the seasons are linked together in family concert, and each being regarded as a demigod, wedded to five Ráginis or nymphs, and the father of eight little genii, called sons. Sir William Jones, the impassioned admirer of oriental learning, says, "The fancy of SHAKESPEARE and the pencil of ALBANO might have been finely employed in giving speech and form to this assemblage of new aerial beings, who people the fairy-land of Indian imagination; nor have the Hindu poets and painters lost the advantages with which so beautiful a subject presented them." He refers to some of their poetic imaginings, and quotes the following sweetly flowing stanza:—

Lílá viháréna vanántarálé,
Chinvan prasúnáno vadhu Saháyah,
Vilási vésódita divya múrtih
Srirága ésha prat'hitah prit'hivyám.

"The demigod Sriràga, famed all over this earth, sweetly sports with his nymphs, gathering fresh blossoms in the bosom of yon grove; and his divine lineaments are distinguished through his graceful vesture."

There can be no doubt that the ancient authors on the art of music, among the Hindus, were men of distinguished talent. Much fertility of genius is said to be displayed in the almost endless diversity of expression which was provided for in the tuning of the víná, and in the modification of the modes. Had the Hindus progressed in civilization and refinement on the basis they occupied thirty centuries ago, what might they not have produced! The political changes, the invasions of foreigners, from Alexander downwards, together with the withering effects of a debasing idolatry, and its accompanying evils, have prevented improvement. The Hindus do not now occupy the ground they once attained in any of the fine arts, and they have failed even to preserve the works of musical genius which were created by their ancient artists. There is but little attention paid to the culture of Hindu music at the present day. Those powers of enchantment possessed by former admirers of the art are not in existence, and it is not likely that Hindu music will again be revived: the civilization, the arts, the science and the literature of the west, we may hope, will hereafter shed their genial influences on Hindu society, and probably, through the English language, convey the treasures of our literature. When the language, the religion, and the refinement of Europe shall be reproduced among the Hindus, the land of the Veda will attain to a higher and purer condition than was ever possible, even in the palmy days of its most distinguished men.

The following *imitative melody*, as selected by Sir William Jones, may well close these brief notes on the music of the Hindus. It is one of the airs suited to the Spring. Its sentiments are as follows:

"While the soft gale of *Malaya* wafts perfume from the beautiful clove-plant, and the recess of each flowery arbour sweetly resounds with the strains of Cócila, mingled with the murmurs of the honey-making swarms; Heri dances, O lovely friend, with a company of damsels in this vernal season, a season full of delight, but painful to separated lovers."

It may be remarked that the time is very rapid, and the air gay and quick.

In estimating the character of Hindu music from what is generally heard by Europeans in India, there would be an obvious impropriety, as is intimated in an article of the "Oriental Quarterly Magazine;" the writer says, "We may add, that the only native singers and players, whom Europeans are in the way of hearing in most parts of India, are regarded by their scientific brethren in much the same light as a ballad-singer at the corner of the street by the primo soprano of the Italian Opera."

PAINTING.

The Hindus are best compared to the ancient Egyptians in the art of Painting. That portraits were taken in ancient times, is inferred from the reference made to them in classical writings; and the frescoes in the caves of Ajunta, and other ancient works of art, show that the Hindus have always known the art, though they cannot be said to have attained to eminence at any period of their history. The modern artists sometimes produce tolerable likenesses; but they will require the instructions of the West, ere they can be said to know much in this elegant branch of the fine arts. Some of their manuscripts are most tastefully illuminated; but the other ornaments are better executed than the likenesses of individuals.

SCULPTURE.

On this subject little needs be said here, since the reference to it in the paragraphs devoted to the temples may be considered sufficient for its elucidation. Though there is great spirit displayed in the attitudes and grace of some of the figures seen in the temples, they are not found associated with those nice discriminative features of the art which one conversant with anatomy, and disposed to copy nature would exhibit, and upon which the art of sculpture depends for its truthfulness and its charms.

MEDICINE.

The most celebrated works on Medicine were written by the Hindus at an early period, as appears from the fact, that commentaries were extant upon their productions in the twelfth century. The Arabians, who translated these medical works of the Hindus into Arabic, acknowledge their obligations to them; and it is remarkable that Hárím-al-Rashíd, in the eighth century, was attended by Hindu physicians.

Their knowledge of medicines, it is admitted, was extensive, nor were they less remarkable for their chemical skill. Dr. Royle, Professor of King's College, gives some very interesting information on this subject.

They prepared sulphuric acid, nitric acid, and muriatic

acid; the oxide of copper, iron, lead, tin, zinc; the sulphuret of iron, copper, mercury, antimony, and arsenic; the sulphate of copper, zinc, and iron; the carbonates of lead and iron.

It would appear that their medical men were remarkable for their skill in the use of the most severe remedies. "They were the first to apply minerals internally, and they not only gave mercury in that manner, but arsenic and arsenious acid, which were remedies in intermittents. They have long used cinnabar for fumigations, by which they produce a speedy and safe salivation."

"Their surgery is as remarkable as their medicine. They cut for the stone, couched for the cataract, and extracted the fœtus from the womb; and in their early works they enumerate no less than 127 sorts of surgical instruments."

They have for ages practised inoculation.

"The Hindu physicians are attentive to the pulse, and to the state of the skin, of the tongue, eyes, &c., and to the nature of the evacuations; and they are said to form correct prognostications from the observation of the symptoms." It is, however, generally admitted, that, in this, as in other branches of knowledge, the Hindus have rather declined than advanced for centuries; so that in medical science they are not even what their predecessors were. They are disposed to follow a beaten track in the treatment of disease; they have recourse to magical arts; consult the position of the planets; and use spells and incantations.

In relation to the present state of medical practice, I have heard it observed by a medical friend, that some of the native physicians possess a great degree of skill, especially in the treatment of the ordinary diseases of their own countrymen; and I have known European (not English) families employ experienced native practitioners, even where European skill was available. The knowledge of the natives of India, in regard to the qualities and powers of the numerous articles of the Materia Medica, is, I have been informed by scientific men, accurate and extensive.

It may be added, that the authorities of the Honourable East India Company, and Her Majesty's government in the island of Ceylon, have for years past done much to provide medical education for the people of their respective territories; and through the measures they have adopted, the Hindus and East Indians are attaining to great proficiency in the healing art; and as practitioners in various parts of the country, their scientific and medical knowledge is productive of the greatest possible benefit to the population. I am personally acquainted with gentlemen of both classes, who have attained to great skill and eminence in the departments of surgery and medicine.

The medical members of the American Mission have also done much in some places to promote the advancement of medical science, and the practice of medicine and surgery among the Hindus. I am acquainted with several Hindus who have been wholly trained by them; of whose intelligence, skill, and successful practice abundant evidence may be adduced.

CHAPTER VIII.

HINDUISM: ITS DIVERSIFIED PHASES—ITS PHILOSOPHIC AND OTHER SECTS.—OPINIONS RESPECTING THE EXISTENCE OF GOD AND THE UNIVERSE.—POPULAR THEORY OF VEDANTISM.—DEVELOPMENT OF THIS THEORY.—THE TRIAD.—PHYSICAL UNIVERSE.—PRETERNATURAL BEINGS.—PERIODIC REVOLUTIONS.

HAVING, in the preceding parts of this work, presented brief and general information on the physical character of India, its population, its social condition, its languages, its literature, and its arts, it is now proposed to offer, in as condensed a form as possible, some account of its Religion. It is intended, in the first place, to speak of Hinduism, a term which comprehends the belief and practice of the Brahmanized portion of the inhabitants of India, because this portion includes the greater part of the inhabitants. The religious condition of the aboriginal tribes may be conveniently described in a separate chapter.

The Brahmanical faith is the national faith of India; and as, in the nations of Western Europe, Christianity has exerted its power in impregnating the mind, moulding political institutions, regulating jurisprudence, and thus affecting all things, civil, and sacred—communicating vitality and direction to much of its literature and science; so Brahmanism has injuriously exerted an influence in every part of India—only to a vastly larger extent, and in a more intense degree.

In a former chapter it was stated, that the religious system of the Hindus was contained in the *four Vedas*, the great Shastras, or books of sacred ordinance, which are said to have proceeded from the lips of Brahma, at the time when the visible universe was called into existence. These ancient and venerated records are, by the bulk of the Hindus, believed to be eternal, as regards the matter of which they are composed. Nothing can exceed the sacredness attached to them. As divinely originated records, they are guarded with profound reverence, and believed to be the fountains of all true religion, and the primeval source of every other species of useful knowledge.

With the Vedas, as we have seen, are connected other sacred records, such as the Vedangas, subordinate Vedas, and the Upangas, or inferior treatises, containing, among matters of speculation, theological teaching. These latter books exercise a much greater influence over the Hindus than the simple records of the Vedas. Those ancient depositories of a simple theism, prescribing no worship but that of ascriptions of praise and invocations in the presence of personified elements, were early abandoned for a more complex and elaborate system of mythology, which, however, the Brahmanical leaders profess to identify with the sacred Vedas, of which they affect to speak with the greatest reverence and veneration. They regard the *Upangas*, or inferior treatises, as the expansion or development of the germinant theological science concealed in the venerated records of the Veda.

It is confessedly difficult to obtain any fixed idea of the Hindu religion as it now prevails throughout India; and great pains and perseverance are necessary to comprehend the diversified and endlessly varied phases of a system that nevertheless possesses something in common. Professor Wilson, than whom no one is better qualified to express an opinion on this subject, says: "An early division of the Hindu system, and one conformable to the genius of all polytheism, separated the practical and popular beliefs from the speculative and philosophical doctrines. Whilst the common people addressed their hopes and fears to stocks and stones, and multiplied by their credulity and superstition the grotesque objects of their veneration, some few, of deeper thought and wider contemplation, plunged into the mysteries of man and nature, and endeavoured assiduously, if not successfully, to obtain just notions of the cause, the character, and consequence of existence." It is admitted, that even the Vedas make a distinction between the practices of a ritual and the speculations of theology.

As will be seen in a subsequent part of this chapter, the Hindu Triad—BRAHMA, VISHNU, and SIVA—occupy an important relation to the moral and material universe, and therefore claim the worship of those who follow the creed of the Brahmans. Their respective worshippers separated into different associations, at a remote period; and in this way, and from other causes never absent from the vagrant tendencies of our nature, distinct and isolated bodies sprang into existence. Whilst preferences for the ritual of the popular divinities separated the Hindus in relation to the popular objects of adoration, conflicting opinions on subjects respecting which human reason has never yet agreed, led to a division among the speculative; this produced the several schools of philosophy, called by the Hindus the six *Dersanas*.

Of these Dersanas, three have been mentioned already in the brief account of the Hindu sacred literature; they were the two *Mimánsás* and the *Nyáya*. Besides those, there are the *Vaishêshika*, the *Sankhya*, and the *Sankhya-Yoga*. These philosophical systems, studied more or less by all Brahmans, present varied subjects of difficult speculation. As we have seen, the *Anterior Mimánsá* relates to ceremonies, the *Posterior Mimánsá* to wisdom, the *Nyáya* to logic; the *Vaisheshika* sets forth an anatomic theory, similar to that of Democritus; the *Sankhya* is a system of universal and atheistical philosophy; and the *Yoga* is very like the *Sánkhya* in some respects, though theistical in principle. Both these systems allow matter and spirit to be the components of the universe. There is also another numeral philosophy of the Puranas, which treats of the visible universe as an entire illusion, resolving matter and spirit into one entity, of which we shall say more hereafter. All the schools of philosophy, however much they may differ in the resolution of difficult questions, agree in their final object, the acme to which they conduct, which is, liberation from matter and final repose. Professor Wilson says:—

"It may be supposed that some time elapsed before the practical worship of any deity was more than a simple preference, or involved the assertion of the supremacy of the object of its adoration, to the degradation or exclusion of the other gods: in like manner, also, the conflicting opinions were matters rather of curiosity than faith, and were neither regarded as subversive of each other, nor as incompatible with public worship: and hence, notwithstanding the sources of difference that existed in the parts, the unity of the whole remained undisturbed: in this condition, indeed, the apparent mass of the Brahmanical order at least, still continues: professing alike to recognise implicitly the authority of the *Vedas*, the worshippers of SIVA or of VISHNU, and the maintainers of the *Sánkhya* or *Nyáya* doctrines, consider themselves, and even each other, as orthodox members of the Hindu community."

Internal incongruities in the system have, however, affected its integrity, and created feelings of animosity among the different sects, which are expressed in the Puranas and other works written to magnify particular deities, or to promote the interests of certain shrines. The worship of Brahma has disappeared amid the strife, while *Vishnu*, *Siva*, and *Sakti*, who now receive the adorations of the Hindus, are chiefly worshipped under their representatives, *Krishna*, *Rama*, or the *Linga*. Quotations from standard works might be adduced to show how the partisans have respectively sought to vilify the objects adored by opposite sects.

Changes in opinion too supervened, and six heretical schools of philosophy arose, and disputed the preeminence with the orthodox: those systems have, however, almost disappeared. Some of those teachers attacked the Vedas and the Brahmans, denouncing the latter as cunning hypocrites, who had invented a religious system for purposes of private gain. Others, too, contemned the sacred books, and their interpreters, and the objects of Brahmanical adoration, and advanced a step further by inventing a set of gods for themselves. These innovations provoked resentment, and ultimately led to the expulsion of Buddhism from India.

There is not only evidence to show that the Hindu religion at the present time differs essentially from that authorized by the Vedas, so far at least as we have ascertained their teaching, but likewise from that which has existed at different periods since the mythological system was invented. It has undergone many variations from time to time, and is now, though one in most of its great features, variously entertained by numerous sects. These sects of the Hindus have been described by several writers, both in the north of India, and also in the south.

From these records it may be seen that the popular divinities, Vishnu and Siva, have long had their numerous votaries divided by various rites and opinions. Many of the sects now existing may be known by their characteristic or sectarial marks, and also by their costume and diversified ascetic practices. The naked mendicant, smeared with funeral ashes, armed with a trident or a sword, carrying a hollow skull in his hand, and half intoxicated with the spirits he has quaffed from that disgusting wine-cup, is one of the most hideous of these very exceptionable classes. The licentious practices of some of the sects are said to be in excess quite beyond belief. The prevalence of foreign rule, and the influence thereunto belonging, has, however, had the effect of diminishing such practices as were formerly common, and where they have not been discontinued, they seek obscurity. Still, we are assured that some of the orgies of the Sactas are of a most disgusting kind.

There are among the Hindus five sects who may be regarded as orthodox, in relation to the fundamental principles of Hinduism. These are the *Saiva*, the *Vaishnava*, the *Saura*, the *Sakta*, and the *Gánapatya*. Those who differ from these five sections of the system are regarded as dissenters.

It would appear that the questions affecting the ritual and the theology, the faith and practice of the Hindus, were discussed about a thousand years ago, by a distinguished religious leader of the name of Sankara Áchárchya. He then decided that the orthodox might entertain certain differences of opinion on great and difficult points of religious belief and practice, without detriment to their fundamental principles. The reformer alluded to did not meditate the suppression of acts of outward devotion, nor of the preferential worship of any acknowledged and preeminent deity; his leading tenet is the recognition of Brahm, Para-Brahm as the sole and supreme ruler of the universe, and as distinct from Brahma, Vishnu, Siva, or any other individual member of the Hindu pantheon; with this admission, and in regard to the weakness of those human faculties which cannot elevate themselves to the conception of the inscrutable first cause, the observance of such rites and the worship of such deities as are either prescribed by the Vedas, or the works not incompatible with their authority, were left undisturbed by this teacher; they even received to a certain extent his particular sanction, and the peculiarities of the five sects were taught severally by some of his disciples. Thus considerable freedom of belief is tolerated by the Brahmanical teachers; and such is the general effect on the Hindu mind, that it is no unusual thing to hear sentiments of toleration in favour of even an antagonistic faith,—the Hindu can believe two opposite creeds, two contradictory propositions.

It is impossible to comprehend within our restricted limits any satisfactory account of the numerous sects who have from time to time been called into existence by the extravagances of Hindu mythology, operating on the depraved and vagrant tendencies of a corrupt nature. Leaving then the vagaries of the numerous sectaries as they affect the parties who are attached to them, we shall endeavour to give, in as compendious a form as may be, the general principles of the Hindu religion. In doing this, it must be understood that the system is professedly based upon the inspired teaching of the Vedas, as they are interpreted by the Hindu theologians themselves.

Those who have always regarded the Hindus as a nation sunk in the lowest depths of a grovelling polytheism, will hear with surprise that the foundation of their religious system is laid in the belief and assertion of the existence of one great, universal, self-existing Spirit, the fount or origin of all other beings, animate or inanimate, material or immaterial. Creation, in the Christian sense, of beings out of nothing is denied. Deity is assumed to be the only essence, and therefore, the formal and material cause of all existence. The incommunicable appellation of this supreme and eternal spirit, viewed in its own abstract and impersonal essence, is *Brahm;* a noun in the neuter gender, not to be confounded with *Brahma*, a masculine noun, and the appellation of the first person of the Hindu Triad.

Nor is this fundamental article of belief found only in the sacred repositories we are referring to; the same doctrine is universally maintained throughout the land; and in almost all the works where the existence and attributes of the Supreme are adverted to, the fullest expression is given to the same verity. He is uniformly spoken of as without beginning or end, eternal; that which is, and must remain unchangeable; without dimensions, infinite; without parts, immaterial, invisible; omnipotent, omniscient, omnipresent; enjoying ineffable felicity.

These utterances of a sublime Theism are not, as we might suppose, the only expressions employed by the Hindus to set forth the character of the Supreme. When he exists as the sole being in the manner just described, the only one, without a second, he is represented as one in a sense which excludes the very possibility, not only of any other God, but of any other being whatsoever. Here we have, in a sense corresponding with the teaching of Christianity, the doctrine of the divine unity: here he is set forth as the only living and true God. The Hindu, however, holds the doctrine of the divine unity under modifications and limits that do not accord with the God of the Bible. The Hindu considers that when Brahm exists in his proper and characteristic state, he is one in such a sense as to exclude not only all other beings, but the possibility of any other being, whether animate or inanimate. In this state, which appears to imply—all quality being denied him—absolute negation or nothingness, he is nevertheless said to be in a state of ineffable repose and enjoyment. In this natural condition, as the sole self-existent being, he must be regarded as an algebraic monad, till the conception starts into being of a possible or desiderated universe. This conceptional or possible universe is, according to the prototypical ideal image, next produced in actual and visible manifestation. On this realization he himself is said to become quiescent, and returns at once into a state of undisturbed repose, such as implies the utter negation of all quality, and yet consisting with being and blessedness.

The question that would hence arise, as regards the universe which we behold before us in visible manifestation, relates to its very being,—what is the universe of beings of which we form a part? Is it a creation out of nothing, of material substance, as we learn from the Bible? Or is it an organization of pre-existent matter into the visible and tangible now exposed to our senses? The latter supposition is already denied in the definition given of Brahm; and it is denied also that existence can arise out of nothing.

So far as I have been able to collect the opinion of Hindu interpreters from personal conference with learned natives, and from the theological writers of India, they may be variously stated. One class of writers contend for the theory of a spiritual or ultra-Pantheism, which represents the apparent realities of the visible universe, and the sentient beings by which it is tenanted, as so many manifestations of the Divine Essence itself; they are so many illusive forms of Brahm. He is said to manifest himself in so many forms, and yet he himself has not any form, as sun-light or moon-light may be reflected from a clear surface, and may appear in any form. He appears possessed of quality, as the clear crystal may appear coloured by the roseate tints of the flower reflected by it. He, though multiplying himself endlessly, remains one, as would the bright sun itself or the moon, although reflected in innumerable mirrors or in numberless vessels of water. He appears to change, yet is immutable, as is the colourless water that may exist in foam, bubbles, invisible vapour, radiant clouds, fleecy snow, stony hail or solid ice. In this way the endlessly varied universe, the visible materialism, and the percipient spectator—the human soul, whom these illusive forms surround, are a manifestation of the Supreme Brahm, diversified into a countless variety of individualities occupying the immeasurable fields of space, and rolling on endlessly through the mutations of time. Such is the theory of absolute Pantheism.

Another theory represents the volition of Brahm as giving separate existence to an energy, which, possessing personality, has the power of separate agency. The propounders of this notion deny that this energy is independent of Brahm, as indeed they deny that any being can be; and they deny that it is identical with him, because the theory sets out with its separated existence and action, ascribing to the energy operations that cannot be predicated of the Supreme Spirit. It needs scarcely be observed, that it is difficult to conceive how an energy can act independently of the subject of which it is an attribute, as in some sense it must be regarded according to the way in which the view is enunciated. This energy first acts on the undivided portions of Brahm in the form of human souls, by virtue of which the soul is led to the illusive belief, in utter ignorance of its identity with Brahm, that it has a separate existence. Its next operation produces in the soul all those feelings, apprehensions, impressions, and persuasions that go to make up the sum total of human experience. By this means the apparent universe, the visible and material creation around us, is supposed a reality. It must, however, be understood that the denial of the real existence of the universe is a fundamental principle of this theory. The impression the percipient soul has of existence is produced by illusion or *Máya.* This Máya is the principle that leads to the belief of existence where no such existence exists. This is illustrated by various similes frequently found in the writings of this school, which are often referred to by the Hindu in his discussions with the western metaphysician. An image in a mirror, the *mirage* of the desert, the objects in a *camera obscura,* the phenomena in a dream, the illusions of fancy, wherein a rope is imagined to be a serpent, and avoided as if real, producing fear and trepidation, are among the facts referred to as considered favourable to the support of the view under notice. Thus the Hindu maintains that it is the effect or operation of *Máya* that produces delusively the impression of an external material universe; and the percipient soul is all the while the mere passive recipient of the impression, just as the mirror or the water are of the images they reflect from the material forms within the range of their surface. And so long as the soul is held under the influence of this actuating Máya, it will be subject to the evils incident to illusion, as the mind is by an imagined spectre, that may torment by its supposed power of evil. This subjection of the human soul to desire and aversion, to hope and fear, this susceptibility of emotion, will necessitate, till true knowledge dispels the illusion, the recurrence of births and deaths, and all the contingencies involved in the successive conditions through which it passes ere it attains emancipation from the power of Máya or illusion. This and similar speculations are entertained by the contemplative, and pursued with the utmost avidity. It is not to be imagined that the profoundly learned are the only persons who are addicted to these subtleties. For, although the system is abstruse and incomprehensible, it is a fact that few educated and intelligent minds are ignorant of its leading features.

The most popular and generally received theory, which contemplates the putting forth of the divine energy for the manifestation of a visible universe, may here conveniently be more fully stated. According to this theory, Brahm produces from himself spirits or souls as rays are produced from the sun, or as sparks are produced by fire. These become individuated as supernals, infernals, men, animals, vegetables, and minerals. So long as these emanated spirits entertain the notion of separate and individual existence, they are moved to action as a consequence, and therefore necessitated to undergo the varying conditions of the metempsychosis. The soul is thus regarded as eternal in its essence, though it began a separate individuality as produced in time; and it is eternal as to the future, because destined to endless being, not as an individuated subject, but as capable of final absorption into the ocean of being. It will be seen that, according to this theory, the soul is not created, but eternal, an effluence from the Eternal Spirit, whose refluence into the fount of being ends but its individuated or separated existence.

From pure spirit it is assumed gross matter cannot emanate, and therefore the advocates of this emanative system have recourse to a successive evolution or expansion of the Supreme Essence. Like many of the subjects connected with Brahmanical speculation, this is one of extreme difficulty, and hard both to state and comprehend; it is made out in something like the following manner: From the essence Brahm—the Eternal One, in the exercise of his energy, the intellectual principle, the seat of intelligence, thought, reflection, reason and other such attributes as may be regarded in essence and subtlety next to pure spirit, the source of future individuated intellects, is produced. From this the principle of consciousness is produced, which involves the notion of personality. "I am," the germ of individuality and the spring of action is hence educed. From this proceed five subtle particles, rudiments, or atoms. These produce in consecutive order the gross elements of which the natural universe is composed. Direct from the principle of consciousness proceeds the etherial; from the etherial the aerial; from the aerial the igneous; from the igneous the aqueous; and from the aqueous the terrene. Thus the Hindu educes from the supreme essence by a fanciful evolution the five elements.

In successive order from the conscious principle are developed the eleven organs of sense and action; these are the five instruments or organs of sensation, as the eye, the ear, &c.; the five instruments of action as the hands, &c. It is to be understood that these are not the gross elemental organs, but a subtle power having its seat in them. To these are to be added mind, intellect, consciousness. These thirteen organs, three internal and ten external, are regarded as so many guards at the portals of the resident essential spirit. The organs receive impressions which are transferred to the *mind*, as an organ of all the senses. The mind delivers over the impressions to consciousness, and that again to the intellect, and that to the spirit which is now made aware by means of these organs of the presence and quality of the thing presented. From the five subtle elements already named, are evolved the five grosser elements which compose the material universe. It does not consist with the necessitated brevity of this work to enter into an elaborate detail of the manner in which the elements are combined from this subtle elemental principle, their source or medium. It may suffice to state that these elements are severally endued with qualities that have their respective relations to the organs which are fitted to appreciate them. The gross elements are ether, air, fire, water and earth, which are evolved and conditioned as follows:—Ether has the property of audibleness, being the vehicle of sound, and is appreciated by the hearing:

Air is endued with the properties of audibleness and tangibility, and is appreciated by the hearing and touch: Fire is invested with the qualities of audibleness, tangibility, and colour, being applicable to the hearing, touch, and sight: Water possesses the properties of audibleness, tangibility, colour, and savour, and is appreciated by the hearing, touch, sight, and taste. Earth unites the properties of audibleness, tangibility, colour, savour, and odour, being sensible to the hearing, the touch, the sight, the taste, and the smell.

Individual souls emanating, as before intimated, from the Supreme Essence, are in the order of things organized, embodied, and individuated, but they are not subject to birth or dissolution. The soul is a portion of the Divine Essence, and as such is infinite, eternal, intelligent, sentient, true. It is governed by the Supreme, and is moved to action, not from within, but from without through the organs; as an artisan, taking his tools, labours and toils, lays them aside and reposes, the soul is active and passive by means of its organs. When emancipation is attained on the true perception of its real character as a part of the Supreme Essence, the soul in its elemental and native simplicity then returns to the ocean of being, where it finds felicity in ineffable repose. Whilst exposed in the cycle of an ever-changing condition it is not independent or free, but under the absolute control of the Supreme, whose behests are regulated by the conduct of the individual subject to his control. Its own real state as to virtue and vice is the measure of his dealings with it, and all its weal and woe, its good or ill, are the allotments of the eternal Arbiter; not that evil is attributable to him, since the anterior dispositions are regared as an infinite series extending into the eternity of the past.

The soul, in its passage through succeeding stages of being, is essentially one, as may be inferred; and although ever changing in regard to organized matter and the conditions it involved, is possessed of a body, a spiritual vehicle or casement, which accompanies the soul throughout its successive stages. This casement, or body, is said to consist of a threefold relation: the first is an intellectual case, which is composed of the simplest elements, and of the intellect, with the five senses. The next is the mental sheath, in which the mind is joined with the preceding. The third casement comprises the organs of action and the vital faculties, consisting of certain airs in the body. The soul, in this combined, subtle frame, migrates; and when it is produced as the result of moral quality in an organized body, that, as we know, whether viviparous, oviparous, or germiniparous, is composed of the gross elements already enumerated.

These few sentences may serve, in some degree, to elucidate this very mystical subject, and show how, from the sole essence, the Eternal Brahm, by the exercise of his own energy, is produced the moral and material universe. The countless orders of beings that exist in the terrestrial, celestial, and infernal regions are thus, in essence, identified with the source and centre of being. The varied forms in the material universe are but an emanation from the same source, expanded, and diffused, and eliminated, being rendered more gross, and dark, and sluggish, as the emanative process is pushed onwards to a greater distance from the essential and transcendental properties of his own spiritual essence. But whatever may be the form or modification under which matter may present itself to the percipient faculty, it is, nevertheless, of the very substance of God. Brahm is at once the *efficient* and *material* cause of all things; and there cannot be, by any possibility, according to the conceptions of a Hindu, any substance or quality that is not in him. The visible creation is an act of his will. Its existence, its continuance and dissolution, are equally under his immediate control. Being, as before observed, the *efficient* and *material* cause of all things, he is the fabricator and the fabric, the framer and the framework, the doer and the work done. All things are resolvable but him. Cloth, however fine or coarse, differs not from the yarn out of which it was made, nor the latter from the cotton of which it was spun. Curds contain nothing that was not in the antecedent milk. The oil contains nothing that was not in its source, the sesamum. The spider's web contains no component that was not in the bosom of the insect from which it was evolved; like deity, it resides in the beauteous and attenuated fabric, as in its own creation. So in like manner are we to regard the universe, moral and material; all that is visible and invisible, real or possible, emanates from, or is educed by, the volition of Brahm, from his own essence. It is to be understood that the philosophers of this school do not intend to insinuate that the material comes from the immaterial. The similes employed for illustration are merely designed to aid the mind in its conception. As the spider's web or thread is produced by, and is an expanded portion of the spider's body,—so truly and really does the universe, through a successive series of emanations, proceed from, and is an expanded portion of the substance or essence of Brahm. Still that essence or substance is truly spiritual, not material. Some writers contend that all things are, at all times, throughout the period of manifestation and of apparent separate existence, still inseparably one with the essential source or fountain of being, as the rays and the sun, the string and the pearls it holds in order and contact, the radii and their centre, &c. When the energy of emanation ceases to operate, all orders of being return, and are reunited to the fountain whence they sprang, and then God becomes the one self and sole existing being, without a second.

The assumed dependence of all things on the source or fount of being, is the occasion of much mystic sentiment to the writers of this school of philosophy, who speak most expressively of the union, the oneness, subsisting between the soul and its great parent essence. Some of the soliloquies indulged under this notion are exquisite and touching, and calculated to soothe and tranquillize the anxious mind amid the turmoil incident to its present agitated condition. Some of the writers of the West, under the inspirations of Christianity, have similarly expressed themselves, as may be seen in the following extract from the poems of Richard Baxter:—

"But, oh, how wisely hast thou made the twist!
To love thee and myself do well consist.
Love is the closure of connaturals;
The soul's return to its originals:
As every brook is toward the ocean bent,
And all things to their proper element;
And as the inclination of the sight,
How small soever is, unto the light:
As the touch'd needle pointeth to the pole,
Thus unto thee inclines the holy soul:
It trembleth, and is restless till it come
Unto thy bosom, where it is at home."

The sentiment here expressed is coincident with what is found among some of the mystic writers of India; but as if Baxter had anticipated the perversion of the sentiment by the pantheist of Brahmanical teaching, he adds:—

Yet no such union dare the soul desire,
As parts have with the whole and sparks with fire;
But, as dependent, low, subordinate,
Such as thy will of nothing did create.
As tendeth to the sun the smallest eye,
Of silly vermin, or the poorest fly;
My own salvation, when I make my end;
Full mutual love is all that I intend;
And in this closure, though I happy be,
It's by intending and admiring thee."

That the Hindu does not mean this ineffable union of a created spirit with its Maker is evident from the remark of a writer who, combating the sentiment of the Pantheist in regard to final absorption into the divine essence, says, "Sugar is good, but where would be the enjoyment, if one were oneself to become sugar?"

It cannot fail to occur to the reflecting mind, how vast are the advantages conferred on the Christian believer by the sublime teachings of the Bible; and it should beget a correspondent feeling of gratitude for the benefit which an authenticated revelation implies: it reveals at once the character of God, and the true character of man.

The unity of the Hindu system has been already referred to as one of the evincements of that sagacity which its originators have exercised in its construction. Its theories and abstractions are well fitted to occupy and gratify the spiritual, the contemplative, the earnest; these as an esoteric substratum of doctrine suit the initiated; whilst the vulgar are provided with an exoteric system, whose symbols and imposing forms and mythological fables are better fitted for an impression, that can no otherwise be made than by a sensuous exhibition and pageant. These must be attached to something, and their enforcement must be identified with something divine and miraculous, otherwise the mind would find no repose in a mere external thing. Hinduism, therefore, connects its altars, its festivals, its relics, its pilgrimages, and its endlessly diversified observances with the theory of emanation, with deified heroes, and with the innumerable legendary miracles recorded in its Puranic stories.

It is now necessary to show how the subtle doctrines already specified harmonize with the mythological system, and are made the basis of the gigantic structure that stands so prominently before us in the literature and religious observances of the Hindus. Assuming that pure spirit cannot act without a medium as an instrumental appliance, and that the exercise of continued energy would be inconsistent with the repose of the Supreme Spirit, Brahm is represented as assuming a form, or the appearance of form; he evolves himself and produces the Hindu Triad—Brahma, Vishnu, and Siva. The great *one* becomes known as three gods or office-bearers: their emanation direct, not as other beings by successive operation, gives them precedence. The evolution here referred to is variously stated by different schools of philosophy. Without entering into the discussion, it may suffice to state, that to the Hindu Triad are assigned the three offices of the formation, the preservation and the destruction of the visible universe. We are not to attach the idea of creation, in its Bible sense, to Brahma, but rather manifestation—he manifests or exhibits the universal order of created things. Vishnu pervades and sustains the expanded universe; and Siva changes, involves, or resolves into primeval elements the visible creation at the end of the successive ages. Attached to these male divinities or office-bearers are three female deities, each represented as the personified energy of the Eternal Brahm, without which no action could be exerted. These personages are invested with three names—Sarasvati, Lakshmi, and Parvati. Sarasvati, the consort of Brahma, is the protectress of the arts, of science, learning, eloquence, poetry, and music. Lakshmi, the energy of Vishnu, is the goddess of fertility and plenty,—a very popular deity throughout India, and famed for her personal charms. Parvati, the mountain goddess, as her name imports, is represented as the companion of Siva, and, like her consort, she is armed with destructive energies. These beings are said to derive their existence immediately from the Supreme Brahm, who, on their eduction from his own essence, confides to them the affairs of the moral and material universe. Hindu writers, according to this system, represent Brahma as drawing from the Eternal Brahm, a being invested with consciousness and all the correlative principles and properties that make up his personality.

In order to supply the germinant seeds and principles of all future things, which, according to their theory, must of necessity have an orderly emanation from one sole essence, the Hindu philosophers have invented a huge seed or egg, in which the elementary or seminal qualities of all future things were nurtured and matured. In order to the production of this seed the Eternal Brahm is represented as assuming a new form, as *Purush* the primeval male; and his energy is sometimes represented as exerted in the production of a plastic principle or female energy, called *prakrit* nature. In the seed of future worlds Brahma resides for an age, or year of the gods, or four thousand three hundred millions of solar years, vivifying, and combining, and expanding its elements. After floating like a bubble on the primeval waters for the period specified, and thus becoming matured, this seed or egg burst, when the perfected product, the collocated, the beauteous, and harmonious universe, the sun, the moon, the stars, and the globe itself with all its furniture, sprang into the depths of space, and commenced the revolutions that we and all our intelligent and percipient fellow-beings behold. Hence it is that the universe is sometimes personified, described as a being in human form, and of amazing magnitude. The hair on this giant form are the forests, his head the clouds, his beard the lightning, his breath the circumambient air, his voice the thunder, his eyes the sun and moon, his nails the rocks, and his bones the mountains.

The physical universe thus produced is sometimes spoken of as three worlds, and sometimes as fourteen. The three are the heavens, the earth, and the interambient air. The fourteen are represented as seven below our own, and seven above, of which our earth is the first, the others being the habitations of the gods; and these in the manner of concentric circles pass beyond each other. The inferior seven worlds are the abodes of all manner of loathsome and wicked creatures. Our own earth is often spoken of as an expanded flower, a water-lily, or lotus, and consists of seven circular islands, each having its own ocean. The central island is the abode of man, around which rolls an ocean of salt water; the next has its ocean of sugar-cane juice; the next an ocean of spirituous liquors; the next an ocean of clarified butter, the nectar of the Hindus; the next an ocean of curds; the next an ocean of milk; and the last an ocean of sweet water. Then comes a region of gold, and this is bounded by stupendous mountains, beyond which nothing exists but regions of blackness and darkness. The magnitude and extent of this wonderful creation are extraordinary—far exceeding the space stretching between us and the most distant planet in the solar system. In the centre of Jamba Dwip, Punyabhumi, the land of virtue—the famed mountain Su-Meru rises to a height of several thousands of miles, in the form of an inverted pyramid, having its upper surface two hundred times broader than the base, and surmounted with three golden peaks, on the loftiest of which the Triad reside. Other extravagant features of this wonderful Brahmanical universe might be specified, were not those already advanced sufficiently marvellous.

The astronomical phenomena of the Hindus are equally surprising, as are those connected with the mundane system briefly described. Of these we may here present a few notices. The second world is between us and the sun; the third is in the space between the sun and the polar star; and in this region are found the moon and all his mansions. The moon is placed beyond the sun. Next come the stars, and then Mercury, Venus, Mars, Jupiter, Saturn, Ursa Major, and the pole star. The four remaining worlds rise beyond these limits, whose intermediate distances are all given with the greatest precision. In these superior worlds are found mansions of glory of varied splendour, the abodes of celestial spirits. In the seventh Brahma resides. How surpassing is the glory of this region! Even the world of Indra, the king of the different ranks of subordinate deities, is described as the most splendid the human mind can conceive. Its palaces are composed of pure gold, resplendent diamonds, jasper, sapphire, emeralds, and precious stones, whose brilliance exceeds that of a thousand suns. Its streets are of crystal fringed with gold. The most beautiful and fragrant flowers blaze in its forests, whose trees diffuse around the sweetest odours. Refreshing breezes, canopies of fleecy clouds, thrones of dazzling brightness, birds of sweetest melodies, and songs of the most delightful harmony are heard in the enchanting walks which are there ever fragrant, ever verdant.

The production of all these glorious visions is the work of

Brahma, or rather he is the appointed agent in their exhibition or expansion. In this mighty work he is represented by some writers as exhausting his powers and unable to proceed. By others, again, he is said to have performed the severest austerities in order to gain power for his undertaking. The tears he shed in despair of being able to accomplish his task are said to have produced a race of hobgoblins that nearly scared him out of his senses. By him the worlds were peopled. The seven inferior worlds are tenanted by savage giants, hydras, huge snakes, among whom Sheshanaga, the thousand-headed serpent, holds a conspicuous place. His head is crowned with starry gems, and his eyes gleam like blazing torches. The superior worlds are occupied by gods, goddesses, and genii, of every order. The superior deities dwell in separate worlds; and the inferior ones chiefly in the heaven of Indra, the god of the firmament. They are said to number three hundred and thirty millions. They are divided into different orders. They hold diversified offices, and perform various functions, and their power extends throughout the universe. They can assume any form and wield any weapon, and even become embodied in anything; hence the advantage which the epic writers have in their great works. You have the god of wisdom, of folly, gods of war, of peace, gods of good, and gods of evil, of pleasure and delight, who shed on their votaries every imaginable enjoyment. There are, too, gods of cruelty and wrath, who must be sated and appeased with blood, and regaled with the shrieks and groans of expiring victims. All things, according to the theory of Hinduism, are placed under the control and guidance of these beings. Everything, animate and inanimate, every function of the physiological system of humanity, breathing, musing, gaping, every joy and every sorrow, all our conduct and its issues, every scene and every object, even the most trivial are supposed to be under their providence and control. Hence the chirping of a lizard, the screeching of an owl, the flight of a bird, a cloud, a fugitive leaf, an empty vessel, a word congratulatory of health, a harsh sentence, a look, nay, almost every circumstance, according to this system of multiplied and multiform preternatural agency, is made to wear an aspect for good or evil.

The manner in which our world was peopled has been already stated in the paragraphs on Caste. It may, however, be necessary to add, that according to the chronology of the Hindus, the present world is destined to last upwards of three hundred billions of common years. This period is divided into four ages, that correspond in some degree with those of the Greeks and Romans,—the golden age, the silver, the brazen, and the iron ages. We are now represented as being in the iron age, an age of corruption, of debasement, and we are told that about half of its period has expired. About half of the entire series of years that constitute the life of Brahma, or the duration of the universe, has passed away.

The Hindu writers speak of disturbances and disorders in the course of one of these ages, that arise from the vices of mankind. In the first age, the true, they are indeed pictured as wholly virtuous, but as time rolls on mutations occur, and floods and storms are sent to punish men for their vices. These catastrophes are spoken of as affecting only our own earth, which, after the administration of righteous retribution is again repeopled and replenished by a virtuous race preserved by a miraculous interposition of Deity. Such was the deluge. But there are other changes occurring at wider intervals. At the end of the great Kalpa, a long day of Brahma, extending through the space of four thousand million years, he is said to repose, and then comes the long night of darkness and inaction, equal in length to the day he has just ended. Then an universal deluge takes place; the seven lower, and two of the upper worlds, are submerged, when Brahma, assuming the form of Naráyana, one moving on the waters, reclines on the serpent Ananta, or Eternity, and reposes in long and awful slumber. Then the vicious of all worlds perish, but the righteous, the immortals, the divine sages, and all orders of celestial beings, with Indra, the king of the firmament, ascend into the fourth of the superior worlds. Others that have been distinguished for their virtue, may ascend still higher, and, unaffected by the catastrophe that has overtaken those in the inferior abodes, enjoy happiness till the day of Brahma dawns, when the course of events already detailed is repeated, and on the gloom disappearing, and the flood subsiding, the world, with its animate and inanimate organizations, again appears. But a period will arise, according to the Hindu writers, at the end of one hundred years of Brahma's life, when the Maha Pralay, the great destruction of the entire universe will take place, and the worlds and all things shall be reduced to absolute nonentity.

At that momentous period the process of emanation or development that has been described, will be reversed, and by a gradual refluence all things will return again to the fount of being. All the visible and corporeal forms throughout the world will be reduced to the elements of which they are composed. The grosser elements will be reduced into the rudimental elements. These in succession will infold themselves into their respective sources, and thus the terrene becomes igneous, and that aqueous, aerial, and etherial, and melting away into the principle of consciousness; and in like manner the eleven organs, or instruments of sense and action. Consciousness is then absorbed in the mass of intellect, and this into the essence of the Supreme Brahm from which it proceeded. Then all spirits of every class and degree are re-fused into the supreme, the imperishable and eternal. Then all that is visible and invisible, everything ceases to exist by being wholly re-absorbed in the eternal impersonal essence of the Supreme Spirit. Time ceases, and the reign of undefined silence and darkness begins. Then throughout illimitable space nothing will remain but the sole, the self-existent incomprehensible Brahm. Yet this essential and eternal one will again conceive the thought and cherish the volition described, and the same mighty scene shall be unfolded. Every succeeding universe is but the repetition of that which preceded it. Evolution and involution, effluence and refluence, succeed each other as day and night, or as the tree and seed, the seed and tree alternating in unbroken succession through the never ending and measureless eternity that is to come. This is the unalterable law of being which has existed from eternity. This is the Hindu theory of the universe. From all eternity past, that ever had a beginning, and to all eternity to come in a boundless progression, shall the Supreme Essence thus expand and disappear at intervals of inconceivable and measureless periods, in a series of alternations that shall never end. Such is the theory of Brahmanism in its most popular aspects. This system is by its advocates entitled the *Vedanta*, a word literally meaning the "end, essence, or purport" of the Vedas, from an affectation on the part of the Brahmans to connect it with those venerable records. Its great authorities are really the *Upanishads*, which are apocryphal appendages to and not parts of the Vedas.

CHAPTER IX.

HINDU THEORY RECAPITULATED.—CONDITIONS OF THE SOUL.—RITES, SACRAMENTS.—DAILY WORSHIP OF THE BRAHMAN.—WORSHIP OF THE SUN.—OTHER RITES AND OBSERVANCES.—CHIEF OBJECTS OF WORSHIP.—NEW DIVINITIES.—CONFIDENCE OF THE HINDU IN HIS RELIGION.

THE theory of the universe briefly but comprehensively stated in the preceding chapter, will prepare the way for further detail in regard to the condition of sentient beings, and especially man. We have seen how souls launched on the ocean of individuated beings are educed from the Supreme Essence or Source of existence, and what their final destiny is. As sparks or rays of light, they are separated from deity, and becoming individuated beings, subject to moral rule, capable of good or evil, and therefore liable to the retributions incident to the moral qualities and actions of which they are the subjects. We have seen how the soul is incased in certain subtle sheaths, wherein it passes through varied conditions in the course of its progress in the metempsychosis, subject, as its moral deserts may determine, to the organizations through which it may, for purposes of discipline, be necessitated to pass, whether in the form of viviparous, oviparous, or germiniparous being. Not only does the soul assume the condition of organized being in this world, but it also visits other worlds when it drops the gross body with which it may have been associated, and there receives the recompence of its deeds, or suffers the penal consequences of moral action. The vicious fall into the regions of torment, and in the realms of Yama they are exposed, for periods more or less protracted, according as their conduct may determine, to the severe inflictions which Chitragupta and other mythological personages are appointed to administer in those doleful shades. The wise and virtuous, when freed from the burden of material forms, rise to the moon, where they enjoy the fruit of their good actions. Thence however they depart, when the rewards of virtue are exhausted; and animating other organized forms, on earth or in ocean, they again suffer and enjoy the consequences of past action and inherent propensity, till, disembodied, they visit other worlds, as may be determined by the righteous award of the Supreme Ruler. Those favoured spirits that have in life paid attention to the Hindu ritual, visited holy places, meditated on the mysteries of sacred learning, and sought the full effect to be realized in the performance of religious duties, are, at death, admitted into the abode and court of Brahma, where, for almost boundless periods, they enjoy the sublime rewards of that transcendent and glorious paradise of Hindu felicity. Even thence, however, they must take their departure, and re-appear on the theatre of secular existence, ere they are finally beatified in the divine Essence. When, however, wisdom is attained and completed, the matured spirit is wholly emancipated from the consequences of action and passion; it becomes thenceforth identified with the divine nature. "As rivers flowing merge into the sea, losing both name and form, so the knower of God, freed from name and form, merges in Him who is the excellence of all excellences." As bubbles bursting are lost in the parent stream, so is the spirit of man, when matured, resolved in the immensity of God. Then, and not before, it attains its final and perfect bliss, the acme of all its aspirations, the end of all the dispensations and discipline through which it has passed; then, unembodied, pure, and free, it finds its fruition in the ocean of being, the source of its existence, where, losing its individuality, it is one with God in Eternity, Intelligence, and Joy.

It may be remarked, that the Hindu is taught to aspire after these various degrees of bliss; and in relation to their attainment, certain religious exercises are prescribed. The absolute freedom from all matter, attained by the perfect, admits the emancipated spirit into the very essence of the Supreme. Before that ineffable enjoyment is realized, the soul may by various religious practices, by austerities, and by intense meditation on the divine nature, acquire supernatural power to such a degree, as to be able to perform the most extraordinary acts. Such are supposed to have preternatural powers, which enable them to evoke the shades of their progenitors, and to translate themselves into other bodies by an act of mere volition, to move through the air, to disappear at pleasure, and to see as if by *clair-voyance* the scenes and circumstances of distant places.[1]

[1] About twenty years ago, a mysterious personage of this character was exhibited in Calcutta. He was in some marvellous way captured, whilst his companions, five in number, escaped, either by flight or by sinking into the earth. The one secured well nigh escaped by entering the solid ground, from which he was drawn by some devout persons who were so fortunate, by reason of antecedent merit, as to be the favoured instruments of presenting him to the admiration of countless multitudes who day after day thronged to do him homage. He was placed on a platform in an upper verandah of a native gentleman's mansion, where he sat cross-legged as in attitude of meditation, with his eyes closed, and as immoveable as a block of marble. His feet were washed by the attendants, and the water poured out or sprinkled over the crowds that thronged around the terrace, who manifested the utmost anxiety to catch, if it were but a drop, of the precious fluid thus purified by application to his sacred person. It was said that he had no sense of touch, was equally indifferent to pleasure or pain, insensible of heat or cold, and that he took no nourishment; yet he looked remarkably sleek. A friend of mine, a medical man, who was in the habit of attending the gentleman of the house, obtained permission to approach the venerated object as he sat on the platform. This gentleman concealed in his sleeve a small bottle of the spirits of hartshorn, and as he passed his hand over the man's face he removed the stopple, and permitted the pungent spirit to come into contact with his olfactory; when taking effect it became evident that he possessed at least one sense, for he gave unmistakable signs thereof by starting and falling

It follows from the principles of the system, that certain acts, certain deeds of supposed virtue or self-inflicted suffering, in the varied forms of austerity and penance, will conduct the soul into intermediate abodes of bliss, such as are provided for the earnest and devout in the mansions of sensuous enjoyment already adverted to; their continuance, however, is but temporary. These stages, these abodes of refreshment and repose, must be quitted on the exhaustion of the merit by which they were attained. Then the soul is again launched on the wide extended sea of mortal birth and secular existence. On this fundamental point of Hindu teaching, much is said by the popular writers; and many of their sayings are as commonly known as the proverbs of the country. One or two of the most remarkable may here be conveniently introduced.

"Of those who swim the wide extended sea of mortal birth, none ever can escape (continued migration), but they who to the feet of God adhere." "Good and bad actions must of necessity be consumed, *i.e.* by retribution; and except as thus consumed, their effects cannot be obliterated by hundreds of millions of ages."

Corresponding with this principle, the system of Hinduism teaches that there is a graduated scale of intermediate punishments, whose intensity and continuance are made dependent on the quality of the actions that conducted the soul to the places of their infliction. The system prescribes the course to be adopted in order to the attainment of any specified condition of future enjoyment. It is never doubted that the performance will be followed by the attainment of the desiderated object. The first award of bliss, or a bettered condition in the next birth, may be obtained by a careful attention to the ritual or ceremonial which forms the service of the temple or exoteric system. A still higher is attained

off the platform. The delusion lasted for many days, but at length it turned out that he was an impostor, who was carefully supplied with every luxury by those who were in the secret.

by acts of religious merit, involving the sacrifice of wealth, and the performance of works and services prescribed in the sacred books. Still higher advantages may be secured—even the condition of the immortal gods, who are not subject to mortal birth. The abandonment of the world, and the practice of austerities, leading the soul by intense meditation on the Eternal Spirit from all that is material and secular, leads to absorption into the Supreme Essence. And the pursuit of any of the varied objects of this elastic system is made dependent on the choice of the individual, at least to a certain extent; for of course he is by destiny compelled to pass through such conditions as his moral state demands. This graduation leads to the assumption on the part of devotees of the diversified lines of conduct, some preferring one object and some another, and hence it is not unfrequently the case, that one class will extol his own peculiar course at the expense of another. Hence, too, the rival feeling of the sects devoted respectively to the popular deities Vishnu and Siva, to which reference has already been made at the commencement of the preceding chapter. Besides this effect of the system, there is another not less remarkable, which may be noticed here. I refer to the existence of a class of writers, who affect to contemn the ceremonial system as conducting to an inferior bliss, and as indicating on the part of the adherents a low spiritual status. It does not, however, follow, as some have imagined, that because this class of writers disparages the lower degrees of the system, that they repudiate the theory of which it is a fact: they, having attained a higher condition, or rather, as the advocates of it, consistently express disparaging views of the symbolic system, as the evidence of indecision on the part of those who are content to remain under the influence of its external and sensuous elements. One of this class of writers, in allusion to the ritual, thus speaks:—

> Formerly how many flowers have I gathered and scattered;
> How many prayers have I repeated in a vain worship!

While yet in the prime of my life, how much water have I poured out!

And, moreover, how often have I encompassed the holy places of Siva!

This I have left off, for the wise who know the true God, the Lord of heavenly beings,

Believe not the Idol of the temples, apparent to the eyes, to be God, nor lift up to it their hands.

While taking up the water and throwing it again into the water (in performing the sandhya, and other rites), what is the object on which you think?

On whatsoever you think you have thrown all the water vainly:

Think on the root, think on the seed, and on the benefit arising from that seed;

When you are thus able to think, you may approach the feet of God.

The following stanza confesses the First Cause:—

It is not Ari, it is not Aren, it is not Ayen;

Far beyond the black (the colour of Vishnu), the white (the colour of Siva), or the red (the colour of Brahmà), soars the everlasting cause;

It is not great, it is not small, neither is it male, nor female:

Beyond every state of corporeal being it is further, further, and further still.

The vast structure of Hinduism is so comprehensive in its principles, and so expansive in its character, that it takes in every peculiarity of religious sentiment. The earnest and spiritual have their intellectual peculiarity more than gratified by magnificent theories, that supply an aliment fitted for their most refined and subtle imaginings: thus it gratifies intellectual pride; whilst the vulgar, the populace, have an attractive and external ceremonial suited to engage their attention in the oft-recurring frivolities of idol worship, and yet the observance needs not, does not generally, abate the pursuit of sensual gratification. The devotee, who abandons all that is sensuous for a spiritual object, and the low and grovelling, who bows down before a shapeless stone or an image of demon form, are equally successful in their respective ends. Each is moving onwards. Thus monotheism and polytheism meet together, and are recognised in this system as consistent parts of a great whole.

It were impossible in a work so limited as the present to enter into all the minutiæ connected with the religious observances prescribed in the Hindu ordinances, as the means for attaining desiderated spiritual and temporal good. Voluminous works have been written in the Sacred language, as already stated, of which versions have been made into the different languages of the country, for aiding and directing the disciple in the object of his desire. It is no exaggeration to affirm, that the study of these works themselves would occupy the lifetime of any one, were he gifted with sufficient acumen, and the requisite philological acquirements and patience, for such a task. Besides which, a very large portion of time must be devoted to the performance of the ceremonial, which is varied with the circumstances and relations of the individual. All the customs, manners, habits, and acts, however varied and minute, frivolous or ridiculous, loathsome or vile, which can by any contingency constitute or characterise, or accompany the doings of an individual, or the modes of intercourse, public or private, between man and man, are prescribed and regulated by the divinely originated Shastras or sacred ordinances. As before observed, all that relates to civil government, to jurisprudence, to the arts, architecture, war, science, law, medicine, music, as including poetry and dancing, grammar, all in fact is communicated to man by the immediate revelation of God. All knowledge is from the Great Supreme, and the language in which these mysteries are conveyed is, too, the language of the immortal gods.

Before introducing the account of the Brahmanical worship, as affording the best example of the daily sacred service of the Hindus, it is necessary to state that there are certain acts of a sacramental character, some of which relate to the Hindu even before birth. These essential parts of the ritual may be conveniently prefixed to the description of the daily ceremonial.

HINDU PURIFICATORY RITES AND SACRAMENTS.

The essential purificatory rites known under the name of Sangskár, are, by some, said to be ten, by others twelve. The performance of these is regarded as essential to the completion of a Brahman, a Kshattrya, or a Vaisya. These are as follows:—

1. The conceptional sacrament, performed, as some say, before the event, and after it according to the testimony of some writers. Some matronly person takes the young wife to worship at the shrine of the family goddess, generally consecrated in the dwelling, where the party is instructed to meditate on the deity in such a manner as may bring her fully before the mind. A cocoa-nut is broken on the occasion, and sweetmeats are offered, and afterwards distributed in the family.

2. The next ceremony takes place some months before birth, and has reference to the vitality of the fœtus.

3. The partition and arranging of the hair. These two rites are performed about the seventh month, and belong to a male child. It may be remarked, that these three ceremonies are confined to the first child, whereas the following rites are connected with every child.

4. The birth-ceremony takes place on the birth of the infant, when the umbilical cord is cut, whereupon ghi, or clarified butter, is introduced into the child's mouth with a golden spoon; and then its nativity is cast by the astrologer.

5. When a month old, if a Brahman or Kshattrya, the child is taken out to see the moon, as its progenitor.

6. The naming of the infant, at ten or eleven days old, is the next sacred rite of purification.

7. When six or eight months old, or when its teeth begin to appear, there is a ceremony incident to giving the child its first rice-milk.

8. At two or three years old, there is a ceremony con-

nected with the shaving of the head, when all the hair is cut off, except a single lock on the top of the head.

9. At some auspicious period between the fifth and the sixteenth year the ceremony for investing the young Brahman with the sacerdotal thread is performed. At or near this time the sacred Gáyatri is repeated in the ear of the youth in a low voice. Generally this important ceremony is performed with festive rites and expensive amusements, as well as with the accustomed religious worship.

10. Marriage is also a sacrament. The Hindu law speaks of eight different kinds of marriage.

Incremation, or the burning of the corpse of the Hindu with or without his widow is accounted an important rite, and by some it is regarded as of a sacramental character.

Besides these essential rites of Brahmanism, there are also the daily duties, which are regarded as the sacraments of the Hindu religion. They are :—1. The worship of spirits, progenitors, gods, the Vedas and mankind, in which offerings of incense and flowers are employed as accompaniments. 2. Obsequial rites, which, when properly attended to, require attention on ninety-five days in the year. 3. Oblations with fire. 4. Meditation on the Vedas. 5. Hospitality.

These very brief notices of the Sangskáras of the Hindus will serve to show how thoroughly religious observance pervades all the acts, habits, and events of life, and also to evince the potent influence it must consequently exercise over the national mind.

It would be expecting too much of human nature to imagine that all the burdensome services of the Hindu ritual are attended to fully. Various degrees of attention are given to the requirements of the system, as its votaries may be more or less earnest, as is the case with the professors of every religion. In Bengal and the northern provinces, bathing of a morning in the river, and the offering up of water to ancestors, with the reading of some portion of the Vedas, are very generally observed. The crowds that may be seen at the Ghats, serve to evince the estimation in which this service is held. Many content themselves with applying holy ashes to the person, or with imprinting on the forehead and other parts of the body sectarial marks—the presentation of flowers and water to the divinity they hold supreme, as Vishnu or Siva—and the repetition of the name of their guardian deity. These acts may be repeated at mid-day and in the evening. The banks of a sacred stream, a portico in a temple on the margin of a tank, are favourite places for these exercises. The worshipper unites with his daily service his petitions for any particular favour he may desire—as health, wealth, or offspring. Persons in business, engaged in the cares of the world, navigators, and labourers, rarely do more than form sectarial marks, with incantations and the uplifting of the hands to the invisible object of worship.

Not to enter into the details of Hindu requirements, even under one aspect of the system, it may suffice to present some particulars connected with the daily ceremonial of a Brahman. To instance the first acts on awaking of a morning: the religious code prescribes for the cleansing of his teeth, and enters into all the particulars as to the instrument, the place, the invocations, and the modifications incident to particular lunar days. His ablutions are so minutely described, and the requisite formulæ so tedious, that a volume might be filled with the detail. The innumerable sippings, the sprinklings, the aspersions, the immersions, are most tedious. The triliteral and monosyllabic AUM[1] contracted into OM, the

[1] OM. This triliteral and monosyllabic name of deity is prefixed to all prayers, and most of the writings of the Hindus. It is compounded of the three letters, A the name of Vishnu, U of Siva, and M of Brahma; it implies the Hindu Triad as three in one. The words following, viz. Bhu, Bhuvah, and Suah, are names of earth, the interambient sky, and heaven, and they stand for fire, air, and the sun. The one essential and eternal one is the soul or principle in all. He is the divine sun, the resplendent light, the great spirit. It may be remarked, that in the judgment of the Brahmans no Sudra can repeat this formula without incurring the severest penalties that can be inflicted on the human soul.

symbol of the Triad, the names of the seven superior worlds, are of special and frequent repetition. And then the sacred GÁYATRI, or holiest text of the Vedas, forms one of the most sacred and efficacious of the Brahman's morning prayers. The repetition of this sacred text is said to be necessary to salvation. As the word Gáyatri signifies *sing to preserve*, it may serve to convey the idea of the all-efficacious character of this holy text. The following is the original of the Gáyatri :—

"Om, bhu bhurvah suah tat savitur varényang bhargo dévasya dheemahe dheeyóyónah prajódayāt." Om, earth, sky, heavens. Let us meditate on the supreme splendour of that divine sun who may illuminate our understandings.

The worship of the sun on each succeeding day is an important duty, and is accompanied by a special ceremonial. The lock of hair on his head being tied, the worshipper takes *kusa*, a sacrificial grass, in his left hand, and three blades in his right, and pronounces the Gáyatri. He sips water, washes his hands, touches with his wet hand his feet, his head, breast, eyes, ears, nose, and shoulders. Should he sneeze or spit, he must not sip water, but as prescribed first touch his right ear. Fire, water, the Vedas, the sun, moon, and air, all reside in the right ear of the Brahman. Ganga, the sacred river, is in the right ear of the Brahman, and sacrificial fire dwells in his nostrils; and whenever either are touched all impurity at once passes away. This explains the touching the ear in the event of contracted impurity; and also shows why it is that a Brahman occasionally suspends his sacerdotal string from the right ear. In this service intense meditation on certain divine forms is enjoined as being of the greatest value. He is to enthrone in his bosom the four-faced Brahma, the sacred form of Vishnu in his heart, and the five-faced Siva in his forehead. He now suppresses his breath by closing, with the two longest fingers, the left nostril, and draws his breath with the right; and then closing the right nostril with his thumb, he holds his breath while he internally repeats to himself the GÁYATRI; and then raising the two fingers from the left nostril, he emits the breath he had suppressed through the right nostril. He next makes three ablutions, using the following prayer:—"As the labouring man drops sweat at the foot of a tree; as he who bathes is cleansed from all foulness; as an oblation is sanctified by holy grass, so may this water purify me from sin." To this succeed other ablutions, with various expiatory texts. He

next fills the palm of his hand with water, and presenting it to his nose, inhales the fluid by one nostril, and after retaining it for awhile, exhales it through the other, and then throws away the water towards the north-east. This is considered as an internal ablution that washes away sin. Then sipping water, he says, "Water, thou dost penetrate all beings; thou dost reach the deep recesses of the mountains; thou art the mouth of the universe; thou art sacrifice; thou art the mystic word *vasha;* thou art light, taste, and the immortal fluid."

These acts prepare the worshipper for the adoration of the sun, which is regarded as one of the most solemn rites. The worshipper takes his position by standing on one foot; resting the other on his thigh, and holding in his hand a cup, containing a smaller one made of dough, and filled with clarified butter, and a lighted wick in its centre, he directs his face to the east; he repeats inaudibly the required formulæ, which includes an ascription of praise to the resplendent fount of light, as the subject of so many qualities beneficial to the world. He next prepares an oblation, consisting of tila, flowers, barley, water, and a preparation of sandal-wood, which is placed in a small copper vessel made in the form of a boat. This is put on his head, and presented whilst engaged in the repetition of holy texts; and he concludes by saying, "His rays, the efficient causes of knowledge, irradiating worlds, appear like sacrificial fires." This oblation is followed by the invocation of the Gáyatri. The following is the form:—"Thou art light, thou art seed, thou art immortal life; thou art effulgent; beloved by the gods, defamed by none, thou art the holiest sacrifice." This is repeated in various forms, and afterwards invoked in these words:— "Divine text, who dost grant our best wishes, whose name is trisyllable, whose import is the power of the Supreme Being, come, thou mother of the Vedas, who didst spring from Brahma, be constant here." After this the Gáyatri is pronounced inaudibly, along with the triliteral monosyllable, and the names of the three worlds, as often as may be practicable, counting the repetitions on a rosary. Some repeat the text a thousand times. The worshipper again presents prayers to the sun, saluting it as the mighty luminary, the cause of day, the foe of darkness, and the destroyer of every sin. He then walks towards the south, in imitation of the sun's course, and terminates his morning's devotions.

By some orders of Brahmans this service is repeated at noon, and by some again in the evening, with a formula of the same general character. Those Brahmans who are householders must, in addition to the ceremonial detailed, daily perform the five great sacraments; these are, teaching and studying the Vedas and other sacred records, in honour of those who composed them; offering cakes and water to the manes of departed ancestors, and the progenitors of mankind; an oblation of fire to the whole assembly of the gods; offering a sacrifice of food to all animated creatures; and performing the rites of hospitality to men. The rites and ceremonies attendant on the performance of these duties are even more minute, intricate, and numerous, than those connected with the daily ablutions and the worship of the sun.

The Hindu, besides these regular and ordinary religious duties, has others that the various events of life necessitate. Marriages, births, funerals, have their respective ceremonials. The rites connected with commemorative obsequies are so numerous, that, if duly observed, they will occupy a portion of ninety-five different days in one year. Then there are the various and complicated ceremonies connected with the temple service, besides the daily ablutions we have described. The latter are performed on the banks of some sacred stream, or on the margin of some artificial reservoir within the precincts of a temple, or elsewhere.

To attempt a detail of the diversified services connected with the Hindu ritual, in regard to all the events requiring religious acts, from birth to the funeral pyre, is quite out of the question: the prescriptions are most numerous, and the directions occupy volumes. The first food given to the infant, the age of the moon, the position of the stars, the hour of the day, the choice and application of a suitable name, are regarded as intimately connected one with another. The first food, the first sight of the sun, the pronunciation, for the first time, of the first letter of the alphabet, are matters involving religious references and ceremonies. In like manner the preparations and observances connected with the various duties of the student of the sacred books; the staff, the mantle, the girdle, and such like externals, must be provided with strict regard to certain observances, certain mystic considerations, without which all would be nullified. The prescriptions to be observed in the choice of a wife, are very particularly laid down. She is not to have any defects; she must have an agreeable name and voice; she must be of graceful proportions and elegant movements, having hair and teeth well proportioned in quantity and size. Deformity, sickliness, an inflamed eye, an inauspicious náme, would always operate as impediments to marriage, as well as anything that might infringe on the respectability of her lineage and descent. Having entered on the onerous duties of a householder, voluminous injunctions and prohibitions now press around him, and call for a great portion of his time and attention. If at home, innumerable things are to be avoided, as eating with his wife, looking at her when she partakes of her food, or when she sneezes, or yawns, or is lounging at her ease, or applying perfumes to her person. If he be abroad, he must avoid standing on certain things, as hair, ashes, bones, seeds of cotton and husks of grain. He must avoid the shade of a tree, if improper persons be near it. If it rain, he is not to run. A rainbow is not to be pointed out to another. He must not interrupt a cow that is drinking. If he pass among cattle that are grazing, he must hold out his right arm, uncovered. He is not to drop saliva or any impurity into water. Should his image be reflected in water, he is not to look at it. He is not to step over a string, or a slipper; nor must he pass over the shadow of sacred images, or of a Brahman. If he come into contact with a mound of earth, a cow, or an idol, or a cup of clarified butter, he must pass, leaving them on his right hand. These are matters of religious obligation.

The numerous rites connected with purification and with diet, it is impossible to specify. The hours of the day, the place, the nature of the food, the manner in which it is to be prepared; the preliminaries to be observed by himself, as well as the prayers and benedictions to be uttered, are all of divine obligation: they are so varied and minute that their enumeration would fill a volume. Although many Brahmans who have leisure may spend several hours a day in the performance of the prescribed ceremonials, it is quite certain that those who have urgent secular duties devolved on them cannot go through the onerous rites we have described. These unite the first and second services together in the morning, and occupy no more than half an hour in their performance. They may repeat the name of their guardian deity,[1] the forms from the Veda, including the Gáyatri, and pour out a libation to deceased ancestors. A writer on the customs of the Hindus, who knew a great deal about them, says,—"The ceremonies most popular are the daily ablutions, repeating the names of the gods, the daily worship of some idol, and visiting holy places. The works of merit are, entertaining Brahmans, building temples, excavating and building tanks, making ghâts,[2] and the offering of expensive gifts in remembrance of deceased ancestors." The Brahman, when devoted to his ritual, is mainly distinguished by a strict attention to ablutions, and the daily service of the object of his special worship, adding, on certain days, the ceremonies incident to the occasion. It may be remarked, that among the

[1] The guardian deity of the Brahmans is Siva; that of the Kshattryas Vishnu; that of the Vaisyas Brahma; whilst that of the Sudras is Ganesha.

[2] *Ghât* denotes here a *bathing* place, usually a slope, or flight of steps, down the bank of a river or tank, sometimes with the addition of a terraced portico of many pillars, which have a fine effect when kept in good repair. It is oftentimes equivalent to a quay, wharf, or landing-place; at others, it denotes a defile or mountain pass.

Brahmans there is a proud and self-sufficient class feeling and correspondent contempt for the lower castes.

These brief and general notices on the habits, the ceremonies, and usages of the Hindus may suffice to show how everything is stamped with a religious character. It must be evident that all the acts and habits of the Brahmanist are placed under the control of his religious belief. On all occasions he is followed by directions, prescriptions, and prohibitions, that require his observance and test his fidelity. It must not, however, be imagined that the mass of the people are able to meet all the requisitions of so burdensome a ritual. The generality select some particular rite as one of ordinary obligation, and this is very often attended to in a very perfunctory manner, and its performance is made subservient to the countless contingencies that make up the daily course of men of business. Hence short and compendious religious observances, such as the application of holy ashes, the painting on the forehead or other parts of his person of sectarial marks, the repetition of some holy text, or the name of a favourite deity, are all that multitudes ever attend to. These may occasionally, as leisure permits, retire to some sacred spot for a more lengthened ceremonial. For this purpose the period of mid-day is often selected for ablution and the associated rites of religious worship, on the side of a tank, or on the banks of a sacred stream. The temple is frequently visited, and the sacred shrine of a chosen divinity is venerated with uplifted hands, reverential sentiments, and the utterance of some sacred word or verse. The priests are in attendance at the temples at certain hours, indicated generally by the sound of the gong, the bell, the sound of the sacred shell, or the shrill sound of the pipe. In extremity, as when a woman is in labour, or when dangerous symptoms threaten the fatal termination of disease, some member of the family, probably its head, will, even in the dead of night, hasten to the village shrine, possibly a mere mud hut, and in lowly reverence supplicate in a hasty petition the beneficent intervention of the powerful being he believes to be there specially present.

Fasts, though not observed with rigour by all, are, nevertheless, observed on stated occasions, as are also the numerous rites which particular periods prescribe. For the purpose of ascertaining these periods an almanac is an indispensable instrument to the Hindu. To this he is obliged to refer in almost every transaction of life, because this is so entirely regulated by astronomical conjunctions and the influence of the spheres. It teaches him how to time the innumerable affairs of ordinary life, so as not only to avoid inauspicious conjunctions, but to seize the precise moment when the aspect of the stars is most favourable. The study of the almanac, as prepared for the Hindu, will afford abundant evidence of the manner in which almost every moment is interfered with by the teachings and requisitions of his religion. A well-ordered Hindu will not neglect the observance of his religious rites, nor overlook the prescriptions of his spiritual guides in the affairs of secular concernment, all of which are, he believes, under the control of preternatural agents and influences.

Whilst the ordinary observance of religious rites secures the benefits attached to its performance, the more severe practice prescribed to the earnest and spiritual is associated with merit, and contributes to advance the soul in its progress towards final beatitude. Accordingly we find that those who aspire after a higher and better condition, after the termination of the present probation, under the impression that certain observances will conduce to that end, resolve on the adoption of certain religious courses, supposed to be peculiarly pleasing to some particular deity. Others, taught to believe that certain deities have the power to bestow on their votaries certain blessings, will engage with special fervour in the worship of that particular deity. Some deities have special functions, and may be sought for special ends,—as for health, or wealth, or offspring, or almost any other temporal object. Some deities are supposed to have power to bless all who propitiate them alike in all places, and are therefore sought by all in every place. Others, again, are considered as having certain power in certain places; and hence pilgrimages to their shrines. Some have no temples, and yet are worshipped. Even demons, having the supposed power of inflicting evil, must be worshipped, and appeased by the rites of demonolatry in seasons of domestic and public calamity. Even disease itself has been personified. It is a fact that in Bengal the Cholera, under the name of *Olábibi*, has been elevated to the rank of a divinity; and the destructive power of this imaginary goddess is adored in terror, and her anger is propitiated by deluded low people. Demonism is the religion of the Shanars, and its rites are their only religious worship. The Hindus also, in accordance with their own system, which contemplates spirits as existing in the form of malignant deities, systematically honour their shrines. And as these divinities are, or have been, distinguished for their vices, their chicaneries, their sensuality, and every species of evil, they are sought as the patrons and abettors of vice and licentiousness. The burglar, the sensualist—even the murderer, in prospect of some deed of darkness—resorts to such in order to obtain aid and protection; perpetrating the foulest deeds under the authority of his divinity; and he does this consistently with his religious theory. In the worship of some of these cruel and licentious objects, emblems, and rites peculiar to their character are prescribed. Hence the bloody sacrifices at the shrine of the goddess Kali, in the suburbs of Calcutta. Hence, too, the self-inflicted tortures, and the sanguinary practices observed in the worship of this horrible divinity at the fanes dedicated to her service. It is on principles of religion that the impure orgies are practised in some of these temples; and the sanctions of religion defend a practice which devotes thousands of unhappy victims to the service of the temples, who, as dancing girls, are doomed to the most degraded occupation. These, by their arts and blandishments, diffuse under the sanction of religion the evils of lewdness and wantonness. The services of the temples are in this way as destructive of morals as are the unrestrained theatricals of the West. Indeed, I have heard intelligent Hindus, who knew the effects of the nocturnal services of the temples, speak of them in the most disparaging manner, comparing them to those of the lowest dramatic exhibitions of the Hindu theatre. Much that takes place under the name of religion in some of the festivals of the Hindus may not be put on record. I have witnessed scenes and heard songs at the natches of the Durga Festival in Calcutta that may not be narrated. And in the interior of Bengal I have seen groups of figures of the most objectionable character, and these not confined to the precincts of so-called sacred places, but in the great thoroughfares connected with the village bazaar. Indeed, the worst obscenities of Pompeii are only counterparts of such spectacles. It is very remarkable that Paganism in every age, and in every part of the world, has been thus characterised by the vilest features of licentiousness.

The position of the Triad, Brahma, Vishnu, and Siva, is universally acknowledged. The preeminent distinction accorded to these office-bearers in the Hindu Pantheon is never questioned. The first of these, being chiefly concerned in the efformation of the moral and material universe at the commencement of the great periods assigned for its reproduction, is not much honoured by public ceremonial, nor, with one exception, am I aware that he has any temple dedicated to him in India. His consort Sarasvati, the patroness of the arts, of science, of music and eloquence, is sung by all the poets, and her auspices are coveted by all emulous of distinction in the fine arts. To Vishnu and Siva, in some of their various manifestations, are dedicated nearly all the great temples that are now popular in India. To these two divinities, who divide the adorations of the people, are daily offered countless invocations, and ascriptions of praise, by millions who engage in their devotions at the numerous shrines consecrated to their service. Their votaries engage in their service in the full belief that these revered personages will eventually confer on their worshippers those future blessings which they themselves enjoy in the mansions they inhabit. The universal belief is, that these acts of devotion possess such an efficacy that they must operate with all the certainty of a physical necessity. The merit of these deeds is such as secures, by a natural sequence, the effects of which they are regarded as the certain cause. To those who have derived their religious belief from the Bible, and whose minds have been imbued with true principles under its hallowed teaching, much that has been advanced will appear incredible. Those whose minds have been enlightened by the lessons of inspiration, and whose moral sense is regulated by the law of God, which is the transcript of his own purity, will find it difficult to comprehend how the religious acts and habits we have described, many of which are associated with so much that is vile, can be regarded as the antecedents, however remotely, of beatitude. Christian minds are unprepared for the announcement; and when it is made they are disposed to suspect some exaggeration. Can it be that a nation so distinguished for shrewdness, so clever and skilful as we know the Hindus to be, can believe such absurd stories as are recorded of their divinities; and in this belief venture their eternal interests on the puerile ceremonies described? Surely there must be some mistake! I can sympathise with these expressions of surprise, and can fully appreciate the scepticism that withholds the mind from a full apprehension of the real power of Brahmanism over its votaries. But many years of intercourse with the Hindus in different parts of the country, in Bengal, in the South, and in Ceylon—not with the low and uneducated merely, but with the intelligent, the refined, the learned, the wealthy—has assured me of the power of the dominant faith of India. When it has really impregnated the mind, and moulded the intellectual and moral character, connected its dogmas—the sacred ordinances of the Shastras—those works of ancient sages, with its ceremonial, with the enchantment of national institutions, with the numerous magnificent and venerated shrines; the hopes and fears of revered parents and valued friends; the daily events of inner life, as well as with immemorial antiquity; then Hinduism commands belief among its votaries as intense as that which they repose in their own consciousness. The Hindu admits that he may not gain all he would by his daily observances, his self-denial, his pilgrimages, his gifts, his prayers, and his manifold efforts, yet he cannot fail, by these means, to advance his own real good to the extent of his known performances. The rites and ceremonies of his religion are the divinely appointed means for the attainment of certain ends, and so far as they are observed, he is secure of his reward; he is in advance in his spiritual condition by the performance, a step is gained, and in the end all will be well. It is the intensity of his faith that inspires the Hindu with his extraordinary attachment to his system. Hinduism is a part of the system of the universe. Its theories are involved in the laws of the world in which he is called to act, and they explain his position and assign him his business. The visible heavens may, nay must fail, but the laws by which they will be re-fused into the Eternal Essence relate to himself as well as to them. With the utmost complacency he resigns himself to the course of events as well-ordered and sure. Who is he that he should be otherwise than passive? What is his condition but that of a bubble that will resolve itself eventually in the ocean of being? He finds himself in a world whose condition he cannot alter, and resigns himself to the order of things around him. Can the order of the universe be otherwise than as determined by the Supreme? Were not the principles of his religion fixed before he became a conscious partaker of their benefit? Is it right for him to question the judgment of his revered ancestors, whose memory he cherishes by his oft-repeated acts and obsequies? Have not all these ordinances emanated from the Supreme? Are they not as certain as the source of being? Must they not, if followed, lead to present, future, and eternal well-being? Here the Hindu reposes.

CHAPTER X.

POPULAR DIVINITIES:—THE TRIAD.—BRAHMA, VISHNU, AND HIS TEN INCARNATIONS.—THE SÁLAGRÁM.—THE TULASI PLANT.—DOCTRINES OF THE VAISHNAVAS.—SIVA AND HIS EMBLEMS.—DOCTRINES OF THE SAIVAS, GÁNESHA, AND OTHER OBJECTS OF WORSHIP.

THE statements given in the last chapter show how the present popular system of Hinduism affects its votaries. The principles, in their application to the external observances, are evinced in the rites considered essential and sacramenta, in the daily ceremonial, and in the occasional religious practices which their hopes and fears may prompt.

In this chapter it is proposed to offer some account of the popular divinities, whose position in the Hindu system is such as to command the homage of the multitudes that throng around their numerous shrines. The supposed influence which astronomical phenomena are believed to have at particular seasons, requires some notice, as affecting the religious observances, and the festivals require some explanation. These matters may form an appropriate introduction to the account it is proposed to give in the next chapter of the temples and their festivals.

THE TRIAD.

The relation in which the Hindu Triad—Brahma, Vishnu, and Siva—stand to the physical and moral universe has been already stated.

BRAHMA.

Brahma, the creator of the universe, is represented as a person with four faces and four hands, emblematic of the four Vedas. He is attended by his consort, Sarasvati, who, as before stated, is the patroness of the arts, the goddess of eloquence. He is generally pictured on his vehicle, the swan, having in his hands a copy of the Veda, a spoon, a water-pot, and a string of beads. He is represented as of a red colour. There may possibly be some reference to the sun, his emblem, and to the all-changing power of fire, in the colour of Brahma.

There are no temples dedicated to this divinity in any part of India. He is, however, reverenced at *Pokher* in *Ajmer*, also at *Bithúir* in the *Doab*, where, at the principal Ghât, denominated *Brahmavertta Ghât*, he is said to have performed the sacrifice of a horse on completing the act of creation: the pin of his slipper, left behind him on the occasion, and now fixed in one of the steps of the Ghât, is still worshipped there. At the full moon in November a festival is held in honour of Brahma, and multitudes assemble, for purposes of piety and secular gain.

VISHNU.

The next member of the Triad, Vishnu, the Preserver, is the most popular divinity of the Hindu pantheon, and in some of his manifestations commands the worship of the majority of the inhabitants of India. He is represented in paintings and sculpture as four-armed. In one hand he holds a club; in another a sacred shell, used for libations, as a trumpet in the temple service, and as a horn in ancient warfare; in a third he holds a discus, used as a missile in war;

and in the fourth hand he has a lotus. He is of the colour of a dark cloud, ornamented with jewels and garlands, and rides on *Garuda*, the prince of eagles, an animal half bird and half man. He is accompanied by his consort Lakshmi, the goddess of fertility and plenty.

Vishnu is distinguished by a thousand names. These are contained in a book entitled "The Thousand Names," which is one of the early school manuals put into the hands of boys of the Vaishnava sect. Some of his names may be specified as descriptive of his attributes, character, or exploits. He is called the enemy of the demon slain by him; the fascinating, the sporting, the supreme, Náráyana, in allusion to his floating on the primæval waters before the creation; the black, cloud-coloured, the fine-haired, the lotus-eyed, the undecaying, the boundless, and the self-existent.

It would exceed the limits assigned to the present work to enter into details on the offices and character of Vishnu and other popular divinities, otherwise it might be shown how utterly at variance with each other are the accounts which are given in the sacred books of the Hindus, of the origin and precedence of the deities that are venerated by the millions of India; whilst the details, as far as they might be admissible into a Christian book, relating to the moral acts of these objects of superstition, would serve to prove irrefragably that they were the most abandoned and flagitious in conduct, and consequently unworthy of either confidence or esteem, much less of divine worship.

The references in the two Indian epics, the Ramayana and the Mahabharat, will suffice to introduce the subject of Vishnu's incarnations, and the details there given will show under what circumstances interpositions of this nature were vouchsafed to mankind. The incarnations of Vishnu are differently enumerated; sometimes they are spoken of as ten, and sometimes as twenty-four; ten is the generally admitted number. Usually a whole Purana, or history, is devoted to each incarnation. The history of Krishna is found in the Bhagavat Purana. This history is sometimes called the

Ocean of Love. It may be remarked that Vishnu as incarnate, in the form of Krishna, is the most popular object of worship in India. I have often heard in the Choultries, at dawn of day, pilgrims engaged in reciting his name to a parrot, the companion of their wanderings. Tradesmen too in the bazaars frequently utter the name several times when beginning to weigh out articles in series; whilst filling the scale they continue to reiterate Ráma, Ráma, Ráma, till the scale is equipoised, when having poured out the contents they proceed with the ordinary enumeration.

The following account of the ten incarnations of Vishnu will show their respective objects. The vignettes attached are engraved from photographs of original drawings, obligingly lent to me by Richard Clarke, Esq., the Secretary to the Royal Asiatic Society. Each incarnation is subscribed with a couplet expressive of its design; these as they appear in the drawings I have inserted in their respective places.

THE TEN INCARNATIONS OF VISHNU.

I. THE MATSYA AVATÁR.

The Fish denotes the fatal day
When earth beneath the waters lay.

The Fish incarnation was vouchsafed to rescue the four Vedas from the grasp of a demon who had stolen them from Brahma, and also for the purpose of preserving the only pious man on earth with his family from the general deluge in an ark. This Avatár of Vishnu is supposed by many learned men to have reference to the general deluge, and indeed it is thought to be the same history disguised in oriental fiction. As the fable of Saturn was raised on the true history of Noah; so it is supposed

that the seventh Manu Satyavrata corresponds with the same scripture personage.

II. THE KURMA AVATÁR.

The amphibious TURTLE marks the time
When it again the shores could climb.

Incarnate in the Tortoise, Vishnu sustained the whole weight of the earth, which was upborne on the back of this animal, when otherwise it must have sunk into the ocean at the time it was churned by the gods and demons with the mountain Mandar for a churn-stick, and a huge snake for a rope, to force it to disgorge the ambrosia it had swallowed. It is imagined by some writers that this Avatár also relates to the general deluge.

III. THE VARÁHA AVATÁR.

The BOAR's an emblem of the god
Who raised again the mighty clod.

The BOAR, with his tusks, drew out the earth, which had sunk in the waters of the deluge, and supported it on them. The general deluge, whose true history is found in the narrative of Scripture, is here presented in the fabulous records of the Hindus under another aspect. The boar is often found in the mythological romances of Greece and Egypt.

IV. THE NRI-SINGHA AVATÁR.

The LION KING and savage trains
Now roam the woods and graze the plains.

Vishnu, incarnate in the man-lion, issued from a marble column to devour a blaspheming monarch, who would otherwise have destroyed his pious son. The latter was engaged in a controversy with his father on the omnipresence of the deity. The incensed father, pointing to a pillar, demanded if the deity were there; on being answered in the affirmative, he began to blaspheme, and in defiance struck the pillar with his sword. The pillar rent asunder, and revealed a power he could not resist, in the form of this Avatár, which destroyed the impious monarch.

V. THE VÁMANA AVATÁR.

Next LITTLE MAN begins his reign
O'er earth, and sky, and watery main.

The DWARF came by deceit to destroy a very good king, who, though he neglected the rites of religion, by his charities was obtaining such merit, that the gods began to fear him. Vishnu, as a dwarf, asked for three steps of land, intending thereby to obtain the sovereignty of the universe, which, when granted, were made to extend over the universe, and for the third there was no place but the king's head. Raja Bali's life was then given as *Dakshina* (a gift), with the gift of his all.

VI. THE PARASU RÁMA AVATÁR.

RÁM with the axe then takes his stand,
Fells the thick forests, clears the land.

Parasu Ráma, the Axe-holder, was an incarnation of Vishnu, who thus appeared as a great warrior to destroy all the Kshattryas with their king, on account of their oppressive rule.

VII. THE RÁMA CHANDRA AVATÁR.

RÁM with the bow, against tyrants fights,
And thus defends the people's rights.

Vishnu as an incarnation appears in the person of a great hero, whose exploits are related in the national epic Ramayana, and whose name has become so common that it is frequently used as a term of salutation instead of the word Salám. He conquered Lanka (Ceylon) and destroyed Rávana, its king. Ráma is used by millions of Hindus as the name for god.

VIII. THE BALA RÁMA AVATÁR.

RÁM with the plough turns up the soil,
And teaches man for food to toil.

Vishnu appears in the person of Bala-Ráma, the Indian Hercules, who with his elder brother Krishna, slew many monsters and demons. He is represented, not only as a warrior, but as a benefactor of mankind, promoting the useful arts of life, and as such, he bears a plough and a rice-beater. It is believed by some that these three Avatárs of Ráma are varied histories of the same person. The question has been raised as to whether the Hindu Ráma was the son of Cush?

IX. THE BUDHA AVATÁR.

BUDHA for Reformation came,
And form'd a sect well known to fame.

Vishnu appeared incarnate in Budha to spread infidelity, and thus counteract the power which many had obtained by austerities, and which they were exercising in a tyrannical manner. It is surmised by some that the Hindus have inserted the name of Budha among the incarnations to attract the Jainas, or to explain the reason why Vishnu allowed so large a body of Atheists to remain in India. Buddhism at one time prevailed almost all over India, as may be proved both by the testimony of history and the monuments its votaries reared. Budha is represented in a posture of meditation.

X. THE KALKI AVATÁR.

When Kalki mounts his milk-white steed,
Heav'n, earth, and all, with them recede.

In his future capacity as reformer of the world, Vishnu will descend, punish the impenitent, bring back the golden age, and restore true religion. He is to appear on a white horse with sword and shield. Expectations similar have been entertained by most ancient nations. The Sybilline and Delphic oracles, the Chinese, the Japanese, and the Siamese, all agree in the event portrayed in the Hindu Avatár.

Vishnu has assumed other forms, among the rest that of the Sálagrám or ammonite-stone, found in the river Gandaká and other streams, flowing from the Himalayas. The reason for the worship of this is stated in one of the sacred books. "Vishnu created the nine planets to preside over the fates of men. Sani (Saturn) proposed commencing his reign by taking Brahma under his influence for twelve years. The matter was referred to Vishnu, who being equally averse to be placed under the inauspicious influence of this planet, requested him to call the next day. The next day Saturn could nowhere discover Vishnu, but perceived that he had united himself to the mountain Gandaká; he entered the mountain in the form of a worm called Vajrakita (the thunder-bolt worm). He continued to afflict the mountain-formed Vishnu for twelve years, when Vishnu assumed his proper shape, and commanded that the stones of this mountain should be worshipped, and become proper representatives of himself; adding that each should have twenty marks in it, similar to those on his body, and that its name should be Sálagrám."

The Sálagrám is usually placed under a tulasi-tree, which is planted on the top of a pillar in the vicinity of a temple of Vishnu, or near a house. Tulasi, a female, desired to become Vishnu's wife, but was metamorphosed by Lakshmi into a tree, a small shrub, called therefore *Tulasi*, or holy basil (Ocymum Sanctum). Vishnu, however, promised to assume the form of a Sálagrám, and always continue with her. The Vaishnava priests, therefore, keep one leaf of the shrub under and another over the Sálagrám, and thus pay their adorations to the stone and the tree. In the evening a lamp is placed

near it. In the month of May it is watered from a pot suspended over it, as appears in the engraving, which represents a person engaged in the worship at this singular shrine.

The worship of Vishnu, which, as before intimated, is more prevalent than any other in India, is supposed to have existed at a period long anterior to the birth of Christ. There are some magnificent temples built to his honour in various parts of India. The celebrated temple of Jaganáth is dedicated to one of the forms of this divinity—to Krishna, as the lord of the world.

No bloody sacrifices are ever presented at the shrines of Vishnu. The offerings are fruit, flowers, milk, money, incense, the lamp wave-offering, food, &c. Prostration, called Ashtánga, so that the eight members of the body come into contact with the ground, and standing with the hands uplifted, in the posture of a slave, are required of the devotee: the eight members are the hands, breast, forehead, eyes, throat, and middle of the back; or the first four, with the knees and feet; or these six with words and mind. The accompanying vignette represents these postures as they may be seen daily among the Hindus.

Though there are no *public festivals* to Vishnu, these being to one or other of his incarnate forms, he is "worshipped at the offering of a burnt sacrifice of clarified butter, in the form of meditation daily used by the Brahmans, when the five gods are worshipped, and at the commencement of each Shráddha."

The festivals in honour of the various forms of Vishnu may be incidentally noticed under the head of religious festivals generally; and in the same connexion may be noticed the worship paid to Lakshmi, the consort of Vishnu, who, as may be seen in the vignette, is associated with him in the paintings and sculptures of the Hindus.

The general doctrines of the Vaishnavas are those of the Rámánuja sect, and they are thus stated by Professor Wilson. They differ but little from the general theory already stated as the Vedanta. They claim for Vishnu, that he is the supreme: "that he was before all worlds, and was the cause and creation of all. Although they maintain that Vishnu and the universe are one, yet in opposition to the Vedánta doctrines, they deny that the deity is void of form or quality, and regard him as endowed with all good qualities, and with a twofold form: the supreme spirit, Paramátma or cause, and the gross one, the effect, the universe or matter. The doctrine is hence called the Visishthádwaita, or doctrine of unity with attributes. In these assertions they are followed by most of the Vaishnava sects. Creation originated in the wish of Vishnu, who was alone without a second, to multiply himself: he said, I will become many; and he was individually embodied as visible and etherial light. After that, as a ball of clay may be moulded into various forms, so the grosser substance of the deity became manifest in the elements and their combinations: the forms into which the divine matter is thus divided are pervaded by a portion of the same vitality which belongs to the great cause of all, but which is distinct from his spiritual or etherial essence; here therefore the Rámánujas again oppose the Vedántikas, who identify the Paramátma and Jivátma, or etherial and vital spirit: this vitality, though endlessly diffusible, is imperishable and eternal, and the matter of the universe, and being the same in substance with the Supreme Being, is alike without beginning or end. Purushottama, or Naráyana, after having created man and animals through the instrumentality of those subordinate agents whom he willed into existence for that purpose, still retained the supreme authority of the universe, so that the Rámánujas assert three predicates of the universe, it consists of Chit or spirit, Achit or matter, and I'shwara, or god or the enjoyer, the thing enjoyed, and the ruler and controller of both. Besides his primary and secondary form, as the creator and creation, the deity has assumed at different times, particular forms and appearances for the benefit of his creatures; he is, or has been visibly present amongst men, in five modifications: in his Archá, objects of worship—as images, &c.; in the Vibhánas, or Avatáras—as the fish, boar, &c.; in certain forms called Vyuhas, of which four are enumerated—Vasudeva or Krishna, Balaráma, Pradyumna, and Aniruddha; fourthly, in the Sukshma form, which, when perfect, comprises six qualities,—*virága*, absence of human passion; *vimrityu*, immortality; *visóka*, exemption from care or pain; *vijighatsá*, absence of natural wants; *satyakáma* and *satyasankalpa*, the love and practice of truth; and fifthly, as the Antarátma, or Antaryámi, the human soul, or individualised spirit. These are to be worshipped *seriatim*, as the ministrant ascends in the scale of perfection; and adoration, therefore, is fivefold,—*Abhigamanam*, cleansing and purifying the temples, images, &c.; *Upádánam*, providing flowers and perfumes for religious rites; *Ijyá*, the presentation of such offerings—blood-offerings being uniformly prohibited, it may be observed, by all the Vaishnavas; *Swádhyáya*, counting the rosary and repeating the names of the divinity, or any of his forms; and *Yoga*, the effort to unite with the deity. The reward of these acts is elevation to the seat of Vishnu, and enjoyment of like state with his own, interpreted to be perpetual residence in Vaikuntha, or Vishnu's heaven, in a condition of pure ecstasy and eternal rapture."

Besides the orthodox worshippers of Vishnu, whose leading tenets have been stated, there are numerous sects who differ from them, and from one another. Some of them are peculiar in their belief, and equally singular in practice. Great scrupulousness is observed by some in regard to dress, particularly as to the material of which it is composed,—they may not eat in cotton clothes. All Hindus are very fastidious about the preparation of their food, and equally so in regard to the place and circumstances of eating. The look of a stranger is sufficient to desecrate a meal, which, under such circumstances, is thrown away or buried. Some of these sects are remarkable for their upright behaviour,—inoffensive, truthful, peaceful, and, as members of a civil community, unexceptionable. In my own experience I have met with persons answering to this description, whom I could confide in with implicit trust. Though the dead are disposed of by cremation, many of these sectarists are so regardful of life that they direct their remains to be thrown into some wild, unfrequented place, as a desert or jungle, to be devoured by beasts or birds of prey, lest insects should be destroyed in the funeral pyre. Ascetic devotion is generally regarded as the most meritorious, and, therefore, its practices are at least professed by the earnest among almost all sects. There is, however, one class of Vaishnavas who regard such habits as no part of sanctity. They are taught to conform to the world in its luxuries and pleasures. Members of the mercantile profession are in some places attached to this sect, and, indeed, some of the religious teachers engage in commercial pursuits, and whilst travelling about in the profession of pilgrims they strive to secure the advantages of secular gain along with those of devotion. Further information relative to the religious sects among the Vaishnavas may be found in an interesting volume by Professor Wilson.

SIVA.

The remaining member of the Hindu Triad is Siva, the destroyer. He, too, has a thousand names, which are intended to express the relation in which he stands to the universe of which he is said to be lord. His worshippers parade this title, and at the point of death it is articulated by them with great confidence as the best security, in the passage to other worlds and new states of being.

Some of the epithets of Siva may be mentioned as significant of the character he bears. He is the three-eyed: one glance of the third is said to consume the universe. He is called the enemy of demons, the moon-crested, the lord of devils, the conqueror of death, the wearer of the tiger's skin, the lord of the hills, the lord of the moon. He is the skull-bearer, and wears a necklace of skulls; the poets represent him as delighting in the battle-field, where he and his attendant demons quaff blood from human skulls, and dance on their mangled corpses. He is fabled to have supported the Ganges when it fell from heaven on the Himalaya Mountains. He is sometimes represented as wearing matted hair rolled up in the form of a cone on the top of the head, somewhat projected over the forehead.

The accounts of the origin or birth of Siva are contradictory. The Triad, of which he is one, is regarded as three forms of Brahm, corresponding to the three qualities of truth, passion, and darkness,—the last quality in its various manifestations of anger, cruelty, and revenge, as may be inferred from his names—predominates in Siva. The precedence of the two popular divinities, as before remarked, is disputed by their respective votaries—the Saivas and the Vaishnavas, and many abusive epithets are found in their writings directed against the deities they respectively worship.

One or two quotations may suffice to establish this assertion: in the Bhágavat we read as follows:—

"Those who profess the worship of BHAVA (Siva), and those who follow their doctrines, are heretics, and enemies of the sacred Shastras."

The following passage occurs in the *Padma Purána*:—

"From even looking at VISHNU, the wroth of SIVA is kindled, and from his wrath we fall assuredly into a horrible hell; let not, therefore, the name of VISHNU ever be pronounced."

SIVA, as the god of destruction, is represented as presiding over reproduction or generation; as a symbol of which he rides on a white bull. Sir William Jones thinks that in this notion of the Hindus there is evidence of some connexion between the mythology of eastern and western Paganism. He refers to the loves and feats of Jupiter Genitor, the white bull of Europa, and the extraordinary title of *Lapis* applied to Jupiter.

The most common symbol of Siva is the *Linga*, the Phallus. Respecting this object of Hindu worship, Professor Wilson states that "it is perhaps the most ancient object of homage adopted in India, subsequently to the ritual of the Vedas, which was chiefly, if not wholly, addressed to the elements, and particularly to fire. How far the worship of the Linga is authorized by the Vedas is doubtful, but it is the main purport of several of the Puránas."

It was the universal worship at the period of the Mohammedan invasion. The idol destroyed by Mahmud of Ghizni was a Linga, a block of stone of four or five cubits in length, and of proportioned thickness. The worship is as prevalent as ever, from one end of India to the other. In Bengal, the temples containing the symbol of Siva are generally erected in ranges of from six to twelve on both sides of a ghât leading to the river. The raja of Burdwan erected at Kalna a circular group of one hundred and eight temples to this object of worship. "Notwithstanding the acknowledged purport of this worship, it is but justice to state, that it is unattended by any indecent or indelicate ceremonies." I have often seen females form the symbol of clay on the banks of the river in Bengal, and worship it, with the accustomed presentation of flowers, &c.

Siva is sometimes sculptured in the figure of a man with five faces and four arms. He holds in one hand a hatchet, in another a deer, while the third bestows a gift or blessing, and the fourth forbids fear; he is seated on a lotus, and wears a tiger's skin. He is sometimes represented riding on a bull, besmeared with ashes, naked, having inflamed eyes, and carrying a horn and a drum. He is also represented as riding on a dog, and in this character he is Regent of Benares, the Holy City of the Hindus.

The doctrines of the Saivas are called the Siddhanta, in opposition to the Vedanta; that meaning the scope of reason or demonstration, and this the scope or purport of the Veda; one system appealing to the sacred records in proof of its positions, the other to the exercise of reason. The advocates of this system of philosophy seem to maintain the co-existence of three entities, all of which are eternal as to the past, viz. God, the soul, and máya or illusion, which is the substratum of the material universe. Some of the works propounding the doctrines of this school are very subtile, and they are regarded with great veneration. They argue analogically, that, as a potter, by his instruments or appliances of a wheel and a staff, forms from the *material cause*, clay, a vessel; so the supreme ruler, or maker, forms from pre-existing *máya*, elemental matter, the visible universe, over which he presides as the arbiter of all things, seeking by the evolutions and mutations, the sufferings and enjoyments of sentient beings, to secure the final absorption into himself of the countless myriads that fill the universe. The psychology of this system differs but little from the Vedanta, already given in detail. Its terminology is nearly the same, and its purport or aim, as regards the liberation of the spirit, is the same. It prescribes vows, penances, ablutions, holy ashes, singing, dancing, genuflexions, recitations of holy names and texts; besides several curious actions that it is difficult to account for.

The practice of meditation, as laid down in some of the books known among the Saivas, promises the most extraordinary results. By assuming certain postures, suppressing the breath, restraining the senses, and devoting the mental powers to the exercise of intense meditation, the prescience of events, and a species of ubiquity, are attained. The veil that is drawn over the mind for purposes of providence is uplifted, and the soul assumes the perspicacity natural to its constitution. A Hindu once endeavoured to show me how the prophets of the Scriptures were thus endowed with supernatural vision, as seers. They are said to acquire, by the practices alluded to, wonderful physical power, and are able to fly, or swim, or penetrate the earth, and see all things as seen by God.

The Saivas regard Siva as a manifestation of the Supreme Being, and worship him as such, denying the independent existence of Vishnu. The Linga, as the component type of the god and goddess, they venerate as an object of peculiar sanctity. It is often enshrined, and attached to the person.

There are numerous sects among the Saivas whose diversified belief and equally varied practice are described in the work already referred to from the pen of Professor Wilson. The members of these different religious orders are met with in every part of the country, and may be distinguished as belonging to the several classes, by sectarial marks on their persons, by the comparative nudity in which some wander about, smeared with ashes, the ascetic practices, involving sometimes self-inflictions of the most painful kind, strictly self-imposed silence, some carrying an earthen pot, some a staff, some in ragged garments of many colours, some with matted, clotted hair, some shorn, others with singularly formed caps on their heads. Some profess preternatural powers, cure diseases by charms, interpret dreams, practise palmistry, sing with musical accompaniments; and others exhibit the singular results of their patient instructions in the tricks of small bullocks or monkeys they lead about. Further references may be made to these sectarists in a subsequent chapter.

We have already seen that each of the members of the Hindu Triad is represented as associated with a consort, who is regarded as the female or active energy of the deity. Brahma is accompanied by Sarasvata; Vishnu is accompanied by Lakshmi; and Siva by Párvati. This latter is far the most popular of the goddesses, as we shall hereafter see.

The right-hand and public worship of the goddesses involves nothing beyond the presentation of offerings of fruit, grain, sugar, milk, and possibly kids. The left-hand worshippers,—by which designation it is intended to intimate that things not to be named are practised,—perform these rites in order to secure superhuman power, and in such a manner as may not be described. It must suffice to state that this worship is generally celebrated by men and women during the night, and includes every abomination that depraved humanity is capable of.

GANÉSHA.

Ganésha, or Ganapaty, is one of the most popular deities, and equally venerated by all sects. He is considered to be the god of wisdom. Ganésha is represented as a stout man, with the head of an elephant, and as attended by a rat. Both these animals are considered by the Hindus as remarkable, the one for sagacity, and the other for cunning. Ganésha in some respects resembles the ancient Janus of the West. He is always invoked at the commencement of an undertaking, whether civil or sacred, and especially in the composition of a book. An example may be seen in the first stanza or invocation of Avveyár's Aphorisms. An artificer in beginning

his work of a morning, always implores the god of accidents and impediments to interpose his effectual auspices to avert mistake. His image may be seen over the doors of houses, and in the bazaars and temples, as a security against the manifold evils that might otherwise visit their occupants. Though all adore Ganésha, some pay him special homage.

SERPENT WORSHIP.

The Hindus venerate the snake, and in this respect agree with almost all ancient nations. The serpent which Moses lifted up in the wilderness, was in after ages worshipped in Babylon. Among the sculptures of Egypt it is one of the most prominent figures. In Persia, in Greece, in Rome, among the Scandinavians, the Mexicans, and the Africans, we learn that homage was paid to this reptile. No doubt the usage has been based on the tradition of the Fall, and perhaps the reputed cunning of the serpent tribe, combining with the malignity of its bite, may have helped to perpetuate the homage paid to it among the Hindus. According to some statements of the Puránas, demigods have sometimes appeared in the serpent form. The Hindus smear the doors of houses with cow-dung and margoso leaves, as a preservative from reptiles. The figure of a serpent is occasionally seen sculptured on a Linga, thus investing the block of stone with a doubly sacred character. The various kinds of Nágas, or the Cobra de Capella, are propitiated by offerings of milk and clarified butter.

Vishnu is said to repose on a serpent couch. The seven inferior worlds are peopled with savage hydras, and huge serpents, "portrayed in every monstrous figure which imagination can suggest, with the dire and tremendous Sheshanaga for their king, whose thousand heads are encompassed, each with a crown of starry gems; while his eyes gleam like blazing torches, and his garments are skirted with yellow flames, and he bears in his arms the holy shell, the radiated weapon, the mace of war, and the divine and immortal lotus." I have witnessed the greatest consternation in some persons when a snake of the Nága kind was about to be destroyed.

In India hundreds of persons are annually destroyed by snakes, which abound in almost every part of the country. Hence on many occasions throughout the year, in some provinces, the dreaded *Manasá-devi*, the queen of snakes, is propitiated by presents, vows, and religious rites. The following extract from an article in one of the numbers of the *Calcutta Review*, will be read with interest:—

"In the month of *Shrábana* the worship of the snake goddess is celebrated with great *éclât*. An image of the goddess, seated on a water-lily, encircled with serpents, or a branch of the *snake-tree* (a species of euphorbia), or a pot of water, with images of serpents made of clay, forms the object of worship. Men, women, and children, all offer presents, to avert from themselves the wrath of the terrific deity. The *Máls*, or snake-catchers, signalize themselves on this occasion. Temporary scaffolds of bamboo work are set up in the presence of the goddess. Vessels filled with all sorts of snakes are brought in. The *Máls*, often reeling with intoxication, mount the scaffolds, take out serpents from the vessels, and allow them to bite their arms. The whole race of serpentry is defied. From the slender and harmless *Hele*, to the huge *Boa-constrictor*, and the terrific *Cobra-de-capello*, all make their appearance, and exert their might to strike dead the playful *Máls*. Bite after bite succeeds; the arms run over with blood; and the *Máls* go on with their pranks, amid the deafening plaudits of the spectators. Now and then they fall off from the scaffold, and pretend to feel the effects of poison, and cure themselves by their incantations. But all is mere pretence. The serpents displayed on the occasion, and challenged to do their worst, have passed through a preparatory state. Their fangs have been carefully extracted from their jaws. But most of the vulgar spectators easily persuade themselves to believe that the *Máls* are the chosen servants of Siva, and the favourites of *Manasá.* Although their supernatural pretensions are ridiculous, yet it must be confessed that the *Máls* have made snakes the subject of their peculiar study. They are thoroughly acquainted with their qualities, their dispositions, and their habits. They will run down a snake into its hole, and bring it out thence by main force. Even the terrible *Cobrá* is cowed down by the controlling influence of a *Mál.* When in the act of bringing out snakes from their subterranean holes, the *Máls* are in the habit of muttering charms, in which the names of *Manasá* and *Maháđeva* frequently occur; superstition alone can clothe these unmeaning words with supernatural potency. But it is not inconsistent with the soundest philosophy to suppose that there may be some plants whose roots are disagreeable to serpents, and from which they instinctively turn away. All snake-catchers of Bengal are provided with a bundle of the roots of some plant, which they carefully carry along with them when they set out on their serpent-hunting expeditions. When a serpent, disturbed in its hole, comes out furiously, hissing with rage, with its body coiled, and its head lifted up, the *Mál* has only to present before it the bundle of roots above alluded to, at the sight of which it becomes spiritless as an eel. This we have ourselves witnessed more than once. But to return; the exhibitions of snakes of which we have been speaking, take place in all parts of Bengal. There is a small village in the district of *Hugli* where thousands of people annually assemble together to enjoy the sight. Skilful *Máls* are always presented by the gaping multitude with clothes and money.

"In giving an account, however short, of the great festival of the queen of snakes, it would be unpardonable were we to omit noticing a circumstance which occurs a day or two before the public exhibitions. Bengali mothers, anxious for the preservation of their children from the bite of serpents, implore the favour of *Manasá.* On one of the last days of *Shrábana*, women may be seen coming out of a village with vessels in their hands, containing a composition of rice, milk, and sugar. Proceeding out of the village, they take their station generally near a tank, and offer their homely presents to the goddess on behalf of their children. The presentation being done, they help themselves to the rice, milk, and treacle; and after thanking the goddess, of whom however no image is set up, they return home with the sure hope of seeing their children preserved, during the ensuing season, from the bite of venomous snakes. In towns and large villages, where women cannot go out, this ceremony, termed *Ban-bhojan*, takes place in the house. In spite, however, of the caution and piety of Hindu mothers, their children are sometimes bitten by snakes. In all such cases the power of *Manasá* is by no means questioned; the blame rests either on the children themselves, who are alleged to have been killed by their irreverence to her, or on the mothers, who are supposed not to have properly propitiated the angry goddess."

It were needless to attempt a description of all the objects that are found in the Hindu Pantheon, since almost all things have been placed there, and consecrated as the objects of worship. This will have become apparent from what has already been advanced regarding the religious rites of India. The following brilliant description is not an exaggeration of the exuberant fertility of the Hindu mind in surrounding itself with objects of veneration. Pantheism deifies all things. Dr. Duff says, in truth,—

"The worlds above this earth are peopled with gods and goddesses, demi-gods and genii; the sons and grandsons, daughters and granddaughters of Brahma and other superior deities. All the superior gods have separate heavens for themselves. The inferior deities dwell chiefly in the heaven of Indra, the god of the firmament. There they congregate to the number of three hundred and thirty millions! The gods are divided and subdivided into classes or hierarchies, which vary through every conceivable gradation of rank and power. They are of all colours; some black, some white, some red, some blue, and so through all the blending shades of the rainbow. They exhibit all sorts of shape, size, and figure, in forms wholly human or half human, wholly brutal or variously compounded, like many-headed and many-bodied centaurs, with four, or ten, or a hundred, or a thousand eyes, heads, and arms. They ride through the regions of space on all sorts of etherealised animals; elephants, buffaloes, lions, deer, sheep, goats, peacocks, vultures, geese, serpents, and rats. They hold forth in their multitudinous arms all manner of offensive and defensive weapons; thunderbolts, scimitars, javelins, spears, clubs, bows, arrows, shields, flags, and shells. They discharge all possible functions. There are gods of the heavens above, and of the earth below, and of the region under the earth.—All the virtues and the vices of man; all the allotments of life, beauty, jollity, and sport; the hopes and fears of youth, the felicities and infelicities of manhood, the joys and sorrows of old age; all, all are placed under the presiding influence of superior powers. Every scene, every element, and almost every object in nature; the bud that bursts forth in spring, the blossom of summer, and the fruits of autumn; meadow and grove, fountain and stream, hill and valley; all have their guardian genii, whose freaks and revelries greatly outstrip, in number and variety, the 'fairy gambols and goblin feats recognised by the credulity of northern superstition.'"

Day&Son, Lithrs to the Queen.

HINDU TEMPLE, TRIVALORE.

CHAPTER XI.

SACRED DAYS.—TEMPLES.—HINDU NOTIONS OF CONSECRATED SYMBOLS. —DESCRIPTION OF A TEMPLE.—IDOL CARS.—FESTIVALS.—CHARAK PUJA.—AUSTERITIES.—SUPPOSED ADVANTAGES OF TEMPORARY INFLICTIONS, TEMPORARY REWARDS.—INTERMEDIATE STATES.—THE HINDU CLAIMS THE SYMPATHY OF THE CHURCH.

THE description given in the preceding chapter of the most popular objects of Hindu worship, may not be inaptly followed by a brief statement of the importance attached to particular times and seasons; this may prepare the way for further information relating to the temples and other places venerated by the millions of India, as the dwelling places of invisible beings; and also for some details concerning the religious festivals.

The days of the week have their distinct recognition, and certain observances mark their recurrence.

ADITYA-VÁRA, SUNDAY.[1]

On Sunday, the sun, both as a luminary and as personified under various titles and aspects, is the great object of Hindu worship. As the most perfect image of the resplendent and transcendent light, the great Supreme, the sun receives special adoration. In some parts of India special praises are recited to his honour; peculiar diet is observed, as milk cakes, &c.; the worshipper sleeps on the

[1] The names of the days used by the Romans and other western nations may be compared with those of India. Dies Solis, Lunæ, Martis, Mercurii, Jovis, Veneris, Saturni.

ground; abstains from lawful pleasure; presents gifts to Brahmans; and avoids the ordinary enjoyments arising from walking abroad.

Sunday is an auspicious day for sowing seed, for commencing a building or residence, for planting gardens, and also for the performance of the Homa, a sacrifice with fire.

SOMA VÁRA, MONDAY.

Soma, the moon, is a male deity, monarch of the stars and planets, of Brahmans, of sacrifices, and of penance. His name is expressive of swiftness and coolness.

The moon is regarded as the presiding deity of the day. It is said that Mahádéva recovered from the effects of poison on this day, and he is therefore specially worshipped on Monday. On particular days in certain months, the worship of Mahádéva is performed about sunset, either at his temple or before an image of him prepared at home. This image is bathed in panchámirta, five-fold nectar, a mixture of curds, milk, clarified butter, honey and sugar. The offering is made of white sandal-wood, white flowers, &c., and placed on the head of the image, which is always white. It is believed that by such religious observances every good may be procured. Monday is an auspicious day for beginning a journey, or for mounting a new horse, an elephant, or a chariot. They are rendered swift and safe by the presiding deity of the day. Whereas the same things begun on Saturday would be proportionally retarded by the influence of Sani, Saturn, for reasons to be hereafter stated.

Besides the fortunes incident to this day in the matters notified, we find similar superstitious sentiments cherished about other periods. As the new and full moon may happen on particular days of the week, there is a supposed influence attendant thereon. The trident of Mahádéva is supposed to be in continual motion over the earth for the preservation of its creatures; therefore it may be encountered if due care be not observed so as not to face it. It were disastrous consequently to travel westward on Sunday and Friday; to the northward on Tuesday and Wednesday; to the eastward on Saturday and Monday, and to the southward on Thursday.

MANGALA-VÁRA, TUESDAY.

Mangal, who is the son of Maháděva, and the Earth, resembles the Mars of western mythology; he is represented as a Kshattrya, a member of the military caste, and is renowned for martial exploits. Offerings at his shrine are supposed to secure the power of cancelling all obligations and debts. Wealth and power are sought from this divinity. His worship promotes fecundity. Tuesday is an auspicious day for fighting a battle. The artificers who use fire in their work regard this day as favourable to. their designs. This day is connected with the exploits of the Simian hero, Hanuman, and regarded with veneration as the birth-day of Parvati. Women present offerings to the goddess Parvati, under the impression that it may promote the attachment of their husbands. Mangala being the colour of fire, coral is his emblem.

BUDH-VÁRA, WEDNESDAY.

Budha is the son of Chandra and Tara. He is the patron of merchants, and therefore the Vaisya caste regard him with veneration. Debts are collected on this day, but not incurred, nor are clothes washed on Wednesday. As an emblem of the yielding disposition of Budha, the bow is worshipped on the day distinguished by his name. Budha and Vrihaspati are worshipped by those who covet the birth of a son; and on their days, Wednesday and Thursday, they delineate a swing, the emblem of infancy, and worship it in the month Sravan. The emerald is the symbol of Budha.

VRIHASPATI-VÁRA, THURSDAY.

Vrihaspati is represented as a Brahman, the pundit or tutor of the gods; and his day is sacred to the worship of all divinities. The mangoe-tree is held sacred, and worshipped on this day because Lakshmi, the patroness of wealth, is fond of its shade. Thursday is regarded as an auspicious day for entering on a new place of business, for putting on new ornaments, for conjugal enjoyments, and for the study of sacred subjects. The topaz is the emblem of Vrihaspati.

SUKRA-VÁRA, FRIDAY.

This divinity, which is symbolized by the diamond, is regarded with peculiar veneration by all Brahmans as the tutor of the Titans. Women, who have been bereaved of their offspring, or, whose children being absent, are anxiously looked for, pay especial attention to the ceremonies of this day.

SANI-VÁRA, SATURDAY.

Sani is stated to be a divinity of a low caste, and, like the Saturn of the west, he is represented as at variance with his parents; he is spoken of as lame, and as being a slow mover, with evident allusion to his motion through the heavens. The sapphire is the chosen emblem of this planet. It is remarkable that in India, as in Egypt and Chaldea, the influence of Sani is considered of an injurious character. Regarded as the ruler and guide of the base and vicious, these pay him honour as their patron, and on the Saturday present offerings at his shrine, to secure his help in their wicked practices. The inauspicious influences of this divinity may be averted by offering various gifts to Brahmans and others on this day. Possibly this may have induced the custom of begging on this day; for it is a fact, that groups of beggars are seen going about on the Saturday in some parts of India and Ceylon.

Certain objects are pursued on this day with special advantage. Magical arts, malicious enterprises, and almost any vicious act derives some potency from the influence of Sani. Vishnu having destroyed a monster of the name of Hiranyakasyapa on the Saturday, those who present on this day offerings of oil and grain will thereby secure the auspices of Lakshmi, the goddess of plenty. The night of Saturday, as indeed every night, is sacred to the worship of Hanuman, Ráma's monkey-hero, who occupied so distinguished a place in the expedition to Ceylon.[1] Sani is the god of attack and enterprise, and may be worshipped with great advantage by those who contemplate these acts.

LUNAR DAYS.

It has been already observed that the moon is a male deity and the monarch of the stars, the planets, of sacrifice and of penance. The eighth, eleventh, fourteenth, and fifteenth lunar days, both when the moon is waxing and waning, are considered fortunate days. The presentation of gifts to Brahmans, and the performance of various religious ceremonies, derive great additional efficacy from the phases of the moon in certain months; therefore the devout Hindu consults the position of the lunar orb and its phases with great attention. Annual and other periodic festivals, likewise, are regulated by the sun, and moon, and planets.

[1] I was once at a festival at Ramisseram, where many thousands of pilgrims were present from different parts of India and Ceylon, when I and my companions were encamped among them on the eve of a great bathing festival, it being Saturday. I heard numerous groups engaged throughout the night in reciting the exploits and singing the praises of the illustrious Ráma and this singular hero. They seemed to enjoy the exercise very much.

We might follow the moon as she forms our months by visiting the lunar mansions, and accompanying her till the earth had performed its circuit of the Zodiac, and almost every day would present some claim to special recognition on the ground of a supposed planetary influence therewith indissolubly bound up. To the Hindu, therefore, an almanac is as necessary as is an ephemeris to a navigator. The ordinary lights of conscience, of experience, and of reason, may not suffice for guidance—he must consult the stars also. It would be interesting to some readers to learn how the Hindu views the changing scenes of the varying year; but space not being available, we must pass at once to some of the magnificent shrines, for which the land of the Veda is distinguished; and having described some of their more prominent features, strive to delineate some of those festivals which they are well fitted to exhibit with so much pomp of circumstance.

TEMPLES.

The popular divinities of the Hindus have their shrines in every part of the country. Some are very humble structures, others are magnificent edifices. The Hindu Pagodas of Southern India are certainly the most imposing buildings I have seen. They are far superior to any of the religious edifices on the banks of the Ganges. It is known that the Mohammedans during the period of their rule destroyed many of the ancient temples in Northern India, which may account for the greater celebrity attaching to those of the south. We might select for description any one of many venerated shrines, as equally suitable for our purpose. At most of the large cities in the Madras Presidency will be found one or more of these structures; but the most celebrated are those of Conjeveram, Tripatore, Trivalore, Chillumbram, Tanjore, Shreringham, Madura, and Ramisseram. No verbal description can adequately express or convey an idea of these religious establishments. Even the temples of Thebes did not produce on my mind a deeper impression than the temples of India. The grand temple at Karnak, for magnitude as well as for the extent of its sculptures, and the Medhinet Habu in Western Thebes, in the symmetry of some of its architectural features, and the extent of its sculptured battle-scenes, are indeed wonderful; but yet they did not impress me so much as the monuments of India. The temples of India are scenes of activity. The officiating priests are to be seen at the shrines, where, amid the din of discordant music, and the smoke of fragrant incense, they are uttering sacred incantations, and presenting the offerings of expectant worshippers. The courts, and corridors, and porticos, are occupied by attendant votaries. The ghâts of the beautiful tanks are in many places crowded with men and women, who are engaged in their ablutions. Everything betokens the existence of a system that commands the sympathies of the people, and one that, in the judgment of the Christian Missionary who has to assail it, possesses a power that nothing human can overturn. The presence of enthusiastic crowds devoted to the religion of their ancestors, gives a significance to the architectural grandeur of a Hindu Pagoda, that cannot now belong to the ruined temples of Egypt, Greece, and Italy.

Like the temples of other ancient nations, those of India are designed to be the abodes of the gods. The Hindus have various names by which to designate the collective buildings, but all convey the idea of a resident divinity. In the adytum, or adyta, if more than one shrine exist, the symbol or idol is deposited. This sacred spot, into which none but the initiated can enter, is generally indicated by a term applied to an inner and special locality. It is also known by a name importing a place of origin, used also in other connexions for ether, heaven, or God. These terms sufficiently indicate the views which are entertained of these places; they are sanctuaries, consecrated apartments, the dwellings of superhuman beings, places of the Divine presence. The symbol of the resident deity is called by various names, indicating body, extension, figure, with evident reference to the assumption of form. The symbols are of various figures, and suited to the divinity therein enshrined; and may be made of any material, such as earth, stone, wood, brass, copper, silver, or gold. The symbol of the deity is placed in the adytum or sanctuary, and consecrated by the priest, who, by performing certain rites, according to the prescription of the Shastras or sacred ordinances, is supposed to have the power of investing the visible symbol with the presence of the invisible divinity. At the consecration the deity is supposed to take up his residence in the idol or symbol. This consecration is effected by the utterance of sacred texts or incantations, and by the touch of the priest. Consecration being completed, the idol becomes an object of worship.

The views entertained of the image after consecration will vary with the intelligence of those who are concerned in its worship. Doubtless there are persons who imagine the visible symbol transubstantiated into the very substance of Deity itself. Having ears, they may be charmed with the symphonies of instrumental music; having eyes, they can behold the prostrations and gesticulations of the worshippers; having nostrils, they may be agreeably affected by fragrant odours, whether of incense or flowers; and having mouths, they may partake of the delicious viands that are spread before them. These are not, however, the notions of the thinking and rational Hindu. He contends, indeed, for a divine presence in the idol; but he regards the divinity present as the invisible fragrance is present in the visible flower; or as fire is present in heated metal. He pervades the idol as magnetic influence impregnates the steel. The visible symbol represents the invisible power, as a vocal symbol or letter stands for an audible sound, which it can by no possibility represent except by conventional usage. Such are the views of the intelligent defenders of idol worship. Had we room, we might state at large the numerous arguments used in support of the system.

From these few observations it will appear that the temples of the Hindus are the consecrated abodes of the divinities to which they may have been dedicated. To these abodes of divinity, therefore, the worshipper resorts for succour in the various exigencies which seem to require the special interposition of preternatural power. The whole system, the consecrated symbol, and the external rites of the ceremonial, are presumed to be of divine appointment, and efficacious in regard to the ends contemplated, because they are divinely authorized. Hence the innumerable terms and similes employed to express the relation in which the external system of worship and its provisions stand to the confiding worshipper. Is he exposed to the wide extended sea of mortal births, and lashed by the storms of secular existence, his divinity is the desired vessel that is to convey him to a haven of security and repose? his divinity is his refuge and asylum in all the difficulties and dangers through which he may be called to pass. Where the elephant-headed Ganésha is contemplated as the divine protector, his expanded ears are poetically regarded as the auspicious raft, by means of which the soul, immersed in the destructive waves of the ocean of sin, escapes to the shores of immortality. Do enemies assail? his divinity is the stronghold into which he escapes for security. Do the floods of secular life threaten to overwhelm and sweep him away? his divinity is the firm branch which he may seize, and by which he may hold on and hold out till the flood abates. In the countless vicissitudes of life, the Hindu confidently relies on the sure, and unfailing, and ever-present lord and guide, locally present in the venerated fane his expectations are directed to. That shrine is his light in darkness, his salvation, his stay, his succour, his bliss, his all. Nothing can exceed the beauty of some of the poetic effusions which the more earnest Hindus have written on subjects connected with the exercises of the mind—its hopes and fears, its joys and sorrows, alternating in relation to a revered divinity. And although the intelligent will avail themselves of the practical value of the sentiments on any occasion and in any place, yet the temple is the seat of special presence. There deity is embodied and enshrined; and, therefore, in the manifold rites and ceremonies of the temple service he is contemplated as the object on whom all that service terminates. The ceremonial of the temple is, in fact, by divine appointment a sacramental service.

It may be remarked, that many of the figures and similes employed by the more spiritual and earnest of the Hindu writers are very much in accordance with those employed by inspired writers. The highly figurative manner in which these convey their sentiments harmonises well with the notions current among intelligent Hindus. The numerous references to God under his appropriate emblem, the sun, found in sacred scripture, are peculiarly forcible to the Hindus. The figure enters into the very substance of the Gayatri, as we have seen. God is that sole, self-existing, and transcendent Sun, whose rays shed their influence on the efflorescing mind, scattering its darkness, and irradiating its powers, as the natural sun diffuses its radiance over the whole creation. It is easy to see that when once truth shall gain an ascendancy over the mind, and give vitality and power to the sentiments here referred to, the oriental teachings of the Bible will have a special significance to the Hindu.

These general observations may serve to show what the Hindu temple is, in relation to the religious theories already explained.

The adytum, or sanctuary in which the idol is placed, is, as in Egyptian temples, very small, and it occupies the innermost, the most secluded part of the building; it is generally surmounted by a pyramidal tower, ornamented with mythological devices. In front of the adytum there is a court, in which an altar is placed; and immediately before this court a flagstaff, and possibly some emblem of a religious character: at Tanjore the colossal figure of a bull occupies this place. The bull, as already stated, is the vehicle on which Siva is said to ride. In the immediate vicinity of the sanctuary there is generally a tank of sacred water for ablutions. The tanks are usually surrounded by a flight of steps, and flanked at the top with a terraced portico, which is provided for the accommodation of the worshippers who may there perform a part of their devotions. At Madura there is a beautiful tank, said to occupy an area of forty acres, whose water is six fathoms deep. It is surrounded by a wall of cut stone, and provided with ghâts, or flights of steps at suitable intervals. In the centre of this expanse of water there is an artificial island, surrounded by a wall, and furnished with flights of steps for the convenience of landing. The isle is planted with choice trees, and a pyramidal tower of several stories high stands in the middle of the grove. This reservoir is used at certain festivals for aquatic processions, when the sacred symbols are conveyed on rafts to the island. Numerous rafts of huge dimensions are provided for these occasions, and to add to these nocturnal fêtes the greater pomp of circumstance, colossal images of elephants are prepared and grouped on the rafts, along with other imposing effigies.

Within the precincts of the same temple there may be several shrines. At Tanjore there are one hundred and eight shrines to one object of worship, the symbol of Siva. Surrounding the sanctuary, in some of the large temples, are quadrangular corridors, which, as colonnades covered in, are used for processions, especially at night. At Ramissoram this corridor is upwards of six hundred feet in length on each of the four sides. Some of the colonnades and courts are singularly imposing. In some of them the pillars are elaborately sculptured with mythological figures executed in bold relief, and in some instances the group is composed of a person mounted on an animal, armed with weapons of defence and attack, the whole being formed out of a single stone. In one of the courts in the temple at Madura there is a cluster of twenty-seven pillars, formed of a single block of granite. Here too, in an adjacent choultry, is a spacious court, on whose pillars are represented the figures of a dynasty of kings. In most of the large Pagodas of Southern India there is a court, whose roof is supported by a thousand pillars, and therefore denominated the thousand-pillared court. A sacred grove is attached to many of these fanes, which is intended for promenade, and also for supplying flowers for the ceremonies.

Glancing at this collection of buildings composed of sanctuaries, courts, corridors, colonnades, and the accompanying tanks and gardens, some idea may be formed of the immense area occupied by one of these extraordinary establishments.

The area or court surrounding the temple is generally paved with large blocks of stone. The whole space is usually enclosed by a high wall of stone, or of brick faced with stone. The temple at Chillumbram has two walls, and that at Shreringam has seven walls, the outermost being four miles in circuit. The enclosure is generally square, each side facing one of the cardinal points. The wall is pierced with magnificent gateways, some of which are forty feet high; that at Ramisseram is said to be one hundred feet high, of proportionate width, and ornamented with pilasters composed of single blocks of stone. These portals are surmounted with lofty towers of numerous stories, sometimes as many as fifteen, and these singular and sublime structures are generally decorated with figures accordant with the legends of Hindu mythology. In most places one or more idol cars are provided for periodic festivals, when they are drawn round the temple by the admiring and enthusiastic crowd. Some of these vehicles are elaborately carved, and formed into several stories, and in some instances are as much as seventy feet in height. It were impossible to describe many of the figures that are exhibited on these vehicles of superstition, such is their obscenity.

The effect which these vast monuments of paganism produce on the Hindu mind is best seen at the great festivals, when, as of old, the people are literally mad upon their idols.

The intense interest manifested by the crowds when the idol car, as presented in the accompanying engraving, begins to move, cannot be described. Then their confidence in the supposed invisible powers associated with such an assemblage of grandeur and magnificence, rises with the occasion to the highest pitch, and is indicated by the most enthusiastic expressions. Every eye is turned towards the venerated object, and, as if some beneficent divinity were about to become visible, for the purpose of conveying whatsoever the worshippers might desire, the most profound attention is paid to the whole ceremonial. The sight of the ponderous and gorgeously decorated vehicle, on whose different stories attendant priests are standing, entrances the spectators, from whom burst forth the loudest acclamations, while the sound of wild, jarring, loud, and discordant music seems to rend the air. Anxious mothers are there with their children, to teach them to hold up their infant and youthful hands in adoration of the all-powerful being they have come to worship. The splendid and ostentatious ceremonial exhibited on these occasions is well fitted to impress the minds of the superstitious and bigoted votaries of the system. Those who come from distant and retired places, where the mind has been more or less prepared by expectation, and confirmed in its confidence by the popular stories, related by vagrant mendicants, concerning the advantages which have been conferred by the resident divinities on certain occasions, are deeply impressed by these pageants.[1]

It has been already mentioned that in addition to the stated daily services prescribed by the Hindu ritual, and which may be performed alike in almost all places; and also periodical festivities, which are observed in most of the temples throughout India under similar circumstances; there are

[1] In some parts of India the Romanists have adopted the car; and make the carvings subservient to the exhibition of legendary stories, the various facts of religious history, and the inflictions of purgatory. These latter are generally contained in tablets, wherein are pictorially represented the consequences arising from the violation of the Divine command or prohibition inscribed below the carving. When the car is used on great festivals, an image of the Virgin is placed upon it.

special festivals at particular places which are regulated by astronomical phenomena. These ceremonies, incident to certain facts of Hindu history and legendary story, are often connected with some particular locality, which on that account possesses, at certain seasons, special sanctity. Attendance at these places, on particular occasions, is regarded as of special advantage, and therefore crowds are attracted to them. The great festivals at Ramisseram, which occur at intervals of twelve and sixty years respectively, are connected with the expedition of Ráma to Lanka (Ceylon), and particular spots are pointed out there which are identified with some of the events in the great national epic, the Ramayana. The precise spot where Sita, the consort of Ráma, went through the ordeal of fire, to test her fidelity to her conjugal duties, is pointed out; and multitudes bathe in the sea at that place, as I have witnessed, in the fullest belief that such ablution will be followed by special favour. On the same principle, the Hindus are taught that if they attend the great car festival at Jugannath, they will be emancipated at death from all the evils of future birth. Hence it is that at these places on the occasions held so auspicious, such multitudes flock together from every part of the land.

There are several shrines dedicated to Hanuman, who is signalized by his exploits in tearing up the mountains, for the construction of the bridge that connects Ramisseram with Ceylon. On our way to one of the holy places in the isle, my missionary brethren and myself looked into a small temple, in which a figure of a black monkey was placed, with immense white eyes, apparently made of cement. There was a boy in attendance, who seemed to be in charge of the shrine. Looking into the interior, by way of ascertaining what there might be within, and seeing nothing besides the image, I asked the boy if there was nothing else—nothing behind the image; to which he replied, with the utmost simplicity, "No, nothing but his tail." Hanuman is sometimes painted in the form in which he is here given, busily engaged in his herculean task of conveying mountains to fill up the sea.

It was computed that thirty-five thousand persons attended the festival under notice. The auspicious moment for ablution was when the sun was half above the horizon, at its rising. We had passed the night amid the songs of the pilgrims, vainly attempting to sleep on the sand. At day-break the multitudes moved on towards the sacred spot, and awaited the moment that was to consummate their pilgrimage. It was a most imposing spectacle. Tens of thousands stood in silence, and every eye was directed over the waves to the eastern horizon. The sun at length appeared, and shed his radiance on the gently agitated bosom of the sea, and soon revealed half of his disc, when the whole mass of living beings disappeared in the waves. Some of the pilgrims present at this festival had travelled seventeen or eighteen hundred miles!

I may here notice another great festival which I attended, with the late Dr. Marshman, of the Serampore mission; it was the *Ratha-Yátrá*, or the Car-Festival, at Mahèsh, about two miles from the above-named place. The vehicle used at this place is a huge car, not unlike the one at *Puri*, in Orissa. The image was placed upon it, and dragged about for the ostensible benefit of an airing. The car was preceded by the usual accompaniment of music, the deep-sounding *tom tom*, and noisy cymbals. There were groups of singers vociferating the praises of Krishna. The utmost alacrity was evinced by the assembled crowd to aid the progress of the venerated relic of superstition, which consists of an armless, ill-shaped image, dignified with the appellation of the "Lord of the World." This festival is celebrated with the greatest pomp at *Puri*, in Orissa. Hundreds of thousands resort to that shrine, the real *Jagannáth*, and before the beneficent spirit of the British government put a stop to the enormities there practised in the name of devotion, deluded votaries stretched themselves beneath the wheels of the car, that by being crushed to death they might obtain admission to Paradise. It has been justly said, however, that, "in spite of this auspicious circumstance, every village car, by the filthy representations painted or carved on it, still exerts a most baneful influence on the morals of the people."

The *Snán Yátrá*, the bathing of *Jagannáth*, is celebrated with equal devotion at Mahèsh. The misshapen block is enveloped in cloth, and carried out of the temple, and placed in a recess built for the ceremony. There, while sacred texts from the Vedas are recited by attendant Brahmans, amid loud acclamations and deafening music, the idol is divested of its garments, and bathed with the sacred water of the *Ganga*, which is poured on his head. At the close of the ceremony the crowds make obeisance, by uplifted hands or by prostration, and entertain the most confident assurance that the auspices of the occasion will secure them from future and numerous evils. The idol being wiped, is placed in his temple, and receives the solemn adorations of the attendant priests and the devoted crowd.

This festival is one of great licentiousness. Most of the abandoned characters from the city of Calcutta, distant only fifteen miles, make a point of being present at this gathering, and thousands make it the occasion of wanton amusement. The most licentious songs and the filthiest language are the seasoning of this religious (?) festival.

These great festivals not only draw tens of thousands for purposes of superstition, but traders in all descriptions of wares are attracted, and the sacred places become marts of business. At Shreringam, near Trichinopoly, in the month of December, the annual festival is a vast fair for the transaction of business. Cattle are brought from the adjacent provinces for sale, and wares of every description are sold or exchanged.

On these occasions snake-charmers, conjurors, jugglers, and such like characters, exhibit their arts, and obtain money from their admirers. Ascetics, who practise austerities, religious mendicants, and deceivers of every description, may be seen on these occasions, brought together from every part of the land. Such appear to spend their time similarly to such characters in the west.

The popular religious festivals of India afford the most fitting exemplification of the tendencies of Hinduism. What we have hitherto advanced is of a comparatively moderate character. Of much we may not attempt a description. Those Bacchanalian orgies, stained with licentiousness and blood, that are practised under the name of religious rites, among some of the sects, are of a nature too gross for description. Ignorance and superstition have inflicted on that fair country the foulest evils that can degrade and pollute the human character. The beneficent rule of a mild and paternal government has interposed for the rescue of the people from some of the horrible crimes that once disgraced the land. The rites of *Sati*, which at one time kindled the fires that consumed thousands of bereaved widows with the corpses of their husbands, have been abolished. The infanticide that once consigned thousands of innocent children to the alligators at Sagur island, has been abolished. Beneficent measures are ameliorating the condition of the aborigines in different parts of the country, and it may be hoped that all which legislation and authority can reach will receive the impress of Christianity. But there is much that government can never effect; and therefore we must look to the operation of that heaven-born truth which alone can emancipate the victims of a voluntary and debasing superstition.

Some of the existing austerities still practised may here be conveniently noticed. Many of them indicate great mental resolution, and impose on their subjects continued suffering, that one could scarcely believe endurable, had we not indubitable evidence of its existence. I propose in this place to give an account of some of the most remarkable instances of self-inflicted torment I have witnessed.

It has already been stated that self-inflicted torture and personal privation are held to be of great efficacy in the Hindu system. In subservience to this doctrine, some sincere persons subject themselves to the inflictions which morbid sentiment may dictate; whilst others, from mere motives of vanity and knavery, adopt the practices of asceticism.

A class of solitary mendicants, called Urddhabahus, may here be named. These extend one or both arms above their heads, till the muscles become rigid and fixed, so as not again to be capable of resuming their original flexibility and use. They also close the hand, and the nails being necessarily suffered to grow, make their way between the metacarpal bones, and completely perforate the hand. These persons wander about from place to place, some in a state of nudity, whilst others wear a small wrapper stained with ochre; they usually belong to the Saiva sect, and twist or mat their hair so as to rise above the head, as already stated. Figures of this class of fanatics are introduced into the sketches of the cave temples of Ellora and Elephanta.

Some of these ascetics retain the use of their limbs, and hold up their faces to the sky till the muscles of the neck become contracted, after which they are, from necessity, compelled to retain the head in that position.

At Ramisseram, on the occasion of one of the great periodic festivals, I saw numerous examples of ascetic practices, many of which, no doubt, proceeded from interested motives, with a view to extort alms from the credulous. Some were literally interred in an ordinary posture, others were buried with the head downwards, and only the legs from the knees above ground; one sat on a frame of iron, in which were fixed iron spikes which pierced his flesh; some had a pan of burning coals on the head, and bore it along in the crowd, whilst others lay prostrate on their backs, with a vessel full of burning embers placed on the breast; and one was performing the penance of the five fires, being seated in the midst of four, with the fifth, the burning sun, pouring its rays on his naked head. One man had an iron collar round his neck, on whose margin were planted iron spikes.

To satisfy ourselves of the sanguinary character of some of the Hindu deities, and of the influence they exert over the deluded victims of superstition, we must witness some of the cruel practices which the popular goddess, Kali, imposes on her worshippers. The most remarkable festival is the one called *Charak Puja*.

This festival derives its name from *chakra*, a wheel or discus; in allusion to the circle performed in the act of rotating, when suspended from the instrument of this horrible superstition. Being desirous of witnessing the ceremony in all its parts, I went to the spot where one of these ceremonies was about to take place. An upright pole, twenty or thirty feet in height, was planted in the ground, across the top of which, moving on a pivot, a long pole was placed. From one end of this transverse beam a long rope was suspended and left to hang loosely, whilst a shorter rope was attached to the other end, bearing a couple of strong iron hooks. A good-looking man, perhaps thirty years of age, came from the midst of the crowd, and doing obeisance beneath the instrument of torture, presented himself as a candidate for the honour he aspired to. The attendant, before whom he stood erect, struck a smart blow on the small of the back, and fixed one of the hooks in the flesh, and then did the same on the other side. The man then laid hold of the rope just above the hooks and held it, whilst certain persons in the crowd, seizing the loose rope, pulled him up, by depressing the other end of the beam. As he rose he relinquished his hold of the rope by which he was suspended, and resigned himself to the rotary motion, by which he was whirled round and round in mid air, suspended by the flesh of his own body. Whilst he was thus enduring the torture incident to this horrid service, at once gratifying the cruel goddess Kali and the crowd of admiring spectators, he drew from his girdle fruits and flowers, which he scattered among the attendants. These were picked up by the crowd, with the greatest eagerness, as precious relics that might avail as charms in cases of personal or domestic extremity. This wretched dupe of a foul superstition remained in the air at least a quarter of an hour, and, of course, in his own estimation and in that of the spectators, gained by this brief infliction a large amount of merit, and consequent title to certain rewards to be reaped in a future state of being. No sooner had he descended, than another was ready for the ceremony. These cruel practices are carried on in various parts of the native town, from day to day, as long as the festival lasts. It not unfrequently happens that the ligaments of the back give way, when the man, tossed to an immense distance, is dashed to pieces. In such cases, the inference is, that the victim of such accident, by virtue of demerit in a former state of existence, was not merely unworthy of the privileges attached to this privileged ceremonial, but destined to expiate his evil deeds by this dreadful accident.

At the festival of *Charak Puja* other acts of violence are also perpetrated under the name of religion. Some precipitate themselves from an elevated platform or from the upper verandah of a house on spikes and knives that are contained in a large bag of straw. By these adventurous acts many are lacerated, and some lose their lives.

Some devotees pierce the skin of the forehead, and suspending in the wound an iron hook, attach to it a lamp; and thus prepared, seat themselves in the open air, and recite the name of some favourite deity till the dawn of the next day.

The following singular vow is performed by some. Stretching himself on the earth on his back, the devotee takes a handful of moist earth, and placing this on his under lip, he plants in it some grains of mustard-seed, and exposes himself to the dews of the night and the heat of the day till the seed germinates. In this posture the man must lie in a fixed motionless condition, without food or drink, till the vegetable process liberates him, which will generally be about the fourth day.

This account of the miserable proceedings of the Hindu devotees may not be closed without a brief reference to some of the extraordinary acts that take place at the temple of Kali, in the vicinity of Calcutta, during the period of Charak Puja. The popularity of her shrine in this particular locality arises from the most extravagant legendary statements that have ever been put on record. They are too long for insertion here; indeed, no good end could be answered by the detail, except as it might serve to deepen the impression, no doubt already made, in regard to the degrading tendencies of Hinduism. That the most absurd stories can be invested with the sanctity and authority of inspired truth, and become the ground of the proceedings we are about to state may well excite surprise: and the emotion will become deeper when it is remembered, that what is about to be related does not happen merely in the retired and sequestered parts of the country, but in the metropolis of our Indian empire, in the city of palaces; for the celebrated temple of Kali Ghat is in its immediate suburbs, and the processions of frantic idolaters we are about to contemplate, I have myself witnessed in the most fashionable thoroughfares of the city, among the mansions of the opulent. Before noticing the processions themselves, it may be convenient to visit the temple itself, and witness what takes place at the shrine. This celebrated temple has no attractions of an architectural character, being totally devoid of the creations of art; its sole attraction consists in the sanctity of the place, and the presence there of a senseless idol, the symbol of a cruel goddess.

On entering its precincts a group of Brahmans is seen stationed to receive the free-will offerings of the people, who flow past on the occasion under notice as a mighty torrent. Opposite this group of collectors may be seen a heap of money, silver and copper, which is received in exchange for consecrated flowers, which have been presented at the shrine, and thence have derived a special sanctity. That presence being attained, the devotees, many of them with phrenzied feeling, knock their heads against the temple wall, if haply they may attract the eye of Kali. And what is the character of this all-commanding object of worship? We will give a brief description: Kali is usually represented as a black or dark blue female, dancing on the prostrate body of her own husband. She has four arms, having in one an exterminating sword, and in another a human head held fast by the hair; a third points downwards, indicating the destruction that awaits all opposed to her; and the fourth is raised upwards in allusion to the future regeneration of nature by a new creation. Her hair is dishevelled and reaches to her feet. Her countenance is ferocious in the extreme, and her tongue protruded from her mouth hangs over the chin. She has three eyes of angry expression, one of which is in her forehead. Her lips and eyebrows are streaked with blood, and a crimson current flows down her bosom. For ear-ornaments she has human victims, and, as a girdle, the heads of the victims over whom she has triumphed; and her necklace is composed of human skulls. Such is the image of the goddess that commands the myriads who throng to pay her adoration!

Let us now witness the acts of devotion wherewith this monster is honoured. Hard by the shrine several men are stationed, with instruments of cruelty, in the forms of iron spikes, canes, rods, &c. The horrible spectacle now to be described will scarcely be believed,—it is however true. One man is pierced through the sides, when a couple of canes are inserted, which being held by his companions, he dances to and fro on them; another has his tongue pierced, and at

HINDU AUSTERITIES.

once passes through the aperture a living snake. Another has his arm perforated, and passes through the opening an iron rod; and another, having his tongue bored through, inserts in the orifice a rod of iron. Thus the work of cruelty proceeds for a long time, group after group, consisting of ten or a dozen, comes up and undergoes the horrible operation. The successive groups pass together to an elevated platform opposite the idol. All being arranged, the crowd having surrounded the sacred precincts, the work of slaughter commences, the goats are decapitated and the court swims with blood. Now the ingredients prepared for the purpose are thrown on the fire, and as the smoke and flame ascend, the music commences from numerous instruments, making the most uproarious and discordant noise that can be imagined. Now the distinguished actors in this bloody and fiendish drama commence their gesticulations, and heighten the cruelty of their voluntary inflictions, by using various methods for giving effect to the meritorious proceedings being enacted. The instruments of torture, be they rods, or canes, or spikes, or ropes, or snakes, are pulled to and fro in the lacerated flesh till it pours forth afresh the stream that is to delight the renowned and beloved object of worship. The crowd becomes frantic with excitement, and in loudest acclaim, cry out, Victory to Kali! Victory to the great Kali! They afterwards parade the chief thoroughfares, accompanied by the horid din produced by trumpets, gongs, cymbals, pipes and drums. The last mentioned are generally surmounted by bunches of black and white ostrich feathers, which give an expression of mock-triumph that is highly suitable to the occasion. No description can convey an adequate idea of the unearthly character of these processions, as I have witnessed them in the streets of Calcutta. The accompanying engraving will aid the reader to form some idea of these horrible spectacles.

It may be enough to suggest the contrast between these scenes of cruel phrenzy and the peaceful tranquillizing worship of the Christian sanctuary. Here, true, there are acclamations of praise, and bursts of triumph; but the jubilant sound is the voice of melody and the sound of them that keep holy day. How different the subjective state, and the objective truth incident to the solemn gatherings for the worship of Almighty God in the church of Christ! The grateful feeling produced by the apprehended mysteries of redeeming love, and the blissful prospects set before the mind by an ascended and glorified Saviour, how they differ from those sanguinary rites and degrading scenes just described! How grateful ought the Christian to be in the enjoyment of such privileges, and how zealous to extend them to those who are brutified by the cruel practices of a merciless idolatry. The superior condition of a Christian population arises, it must never be forgotten, from the gospel of the grace of God. This record of saving truth reveals at once our miseries, the wants of our nature, and the remedies which have been provided for our benefit. On the diffusion of the truth, and the consequent application of the grace of God, depend the restoration of man, whether degraded by Brahmanism or Druidism. And it ought to be borne in mind that the appointed instrument for the demolition of every system of idolatry and superstition is put into the hands of the church to be used. It must surely be a matter of deep interest to every enlightened Christian to hasten the proclamation of that gospel which alone can effect the deliverance of our fellow-men from the cruel bondage in which they must remain willing captives till its sound reaches their ears. What the church in ancient times did for the victims of a horrid and soul-debasing Druidism in Britain, that church, if baptized into the same spirit, must feel impelled to attempt for the millions of India who are still the hapless bondsmen of an equally degrading system—Brahmanism.

A superficial glance at the system will suffice to show that Hinduism is admirably fitted to comprehend within its grasp every peculiarity of character, every phase of mind. Its flexibility adapts it to every condition of the moral and even immoral feelings. The system has something to offer every adherent as the reward of even the most perfunctory performance of any part of its varied ceremonial. The present act, whether civil or sacred, is either connected with the past as the reward of merit, or the result of demerit, or it is the seed corn of future awards; it must germinate and bring forth fruit correspondent with its own moral quality. The graduated scale of religious merit has its correspondent awards in the pleasures and pains of future being; these must be realized in the future with all the certainty of a physical necessity; all, however, admit that the final emancipation of the spirit is the summum bonum, the all-absorbing object to be aimed at in all the acts and habits of life. The attainment of this is not possible by works. This final beatitude can only be attained by Divine knowledge, the knowledge of the Supreme Brahm or essential Spirit. This knowledge consists in the perception of the sole self-existing and essential Spirit as the all-pervading, all-sustaining, and all-comprehending being, the all in all. He is the essence of the visible and tangible around us. The desiderated knowledge consists in the full apprehension of the theory of existence, and by this means intensely to realize the fact that there is nothing apart from or besides God. To be absorbed in the sublime truth, "I am He;" not "I am one with Him," in happy union, although this is a high state they admit, but I am He. While aught is conceived of as divided or divisible, there is no true knowledge, and consequently no liberation.

This knowledge, this deifying element, is to be sought in the intense study of the sacred ordinances contained in the Vedas, or in works that embody their principles. Devotional exercises aid the attainment, and hence the ceremonial: ascetism, or the practice of austerities, aids the object, and hence the self-inflicted torments of the devotees, the aspirants after the acmé of Hindu felicity. There are some who maintain that by the exercise of profound meditation, the knowledge of the Supreme Spirit may be attained; and works giving directions for the postures, gestures, and varied physical means for the desired end are read by the earnest and spiritual. By such means the Hindu is taught to believe that he may attain union with God when God will be seen in all things, and all things will be ascertained to be but the expansion of the divine unity. It is admitted that but few attain this supreme felicity. The following simile is used to express the extreme difficulty in the way of its apprehension. Supposing a yoke, used for uniting a couple of oxen in a plough, were cast adrift on the ocean, it is conceivable that in the course of time a turtle might insert its head in one of the several apertures existing in this piece of wood. But when the yielding and restless ocean is the place where such a contingency is contemplated, there does not appear much chance for the occurrence of such an incident; so rare is it for souls to attain to the knowledge that leads to beatitude.

Yet this finality of the Hindu is pursued by the votaries of the system as a possibility. In the use of the appointed means, the soul will ultimately attain the true knowledge, when the illusion which now enthrals it will be dispelled. Then the ethereal principle, no longer bound by the gross elements which now entangle it, will be absolutely enfranchised and emancipated by the attainment of the truth. It will be precipient of the truth now concealed, that Brahma, Vishnu, Siva, the moral and material universe, however efformed,—whether by the expansion of the divine essence, or by an illusive energy, or by a materializing emanative process,—is indeed nothing but the one sole, self-existing, and essential spirit, and must merge into the ineffable ocean of being, whence it was educed as the foam on the water. Thus as foam resolves itself into the productive fluid whence it was lashed into being by external energy; or as water taken out of the ocean and confined on its surface in a vessel may, by the subsidence of the storm, or the fracture of the vessel, return to the bosom of the ocean of the parent waters; so the soul that has been launched on the sea of births, and confined in vehicles more or less gross, pent up in those intellectual, mental, and organic casements already described, when matured by true wisdom, will burst from the prison-house, emerge from the subtle frame in which it has migrated, it may be for almost boundless cycles, and find its supreme felicity in God. Then the germ of existence that had been confined in material forms, like the germ of a seed in a husk, having exhausted, by endlessly varied sufferings, and enjoyments, and mutations, the causes that shaped its destiny, shall put off the tabernacle, and unclothed, a pure spirit, will return to the bosom of the Eternal.

Analogous to the doctrine of rewards to be attained in one of the fourteen worlds, and like those, temporary in their character, is the doctrine of punishments taught by the Hindu Shastras. The violation of the ordinances prescribed with reference to the various relations of life as regards caste, religion, or moral duty, will involve correspondent penal consequences which must either be endured or consumed, by passing through aggravated conditions in future births, or satisfied by the retributions of intermediate places of torment, or by the prescribed atonements or penances connected with the Hindu religion. The detail of these matters would, like that relating to the ceremonial, occupy too much of our space, and therefore it must be here omitted. The various afflictive circumstances incident to our present economy, that of human existence, are explained in accordance with this dogma of the Hindu schools. An elaborate treatise exists among them, which professes to show the effects of certain moral actions done in this life. By consulting this, much may be inferred relative to the causes of personal defect, as blindness, deafness, lameness, or maimedness. The question put to our Lord had reference to this view of pscychology, and related to the doctrine of the Metempsychosis, a doctrine not unknown among the Jews, as may be seen from its occurrence in one of the apochryphal books. "Who did sin, this man or his parents, that he was born blind?" The Hindus state in certain cases what will be the result of particular acts. If a man has robbed a priest he is born a crocodile. If he has stolen grain in the husk, he is born a rat. The spirit now conditioned as a man, or even one of higher auspices, may become a blade of grass, a shrub, a mineral, an insect, a nymph, a god.[1] Some conception may be formed of the various destiny to which the soul may be subjected when it is known that the propensity, or passion, or action, of the preceding actuates the following birth, as to form or condition, and particularly when it is remembered that the soul may be transmitted for purposes of expiation through the whole range of the animate and inanimate creation. Should these degradations be not, in value or degree, equal to the demerit, the unhappy spirit is doomed to *Naraka*, hell, the realms of Yama, those

> "Regions of sorrow, doleful shades, where peace
> And rest can never dwell."

There the soul is subjected to the positive inflictions of meet

[1] Some years ago when engaged on a manuscript of a version of the Book of Genesis, I called in a learned man resident in the neighbourhood, in order to read the manuscript with him for purposes of philological criticism. He was a very rigid Hindu, and though well acquainted with the scheme of Christianity, performed the religious duties of his own system with great zeal and equal confidence. Occasionally we blended with our mutual conferences on language remarks on the respective claims of Christianity and Hinduism; and therefore he always felt at liberty to offer his opinions on any of the doctrines, or characters of the Bible. When we were reading the history of Jacob, and had nearly finished it, he observed, that, in his judgment, the narrative of that patriarch, assuming its truth, might be taken as inferring the doctrine of the Metempsychosis. "For," said he, "it is very clear from the whole career of the man in this birth, so exceptionable was it in regard to the requirements of morality, that Jacob was not in any wise entitled to the auspices under which he was placed, and the inference, therefore, is, that he had in a prior state of being acquired such merit as to secure, notwithstanding his questionable expedients, the signal interpositions of God, and the successive manifestations of Divine favour with which his life abounded."

retribution; but, like the rewards reaped in the celestial and sensuous mansions, the duration of these torments will be but temporary; those purgatorial fires will not burn for ever. From those regions of lamentation and woe, the spirit will again emerge, and embodied again appear on the sea of mortal births, and if needs be, again and again through the endlessly varied mutations and migrations of the vast cycle of the Metempsychosis, seek its supreme end, absorption, in the divine Essence.

In the consideration of the doctrines and theories of Pantheism, we are made acquainted with a nomenclature, with an array of theological terms, that we might mistake for those employed by the inspired writers of the Bible; and we are ready to conclude that we are about to be conducted into the glorious temple of truth, there to enjoy further revelations of the transcendent attributes of God, natural and moral, and of the laws of the intellectual and moral universe; but how are we disappointed as we advance into the deductions, the speculations, and the issues of the system! And in like manner, when we hear of final beatitude, and ineffable felicity, and unbroken and eternal union with the Godhead, and the inexhaustible fruition of paradise, we are disposed to imagine ourselves on the margin of perennial delights; and that there is something in Hinduism that may avail for the satisfying of the immortal cravings of a deathless and intelligent being. We find, however, as we analyse the terms, and examine the things for which they stand, that we are presented with little more than what may be denominated annihilation in the final beatitude of the Hindu religion. Though the Brahmanist will not admit with the Buddhist that cessation of existence, or extinction of being, is the acmé he aims at, yet the loss of individuality by the refluence of the spirit into deity, would appear to differ but little from the finality of that theory. The system holds out no prospect of conscious felicity amid the rewards of a changeless state. The intermediate conditions of the spirit are those incessant changes from birth to birth through an almost endless cycle of migration; and if the highest state be ever reached, it consists not with consciousness; really it amounts to nothing better than annihilation. That this is the doctrine of the Hindu may be inferred from one of the passages which Krishna addressed to the hero Arjuna on the battle-field. The views he there expressed are contained in that ocean of words, the Mahabharat, one of the national epics already described.

Thou mourn'st for those thou should'st not mourn, albeit thy words are like the wise,
For those that live or those that die, may never mourn the truly wise.
Ne'er was the time when I was not, nor those, nor yonder kings of earth;
Hereafter ne'er shall be the time, when one of us shall cease to be.
The soul within its mortal frame, glides on through childhood, youth, and age;
Then in another form renew'd, renews its stated course again.
All indestructible is he that spread the living universe;
And who is he that shall destroy the work of the indestructible?
Corruptible these bodies are that warp the everlasting soul—
The eternal, unimaginable soul. Thence on to battle, Bkarata!
For he that thinks to slay the soul, or thinks the soul is slain,
Are fondly both alike deceived; it is not slain—it slayeth not;
It is not born—it doth not die; past, present, future, knows it not;
Ancient, eternal, and unchanged, it dies not with the dying frame.
Who knows it incorruptible, and everlasting, and unborn,
What heeds he whether he may slay, or fall himself in battle slain?
As their old garments men cast off, anon new raiment to assume,
So casts the soul its worn-out frame, and takes at once another form.
The weapon cannot pierce it through, nor wastes it the consuming fire;
The liquid waters melt it not, nor dries it up the parching wind;
Impenetrable and unburn'd; impermeable and undried;
Perpetual, ever wandering, firm, indissoluble, permanent,
Invisible, unspeakable. Thus deeming, wherefore mourn for it?

We must take leave of the subjects that have occupied attention, as we have endeavoured to depict the character of Hinduism, a system of religion confessedly the most stupendous—whether we consider the boundless extent of its range, or the multiplicity of its component parts—that ever engaged the mind of man. An eloquent writer, already quoted, very lucidly presents its features in a passage which may be here conveniently placed before the reader: he says—

"Of all systems of false religion, it is that which seems to embody the largest amount and variety of semblances and counterfeits, of divinely revealed facts and doctrines. In this respect it appears to hold the same relation to the primitive patriarchal faith, that Roman Catholicism does to the primitive apostolic faith. It is, in fact, *the popery of primitive patriarchal Christianity.* All the terms and names expressive of the sublimest truths, orignally revealed from heaven, it still retains; and under these it contrives to inculcate diametrically opposite and contradictory errors. Its account of the *creation* and *destruction* of the universe,—of the *floods* and *conflagrations* to which it is alternately subjected,—of the *divine origin, present sinfulness,* and *final destiny of the soul,*—together with many *cognate* and *subsidiary* statements, must be regarded as embodying, under the corruptions of tradition and the exaggerations of fancy, some of the grandest truths ever communicated by the Almighty to man, whether before or after the fall. Its nomenclature on the subject of the *unity* and *spirituality* of the one great, supreme, self-existent Lord, is most copious; but, when analysed, it presents us with nothing better than an infinite negation. Its vocabulary, descriptive of the *natural attributes* of the Great Spirit, superabounds to overflowing; but it evacuates every one of them of *absolute perfection.* There is *unchangeableness;* though constantly subject at the confluence of certain cycles of time, not merely to alteration of plans and purposes, but to change of essence. There is *omnipotence;* but, bereft of creative energy, it is limited to the power of eduction and fabrication. There is *omniscience;* but it is restricted to the brief period of wakefulness, at the time of manifesting the universe. And so of other natural attributes. Instead of possessing *moral attributes,* the Supreme Spirit is represented as assuming, when he awakes, certain *generalised active qualities,* which admit of being predicated of *fire*, or *air*, or *water*, or any other material substance, as well as *spirit!* What a *contrast* to all this do the statements of the Bible exhibit!" The God of the Bible is possessed of independent personality, of freedom of will, and of absolute power. There is a natural and moral attractiveness in Jehovah that invites the conscious sinner to draw nigh with confiding trust. The propensions of mercy, and its provisions too, are all clearly revealed in the Son of his love. Here all is solid rock. In Hinduism there is nothing but theory—nothing real—nothing satisfactory.

The voice of conscience, and the fragments of patriarchal truth traditionally conveyed to all nations, have indeed taught the Hindu that, to meet his legal destitution, some mode of expiation is absolutely necessary, to free him from the felt guilt of sin; and some laver of regeneration equally needed, in respect to the degradation and corruption of our moral nature. In accordance with these absolute truths, he seeks expiation by the endless ceremonies of his ritual, and he strives to appease the anger of revengeful and sanguinary divinities, not only by victims immolated at their shrines, but by self-inflicted tortures of the most shocking and horrid description. To procure the inward purity, without which all his rites and ceremonies must go for nothing, he has recourse to the supposed efficacy of oft repeated ablutions. By these he hopes to purify his spirit, and to prepare it for immortality. That he may elevate his soul, and assimilate his mind to the purity and dignity of the divine nature, he has recourse to continued and intense meditation. By these moral acts he endeavours to enthrone deity in his affections, and to attain divine attributes. In this effort, however, there is no tendency to intellectual and moral expansion, or the ennobling of the faculties, just the contrary. He is engaged in the constant endeavour to repress the natural and immortal aspirings of his nature, and to render himself insensible to those genial motives that alone can avail as the instruments of moral elevation. And the natural longing for immortality, which his system seeks not to eradicate but to pervert, he is instructed to cherish, and to cultivate in connexion with expectations of almost endless mutations and migrations in successive births. The finality attained, and he is re-fused into the infinite and eternal essence of the great Supreme, where, bereft of consciousness as of individuality, he loses himself in what seems little better than cessation of being.

Such is the practical issue of the elaborate system contained in the records of Brahmanism. How vastly superior do the teachings of the Bible appear! Here we have the grateful and tranquillizing announcement of "One God, and one mediator between God and man, the man Christ Jesus, who gave himself a ransom for all." How attractive is the character of God as exhibited in the Bible. His natural attributes sustain so fully, and harmonize so perfectly, with the moral qualities of his nature. His exuberant charity expands into the pitying and redeeming economy of vicarious atonement, renewing and sanctifying grace, salutary and saving discipline, hallowing and elevating and immortal hope, guarding and guiding providence. Here we have even the tomb illumined by the lamp of his love, beyond which we see, stretching into the depths of a boundless futurity, fields of intellectual and moral splendour, the glories of the beatific vision, the presence of the King Eternal; and all the endless felicities of those mansions which the glorified Redeemer has gone to prepare for those who confide in the infinite merits of his atonement. The objective and subjective glory will consist alike with individuality and with consciousness.

Having these hopes freely bequeathed to us in the course of a merciful providence, and taught as we are, that "He," whom we have by happy experience ascertained to be gracious, "by the grace of God tasted death for every man," shall we conceal the secrets of redeeming love, put the light under a bushel, and allow our fellow-men, our fellow-subjects, in India, to descend to death bound by the adamantine chains of a merciless and destructive superstition?

NASIK ON THE GODAVERY.

CHAPTER XII.

HINDUS, THEIR EARLY CIVILIZATION.—SKILL IN THE ARTS, AGRICULTURE, TANKS.—ASPECT OF THE HINDUS.—COSTUME.—HOUSES.—FURNITURE. — VILLAGES. — CHOULTRIES. — TOWNS. — INDUSTRY. — FOOD.

THAT the ancient Hindus had attained to a high degree of civilization, and equal eminence in the arts of social life, at a period long anterior to European history, has already been proved. The testimony of other ancient nations in regard to India, their commercial intercourse with its inhabitants, its manufactures, its own languages, literature, and science, all combine to show that its people occupied a distinguished place among the early nations of mankind. Though it is not the intention to enter into lengthened details on the arts, the manners, the customs, and the character of the Hindus, either as regards the past or the present, the scope of this little work requires some reference to these points. The refinement, the opulence, the splendour, and the luxury of the urban population of ancient India may be inferred from the following description of one of its cities. Being presented in a poetic form, there may possibly be some degree of exaggeration in the picture; yet the semblances will enable us to form a tolerably correct idea of what the social condition of the Hindus was three thousand years ago.

"On the banks of the *Sarayu* is a vast, fertile, and delightful country, called *Cós'ala,* abounding in corn and wealth. In that country is a city called *Ayódya,* greatly famed in this world, and built by *Manu* himself, the lord of men.

This great and prosperous city was twelve *yójanas*[1] in length, and three in breadth, and stored with all conveniences. The streets and lanes were admirably disposed, and the high roads were all sprinkled with water. In this city lived *Dasaratha*, the most potent of monarchs, even as *Indra* lived in Amaravati.[2] It was adorned with arched gateways and beautiful ranges of shops; it was fortified with numerous defences and warlike machines, and inhabited by all sorts of skilful artists. It was crowded with bards and musicians, filled with riches, and shone forth with unrivalled glory; it had lofty towers stored with fire-arms, and adorned with banners. It was constantly filled with female stage-players; it was beautiful with gardens and groves of mango-trees, and enclosed with high walls. It was surrounded by impassable ditches, and secured by fortifications difficult of assault by foreign kings; it was full of horses, elephants, cattle, camels, and mules. It was ornamented with palaces of exquisite workmanship, lofty as mountains, and enriched with jewels, abounding with beautiful houses consisting of several stories, and it shone like *Indra's* heaven. It was crowded with tributary princes, purified with sacrificial rites, and filled with merchants of foreign countries. Its aspect had an enchanting effect, and the whole city was diversified with various colours, and decorated with regular avenues of sweet scented trees. It was full of precious stones, and resplendent with stately edifices and beautiful apartments. It was filled with buildings erected close to one another, and without intermediate voids, and situated on a smooth level ground. It abounded in delicious rice, and water sweet as the juice of sugar-cane. It incessantly echoed with the sounds of kettle-drums, tabors, cymbals, and lutes; this city truly surpassed any that was ever beheld on earth. The houses which it contained resembled the celestial mansions which the Sidd'hás obtain through the virtue of their austerity."

The professions mentioned incidentally in numerous works

[1] One yojan=9 miles. [2] The capital of Indra, the regent of heaven.

show advancement in all that relates to a high civilization. The gems, the golden ornaments, the embroideries, the silks, and other fabrics, the perfumes, as well as the more useful articles connected with domestic life evince their artistic skill. "Their palaces, their temples, the stupendous pyramidal gateways, leading to the latter, the colonnades and porticos with which they are surrounded; some of 'a thousand pillars,' others equally remarkable for their elevations, richness, and grandeur of design, have for ages been the objects of admiration to the traveller in the east." These still serve to attest their former skill and resources, as may be inferred from the illustrations of this volume.

One of the most remarkable facts connected with the arts among the Hindus, is the extreme simplicity of the appliances in general use in their execution. The cabinet-maker, the goldsmith, the blacksmith, the mason, the spinner and weaver are all, in regard to their tools and machines, equally remarkable for the skill they evince in producing, by means apparently quite inadequate, effects the most wonderful. This it must be confessed is an unquestionable proof of superior skill. The arts and implements relating to agriculture are those bequeathed by the earliest ancestors of the race. True, for the most part, the nature of the soil and the amenity of the climate favour this. The plough employed for turning up the soil is of the simplest kind, and so light that the husbandman may be seen bearing it on his shoulder to the field, driving before him the couple of bullocks that are to be yoked to it on his arrival there. The spade is not in use; a hoe, varied in shape in different provinces, is used instead. The sickle, the bill-hook, the axe, are similar to those in use in the west. Cattle are employed for treading out the corn, and may be seen at the end of harvest sluggishly moving over the mass strewed on the ground, and eating as they list. In some parts of the country the crops are wholly watered from the clouds. In hilly districts the declivities are terraced, and the land is formed into a succession of steps—

irrigation being promoted by diverting the mountain torrents into the patches of cultivated ground. Where rivers afford the means of irrigation, as in Bengal and other parts of India, the water is conducted into the smiling fields as they may require its fertilizing streams. In some provinces the waters of the periodical rains are reserved in artificial tanks, whence they are transmitted, as may be necessary, either by channels direct from the reservoir, or after being raised by simple means to a higher level. Some of the artificial works constructed for irrigation, and some of the tanks prepared for ablutionary purposes, are among the most remarkable works of art found in any part of the world. They are of two kinds, one excavated, and the other formed by embankments thrown up or constructed across a valley. Those of the former description are formed in the precincts of temples, choultries, or in the suburbs of towns, and are used both for religious purposes and for irrigation. They are generally surrounded with steps for the convenience of those who resort to them. In most cases temples surround these works of art, and in many places shrines are erected along the flight of steps down to the water's edge. When these tanks are crowded with living beings, some in the water engaged in bathing, others in acts of worship, perhaps up to the middle in the water, and reverently employed in reciting holy texts to the resplendent sun,—others seated in the porticos engaged in the performance of some ceremony, that either the accustomed ritual imposes, or that earnest devotion has decided to attend,—others reading one of the sacred books, whilst Hindu females are going to and fro in brilliantly coloured garments carrying on their heads brazen water-pots, sometimes one above the other, on their ample tresses loosely disposed in their own convolutions—when such scenes are really witnessed at these magnificent sheets of water, the mind is deeply affected with the living plastic character of Hinduism.

Some of the wells are as remarkable as the tanks. These are often of great depth and of different forms, some round, others square. They are sometimes surrounded to the bottom with galleries in the strong and massive style of Hindu structures; and they have also a flight of steps, or an inclined plane, leading from a considerable distance to the water.

The tanks, or reservoirs formed for purposes of irrigation, are quite as wonderful as those just described, and generally very large, some being many miles in circumference. The embankments are works of immense extent, and in their formation there is often an evincement of extraordinary skill.

In the Island of Ceylon the early inhabitants constructed some of the most wonderful works of art for purposes of irrigation. These as monuments of ancient skill and industry afford the most extraordinary evidence of former power and greatness. They, like those in India, are formed by embankments thrown across the valleys. One of these occupies an area equal to fifteen miles by four; the embankment being six miles in length, and of an average height of sixty feet. The reservoir known as the giant's tank was originally as large as the Lake of Geneva. It has been ascertained that in one province of that beautiful island there are not fewer than seven hundred tanks or artificial reservoirs. The ruins of the ancient city of Anurajapore, with which many of these works were connected, covers an area of sixteen square miles. Some of the antiquities of this once populous, but now almost desolate, region are very remarkable, and serve to show that the people who raised the now ruinous fabrics were a refined nation. It is remarkable that this city was near one of the emporia of Eastern commerce, situated on the west coast of Ceylon in the vicinity of the Pearl Fishery.

For raising the water from tanks and wells, the common well-sweep or lever is used extensively, as it is also on the banks of the Nile in Upper Egypt. Another simple plan is the employment of a large ladle or scope suspended by a rope, which being depressed as its mouth approaches the water takes up the element, and as it describes its segment elevates it to a higher level, where it is ejected by a simple action of the hand.

Fields are rarely separated by hedges. Divisions are made by low embankments of perhaps a foot and a half high, and of equal breadth, which serve at once to define boundaries, to retain the water needful for the crop, and often as the means of communication from one village to another. When the full crop is growing, a boundless expanse of waving vegetation may be seen stretching in uninterrupted grandeur like the surface of the sea. Alluding to the disappearance of the boundary lines with the rising crops, a native Christian teacher once observed to me when speaking of the evils of sectarian division in the church, "These are not perceived when believers abound in 'the fruits of the Spirit,'—they are made prominent in proportion to our sterility."

Soils are distributed into various classes, as suited for different sorts of culture, the kind being generally specified in deeds of conveyance. Great attention is paid by the Hindu to the quality of the soil, the requisite means for improving its fertility, and the order to be observed in the rotation of crops. Rice is in some places extensively cultivated by transplanting. The seed is sown thickly in a favourable situation, and when of a proper growth, the due preparation of the soil being observed, the young grain is taken up and planted out, of course involving much care and trouble, but, from the abundance and cheapness of labour, not very great expense.

There can be no doubt that the Hindus have from the earliest times shared largely in the comforts and luxuries of life. The fertility of the soil, and the amenity of the climate, favoured the production of those supplies which were obtained as the fruits of the ground; and the skill of the Hindus in manufactures contributed corresponding advantages. The arts of spinning and weaving were early carried to great perfection, and raised them to a commercial position, which as we have seen brought the civilized world to their markets. They have always been distinguished for their gold and silver brocades, of which they were in all probability the inventors. Their skill in the fabrication of ornaments, and their delicate works in gold are also well known.

The references in the most authentic of Hindu writers to the wealth and splendour of her rulers, and to the brilliancy of their courts, may be considered as sufficient to set this matter at rest. The variety of articles used for dress mentioned in the Periplus may well astonish us. At the time of Alexander's invasion of India the people are described pretty much as we would describe them now in all that relates to costume and external appearance. The princely presents mentioned in Hindu writings as consisting of woollen-stuff, furs, precious stones, fine silks, and vestments of divers colours, princely robes and sumptuous carriages of every kind may aid our conception in forming a notion of the opulence, grandeur, and magnificence of that early seat of civilization. And now that the advantages of the west have by a retrocession of the tide-wave of civilization been conveyed back to their ancient source, the Hindu artisans are exhibiting a skill and ability in the arts of building, cabinet-making, and the kindred branches of human industry that cannot be surpassed by the artificers of Europe. The amenity of the climate is favourable to the flexibility of the muscle and the elasticity of the mind, and the physiological structure of the Hindu, too, is favourable to their progressive advancement.

The natural advantages of the country at once promoted the wealth of its inhabitants and their commercial intercourse with other nations. The necessaries, conveniences, and luxuries indigenous to itself brought into it by traffic the advantages which other nations could confer: hence we find in the code of Manu laws were made for commerce three thousand years ago. On his entry into his capital, Ráma, a historic personage who flourished thirty centuries ago, is met by all the men of distinction, together with the merchants and chief men of the people; and the procession is closed by the warriors, tradesmen, and artisans. In one of the epics of

Southern India one of the chief personages who figures in the history is a merchant, whose shipwreck is detailed, and the subsequent repairs of his vessel are also particularly mentioned. The internal commerce of India must have been considerable. From the Gangetic valley grain was doubtless exported to various parts of the Peninsula, which in return sent back the productions of the south.

In forming an estimate of the civilization of the Hindus, and contrasting the present with the past, it may be said that although they are not now in the high condition either intellectually or morally which they attained in the best days of the nation, yet they are at least equal to any other people except the refined nations of Europe. Many causes have operated to prevent advancement, and some to hasten decline. The religious and social constitution of the Hindus is opposed to change and favourable to inaction. Caste is peculiarly opposed to change, and consequently to the advancement of the classes. The government, whilst Hindu, operated to check progress, and when that was broken up by Mohammedan invaders and their unmitigated despotism, the people were certainly not in a position more favourable either to the conservation of what they had attained, or advancement to a higher point.

It is thought by the most competent judges that the Hindus attained their highest point of civilization before the period of Alexander's invasion; not indeed in learning, for the most flourishing period of Hindu literature was later, though anterior to the Christian era. In works of standard value little has been added to the productions of the ancients since the period of the Mohammedan invasion, yet the classical authors are studied with avidity and love of learning; and a high appreciation of scholarship are still marked features of the Hindu mind. It may be assumed that the external circumstances and general condition of the inhabitants of India have suffered but slight, if any, change for more than two thousand years, and therefore the study of their character, and an examination of the existing manners and customs, places us in the midst of realities enabling us to judge of the actual state of their ancestors before the Christian era. Under these circumstances India must be regarded as a country in which the student of human nature must feel a deep and lively interest. In visiting other seats of early civilization, such as Egypt, Assyria, Greece, and Etruria, we are struck with amazement at the remains of ancient splendour. We gaze on the imposing monuments, the temples, the palaces, the Mausolea, the statuary, the paintings, and through the latter gain some insight into the condition of those whose skill and perseverance produced them; yet we are able to acquire, even from the researches of the most learned, but very imperfect notions of the social, intellectual, and moral condition of those primeval nations. The case is otherwise in India. As in Egypt, so in India, we have ancient monuments whose date cannot be ascertained,—and some of them are of the most stupendous character; we have languages the most refined, and in them an ancient literature whose merits will not suffer by comparison with the best classical productions bequeathed to us by the Greek and Roman writers; and we have arts,—true they are simple, but they are the more remarkable on that account, since they are efficient in the production of the most beautiful specimens of human skill; we have a higher degree of civilization than exists in any other country, except the more refined portions of Europe, that harmonizes with that of the same race, as it was exhibited in the capital where Ráma held his court three thousand years ago. There we may study antiquity as it is preserved in the unchanged society, the habitudes, and national institutions of a living people. India presents itself to us, as it did to the Macedonian conqueror, the Arabian navigator, the Tyrian, the Byzantine, and the Roman merchants. The aspect of society as regards domestic order and religious rites remains unchanged. Her rural and urban population, in its customs, manners, habits, and general condition, may be taken as the living and practical exponent of what we read in her code of ancient law, and in her national epics. This fact renders the study of almost all that relates to Indian antiquities comparatively easy. We read on the expanded page of every day life the lessons that have been stereotyped for ages. In common with all ancient nations, the Hindus are an interesting people, and pre-eminently so, because of the manifold peculiarities that distinguish them from all other nations, and the superior civilization by which they are characterised. For ages it has preserved its integrity, whilst other empires have risen, flourished, decayed and perished. Not indeed without chastisement. It has been made a spoil, and overrun by rapacious and cruel invaders; it has experienced repeated inflictions from their relentless and oppressive despotism. Her villages, cities, temples and palaces have again and again been reduced to heaps of smoking ruins. At length, however, deliverance has been vouchsafed. India has received the blessings of a mild, paternal and Christian rule; and if her sons should appreciate the day of her visitation, she will rise to the dignity and happiness of a free and virtuous people. To Christian England has been assigned the enviable distinction of effecting, under God, her intellectual and moral, her social and political, regeneration.

The Hindus are of the Caucasian type, and in personal appearance agreeable. The colour varies in different parts of the country, but, as a general complexion, brown in its various shades predominates. Some of the northern tribes, and most Brahmanical families, wherever located, and some of the inferior castes too, are light, not very different from gold-colour. In stature they are generally lower, yet much like Europeans; more slender, but not very different in feature. Both male and female are for the most part distinguished for elegance of figure, graceful limbs, fine hair, and beautiful eyes. Symmetry of outline, the form and expression of countenance, and all that is included in personal beauty among Europeans, will be equally appreciated by the Hindu. The race of the Hindus being identical in origin with our own, it is not surprising that their notions of beauty are found to harmonize with our own ; nor that many persons are met with among them that remind one of friends in Europe. In accordance with the laws of human physiology, that the most barbarous tribes are the ugliest, it will follow that a nation like the Hindus, enjoying for so many ages the ameliorating effects of a high civilization, should possess the lineaments of personal beauty. From the poets and other writers, as well as from the observations constantly made in the intercourse of society, it is quite evident that personal appearance has among the Hindus its wonted place. The following quotation from one of the classical writers may be taken as a specimen of feeling on this subject. In allusion to the personal appearance and graceful attitudes of a female under notice, the poet says :—

> "Her silken curls
> Luxuriant shade her cheeks; and every limb,
> Of slightest texture, moves with natural grace,
> Like moonbeams gliding through the yielding air."

The costume of the Hindus is distinguished by simplicity, fitness, and elegance. The ordinary national dress consists of a scarf, a piece of cloth varying from two and a half yards in length for men, and often as much as nine or ten yards for women, which is gracefully put round the waist, loosely gathered and tucked in at the front. In some instances the men have a light scarf, which is thrown over the shoulder, and suffered to hang down before and behind in graceful festoons. Those who are employed in public offices or in business, wear a jacket which is tight about the shoulders and sleeves, and long and loose in the skirts. A turban is the appropriate head-dress,—white muslin is generally used, and sometimes crimson. To these articles of dress a pair of slippers. red or yellow, turned up at the toe, must be added, and then you have the ordinary dress of respectable native men, in the chief cities. Men who can afford the cost, may have a couple of brilliants in the ears, and a precious stone of some kind—perhaps an emerald—pendant from the upper lobe of the ear. One or two gold rings may be seen on the fingers, one of which may have on it the initials or name of the wearer. The hair is sometimes shaved, except a tuft on the top; in some cases it is partially removed from the top, and allowed to grow bushy round the margin of the turban, especially in Bengal, while in some places it is permitted to grow long, like that of the female, and tied in a knot behind by the married, and on the side of the head by bachelors. The *mustachio* is generally worn.

The female puts on her dress cloth in a manner similar to that of the men, but its greater length enables her to wear a fuller skirt, and, in the absence of a bodice, a portion of the garment is gracefully disposed across the breast, and passed over one shoulder, as before described. Sometimes, when abroad, the female may use this as a hood, in lieu of a bonnet or veil. Many native females, especially in towns, wear a tight bodice with short sleeves, reaching half way from the shoulder to the elbow. The costume of a Hindu female is singularly beautiful, and generally her carriage is equally graceful, whilst her expression of countenance is modest and gentle.

The women are characterized by extreme fondness for jewellery, and many of them wear a profusion of ornaments. The ears, the nose, the neck, the wrists, the ankles, the toes, and the fingers, are all provided with their appropriate appendages.

It is not uncommon for all the personal estate to be invested in ornaments, which, in case of necessity, can be pledged for money, or, in the event of absence from the homestead, borne in safety on the person. Children are often loaded with ornaments, which excite the cupidity of the vicious; and not infrequently children thus decorated are murdered for the sake of the treasure they wear.

The hair of the native female is generally combed back, and variously disposed at the back of the head. Sometimes a supporting band is formed, by detaching a portion of the hair behind each ear, which is tied behind, into which the tresses are put, and by which they are confined in a not ungraceful mass. The hair is usually most luxuriant, beautifully black, and extremely glossy. When the dress is of coloured material, whether silk or cotton, the Hindu female appears a striking object. The vestments are generally of brilliant colours, in which crimson, full blue, yellow, or green are prominent, and having an elegant and appropriate margin, as well as an elaborately ornamented border. The colours are well blended, and they are seen to great advantage in the brightness of an Indian sun. Viewed for the first time by a stranger, perhaps on her way from a well or river with a brass water-pot on her head, the Hindu female appears peculiarly striking. The outline of her person is full before you. The water-pot on her head secures her erect posture. The placid composure of her countenance, and the graceful measured step, indicate the submissive and dependent relation in which she is nationally trained from infancy. Here you have the living prototype of the sculptures and the frescoes of Ellora and Ajunta. Ancient India is as much before you as it was before the eye and imagination of the ancient sculptors, painters, and national poets.

In manners the Hindu is inoffensive, gentle, mild, pacific; graceful and dignified in mien, in his ordinary communication with his equals; polite, courteous, and deferential in his intercourse with strangers, and especially with his superiors;

and like most Asiatics he is skilled in the arts of adulation. This last trait is so deeply inwrought into his composition, that he not infrequently sacrifices truth as well as modesty in its exhibition : forgetting the claims of ingenuousness and truth, he is in danger of becoming servile to his superiors.

Perhaps no people are more distinguished for their love of learning, and none are more impressed with the persuasion, that to give and receive instruction should be the sole and ultimate object of life. This is easily accounted for, from the fact that the attainment of true knowledge and beatitude are identical. Ignorance is regarded as one of the greatest of evils, and the source of all misery. In much of the popular literature this is strongly insisted on. Innumerable quotations might be produced to show that in the estimation of the Hindu, knowledge is the best of all possessions, the true end of existence. This feature of the Hindu mind accounts for their extensive and refined literature, and is the security for its continued diffusion. When their love of learning shall be cherished in subservience to true science and revealed truth, the Hindus will rise to a high position among the nations of the earth.

These are the better, the external features of the Hindus, as they show themselves to the superficial observer. It is not from this that we are to conclude, as has hastily been done, especially by writers of a former age, that the exterior, the mildness of demeanour, and the freedom from offensiveness and grossness, always infers a correspondent freedom from vicious principle or the malign affections. Evidence abounds of their innate depravity, and also of the degrading tendency of their religious system. The malign affections are frequently in fearful ascendency, and show themselves in the jealousy, the slander, the litigation, conspiracy, perjury, and revenge that are always more or less at work among them. These evils are the staple of the courts of justice. In the relationships of domestic life, internal differences, bickerings, strifes, and animosities too frequently destroy all happiness. Among neighbours these passions sometimes break out, and when they do, the women take the lead; and the most astounding rage, and the most furious invectives, are vented amid railings unspeakably virulent and obscene. Often do the groves ring with such outrageous quarrels. Disgusting vices, brutalizing crimes, gross debauchery, such as are seen in some parts of Europe, rarely occur; but licentiousness, falsehood, deceit, and petty thefts, are vices the prevalence of which excites no more surprise than do drunkenness and profane swearing among the same class of Europeans.

The houses of the Hindus are as various as their means. In general, the dwelling of the poor consists of no more than a single apartment, it may be a shed covered with the leaves of cocoa-nut, or palmyra-palm, or grass, and in many cases surrounded with walls of the same material, or mud; the floor in such cases will be of earth, and kept clean by means of a solution of cow-dung, with which it is periodically smeared. The use of cow-dung for purposes of cleanliness may sound strange to a European; it is, however, one of the best preventives that can be adopted in regard to insects and vermin. A native house or any apartment with a mud floor smeared once a-week, is very comfortable. As a general rule among the lower classes, it is preferable to other kinds of flooring. I have been informed that bugs, very prevalent among the lower orders, are best kept away by the regular use of cow-dung. In some native houses where a rude bedstead is used, with reference to the dampness of the ground, if made of split bamboo, it will be plentifully inlaid with cow-dung as a defence against vermin. Such is the amenity of the climate in most parts of India, that a small shed, especially if in a grove, is one of the most agreeable places one can desire for the conduct of ordinary business. In such situations I have spent large portions of time when engaged in absorbing intellectual pursuits.

The better kind of houses, among the agriculturists and others, are built of mud, brick, or stone, in a square form, with an open central court, something after the manner of the Roman atrium, around which the apartments, or very commonly the open verandah, offers accommodation for the different members of the family. Slight screens, made of mats, may be interposed as a substitute for walls, and thus compartments are made. On the outside of this square edifice, a verandah is frequently formed all round, by projecting the eaves, and raising an elevated terrace, for the convenience of the family and visitors. The inner court is entered by a single door, generally low overhead, a lofty doorway being regarded inauspicious ; the entrance should not be in the centre of the building, but a little to the left of the middle. The outer wall is used for suspending unused agricultural implements and spare timber, or any other articles not likely to attract the cupidity of dishonest persons. On this outer wall, if of stucco, rude frescoes are sometimes painted, and even on red mud plaister, devices are formed, or broad streaks of white and red. When in the middle of a garden, such houses are very agreeable. On the elevated outer verandah the master of the house may be frequently seen seated, if alone, possibly counting his beads, or looking over his accounts. Here he receives his friends. If the evangelist approaches, he may, if of the proper caste or a European, be invited to sit down on a mat, or deer, or tiger-skin, and in case there be no verandah, as in the common one-roomed huts, the rice pounder is turned upside down under a tree, and he is invited to be seated on it. The houses of the better classes have an air of neatness and cleanliness about them that is very agreeable, and indeed they are really so. The inner corners of the homestead may not be attended to with so much care as the parts more exposed to view, but generally the natives of India are distinguished for sanitary habits. It is not uncommon to see, at an early hour, the matron engaged in cleansing the open space opposite her door, and ornamenting it with a device somewhat in the form of a flower made on the hard ground by a solution of lime or chalk. This is at once ornamental and religious, having reference to certain divine auspices that are supposed to be hereby secured.

The furniture in the ordinary dwellings of the Hindus is very simple. Among the poor a rice-pounder, a large pestle and mortar, for beating the rice out of the husk, a few earthenware cooking vessels, sleeping mats, rolled up and deposited in a corner, or hung up in slings under the eaves, and a box with a lock on it, make up about all that a native family really requires. The box will contain the better articles of dress, possibly copies of nativities, and some other documents, such as agreements and marriage deeds. The wealthy have possibly a chair or two, a table, and it may be in place of the ordinary box, a large family coffer, bedsteads, rugs or carpets, metal vessels for culinary purposes, &c. In some families a separate set of vessels is kept for religious festivals. As a general rule, the natives sit on the floor in the posture of the Buddhistic images. This mode is suited to the climate, and where the dress permits the free use of the limbs, it is not uncomfortable. It may often be seen when a native, unaccustomed to a chair, is seated on one, that he will instinctively draw up his feet and assume the posture referred to.

In the large cities the wealthy natives live in great splendour. Their houses, though retaining the Eastern arrangement, are many of them elegant mansions, sumptuously furnished. Their doorways are hung with quilted silks, and the wood-work in the halls and corridors is richly carved. Expensive chandeliers, ottomans, and other articles, with every possible decoration, are provided in profusion. The equipages of such are among the most remarkable for elegance, their dress is costly, and their ornaments profuse. The Anglicised Hindus—that is, those who have acquired in the various institutions of learning an acquaintance with the English language, literature, and European science—have, in some instances, imbibed a taste for western manners, which is indicated in the modification of their costume, and in their domestic arrangements. In some instances the restraints of caste and the restrictions of Hindu habits in regard to diet are abjured. Not infrequently are these ultra proceedings connected with the adoption of habits of extravagance that indicate a progress decidedly in the wrong direction.

In regard to the habitations, the conveniences, and usages of the Hindus, there may be, especially among the poorer classes, little that accords with European ideas of comfort; yet no people are more characterized for personal and domestic cleanliness than the Hindus. They are peculiarly careful in all that concerns their food and its preparation. No people on earth, it may be averred, secure with the same means, or even with greater, a larger amount of physical comfort and enjoyment. The Hindu contends that eating from a fresh, clean leaf is a more delicate habit than eating from a porous vessel, that is charged with an infusion of various articles of diet. Passing the food to the mouth with the hand, properly cleansed, he holds to be better, and more free from objection, than by means of a spoon, which is alternately passed into the mouth and into the food, possibly a fluid, of which the person is partaking.

When the number of houses is sufficient to form a village, there will generally be a bazaar or two, where may be procured grain, condiments, tobacco, cloth, firewood, and other articles for domestic use. If the village be large, there will be a division of the trade into separate branches, one selling grain, another cloth, another earthenware, &c. In the village there will be a small temple, and a choultry, or public place of accommodation for travellers. These choultries are of various descriptions. In some places they are no more than a simple apartment, formed by a wall, either carried to the roof or half way, covered with leaves or tiles, having generally a good floor. This apartment will be open on one side; and as there is, ordinarily, a well connected with these places, they are found extremely convenient to travellers, either as places for refection and rest in the day, or for sleeping during the night. Some of these edifices in the south of India are large and elaborately ornamented places, built in the form of the square house already described. When surrounded with trees, and in the neighbourhood of a reservoir or river, they are of great convenience to those who are compelled to travel. Some of the choultries are open courts, or apartments open on one side, built of cut stone, with flat stone roofs, supported by sculptured pillars. The floors are generally good. But many of these places are untenable, either from their want of ventilation, or from the smell of smoke, some one having recently cooked his food in the corner, or because of the obscene character of the sculptures on the pillars. The propensity to scribble on walls, it may be remarked, is here, as in similar places, whether in ancient Pompeii or Egypt, abundantly evinced, and not infrequently in several languages.

Connected with the village choultry, there will sometimes be a shrine as well as tank, and it is therefore convenient as the place of resort; those who have leisure can repair to such a locality for the purpose of ablution, and the performance of religious service. The village school may, in some cases, be taught in the choultry. In such places the itinerant evangelist may occasionally have an opportunity of inviting the people of the village to meet him for the purposes of religious conference, and, screened from the rays of a mid-day sun, he may there expound the oracles of God. In an extended tour, the missionary often finds such places of great convenience for temporary abode and public communication with the natives.

European travellers are generally provided for, on the great lines of road, by commodious rest-houses called travellers' bungalows, erected at convenient distances of from fifteen to twenty miles. These structures are built by the Government, and generally consist of two apartments, surrounded by a verandah, with bath-rooms attached. There are offices within the enclosure. Most of these places of accommodation are kept by a pensioned sipahi, who resides close by. He opens the door on the approach of a traveller, and is in attendance to procure any needed supplies, as poultry, milk, eggs, &c.

No fee is demanded. The traveller may remain a day or night, or even longer, if necessitated to delay his journey; and on his departure enters his name in a book, stating his starting point, his destination, and his official position. He is expected also to state his opinion as to the cleanliness of the place and the attention of the keeper. Facetious persons sometimes indulge their humour by remarks, either on the journey, or the place, or possibly on the party who may occupy the apartment at the other end of the bungalow.

His Highness the Rajah of Puthucotie, near Tanjore, has an open house for Europeans, well furnished in European style, and provided with every convenience and luxury for travellers. The servants in attendance receive instruction from the party, on his arrival, as to what is desired, either for breakfast or dinner, or both, and immediately set about preparation, as if they were his own attendants in his own house. This is genuine oriental hospitality.

Towns are, in point of composition, the same as the large villages, with the difference that exists in all countries between a village and a town. Everything here wears an air of vivacity. The handsome figures of the respectable natives, in garments white as snow, contrast singularly with those who are naked from the waist. The showily, but neatly attired, slim figure of the active Hindu females, bearing on their heads various burdens, as water, grain, sweet-meats, fish, fruit, and possibly a young child on the hip; the grave and philosophic Brahman, invested with his sacerdotal string, his newly shaven head glistening in the sun-beams, are notable objects in the crowded avenues. The sectarial marks of the Hindus serve to show the divinities to which they may be attached. They consist of various streaks on the forehead, breasts, and arms. The Vaishnavas use a species of calcareous white clay, which ought to come from Dwáraká, where it is obtained from a pool in which the shepherdesses drowned themselves when they heard of Krishna's death. Some of this class of Hindus imprint two perpendicular lines from the root of the hair to the eye-brows, with a transverse streak uniting them between the eyes; and add a central perpendicular red line, with a preparation of turmeric and lime. They have also marks on the breast and on the arms: these marks are supposed to represent the weapons of Vishnu, and the goddess Lakshmi. Some wear a necklace of the wood of the tulasi, and carry a rosary of the seeds of the same plant, or of the lotus. The followers of Siva wear sectarial marks made by the ashes of burnt cow-dung, which symbolize the destruction of sin, the desiderated benefit to be sought by all religious usages.

In the streets are seen wandering half naked mendicants, smeared with ashes, distorted ascetics, comedians, jugglers, musicians, monkeys on the towers of the temples or on the tops of the houses; possibly a palanquin, occupied by a native official, is borne along by a set of lively bearers, shouting hoo-ha, hoo-ha, hari bháe, at the top of their voice, and preceded by one of their number, who clears the way for the great person, as he runs before him. A bullock-cart, drawn by a couple of handsome bullocks, may be slowly moving through the crowd. A peon, or police officer, dressed in white, with his capacious crimson turban, or a crimson girdle round his waist, and a belt across his shoulder, with a sabre attached, and having a silver plate on it, bearing an inscription of his position and office, may be witnessed in the principal streets. The sides of this avenue consist of shops or open verandahs, with the commodities disposed in full view, with their owner or salesman seated in the midst, within reach of almost all that surrounds him. The customer stands in the street and makes his purchases, probably just able to occupy a small space under the temporary shed that hangs over his head. This shed of leaves or grass is so attached to the front of the verandah, that it serves as a door or covering of the shop by night, and when lifted up and kept aloft by props in the day, it answers the purpose of a canopy.

If the town be a place for the manufacture of fabrics, some of its streets will wear an aspect peculiarly interesting to those who have been accustomed to such pursuits in the manufacturing districts of Europe. Weavers may be seen at their rude looms within their huts, while others are dressing their warps; winders are busily moving to and fro, under the shade of the trees, with the brilliantly coloured thread; men, women, and children are all engaged in the preparation of fabrics for the consumption of home and foreign trade. The streets are beautifully clean, and all the houses wear an aspect of thrift, indicating the prosperous condition of the inhabitants.

In the towns, and even the villages, there will be the appointed head men, to whom all matters of public concernment must be referred. In the larger places the authorities are more numerous, and the graduation more extended. Bankers, merchants, and all the professions needed to make up a civil community, will have their respective pursuits in these busy centres of Hindu industry and activity.

Those who are engaged in the ordinary pursuits of life are generally well ordered and industrious in their habits. Early in the morning the labourer rises, performs his ablutions, repeats his religious formulæ, and proceeds to his avocations. His morning meal, if any be taken, will, in some provinces, consist of cold rice left the preceding night, and preserved in cold water in an earthen vessel. In the middle of the day the labourer generally reposes, for at least two hours, and in some places, when no breakfast has been taken, it is customary to take a full meal of warm rice, or such solid food as may be ordinarily used. In the evening he desists from labour, about sunset, when he may bathe, sit and chat with his neighbours till his principal meal is ready. Having consumed that, he takes a little betel leaf, and, after talking over the events of the day with the members of his household, he retires to rest. In rural districts I have often observed the habits of the Hindus, and witnessed the same play of the home affection as are found among the best ordered peasantry in western countries. The husband and wife seem to be on the same terms of equality as those which obtain where the ameliorating influence of Christianity has exerted its power. In cases of domestic affliction I have seen the same solicitude manifested among the Hindus as elsewhere; the same alternations of hope and fear, as the symptoms of disease have changed their aspects; and, in some cases, I have known the husband, even at midnight, to visit the village shrine to offer up a hasty petition for relief when his wife has been exposed to the fatal consequences of a dangerous crisis.

The women, in general, attend only to domestic matters. They pound rice, carry water, cook, spin, weed the fields, and aid in time of harvest. They are deferential to their husbands, and peculiarly attached to their children, showing the greatest solicitude for their well-being and happiness.

Averse as the Brahmanised population is to the shedding of blood, as might be expected a vegetable diet is the rule—yet there are some who eat poultry, and even mutton. It may be said that the millions of India never taste through life any kind of animal food, nor do they drink anything that could intoxicate. I know members of the Christian Church who are strict vegetarians, not because they think it an impropriety to eat animal food, but because they have been from infancy unaccustomed to it. Fruit generally abounds, and may be had at a cheap rate, and therefore its use, as an article of diet, is very common for children. The prejudice of some Hindus against the practice of eating flesh is very strong; and the views they entertain of those natives and tribes who indulge in animal food are not very unlike those which the civilized entertain respecting cannibals. Soon after my arrival in the country I was conversing with a learned and rather rigid Hindu on various subjects, and incidentally mentioned the use of animal food. I asked him what the general practice might be among his own class. He replied with great emphasis, in a carefully constructed English sentence, and in a manner at once sarcastic and grave, "We Hindus do not bury the dead in our stomachs; we do not make our stomachs into burial grounds."

CHAPTER XIII.

AMUSEMENTS: CHESS, CARDS, FESTIVALS, THE DRAMA.—FEMALE AMUSEMENTS: MUSICAL RECREATION.—MARRIAGES.—FUNERALS.—BURNING THE DEAD.—THE SATI.—CHARACTER.—SOCIAL CONDITION OF HINDU FEMALES.

THE amusements and diversions of the Hindus, like many other matters connected with a people occupying so large a surface, influenced by so many circumstances incident to climate, language, literature, and various modifications of religious belief, are, of course, diversified. To attempt an account of the habits of even a large province, would be inconsistent with the design of this little work, to say nothing of so vast a continent; yet some few notices of the recreations common among the people of India seem necessary. Those who have had the opportunity of acquainting themselves with the Hindus, when they have thrown off the cares and business of life, cannot be ignorant of their vivacity. Their religious festivals, many of which are more like the merry-makings of a country wake or fair than aught besides, their various diversions, sports, and pleasant domestic or village conversations, all serve to prove that they are by no means dull and torpid.

Since one of our greatest oriental scholars, Sir William Jones, ascribes the origin of chess to the Hindus, it may not be out of place to notice, first and foremost, this intellectual game as one common among them. This game requiring, in order to efficiency, so much intelligence and sagacity, is peculiarly fitted for the mind of the Hindu, in which perspicacity and shrewdness are so strongly marked. The pieces in the Indian chess are the same in number as in Europe, but differently denominated. They stand thus:—The king, his minister; two elephants; two horses; two boats; and eight soldiers. The moves are similar to those of European nations.

Another military game, called the Pàshà, is played amid great excitement and vociferation, in marked contrast to the quiet thought and silence of the chess paper or cloth. It is played on ninety-six squares with sixteen pieces, and the moves are regulated by the throws of three dice of the usual form, and commonly made of ivory.

Cards are a source of amusement among some of the middle and upper classes; they were, in all probability, introduced from the west. European cards are used, though not exclusively, for, in some places, cards are produced with the figures of gods and goddesses, &c. upon them, instead of those common in Europe. That gaming existed in India in early times appears certain, from the statements of ancient writers, who mention monarchs that were so addicted to the vice as thereby to bring down ruin upon themselves. Among the peasantry at the present time, when games of hazard are connected with gain and loss, they rarely go beyond the value of a few shells, which in some provinces pass as money.

The Hindus are generally a sociable people. The bond of caste, while it repels those who do not belong to the class, has the effect of promoting among the members of the same caste a fellow feeling and union. And such is the disposition to social intercourse that the Brahman even may be seen laying aside his pretensions to exclusiveness, and uniting with the Sudra in the same amusement. In the open verandah of a private dwelling, in public places on the sides of roads, or under the protection of some shady tree, may frequently be seen little knots of natives brought together by love of society and gossip; and there are not wanting in most places those who spend their time, as did some of the Athenians, in telling and hearing some new thing. This disposition of the Hindu becomes evident to those who are accustomed to travel. In almost all places the traveller is visited in his temporary abode by some busy-body, whom it is often difficult to repel, unless, indeed, he may call to his aid one of his attendants, who, less scrupulous about giving offence, will signify, often in very plain terms, that the intruder had better be about his own business.

The annual festivities at Durga Puja, especially in Bengal, are of a social as well as religious character. They continue for about eight days, during which period every kind of business is suspended. The jubilant character of this festival exceeds all ordinary bounds. The demonstrations are universal. In all the large towns, in the villages and hamlets, music is everywhere heard, and the mutual expressions of goodwill circulated among the votaries of the celebrated goddess, remind the European of the season of Christmas in Christian lands. Though the Durga Puja is a religious festival, it is one of the most exciting occasions in the Bengal year. Every one vies with his fellow in producing his best on this occasion. There is now, if at all, a display of wealth, in order to give all the pomp of circumstance to the great annual observance. The year's thrift is dissipated in a few days. As the ceremonies of this annual celebration, under its general religious aspect, are noticed elsewhere, I shall in this place allude merely to its influence on the enjoyments of home. Some of them are of a very questionable character as will appear from a few details.

The image of the goddess is placed on one side of the inner court of the house in which the festivities take place. The goddess is worshipped from day to day, and on the third day bloody sacrifices are presented to her. At the conclusion of the daily ceremonies, Brahmans and friends are feasted with various kinds of sweetmeats, fruits, and curds.

In the large mansions of the wealthy, provision is made for the entertainment of distinguished European visitors, who were in former days, more than latterly, wont to honour this festival with their presence; the object with such, being to witness the natches or dances. On these occasions the saloons are brilliantly illuminated, and the refreshments, prepared after the European style, are laid out in great

profusion. Under such circumstances the songs and representations will be restrained within the bounds of propriety, out of deference to the refinements of European visitors; but when no such motives prevail, the songs are of the most filthy character, and the movements that accompany the music are objectionable in the highest degree. Of course the nature of the amusement varies with the character and tastes of the parties who conduct the ceremonies. In some houses several groups of musicians and natch-girls are placed in different parts of the same area. The opulent procure the most distinguished performers, and not infrequently large sums are spent in procuring the attendance of girls from distant parts of the country. Some of the finest young women engaged in this service come from Cashmere. They are generally distinguished for great personal beauty, and large sums are laid out in their dress and ornaments. They are attired in fabrics the most delicate, almost to transparency, so that the movements of every limb, and almost every muscle, are visible. They perform before the musicians, who are seated in a group on rugs close to the wall of the court, and effect their movements and gesticulations, often indecent in the extreme, with gentle and measured pace, uttering with the sweetest accents the most filthy songs that the most refined in pollution have composed for these occasions. You may pass on from one degree to another as regards the mode of celebrating this great festival, and witness in the course of the same round of visits the most extraordinary exhibitions that sound and gesture can produce. In some of the homesteads, the air is filled with the loudest and most uproarious songs, teeming with the foulest language. The female inmates of many of these houses, the matrons, the young girls, all may be observed peeping from behind the crowds that throng the apartment, giving expression to the most delighted sensibility. The moral effect of these licentious amusements and impure representations is most pernicious. Combining, as the great festival does, the grossest idolatry, boisterous and obscene merriment, indecent exhibitions, and every form of licentiousness, it may be regarded as one of the most injurious of the Hindu usages to the moral health of the community at large. It may be remarked here, that except in the form of the natch, domestic dancing does not exist among the Hindus: it is considered highly indecorous for a woman of good character to dance. The English ladies would consider themselves ill complimented, if they could hear what the Hindus say of their nocturnal movements in the dance.

Theatrical representations among the Hindus are very much like the exhibitions just noticed. The dramatic art about the period of the Christian era, it is admitted, was of a respectable character, but at the present time it is greatly degenerated. In some parts of the country, these amusements are got up in the open air, or with the simple accommodation of a temporary shed in a grove. The indecent passages in the histories of some of the popular divinities are the most prominent staple of these demoralizing scenes. On some occasions I have known in my vicinity these amusements kept up with the greatest spirit from eight or nine in the evening till the dawn of day. It may be necessary to say, that at these nocturnal amusements no females are present except those of abandoned character.[1]

The public reading of popular literature, as a source of amusement, is not uncommon in some parts of India. Some wealthy person engages a couple of learned persons to perform the task, and where the populace is permitted to share in the benefit, these persons take their places on an elevated verandah, which is duly lighted up for the occasion. The reader is seated, and in musical cadence recites the verses in consecutive order. The expositor then takes up the stanza, and reciting the lines one by one, gives a free translation of them, interpolating his version with such elucidatory matter as his genius and scholarship may suggest. The people, in

[1] The Roman Catholics in Southern India and Ceylon long ago introduced religious dramas, which were exhibited in the vicinity of their churches. I once saw a stage connected with one of the churches near Trichonopoly; and a friend of mine informed me that a similar stage existed after the commencement of the present century in one of the old churches of North Ceylon.

large numbers, seat themselves around under the trees or verandahs within a convenient distance for listening, and in this manner become acquainted with celebrated Hindu works illustrative of the mythology, the festivals, and the popular superstitions of the country.

This very brief account of the pastimes of the Hindus would be imperfect, if it included no notice of those in-door amusements, which are almost exclusively pursued by the female part of the population and children. Some notice may be interesting, not merely as showing the habits of an ancient people, but as illustrating to some extent the condition of the Hindu female, concerning which it is confessedly difficult to procure and set forth a correct account.

The females of the upper classes in northern India, as well as the males, engage in some of the in-door amusements already named; cards, for instance, are sometimes used by the females of the superior classes. The following games are likewise indulged in by both sexes in the upper ranks of society in Bengal:—

Ashtá-Kashte. This game is played on a board of twenty-five squares, with sixteen pieces of small *cowries* (shells), which are placed on four sides of the figure. For regulating the moves of the pieces, four large cowries, instead of dice, are used. The pieces have the same motion. The throws are only five in number—one, two, three, four, eight; the first being called Kashte and the last Ashtá, and hence the name of the game. It is played by four persons, and is said to be finished, when all the pieces, traversing through the length and breadth of the board, enter into the central square—the heaven of rest and undisturbed repose; and those persons whose pieces first attain this position are said to win the game.

Mongul Patán. This is a singular game, especially for ladies, since it is wholly of a military character, and is therefore a military pastime. It is the representation of a battle between the Monguls and the Patáns. The battle-field is accurately drawn, consisting of sixteen squares; within this figure is inscribed a large square. On one side is arranged the Mongul army in a triangular form, and on the opposite side the Patán army. Each army consists of sixteen pieces, the moves of which are regulated, not by chance, but by the skill of the players. It is less ingenious than chess, inasmuch as the moves of the pieces are uniform. The fascination, nevertheless, which this less complicated game produces on the softer sex, is fully equal to that excited in more robust minds by the pastime called *par excellence* royal.

Das-Panchish is another favourite game of native women. Its board is similar to that of the Páshá; the moves of the pieces, which are sixteen in number, are, however, regulated, not by their dice, but by seven cowries, thrown either on the floor or against an inclined plane. The throws are two, three, four, six ten, twelve, and twenty-five, the game deriving its name from two of them, ten (Das), and twenty-five (Panchish). This play is as exciting as the Páshá; its animating character renders it one of the most favourite games of the ladies of Bengal.

There are other pastimes of a similar character to those described, by means of which the Hindu female, whose time is not better employed, seeks to beguile her leisure. The prescribed limits of this little book do not, however, permit any further account of these matters.

Among the peasantry are found various amusements. The sling, kite-flying, a game similar to bat and ball, played with two sticks, one longer than the other, wrestling, and various other sources of recreation are seen in every part of the country, especially among the rural population.

The itinerant jugglers, both men and women, are everywhere patronized by the natives of India; and some of them perform the most extraordinary tricks by sleight of hand.

Musical recreations are among the most common in the country; not in the temples and on festive occasions merely may the most jubilant sounds of instrumental music be heard, but in the homestead, even of the humblest, sounds everywhere greet the ear. Where instruments are not practicable, the voice of melody(?) is substituted. Hence the cultivator, as before stated, in drawing water, regulates his acts by musical cadences. The common cart-driver, the boatman, the shepherd, all seem to enjoy the pleasures of song. It may be safe to say that few excel in music, either vocal or instrumental, although it is equally so that the Hindus are extremely fond of it, and generally prefer their own to that of Europe. This preference may, in part, arise from habit, and partly from the character of their vocalism, which generally may be said to be adapted to aid the sense designed to be expressed. The Hindus often succeed in giving great effect to certain sentiments by the animated and measured tones in which they recite or chant their pieces. The utter want of clear enunciation in song, which often in Europe attends even church psalmody, is perhaps to be regretted, as at variance with the design, especially of sacred song. I have heard intelligent Hindus animadvert on this feature of European singing with great force. I remember when in Calcutta, during the period of the late Lord William Bentinck's administration, it was said that on the occasion of a general gathering of the native and European gentry at the Government house, his lordship had taken special pains to provide a good band; in the course of the evening one of the native gentlemen, when the conversation turned on the character of the English, and their superiority over the Hindus, observed, that he thought the superiority could not be denied except in regard to music, in which he thought the Hindus had the advantage.

Marriage ceremonies among the Hindus are conducted with great display; even the poor on these occasions do all in their power to secure such accompaniments as may call attention to the joyous event. Where the property of the parties amounts to nothing in reality, it is not uncommon to see the bride especially decked out in a profusion of jewels, borrowed for the occasion possibly from a native Banker, with whom they had been deposited as security for money lent.

Among the wealthy in Calcutta it is not unusual for a marriage ceremonial to cost something like a hundred thousand rupees.

Marriage, as before stated, is one of the sacraments of the Hindus. To detail even one of the forms of celebration would far exceed our limits. The following recapitulation of that mostly observed may suffice by way of example. Colebrooke thus states the leading circumstances of a Hindu marriage :—

"The bridegroom goes in procession to the house where the bride's father resides, and is there welcomed as a guest. The bride is given to him by her father, in the form usual at every donation, and their hands are bound together with grass. He clothes the bride with an upper and lower garment, and the skirts of her mantle and his are tied together. The bridegroom makes oblations to fire, and the bride drops rice on it as an oblation. The bridegroom solemnly takes her hand in marriage. She treads on a stone and muller. They walk round the fire. The bride steps seven times, conducted by the bridegroom, and he then dismisses the spectators, the marriage being now complete and irrevocable. In the evening of the same day the bride sits down on a bull's hide, and the bridegroom points out to her the polar star, as an emblem of stability. They then partake of a meal. The bridegroom remains three days at the house of the bride's father; on the fourth day he conducts her to his own house in solemn procession. She is there welcomed by his kindred; and the solemnity ends with oblations to fire."

Hindu legislators insist on the duty of the father to provide a suitable match for his daughter, and it is considered improper to defer the choice till mature years permit the parties to exercise their own choice, or to express their sentiments on the subject. The rule is for the parents to settle the matter whilst the parties are children. The ceremony should take place before the tenth year. It is rare, therefore, for a marriage to be consummated till long after its solemnization. The recitation of prayers on this occasion constitutes it a religious ceremony.

The ceremonies observed at funerals are worthy of a brief notice. The moment it is ascertained that the spirit has departed, the near female relatives indulge in the most dismal expressions of grief and lamentation. It is remarkable, however, that in seasons of general pestilence no such demonstrations accompany the solemn event. Regarding such visitations, like the Jews, as special inflictions from the Almighty, they are silent amid the direst bereavements. There are several touching references to a similar usage among the Jews, as may be seen by reference to the major and minor prophets. On these solemn occasions the whole neighbourhood rings with the doleful expressions of sorrow. The body is bathed, perfumed, decked with flowers, and deposited on a temporary bier, or litter, which is also decorated in a tasteful manner by means of leaves, &c., and generally this is overshadowed with a canopy. I have seen some of these funeral litters of the most imposing dimensions, rising perhaps twenty feet above the ground, the body being dressed as in life, and stretched upon a platform constructed for its reception. This shrine, borne by a sufficient number of men, moves along the chief thoroughfare, preceded by men who spread the way with cloths, that the procession may, throughout the length of the last journey, pass over a carpeted surface to the tomb or funeral pyre. On these occasions several cloths are used, so that by taking up the one just passed over and carrying it forward, there is kept up an uninterrupted expression of respect for the deceased.

The funeral pyre, formed of firewood, may be three or four feet high, as many wide, and sufficiently long for the corpse. Clarified butter and scented oils are poured on the pyre to give intensity and fragrance to the flame. After the Brahmanical ceremony is over, a near relative applies the fire and the body is consumed. The parties who are in special charge may seat themselves for a time to watch the progress of incremation, possibly indulge in the expression of common-places on the vanity of human life, quoting well-known lines from the popular writers on religious and moral sentiment; they afterwards purify themselves by prescribed ablutions.

Several of the female relations and friends meet on the eighth day after the death, and renew their lamentations, alluding generally to the virtues, real or assumed, of the deceased. In this custom some women excel greatly in the skill they display in enumerating the good acts and habits of the deceased, and the importance that attached to him in relation to the bereaved survivors. He is compared to all things animate and inanimate, esteemed useful, ornamental or valuable to man in social life, and to the immortal gods themselves, whose envious dispositions are sometimes represented as the cause of the calamity that has come on them. Some of these laments are touching and exquisite.

It has been stated that the funeral ceremonies of some illustrious persons have been known to cost fifty thousand pounds sterling. The annual ceremony performed to a deceased ancestor, is an important one, whose due observance is regarded as specially beneficial to the deceased. When Brahmans are feasted on the occasion of these obsequies, the spirits of deceased ancestors are said to be present as the invisible spectators of these approved acts of devotion. Under this and similar sentiments, the Hindu is most solicitous about male offspring that this ceremony may be duly performed. The name of a son, Puttra, literally refers to the supposed virtue of his act as the performer of the obsequies; the word means literally one who liberates from hell.

The practice of *Sati*, the burning of the widow alive with the corpse of her deceased husband, once so prevalent in India, has been abolished throughout the British provinces. The distinguished statesman before named, Lord William Bentinck, put an end to the cruel practice. It is said occasionally to take place in provinces beyond the influence of British rule, but it is believed the cases are few. For ages the foul rite was practised; and however incredible it may appear to us, there can be no doubt that the ceremony of self-immolation was often entered on by deluded victims of superstition with the greatest alacrity. A case is recorded that happened at Korimbazar, in Bengal, wherein the party not only refused the admonitions of relatives, friends, and Europeans of distinction; but as a proof of heroic courage, she put her finger into the fire, and held it there for a considerable time, afterwards putting fire into one hand by means of the other, she sprinkled incense upon it, and fumigated the attendant Brahmans. The preparatory ceremonies being completed, this heroine, with a firm step, mounted the pyre, and prostrating herself on the corpse, she embraced it, and resigned herself to destruction under a canopy of smoke and flame. Eight females attached to one man have been known to devote themselves to death on his funeral pyre. How, it may be inquired, can we account for such acts as these? What is the all-impelling motive that induces such self-sacrifice? It is the dogma enunciated by false and selfish priests, who teach that such an act of virtue possesses a merit sufficient not only to rescue the deceased husband from the abodes of torment, but to secure re-union and the positive enjoyments of a sensuous paradise for an almost boundless period—for thirty millions of years in the heaven of Indra. With a belief so monstrous, we are not to wonder that before British beneficence interposed its authority, there were found thousands who were content to brave the devouring flames of the funeral pyre to obtain such a boon.

From what has appeared in the brief references made in this volume to the usages, civil and religious, and the manners and customs of the highly civilized and ancient people whose institutions have been imperfectly considered in these pages, we must conclude them to be in many respects an extraordinary and interesting people. Such they are, as seen from almost any point of view; it is however difficult, if not impossible, to present, under one general definition, adequate ideas of the character of the Hindus. Forgetting the extent and diversified climates of the vast area included under the single term India, persons who judge of it from limited information are apt to come to very imperfect, and even erroneous, notions of its salubrity and productions. In like manner those who have seen but little of its inhabitants, except as official duty, or commercial intercourse, may have brought them into contact with, perhaps, the most exceptionable portion of the community; or those who have gathered their opinions from books, written possibly by the partially informed, may form very imperfect and equally incorrect notions of the people of India. Foreigners ordinarily can but obtain a very limited knowledge of any people. In India there are peculiar difficulties in the way of our becoming intimately and extensively acquainted with its inhabitants; religion and superstition, and exclusive social habits repel the foreigner,—these draw a veil over the inner life of the millions of the people of that country. We may not penetrate into the family of the Hindu, and we cannot therefore see the character where it has its fullest and best manifestation. When seen in places of business, under the influence of selfishness and passion, men do not generally appear to the best advantage; nor are always the better portion of a community found in such circumstances. Travellers are well aware, that it were highly irrelevant to judge of any nation from what is met with in the intercourse incident to the superficial contact which travel permits. It would be so at home. How much deception, how much selfishness, and carelessness prevail among those the traveller has to do with almost everywhere! Amid the conflicting opinions that have been recorded concerning the Hindus, it becomes one to observe modesty in the expression of any very decided judgment. It may be said to their advantage that those who have had the greatest opportunity for observation, and the most extensive intercourse with them, being at the same time in a position, from an extensive acquaintance with other nations, to offer an opinion of them, are disposed to give the best report of them. The more extended the knowledge of human nature is, the greater is the advantage under which the Hindu character appears.

There are, however, characteristic differences in the various provinces which need to be duly weighed in relation to the physical causes that originate them. Nothing can be more manifest than the difference existing between the Bengali and the Hindu of the north-western part of India. In Ceylon the superior manliness of the mountaineer over the Cingalese of the maritime provinces is most remarkable. Where climate and other circumstances necessitate their cultivation, we find traits vigorous and active are produced; whilst in a warmer region, fertile, moist, and enervating, there is a greater tendency to indolence and inaction. It is not the heat alone which produces the greater lethargy; the deserts of Arabia produce no such effects, because their sterility obliges action: and in India, both among the agricultural and commercial portions of the communities, the most persevering activity and industry are met with. The Hindu peasantry, in many parts of India, will not suffer in comparison with any peasantry in any part of the world. There will be found among them a great amount of simplicity, and some of their social virtues entitle them to admiration. Their industry and perseverance are often as remarkable as are other excellent qualities. What an amount of labour the palanquin bearer is capable of! Some of the coolies, on journeys bearing heavy burdens, will travel an incredible distance within a comparatively short time. The native troops in our Indian army have signalized themselves on many occasions by deeds of valour that would have given lustre to any arms. Under adequate motives the native of India is capable of almost any achievement.

The remarks just made are equally applicable to European residents; though it may be true that some suffer the greatest lassitude, and may be able to exert themselves but very little in India, it is also true that the majority of Europeans are there as fully engaged, and do as much as they would in their native land. In the office, in the study, in the school-room, or abroad in travel, I have known many who perform as much as any men could possibly accomplish under the most favourable circumstances of climate. Where intellectual and moral vigour are associated with a sound constitution and industrious habits, Europeans in India effect as much as their contemporaries in any part of Europe.

In estimating the character of the Hindus, it cannot certainly be said that love of truth is a national virtue. It is astonishing how strong the tendency is to falsehood. There seems to be an instinctive distrust of truth even where its fullest expression would best serve the party who has to bear his testimony. Even then his disposition to exaggeration and falsehood is apparent. This is so well known by those who have had much to do with the Hindu, that testimony is not generally regarded as evidence. It requires not much sagacity to see how the political history of the country has tended to induce and confirm this trait of character in its inhabitants. The despotism in one form or other that has so long prevailed, and the consequent oppression attendant thereon, must have rendered it difficult to make way without fraud. Deception and arts of cunning, under such circumstances, being the only means at the command of the inferior portions of the community for gaining their ends, and securing the plainest rights, they would resort to them as only way of avoiding certain ruin.

The natives of India have suffered immensely from the absence of salutary political institutions ; systematic oppression has for ages paralysed their energies, deprived them of their natural manliness, and reduced them to the lowest condition consistent with the preservation of the race. Their own countrymen, the Zemindars, have degraded them to the abject condition of brutes ; these are the men who have most cruelly oppressed them, and must be considered the greatest enemies they have. The average return for labour in some agricultural districts does not give a much greater sum than two shillings a month! This is a speaking fact.

For centuries India had no equitable laws, no stable government; it had no salutary religious instruction enforced by the sanction of divine authority, and therefore, that its people became false and vicious is not to be wondered at.

The Hindus are a clever and acute people; their languages, their literature, their arts and manufactures, prove this. Some of the common labourers evince a readiness and skill in various ways that is most remarkable; a gardener, or ordinary labourer, will take his place among carpenters or masons, when circumstances authorize it, and execute the rougher kinds of work in a very satisfactory manner. A common Cooly, accompanying one as a porter through the jungle, will cook an excellent meal of rice and curry, with the simplest appliances. Generally, as servants, they are unequalled. Their attention, in cases of sickness, is remarkable, and, excepting in the matter of veracity, they may be trusted to any extent; their attachment to their master, and their instinctive anticipation of his wants, are equally admirable.

The Hindu possesses great tact in devising means for accomplishing his ends, and often they are as simple as they are effective. His pocket knife, with its stylus, is almost equal to the axe of the divine architect that fabricated the idol at Jagannath. He requires no time-piece; for by day he marks the extremity of his shadow with his eye, in relation to a stone or something before him, and then measures its length by his bare feet, and from a poetic formula that fits the solar year, he ascertains the time; or he may erect the second finger on one of his hands by its middle joint, and allowing the shadow to fall on the joints of the other fingers, he determines the time within a few minutes: the hand is placed flat on a plain surface. In the night you call him up to ascertain the time, and he will consult the constellations, and in their absence he will tell you, possibly, from the state of the dew on surrounding objects, that may fall at certain known periods. As a servant, the Hindu is, as it were, yourself reproduced, an agent or instrument instinct with your own volition: he is what you have power to make him.

There is a vein of pleasantry generally combined with thoughtfulness and courtesy, that renders the Hindu very agreeable, and often highly amusing: of course, this is not frequently seen by Europeans, because their relative position generally forbids unrestrained freedom. His perception of the absurd, the ridiculous, the pretentious and the hypocritical, in speech or conduct, is remarkable; and the manner in which he can rebuke such exceptionable traits with appropriate national proverbs, is often amusing and instructive.

The Hindu is distinguished for his keen insight into character, and combining with this faculty the most dogged perseverance in the pursuit of his ends, he rarely fails of success for want of perspicacity. He is not generally very scrupulous about his means, and he is, therefore, ready to adopt any manœuvre to secure his object. He perceives instinctively the character of the person he has to deal with, marking his idiosyncrasies, his temperament, and his weaknesses, with the greatest readiness;—he will either soothe or irritate as may best avail to secure the end in view.

The Hindus are generally extremely litigious, and often spend in the maintenance of a lawsuit a larger sum than is to be gained by a successful issue of the case. Mock trials are sometimes got up in secret for the purpose of training the witnesses for their appearance in the real court. In the event of a false case being got up, nothing is thought of a defence based alike in falsehood. A friend of mine informed me, not long ago, that in a claim made in a district court by a plaintiff for a certain sum, the case was decided in favour of the defendant, on the ground of a receipt he filed, showing that he had paid the money. It came to the magistrate's knowledge afterwards, on the best authority, that the claim was false, and the defence equally so: the party adopted the defence he set up, because it was the only method he could adopt for avoiding the loss he was exposed to.

There is much truth in the following judgment of the Hindu character; its author had enjoyed ample means for forming an opinion, and it is quite certain that he had made the fullest use of his opportunities for arriving at the decision recorded. He says,—"Their great defect is a want of manliness. Their slavish constitution, their blind superstition, their extravagant mythology, the subtleties and verbal distinctions of their philosophy, the languid softness of their poetry, their effeminate manners, their love of artifice and delay, their submissive temper, their dread of change, the delight they take in puerile fables, and their neglect of national history, are so many proofs of the absence of the moral robust qualities of disposition and intellect throughout the mass of the nation." But notwithstanding the deteriorating effects of religion and the prevalence of blind superstition, the demoralizing influence of political despotism and oppression, the Hindus are possessed of many estimable qualities: some of the tribes are endowed with a high spirit, enthusiastic courage, and generous self-devotion, and almost all are distinguished by gentleness of manners and softness of heart. If affectionate attention to their families, kindness to neighbours, inoffensiveness and amiability, be social qualities that entitle their possessors to our esteem and approbation, then the Hindus, at least many of them, and especially the rural population, are worthy of occupying a high place among civilized nations.

SOCIAL CONDITION OF HINDU FEMALES.

The account which has been given of the social characteristics of India would be imperfect without some further particulars on the condition of the Hindu female. It is a subject of considerable difficulty, concerning which exaggerated notions are entertained, both in India and in England. That the females of India do not occupy that position in society which has been attained by the women of European countries may be conceded, but it is not true that she is degraded to the extent which is frequently represented. Some of the sayings quoted in proof of the depressed condition of the females of India might seem to prove her utter bondage and servitude. One has heard her represented as occupying much the same place in the homestead as that assigned to cattle; and as the victim of unrelenting oppression, even worse than the inferior animals in condition, because possessed of instincts and sentiments of which they are not capable. That they are immured to an extent not common in Europe is certain, and that in the remote periods of Hindu history women occupied a different position in society is clear from the testimony of their own writers, and the pictorial representations of domestic manners which are now extant. It may be difficult to say what has led to the alteration which has taken place. The political changes, the invasion and despotism of the Mohammedans may have obliged the seclusion of females, now so general. That Hindu females at one time enjoyed the advantages of intellectual culture is certain. The being deprived of this privilege at the present day, is the chief disadvantage under which Hindu women are placed. Were they allowed the privilege of cultivating their minds by the salutary exercises of reading and writing, they would, notwithstanding their exclusion from some of the habits of Europeans, such as greater freedom of intercourse with society, be on a footing of equality with the majority of European females. Some of the usages of the Hindus throw around the female character guards which are of the greatest advantage both to her and society. From observation and comparison with the state of things in Europe, and the facts of social life in India, I confess that in the latter country the female, among the lower orders, is under restraints, and protection, and guidance, that if introduced into Europe would go far to remove some of the most fruitful sources of domestic disorder and discomfort now experienced. The independence of the youthful female, which some plead for, is a serious injury to herself and society, as might easily be proved by any one conversant with the state of things among the labouring classes of England.

That misconception as to the real condition of the Hindu female exists in England is certain, as appears from what is written, and also from the opinions frequently expressed on the subject in conversation. Much that is written is unguardedly stated, and liable to be misunderstood, especially by those who have not had the means from personal observation of judging of the real value of such statements; and much that is said is not infrequently the result of false inference from known facts, or from the want of a larger and better acquaintance with the real state of Hindu females in the homes of India. A remark made by a lady some months ago suggests this paragraph. Speaking of the condition of women in India, she said, that an officer, who had recently come to England, had been giving some account of their condition among the native troops, and he had stated that such was the utter disregard of propriety, that the men thought nothing of transferring their wives from motives of the most unworthy kind. It may not be imagined that the officer who made this statement intended to deceive, or to misrepresent the actual state of things; it is more probable that he was really unacquainted with the relation in which the women of the camp stood to the native troops, and therefore inferred that some transaction that had passed under his notice was a case of transferring a wife, whereas it is certain she could be no other than an abandoned common woman. We may take the following statement made by an Indian official, who, in a work containing an account of his own rambles and recollections, gives a very different view of the native soldier, and the condition of his wife. Colonel Sleeman, whose testimony we are about to introduce, is, let it be understood, an honest and unprejudiced writer, whose experience of Indian matters was derived from long and intimate connexion with the country. Speaking of one of the most "honourable characteristics of the native soldier,—one which contrasts most favourably with the selfish, and often brutal prodigality of his European brethren in arms," he says,—"They never take their wives or children with them to their regiments, or to the places where their regiments are stationed. They leave them with their fathers or elder brothers, and enjoy their society only when they return on furlough. Three-fourths of their income are sent home to provide for their comfort and subsistence, and to embellish that home in which they hope to spend the winter of their days. The knowledge that any neglect of the duty they owe to their distant families will be immediately reported by their native officers and brother soldiers, and ultimately communicated to the heads of their families, acts as a salutary check on their conduct; and I believe that there is hardly a native regiment in the Bengal army in which the twenty drummers, who are Christians, and have their families with the regiment, do not cause more trouble to the officers than the whole eight hundred Sipahis."

The circumstances of the Hindu female are confessedly difficult to depict, and the more so, because of the apparently contradictory positions she may be represented to occupy. The degradation of the Hindu widow is perhaps the most deplorable. The laws and usages relating to marriage among the people of India are such, that we, as Europeans, can hardly conceive how they affect the mind of a native. On the death of her husband, the widow is stripped of her ornaments, her head is shaved, and she is thenceforth and for ever clad in the robe of widowhood. These conditions to a Hindu female are in themselves sufficiently grievous, fond as she is of ornaments, and most particularly proud of her luxuriant tresses. She is not merely bereft of these externals, but deprived of all sympathy and respect; and may be loaded with reproaches and execration as the cause of her husband's death, by reason of her evil destiny, thus fulfilled by an infliction that makes her a widow, and the parents of her deceased husband child-less. If the widow be a Brahmani, she is permitted only one meal a-day. She may not contract a second marriage. Nothing could be more heinous, nothing more reproachful to herself and her family. The Hindu female is thus by the institutions and usages of her country subjected to every species of degradation that can befall a human being in society; and we may therefore infer that, with such prospects before her, the bereaved have sometimes chosen self-immolation to continued existence under such circumstances.

This condition of the Hindu female, in relation to marriage and widowhood, may induce a severe view of the position of the sex generally; and the more so, when it is recollected that in some places the custom to betroth the future wife to her future husband when a mere child, not only deprives her of all right of choice; and of the exercise of private judgment in a matter involving the most important of all relations; but in the event of the man's death before the marriage is consummated, the betrothment being held of the essence of a marriage, she becomes by his decease a widow, and as such she is treated. She may not in future marry, and is therefore subjected to the thousand vexations, mortifying annoyances and indignities peculiar to this condition. This being the case, the usage, the custom of immemorial antiquity, there are thousands of widows in that fair land of ten or twelve years of age, yea, of the tender and helpless age of comparative childhood. In such abhorrent usages and practices we have considerations well fitted to move our sympathies and indignation too, and hence we may derive very powerful motives for promoting every means that may tend to place the Hindu female in her legitimate social position.

In estimating the character and condition of the Hindu female, some are in danger of a wrong judgment, from ascribing too great an importance to matters that are purely adventitious. Climate and religious sentiment, and the moral and political circumstances of a people, have all more or less to do with national usage and national taste. The degradation of a race does not arise from matters that are connected with the free choice of individuals. The majority of Hindu females, it may, we think, be safely affirmed, are as content with their lot, and in a condition quite as agreeable to themselves as are their European sisters; and the majority have quite as much influence, in all that relates to the sphere of female duty, as any enlightened and educated woman would wish to exert. She may be accustomed to eat alone, and after her husband, to walk behind him when abroad, and to be deprived of intercourse with strangers, but these things she prefers. We are not to seek her disadvantages in these external and accidental usages—they are to be sought and found too in other matters to which attention may now be briefly directed.

The Hindu female is degraded and disadvantaged chiefly because she is deprived of mental culture. She is not permitted to see the world, nor has she any desire to do so. In youth, by her docile and industrious habits in the common offices of domestic life, she seeks to please her parents and her superiors. When she becomes a wife, her only gratification arises from the attention her husband bestows on her, and from those in-door amusements in which she may choose to take a part. Her mind is not exercised on any object beyond those of immediate interest. The resources of books and society she has not. The ornaments with which she decorates her person are the substitutes for the mental culture which would form a far higher and more valuable embellishment. Her moral faculties are not more ennobled than her mental powers. The virtue she strives to preserve inviolate is that of continence; and in respectable families, as we are informed by competent and unquestionable authority, the Hindu female is rarely chargeable with a breach of conjugal fidelity. Beyond this the moral sense is but little exercised, and the religious feelings are but partially, if at all, cultivated or developed; she is just what prejudice and superstition can produce. Of necessity her notions of God are exceedingly scanty; the necessity for atoning mercy never enters her thoughts. She visits a temple at some special festival, possibly frequents a sacred stream or reservoir for ablutionary purposes, and she may habitually perform some trivial ceremony, to avert evil from herself or infant. She is devotedly attached to her offspring. Her attention to its wants and whims is most remarkable. She will submit readily to any self-sacrifice or to any amount of inconvenience to promote its comfort or to obviate its sufferings. In maternal kindness the Hindu female is not surpassed by any female in the world, whether savage or civilized. In many respects the Hindu female ordinarily occupies a position that cannot be greatly excepted to by the most fastidious. In her relation

to her family, in her freedom as regards the instincts that connect her with domestic life, generally as the object of conjugal affection, and always as the revered object of filial love and obedience, the Hindu female inherits a large share of domestic enjoyment. But destitute as she is of intellectual culture and religious knowledge, the maternal instinct, for which she is so eminently distinguished, often leads to laxity of discipline; and her superstition is her only measure, as the spiritual instructress and guide of her children. It will, however, be found that her natural sagacity, her aptness to imitate the examples she may have witnessed, and the depth of her moral feelings, often raise her to a justness of perception in matters of ordinary concernment that combine to form a superior woman. And when conscience, the internal monitor which never fails to make known the work of the law written in the heart, is consulted and followed, as doubtless it is in many most remarkable instances, you have in the Hindu housewife a wonderful example of conjugal fidelity, maternal love, scrupulous cleanliness, domestic economy, kindness, and good neighbourhood. It is often very pleasing, in extended and intimate intercourse with the Hindus, to see so much in the husband and in the son respectively of profound regard for the judgment and well-being of the wife, the mother; and as opportunity may occasionally permit us to witness, of its reciprocation on her part. A highly cultivated Hindu of my acquaintance, who was in the habit of speaking of his father and mother in terms of great veneration, told me that on one occasion, as a boy, he was travelling by palanquin with his mother, and on the way he manifested some impatience at the slowness of their progress, and objurgated the bearers in somewhat harsh terms. When they put down the palanquin opposite the portico of a temple dedicated to Ganésha, to permit their drinking water at a well close by, she expressed her sorrow that he had used such language to those who were so usefully engaged in promoting their comfort by bearing him on their shoulders, and told him to get out of the palanquin and join his hands and ask forgiveness at the shrine of Ganésha Other examples I have often witnessed equally remarkable, in proof of the existence and exercise of much that is admirable in the several relations of domestic life.

Possessed of so many worthy characteristics as the Hindu female is, it may easily be conceived how overwhelming is her grief in the hour of affliction. When bereft of husband or of child, she has not those sources of consolation which, among Christians, have created so wonderful a change in the aspects of the tomb. Neither the transcendental doctrines of Pantheism, nor the theory of Metempsychosis, can alleviate the pangs of separation, or irradiate the darkness of the grave. When once the animating spirit is departed, all hope of future union is gone. The prospects, boundless and eternal, that faith opens into the inheritance of the saints in light; the glories of the many mansions in a Father's house; the ineffable realities of the beatific vision; the crown of righteousness, the palms of victory, the eternal weight of glory, that lie beyond the brief sleep of the grave,—have no place in the Hindu system. Nor can that system authorize the entertainment of the touching sentiments contained in the numerous epithets found in the Book of God, wherein the Eternal is presented as the Father of the fatherless and the husband of the widow. The Hindu female is absolutely hopeless as regards the beloved objects she mourns; she pours out her soul in the most touching strains, and overwhelmed with sorrow contrasts her former enjoyments with present bereavement. It may be in running through the numerous traits of excellence that attached to departed worth, she extracts additional pain from the beautiful similes in which she arrays the beloved one she laments, but in all this fertility of grief that magnifies her loss, she utters no sentiment such as we find in the simple inscriptions on the tombs of early Christians; future re-union in eternal life Hinduism cannot promise. Here then we may seek, and here we may find, the destitution of the Hindu female. And need it be added, there remains one only means of meeting that destitution? The Gospel of the grace of God alone illustrates life and immortality.

Efforts for the education and enlightenment of the Hindu female, it were almost superfluous to say, must spring from without, either directly or indirectly; for although there is no absolute prohibition against a female acquiring knowledge educationally, such is the innate and hereditary prejudice against it in society, that it amounts to a moral and almost sacred dissuasive. Usage, which among Asiatic nations generally is so potent, so far as the efforts of her nation are concerned, has stamped her destiny in relation to useful learning and authorized religious teaching. Till Christian benevolence originated them, no schools existed for the instruction of Hindu females. None but those abandoned women who are connected with the service of the temples, were permitted to learn to read; at least not since the present phase of Hindu society obtained its ascendency. The unhappy women alluded to acquire letters that they may the more readily acquaint themselves with the lyrics of their service. This exclusive custom may have exercised some influence on the usages of society. The fact that none but the abandoned read, may have led to its discontinuance among the virtuous. And it is not improbable that the production of an inferior and exceptionable literature, not at all fitted for female reading, may also have had something to do with the present restriction.

Be the origin of the present exclusiveness what it may, there can be no doubt that the subject demands the serious consideration of the Christian philanthropist. The position of the female in the social economy in all countries, demands that she should be possessed of the highest mental and moral culture,—I am not now alluding to accomplishments,—and especially is it important among the Hindus, because, as may be demonstrated, women among them have a most extraordinary influence over the young. It is indeed gratifying to know that there are now perhaps twenty thousand girls in the different schools supported by the beneficence of European and American Christians; but what are these among seventy-five millions of females in India? Besides the efforts made by the benevolence of Christian friends, there is now at Bombay a Society formed among the educated natives, whose object is to promote female education among the natives of that Presidency. The young men of that city, who enjoy the advantages of intellectual training, and consequently know how to appreciate them, have organized schools which, when I passed through Bombay a few months ago, contained some hundreds of native females. There can be no reason to doubt that, as education and western civilization advance among the male portion of the wealthy and influential classes, the want of intellectual culture will proportionally be felt, in relation to the female portion of the population. It cannot be overlooked that she, who is the appointed friend and companion of man in the duties of life, ought to have that mental culture, which alone can qualify her for the important relations in which she stands to society and to posterity; the fact that at Bombay we have an example in this important and desirable object, may be regarded as a pledge of still greater movements in the same direction. When the native mind shall become emancipated from the fetters that have so long confined it, and emerge from the darkness in which it has groped for ages; and when it shall be freed from the ignorance and superstition that have so long chained it down, there can be no doubt that it will exert its powers to diffuse among the female population the ameliorating influences of useful knowledge. The general diffusion of intelligence will doubtless open the way for extensive efforts in the cause of female education. The thing is practicable; this is a joyous thought. We have pledges of eventual success. The Church may prosecute its laudable and beneficent efforts in the full assurance of hope. Happy day, when the seventy-five millions of Hindu females shall be enfranchised, and admitted to the privileges of intellectual, moral, and Christian freedom!

CHAPTER XIV.

ABORIGINES OF INDIA—THE SHÁNÁRS—THEIR DEMONISM, AND ITS RITES—THE TUDAS OF THE NIELGHERRY HILLS—THEIR SINGULAR CHARACTER—THEIR MANNERS AND CUSTOMS BRIEFLY REFERRED TO—FUNERAL RITES—POLYANDRY.

In the chapter on the population of India, some account is given of the aborigines, and the characteristic differences existing between them and the supervening Brahmanical race are pointed out. As there proposed, it is here intended to furnish some information concerning the religious belief and practice which prevail among them. It may be observed that our acquaintance with the various aboriginal tribes is very limited, and consequently the account here to be presented must be very imperfect. The object in the brief sketch it is proposed to give will be to describe the most interesting religious peculiarities which have been ascertained to exist among the tribes best known.

The aborigines of India are now represented by the Shánárs of Tinnevelly, possibly also by certain wild tribes in Ceylon, called Veddahs, and especially by the numerous rude and barbarous tribes who occupy the inaccessible mountain ranges and impenetrable jungles of the country. They have no literature, sacred or profane, oral or written. Their religion is that of a simple system of superstition, resting as much on the natúral and suggestive fears and desires of the human mind, as on traditions which are handed down from father to son, alike without the embellishment of song, or the precision of the established chronicle, or exciting romance. Their imagination fills their gloomy forests with malevolent spirits of every kind, and especially the ghosts of their own ancestors; and some see in the earth and in the heavens powers capable of inflicting evil and of conferring good. Their worship, conformably with their notions, is principally a deprecation of evil conducted by bloody sacrifices, sometimes of human victims, and by peace offerings to the beings, seen and unseen, from whom they apprehend injury. When they rise above this devotion, it is principally to take cognizance of the multifarious powers which they suppose direct and control the various objects of nature, and occurrences of providence, and occupations of savage life, with which they are most familiar. They have not even, in general, a regular and established priesthood. Their principal religious ceremonies and services are conducted by the aged and honoured persons of their community, both male and female. In this condition, in India, there are, perhaps, eight or nine millions of our race, the descendants of the most ancient inhabitants of the country, who have never yet submitted their necks to the oppressive yoke of the Brahmans, and who, in their remote and frequently noxious retreats, defy the power of that dominant class of religious teachers.

THE SHÁNÁRS.

Of these aboriginal inhabitants the Shánárs are an interesting tribe; and, as they are more or less mingled with the Hindu population, their peculiarities are well known, and may be first noticed. Their geographical, political, and social position gives them a prior claim.

The Shánárs have of late been brought under the notice of the Christian public in England, as well as in India, by means of the missionary notices connected with Tinnevelly, where this people are more numerous than in any other part of the peninsula. The Tinnevelly Shánárs represent themselves as immigrants from North Ceylon, where the same class now exists; few, it is true, and generally respectable, and mingling more or less with the Hindus. They are cultivators and climbers of the Palmyra-palm, from which they extract the juice for the preparation of sugar. It is generally admitted, that the Shánárs are intellectually of the lowest type of all the inhabitants of India. They are, however, an interesting example of a people resisting successfully the religious influence of a supervening and dominant class of teachers, whose dogmas they have not received. The authority of the Brahmans they have never acknowledged, and they are therefore regarded by them with supercilious disdain as a low and degraded race. The Shánárs cherish the superstitious opinions of their ancestors and follow their practices. Some account of these will prove acceptable.

Though the Shánárs speak of God as the Supreme Ruler and Arbiter of the events of life, acknowledging his mercies in the benefits enjoyed, and impugning him as merciless and blind when they do not get what they wish, yet it does not appear that they entertain any distinct or just notions of his existence, and none of his natural and moral attributes. They make frequent references to the various divinities of the Hindus, but do not venerate their shrines, nor seek their favour. The religious ceremonial of the Shánárs has exclusive reference to the influence which it is supposed disembodied spirits have over the condition of the living. They seem not to have any definite idea of a future state of happiness or misery. In the event of a person suffering a violent death, especially if distinguished for wickedness during life, they imagine that his spirit may haunt the abodes of the living, or it may be he has assumed a demon and malevolent form; and they believe that such possess superhuman power and malignity. Their demonolatry is based upon this vague notion. Demonism is the religion which exercises its power over the imagination of the Shánár, and gives sentiment to his religious worship. In some instances they erect temples to a goddess they call Amman, mother, especially in North Ceylon. It is, however, thought that this is done in imitation of the Hindus; and it is not improbable that the usage derives its origin from the worship of Kali, the cruel goddess, whose Bacchanalian orgies have been described in a former part of this work. The following engraving represents an image in Tinnevelly of a female Pè, a demon called Nallamadathi. It is cut out of stone, about five and a-half feet high, and represents the demon in the act of destroying a child. When the drawing was taken, it had on its shoulder a wreath of red and white oleander flowers.

The demons whom they seek to appease, as occasion may require, are supposed to have been human beings, and are therefore either male or female, indigenous or foreign. All are powerful and malicious; they are fond of bloody sacrifices and frantic dances. Some recognised peculiarity in the demon to be propitiated may require to be regarded in the sacrifice offered and the service performed; some require a goat, some a hog, others a cock, and possibly a libation of ardent spirits. These demons dwell in trees, wander to and fro, and take special delight in uninhabited places. Sometimes they are said to take up their abode in houses tenanted by man; in which case the dwelling is totally abandoned. Many such houses I have seen in a state of ruin and decay. They are also believed to take up their abode in one of their own votaries, of which unmistakable symptoms will be given. He screams, foams at the mouth, stares, and utters oracular sayings. The individual consciousness and responsibility of the possessed is supposed to be suspended, and all that takes place under these circumstances is attributed to the presiding demon. During the prevalence of a visitation of the cholera, which decimated the population of the neighbourhood in which I then resided, my own servant, who was professedly a Romanist, but a man of the Shánár tribe, I believe, was affected in such a way that his relatives regarded him as possessed by a demon for a time. He was treated with a species of veneration, and his incoherent expressions were by his superstitious friends and neighbours regarded as of oracular import. These demons are supposed, in some places, to assume aërial forms, and to move about in troops. Some appear in the form of decrepit and aged females. Others move along the highways and byeways, invisible to human eyes, and somewhat above the ground; against whose malignant influence protection is sought by charms of various kinds. The leaves of certain trees are efficacious.

The numerous ills of human life are attributed to these demons; and a sacrifice, with the accustomed ceremonial, is regarded as the only efficacious method for obtaining deliverance. When disease of a serious and dangerous kind visits a Shánár, the physician is called in, that he may exercise his professional skill for the removal of the malady. The hill tribes in the district of Madura, and the more barbarous Khonds, do the same. The physician tries various methods for the relief of the sufferer; some are natural, as the exhibition of probable remedies, others are preternatural, as the utterance of incantations; and in the event of a failure of all ordinary means, it is concluded that the patient is possessed, when the physician recommends the more efficacious remedy, a demon dance. The union of the priest and physician in the same person, is a remarkable fact among the aborigines of India, as also among other ancient nations. In order to dispossess the individual of the demon, extreme measures are not always at once adopted: they may get up a dance, and induce the demon to utter responses, and also prophecies relative to some matter of personal or family concernment. In some instances the possessed is struck violently, and shook, the bystanders using the most opprobrious language at the same time, in order to eject the malignant intruder. Thus bidden away, the demon may yield in some degree, and say, "I go," intimating at the time why he came, also that he requires a sacrifice; and then producing on the party violent contortions and convulsions, he leaves his victim. The spirit being thus appeased or laid, the possessed awakes, and professes to know nothing of the events that have taken place.

These are some of the proceedings connected with the demonistic notions of the Shánárs. But they go beyond this, and systematically worship the supposed preternatural authors of evil. In Tinnevelly and Travancore, places called Pè Kòvil are provided for the worship of demons. Generally these consist of a small pyramidal pillar of mud, six or seven feet high, and constructed with their faces to the cardinal points: these are sometimes in the vicinity of a tamarind-tree. Before the pillar there is a smaller erection of mud, with a flat surface for sacrificial purposes. These mementos of the system, of which I have seen great numbers in Tinnevelly and Travancore, are not unlike models of the obelisks of Egypt.

Two acts seem essential to the demon worship of the

Shánárs, dancing and bloody sacrifices. They have no priest. The person who conducts the ceremony, which is undertaken from choice, is called the rotator of the demon. The head man of the village, or any other person, male or female, may officiate. The dress is grotesque, consisting of a sort of coat of various colours, a cap, and other vestments, arranged so as to strike the spectators with their comic appearance. In this service several musical instruments are used, but the most notable among them is one called a *bow*. It consists of a bow strung and ornamented with bells. This is placed on a brazen vessel of a globular form. The bow is struck with a plectrum, and the bass is produced by the application of an instrument to the brazen pot, another person keeping time by playing a pair of cymbals. The jarring, discordant, uproarious and cacophonous character of this musical accom-

paniment exceeds description, and when the parties are vieing with each other for pre-eminence, it is indeed the most horrid din that can be produced. At first the movements of the dancer may be slow, but, as the music waxes louder and takes effect, he becomes gradually more excited, urging himself to phrenzy by striking himself violently, and applying his mouth to the neck of the decapitated sacrificial victim, he drinks its blood, and possibly a potation of ardent spirits. The afflatus thus acquired, its effects become visible in the frantic glare and the convulsive gesticulations of the possessed. This is greeted by the spectators in the loudest acclamations. The dancer is now deified or demonized, and he is consulted by the eager and delighted worshippers who do him homage. Each one puts his questions as his fancy or his needs may dictate. The possessed or demonized dancer, being more like a maniac than aught else, and subject to various contortions of body, utters his oracles with much indistinctness, rendering it necessary that some one initiated into these mysteries should interpret his wild and incoherent utterances. His ambiguous sayings and curious inuendos are so indefinite as to need interpretation.

As in the instance of my own servant already noted, persons sometimes receive the afflatus without the demonolatrous rites just described; in which case the symptoms will be much the same, indicated in the peculiar stare, the gesticulations, and involuntary movements of the party. Being perceived by the friends and associates, fruits and flowers are immediately presented, and possibly a cock may be sacrificed.

In a former chapter, in which the characteristic differences between the aborigines and the Brahmanists were pointed out, it was stated that whilst the latter abhor the spilling of blood, the former conceive no religious or domestic ceremony complete without blood-shedding and the offering up of a live victim. The demon worship of the Shánárs affords us a good example of the fact. The victim may be a goat, a sheep, or a fowl. The animal selected for the auspicious service is ornamented with red ochre, and adorned with chaplets of flowers, and is thus led to the altar. There its head is severed by one blow of the sacrificial knife, and the lifeless trunk is suspended over the altar that the blood may be poured out thereon. The flesh is then cut up and cooked, and along with rice is consumed by those who have been engaged in the sacrifice. The sacrificial act is supposed to appease the angry demon, and induce him to remove the evil he has inflicted, or abstain from the infliction he may meditate. The sacrifice has no reference whatever to guilt; it is not intended to expiate sin. The demon is supposed to thirst for blood, and it is thus supplied. Indeed it is the same as the sacrifice offered at the shrine of Kali. The Shánár assumes that the demon seeks his life, and he propitiates it by offering that of an animal. We shall see as we trace the usages of some of the wilder and less civilized branches of the aborigines on the hills, that they do not rest in the presentation of animal sacrifices, but pay the rigid satisfaction—life for life—by immolating human victims.

The religious and moral condition of the Shánárs of Tinnevelly has been fully elucidated in a very able pamphlet, written by the Rev. R. Caldwell, B. A., originally published at Madras: it has been reprinted in London.

In illustration of one phase of the religious belief of the Shánárs, Mr. Caldwell gives the following paragraph. He says:—

"One of the clearest proofs of the un-Brahmanical origin of devil-worship is obtained by a reference to the history of the devils themselves. The process of *demonification* is still going on amongst the Shánárs; and in every case the characteristics of the devil and his worship are derived from the character and exploits of his human prototype. There is a continual succession of devils claiming the adoration of the Shánárs, and after a time sinking into forgetfulness; but not one of the more recent of the race has any connexion with the legends of Brahmanism. One of the demons most feared at present, Palavéshum, was a Maraver of a servile family, who made himself celebrated for his robberies and outrages 'from Madura round to Quilon,' during the latter period of the Mohammedan government. So celebrated has he become already, that thousands of persons are called after his name. Mohammedans also, who certainly have no connexion with Brahmanism, are supposed to have become devils. But it is a still more remarkable fact, and one which I suppose cannot easily be paralleled, that in the district of a neighbouring missionary, an European was, till recently, worshipped as a demon. From the rude verses which were sung in connexion with his worship, it would appear that he was an English officer, a Captain Pole, or some such name, who was mortally wounded at the taking of the Travancore lines in A.D. 1809, and was buried about twenty-five miles from the scene of the battle, in a sandy waste; where, a few years after, his worship was established by the Shánárs of the neighbourhood. His worship consisted in the offering to his manes of spirituous liquors and cheroots!"

THE TUDAS.

On the Nielgherry hills, a portion of the Western Ghauts, lying between the 11° and 12° of north latitude, and the 76° and 77° east longitude, there are several tribes of aborigines, of whose customs some brief notice may not be uninteresting. The Nielgherry hills rise to a height of about nine thousand feet, and present, along with a delightful climate, the most beautiful scenery, and in wild spontaniety the strawberry, and other delicious fruits that are not found in the maritime provinces. These hills have for some years been the resort of European invalids as a sanitarium.

The Tudas are the most remarkable aborigines of these beautiful mountain heights. They are tall and athletic; their countenance is open, expressive, and ingenuous; with a large full eye, a Roman nose, and fine teeth. They have no covering on the head, wearing the hair six or seven inches long,—parted from the centre, it forms into natural bushy circlets all round. Their costume is simple, formed of a short garment round the waist, fastened by a girdle, with an upper mantle that covers the whole person excepting the head, legs, and right arm. The women are fine in person, with a feminine expression of countenance, and distinguished by beautiful long black tresses, which flow in unrestrained luxuriance over the neck and shoulders. They are modest and retiring in demeanour; but, when circumstances require it, they converse with strangers in a manner unembarrassed by the timidity common in some provinces. Their dress is similar to that of the men, but it covers the whole person. The Tudas do not congregate in villages, but live apart, there not being generally more than four or five habitations together: this is suitable to their pastoral habits. They breed no animals but the buffalo. Their food consists of milk, meal, parched grain, and butter. When the herd is brought into the enclosure near the dwelling of an evening, they make a species of obeisance to the buffalos, by rising the right hand to the head, the thumb lying on the nose, the fingers being expanded. They practise the same obeisance to the lamp when lighted of an evening.

The Tudas of the Nielgherries have no knowledge of the Hindu religion. Their dairy, or lactarium, is partly consecrated to the offices of religion. It is divided into two apartments, one of which, a dark chamber, contains a rude stone. They have several sacred groves, where a priest called Pálál, and his assistant denominated Kávalál, are in attendance. They enter this vocation not by descent, but by their own choice, and are required, in order to the performance of their sacred functions, to pass through the rites of consecration. The consecration is singular: the aspirant retires into the depths of the forest to the border of some stream, casts off his garments, and remains in a state of nudity. He peels off the bark of a certain tree, expresses from it a liquor, which he uses partly as a drink and partly to smear himself. After this, he bathes. He remains several days, wears no clothes, and during this time he partakes of nothing but parched corn, which he takes with him. At the end of eight days, he receives about two yards of the coarsest cloth, half a yard wide, which he fastens round his waist as a garment. He is now no longer a secular person; he is devoted to the sacred office. He lives a life of celibacy, and may not see any of his family. He is supported by tithes, which are paid in return for his prayers and religious services. No other Tuda will approach him nearer than ten or twelve paces. Should he, however, call to any one, he may approach, which he does with reverence and profound respect. A bell, kept in a niche of the temple, is the only object of worship. To this they pour out libations of milk. It does not appear that they regard the bell as possessing any preternatural powers. To each sacred place is attached a herd of buffalos, whose milk is never drawn off, but left for the calves. One of these is chief. Should it die, and leave a female calf, that succeeds to the sacred relation. If the buffalo in chief had no female calf, another one is selected, the sacred bell is attached to its neck one day, and the succession is established. The Pálál milks one portion of the herd of a morning, carries the milk to the temple, laves the bell, and the milk is then consigned to ordinary use. The Tudas can give no reason for these usages, but believe them of divine institution. The temples in the sacred grove are conical in form, covered with thatch, and surmounted with a stone about a foot in diameter. One temple visited by Captain H. Harkness, from whose work on the Nielgherries these paragraphs are abstracted, contained nothing besides four bells. One or two persons were observed engaged in prayer, with the hand put up as before described, and directing the face not towards the temple, but towards the heavens. He mentions also another instance of prayer put up by an old lady who was sick. Some one present enjoined her to pray for alleviation. She did so for a few minutes, and then cheerfully remarked that she should soon be well.

The funeral rites of the Tudas are peculiar. When it is evident the sick person must soon die, near relatives ask what may be his dying wishes; then among other matters he names certain buffalos which he desires may accompany him. The body is kept three or four days to allow time for the requisite preparations. They also entertain a lingering hope that till putrefaction commences, reanimation may possibly take place. Fasting, cutting off the hair, putting off ornaments, chanting morning and evening laments, mutual condolence, falling on the corpse, with other expressions of grief, are observed on the death of a Tuda. On the day appointed for the burning of the body, a bier is prepared of boughs of trees, on which the body is laid, dressed in a new garment and mantle, and wearing the ornaments the deceased had been accustomed to. The body is borne along, followed by the mourners, male and female, chanting the lament, and after these a multitude follows bearing bundles of wood for the pyre, and small sacks of grain, cups made of leaves, filled with milk variously prepared, and butter, with cooking utensils. At a distance a herd of buffalos moves along, intended for the obsequies.

The bier is put down at a little distance from the place of burning, when the friends and relations take up earth, and with much ceremony sprinkle it on the body, and seating themselves around, continue their lament. Others are preparing the pyre, and some are engaged in preparing food. The Cohatars, the buffalo-slayers, a singular race of aborigines with attenuated forms, unseemly garb, and loosely flowing hair, await the moment when they hope to sate themselves with the victims they anticipate.

The following is a description of the remaining part of the ceremony, as witnessed by Captain Harkness. He says:—

"The greater part of the village had assembled, and many others, relatives and friends, from distant villages. The musicians, five in number, who were Cohatars of the circle to which this village belonged, now commenced the wail, and to this the whole party kept time, as, with a measured step, they moved round the body, mourning and lamenting. A milch buffalo was then forced round the bier in the circle, a little milk drawn from it, and poured into the mouth of the deceased. This buffalo was then liberated, and another one brought up, the same ceremony observed with it, and with others to the number of ten or twelve. Parched barley, and various kinds of millet, were then put into the mouth of the deceased, and some of the party taking up the bier, the procession moved towards the place of burning, the musicians proceeding at some distance in advance, the female relatives fanning the body, and the males running a short way in front, turning round, and prostrating themselves before it. Arriving near the spot where the pile was constructed, the bier was set down, and the son or representative of the deceased, carrying in his left hand a small bar of iron, went up to the deceased, and again dropped a little grain into his mouth; the remainder of the relatives then approached, and observed the same ceremony. After this, the representative seized a calf which had been brought here for the purpose, and addressing it, besought it to mediate for the departed, that the gates of heaven might be opened to him, and that his sins, and the sins of his generation, might be forgiven.

"The calf was then let loose, and, glad enough to get away, ran off with all the speed it could attain; the representative, and the whole of the party, shouting out to it at the same time,—'away, away, away!' The idea of this ceremony is, that the sins of the deceased enter the calf, or that the task of his absolution is laid on it. They say that the calf very soon disappears, and that it is never after heard of. In this case it did not run off a great way before it stopped, and as it is always one which has been purchased for the purpose, generally from the Cohatars, they do not, of course, allow it to wander far in want of an owner. The bier was now divested of all its ornaments, and the cloth or pall with which the body had hitherto been covered, taken off; a cubit of it given to each of the Cohatars, and to the Toriahs, and the remnant again thrown over the body, which was now placed

on the pile, the face downwards, the head to the north, and a sort of pent roof raised over it, composed of logs of wood. On these a large quantity of ghi was poured, and the whole being encircled with little heaps of different kinds of grain, fire was applied to it by the representative of the deceased, and then by others of the party.

"All the females who had attended the funeral remained on the spot where the bier had been first set down, excepting the widow of the deceased, who, endeavouring to approach nearer to the pile, or rather making a show of doing so, was surrounded by the other relatives, and made to divest herself of her upper garment and a part of her jewels. These were thrown on the pile, and a new garment being given to her, she was escorted back to her home. After they had remained for some time, and until the body was nearly consumed, the whole party returned to the village, and mixing up a little cow-dung and water, sprinkled themselves with it, as a means of purification.

"We understood that the party would return to the burying place the next morning, for the purpose of sprinkling a little water on the pile, collecting the bones of the deceased, and such portion of the metal which had composed the ornaments as they could find, and putting the former into an earthen pot, that they would bury it some three or four feet deep, marking the spot with a circle of stones. If, as in this instance, the deceased was a male, the metal collected from the pile would be given to the nearest male relative; if a female, to the nearest female relative, for the purpose of being again worked up into ornaments. We also understood that the funeral of a female is conducted in much the same manner as that which we had now witnessed, excepting that the winnow, the pestle, and such like articles, over which she has had control when living, are put on the pile and burnt with her."

The funeral obsequies are accompanied by the sacrifice of a number of milch buffalos, which are forced into a circle round the body, and there slain; and as each of the victims falls, the deceased is addressed by the party sacrificing, who mentions the name of the animal, saying that it is sent to accompany him. The accompanying engraving represents the sacrificial part of the funeral obsequies of the Tudas.

After the sacrifice, a near relation cuts off two or three locks of hair from about the temples, when the body is conveyed to the recess of the wood, taken off the bier and placed on the pyre, the feet to the south, the face downwards, and without any of the dress or ornaments being removed. The relations and friends now throw over it handfuls of parched grain, of various descriptions, and of coarse sugar; other logs of wood being then heaped over the whole, the pyre is ignited, in the first instance by the person who cut off the locks of hair, and then by the other attendants.

These brief notices of the Tudas may not be closed without some reference to the singular custom prevalent among them of a plurality of husbands. A woman may have two or three husbands and as many cicibeos as her husbands may permit her to contract engagements with—their consent is rarely withheld. A man may only contract marriage with one woman, but he may be the cicibeo of many. It would appear that the wife takes up her abode with each husband in succession, remaining a month or more as the case may be with each.

There are several distinct tribes of aborigines on the Nielgherry and other hills in the south, whose social and religious usages are of a highly interesting nature.

CHAPTER XV.

THE ABORIGINES OF INDIA, *continued*—THE KHONDS—THEIR RELIGIOUS DOCTRINES—SUPERIOR AND INFERIOR DIVINITIES—GOD OF THE DEAD —NOTIONS OF VIRTUE AND VICE—ORIGIN OF HUMAN SACRIFICES— THE KHOND WORSHIP—THEIR PRIESTS—WORSHIP OF THE GOD OF LIGHT —WORSHIP OF THE EARTH-GODDESS—MERIAH SACRIFICE DESCRIBED— FEMALE INFANTICIDE—SUMMARY OF THE KHOND RELIGIOUS BELIEF— INFANTICIDE IN RAJPUTANA AND OTHER PARTS OF INDIA.

BEFORE describing the condition of the semi-barbarous tribes of the hills, among whom the practice of female infanticide and human sacrifices prevails, it may be useful to direct attention to the map. By referring to that, it may be seen that a chain of mountains, called the Vindya mountains, extends east and west from Guzerat to the Ganges. From the east and west ends of this chain, a range of hills runs in the direction of Cape Comorin, at an average distance from the coast of from fifty to a hundred miles; these mountains are called the eastern and western Ghauts. Taking for a point of observation the upper end of the Gulf of Cambay, and looking across the plains direct in front, may be recognized, at a distance of nearly three hundred miles, the insulated Abu, the Saint's pinnacle, a lofty mountain. A little to the east of this, the range of rugged and elevated hills, called the Ara Valli, starts and runs on in a north-easterly direction, nearly as far as the imperial city of Delhi. The country lying between this ridge and the Vindya chain exhibits every variety of surface;—districts the most fertile, where genial nature shoots forth with exuberant, and almost spontaneous luxuriance, and where cultivation is carried on with incredible ease. The surface has all the features of a garden: but we cannot be permitted to dwell on this charming scene; it is not the prospect, however pleasing, that we are to gaze on, but the degraded occupants of this scene of riches and beauty, who, by reason of the painful contrast, appear the more vile. These hills are occupied by various aboriginal tribes, known by different names as Koles, Bhils, Khonds, Sourahs, Kulis, Tudas, already alluded to, Conravárs, &c. Those found on the elevated ridge in the south, on the Pulney, Shevroy and Nielgherry hills, are, as we have seen, inoffensive and harmless.

These various tribes, the scattered portions of the primitive population, were never subdued by the conquering Brahmanical invaders. Physical circumstances specially favoured their resistance to force; and also secured them against the pressure of those moral influences which might have assimilated them to the supervening and dominant classes. The regions just pointed out on the map were highly favourable to the preservation of the aborigines from the power of the invaders. Some portions of these aboriginal tribes that were exposed to more intimate contact with the conquering race have, indeed, in some degree been assimilated to them in manners and religion. They have become peaceful and settled, engaging in agricultural, pastoral, and mercantile pursuits, paying the exacted tribute, and rendering homage to the lords of the soil: but beyond the sub-alpine regions occupied by these, in the higher and wilder tracts of country, among the central ridges, and the interjacent valleys of the Ghauts, large portions of the primitive races have been but very partially, if at all, subdued; and some have maintained their independence from the earliest times.

Those whose peculiarities we now propose to notice, are the aborigines, who roam about in the province of Orissa, a country lying on the eastern coast of India, at the upper part of the Bay of Bengal. In the northern division of this province, the Koles are found, in the central part the Khonds, and in the southern portion the Sourahs prevail. On the eastern side of the Ganjam district, bordering upon the Chilka lake, the Khonds are met with in considerable numbers. On the north-west they are found on the borders of the Gondwana. Throughout the hitherto unexplored territory of the Nagpore state, they enjoy their primitive independence. In parts of the peninsula, even as low as within the tenth degree of latitude, the Khonds exercise their wild dominion.

The account of the first intercourse between the English and these aboriginal tribes is highly interesting; it may be seen in a report which was written for the Madras Government by Captain S. Charters Macpherson of the Madras army. This gentleman, who evidently possessed qualifications of a high order for the enterprise, was entrusted with a commission by the Supreme Government of India, with the design of suppressing the Meriah Sacrifice and female infanticide among the wild tribes under notice. Captain Macpherson, from successive visits and temporary residence among the Khonds, became better acquainted with their social condition and religious peculiarities, and eventually furnished a most interesting paper to the Royal Asiatic Society, which has been published in the Journal of that body. From that paper, and incidental notices that appeared in the *Calcutta Christian Observer* and the *Calcutta Review* the present brief account is prepared.

It may be remarked in the outset, that as the details of doctrines and of rites, of legends and of narratives, vary in almost every district, it must be exceedingly difficult to arrive at certainty on the subjects of inquiry, and proportionally so, to reduce to an embodied form the oral traditions collected. There being no hereditary or organized priesthood among the Khonds, the ceremonials of the gods, composed of rites, invocations, hymns, legends, and recitals, are the only repository of materials doctrinal and ritual, from which the main outlines and spirit of the superstition can be deduced.

THE RELIGIOUS DOCTRINES OF THE KHONDS.

The Khonds believe in the existence of One Supreme Being, self-existing, the source of good, and Creator of the universe, of the inferior gods, and of man. This divinity is known in some districts as Boora Pennu, or the god of light; in others, as Bella Pennu, or the sun god; and the sun, and the place from which it rises beyond the sea, are his chief abodes.

In the beginning Boora Pennu created for himself a consort called Tari Pennu, the earth goddess and the source of evil. He afterwards created the earth. As he walked forth upon it with his consort, she was found wanting in her attention to him, refusing to scratch Boora Pennu's back when requested to do so; he resolved to create from the substance of the earth a new being, Man, to pay him due homage; and, for the benefit of this new race, the Supreme called into being the vegetable and animal kingdom. Tari was filled with jealousy, and attempted to frustrate his purpose; she, however, only so far succeeded as to change the intended order of the work, as preserved in a generally received legend: Boora Pennu took a handful of earth and cast it behind him to create man; but Tari caught it and cast it on one side, when all the varieties of vegetable life sprang into being. He repeated the act, and she did as before; casting the earth into the ocean, when fish, and all things that live in water, were formed. Boora Pennu took a third handful and cast it behind him; this she caught and flung aside, when animals wild and tame sprung into life. The next handful she seized and threw it up into the air, from which proceeded the feathered tribes. Boora Pennu now perceived what Tari had done to frustrate his purposes, and laying his hand on her head, placed a fifth handful of earth on the ground from which the human race was educed. Tari Pennu then placed her hands on the earth and said, "Let these beings you have made exist; you shall create no more." Then a sweat exuded from Boora Pennu's body, which he collected in his hand, casting it around said, "To all that I have created," whence arose the distinction of sex, and the continuation of the species.

In that primeval state all was harmony and bliss. No evil existed, and man enjoyed communion with his Maker. Unclothed and unencumbered, he was able to move through earth and air and ocean.

The earth goddess, Tari, became incensed at this, and broke out into open rebellion against Boora, and resolved to introduce evil into the world. She succeeded in producing moral evil, and sowed the seeds of sin in the heart of man, as seeds are cast into a ploughed field. She, too, was the source of physical evils and disorder as they now exist. Boora Pennu, by the application of antidotes, arrested and held in abeyance the elements of physical evil; but he left man free to receive or reject moral evil.

A few individuals only preserved their primitive purity; to whom Boora Pennu assigned the condition of gods, whilst the masses became degenerate. The sinless few he exempted from death, saying to them, "Become ye gods, living for ever, and seeing my face when you will, and have power over man, who is no longer my immediate care." On the wicked Boora inflicted sundry and manifold evils, physical and moral, and withdrew the antidotes by which their force had been abated. He withdrew from mankind, and all became subject to death. He also ordained that all who commit sin should suffer death as a consequence. Social order disappeared, and discord and rapine and war supervened. All nature became disordered. The seasons became irregular, the earth no longer yielded spontaneously its fruits. Disease ensued; the serpent tribe became poisonous, and animals became savage and destructive. Man now assumed outward clothing, lost the power of moving through air and ocean, and became subject to misery, disease, and death. Moreover Boora and Tari fiercely contended for superiority; their terrible strife raging throughout the earth, the sea, and the sky; their chief weapons being mountains, meteors, and whirlwinds.[1]

[1] The comet of 1843 was watched by the Khonds with the most intense interest, each of the opposite parties regarding it as a new and prodigious weapon in the hand of the deity to which their own particular worship was chiefly paid.

Up to this point, the Khonds hold the same general belief; but from it they divide into two sects, directly opposed, upon the great question of the issue of the contest between Boora and his rebel consort, involving the whole subject of the practical relation between the two antagonist powers with reference to man, the source and subject of their strife.

The sect of Boora believed that he proved triumphant in the contest; and, as an abiding sign of the discomfiture of Tari, imposed the pains and cares of childbirth on her sex. Her rebellious will, however, her activity as the source of evil, and her malignity towards man, remain unabated, and are ever struggling to break forth; but she is so subjected to control, that she is employed as the instrument of Boora's moral rule, being permitted to strike only where he, as the omnipotent ruler of the universe, desires to punish.

The sect of Tari hold, upon the other hand, that she remained unconquered, and still maintains the struggle with varying success. They recognise the supremacy of Boora as the Creator of the world, and the sole source of good, invoking him first on every occasion; but they hold that his power, exerted directly and through the agency of the inferior gods, is insufficient for the protection of man when Tari resolves to inflict injury or destruction; and moreover, while they regard Tari as the original source of evil alone, they nevertheless believe that practically she has power to confer every form of earthly benefit, both by abstaining from the prevention of the good which flows from Boora, and by directly bestowing blessings.

DOCTRINES OF THE BOORA SECT RESPECTING THE INFERIOR DIVINITIES, THE SOUL, AND THE DEAD.

In order to secure the partial happiness of man on earth, and the final happiness of the good, Boora resolved on the creation of inferior divinities to occupy the place of guardians, who are entrusted with authority over the various powers of nature. These inferior gods are to be worshipped in subordination to the supreme being Boora, and Tari his consort, who are always first invoked.

The inferior gods are of two classes, distinguished by their origin, attributes, and authority.

The first sprang from Boora and Tari. They are unchangeable, and to them is assigned a general jurisdiction over all that relates to the well-being of man. These deities are as follows:—

1. PIDZU PENNU .	The god of rain."
2. BOORBI PENNU .	The goddess of new vegetation and first-fruits.
3. PITTERI PENNU .	The god of increase and of grain.
4. KLAMBO PENNU.	The god of the chase.
5. LOHA PENNU .	The god of iron—of war.
6. SUNDI PENNU .	The god of boundaries.

The seventh of the first class is an inferior god, DINGA PENNU, the judge of the dead: he is unchangeable and immortal.

The second class of divinities are the deified sinless men of the first ages. These are invested with immutability, and are the tutelary gods of tribes.

The third class sprang from the gods of the two first classes, having power over the functions of nature. Their number is unlimited. They guard the hills, groves, streams, fountains, paths, hamlets, and are cognizant of every human action, want, and interest, in the locality in which they may preside.

The following are the chief of this class:—

1. NADZU PENNU	The village god.
2. SORO PENNU	The hill god.
3. JORI PENNU	The god of streams.
4. IDZU PENNU	The family, or house god.
5. MOONDA PENNU . . .	The tank god.
6. SOOGA PENNU	The god of fountains.
7. GOSSA PENNU	The forest god.
8. KOOTTI PENNU	The god of ravines.
9. BHORA PENNU	The god of new fruits.

We may conveniently here introduce the sentiments which the Khonds entertain respecting the soul. Men are endowed with four souls. First, there is a soul which is capable of beatification and restoration to communion with Boora. Secondly, there is a soul which is attached to some tribe upon earth, and re-born for ever in that tribe, so that, upon the birth of every child, the priest declares, after inquiry, which of the members of the tribe has returned. Thirdly, there is a soul which endures the sufferings inflicted as the punishment of sin, and performs the transmigrations imposed on that account. This may, at the bidding of a god, temporarily quit the body, which thereupon becomes sick and languid. Thus, when a man becomes a priest, this soul for a time passes into the presence of divinity, to receive instruction in relation to his office. When a man, aided by a god, becomes a tiger, this soul animates the assumed animal form. Fourthly, there is a soul which dies with the dissolution of the body.

The judge of the dead, Dinga Pennu, resides beyond the sea, on a slippery rock called Grippa Valli, *the leaping rock*, around which flows a black unfathomable river. Souls on quitting their bodies proceed directly to that locality; and in the attempt to leap the awful gulf and gain a footing on that rock, frequently suffer various injuries, involving the loss of an eye, or other privations, which may be expected to appear in the body next to be animated by them. Upon that rock Dinga sits, and is engaged day and night in adjusting the accounts and the awards of souls. There he registers all things, and as souls arrive they are disposed of according to his inexorable decisions. If a soul be entitled to final beatification, it passes at once to the society of the gods; but if not fit for that sublime reward, it passes again, after certain inflictions at Grippa Valli, into another body for probation: it reappears in its appropriate tribe.

The punishments which Dinga Pennu inflicts are various. Epilepsy, poverty, privation from male offspring. Bodily defects are regarded as peculiarly afflictive among the Khonds, who above all things covet beautiful and brave children. No curse, however, is so much deprecated as that connected with cowardice and other base qualities, such as falsehood, which bring upon their subject infamy in his tribe.

The following enumeration of virtues and vices will indicate the character of Dinga's rule, and also of public sentiment among the aborigines of India.

It is regarded as heinous :—

1. To refuse hospitality, or to abandon a guest.
2. To break an oath or promise, or to deny a gift.
3. To speak falsely, except to save a guest.
4. To break a solemn pledge of friendship.
5. To break an old law or custom.
6. To commit incest.
7. To contract debts the payment of which is ruinous to a man's tribe, which is responsible for the engagements of all its members.
8. To skulk in time of war.
9. To betray a public secret.

The commission of any of these sins involves future birth, and possibly the disadvantages incident to bodily defect, or bad mental or moral qualities.

The most distinguished virtues are :—

1. To kill a foe in public battle.
2. To fall in public battle.
3. To be a priest.
4. To be a victim to Tari.

The souls of the virtuous enjoy communion with the gods, and are much in the same condition. Every tribe invokes, as well the god and the souls of deceased, and especially virtuous ancestors, in all religious ceremonies. They imagine the souls of deceased virtuous ancestors to possess the privilege of intercession with the gods.

DOCTRINES OF THE TARI SECT.—ORIGIN OF HUMAN SACRIFICES.

This sect ascribe to Tari the same propensions and beneficence which the adherents of the Boora theory attribute to him.

She, to accomplish her purposes, assumed a feminine form, under the title of Umbally Bylee, communicating immediately from herself, and through her priests, revelations to man, who she permits to receive the benefits conferred by Boora through the inferior gods. Hence the Tari sectarists worship the inferior divinities. They further hold that she continues to mankind the enjoyments of earth, on the condition of receiving their homage and human sacrifices, the latter being her food.

The following legend accounts for the horrible rites to be detailed. When the earth was soft, and utterly unfit to yield its increase, Umbally Bylee appeared, cutting vegetables with a knife. She wounded her finger, and as the blood trickled down upon the earth, it became dry and firm. She said, "Behold the good change; cut up my body to complete the process." They refused, lest, as she was one of their own tribe, the race might become extinct: they determined to procure by purchase victims from other tribes, and did so. Then, they say, the social economy of family and government, and the varied ties of life arose; and the knowledge of agriculture was imparted to mankind.

Tari introduced venatical pursuits, the use of iron, the art of war, and the fabrication of its weapons.

Thus all the benefits enjoyed by mankind spring from Tari. At first the good was restricted; whereupon they complained to her that wealth was little, anxiety great, children few, and noxious reptiles and thorns abundant, and she was graciously pleased to extend the advantages of her kind rule to all our race. The followers of Tari believe that their rites now procure the auspices under which we live.

Those attached to the worship of Boora regard with horror the rite of human sacrifice as the greatest of crimes; into which they regard its perpetrators as drawn by the delusive wiles of Tari. They believe themselves to be preserved from the delusion and crime by the favour of Boora.

LEGENDS CHARACTERISING THE KHOND DIVINITIES.

The forms assumed by the gods of the Khonds are human, but of great stature, and of ethereal substance. They can assume any shape or colour, and except Boora, Tari, and Dinga Pennu, they reside on the earth, moving about two cubits above its surface, and though invisible to men, they are seen by animals. They are subject to all the passions of mankind, and to their consequences. The inferior gods are subject to a species of decay and dissolution; but on becoming disembodied, they are instantly re-born without the suspension of consciousness. The gods live upon the essences and flavours of offerings presented to them by their votaries, and on those extracted from animals which they kill for themselves, by inflicting disease. They can extract the corn from the ear or from the garner, and feast upon that. The inferior divinities procure sustenance for Boora and Tari.

WORSHIP OF THE KHONDS.

The Khonds regard as absurd the erection of temples as the dwelling-places of their divinities, and identify their special presence with sacred groves, barren rocks, the banks of streams and fountains. They regard the making and setting up of images as the most signal proof of conscious removal from all communion or fellowship with the unseen. Where, however, they have been brought into contact more or less with the Hindus, they may set apart in a rude building a stone or a piece of iron as a symbol of a revered divinity.

The priesthood among the Khonds, like every other priesthood, lays claim to divine institution. The inferior deities, as the mediators between man and Boora and Tari, resolved that a class of men should be specially instructed in divine things, and enjoy a more intimate communion with themselves, that they might be specially qualified to aid mankind in the concerns of the soul. Each deity appoints his own ministers, calls into his presence the third or movable soul of the persons selected, and instructs them in their duty. The priests first taught to their sons and disciples the mysteries of religion, and the gods have since kept up a succession of men, selecting them either from the initiated or from others. The priesthood may be assumed by any one who chooses to assert his call to the ministry of any particular god. His pretensions are authenticated by his sinking into a state of stupor,—a dreamy confused state,—for a period varying from one to ten or fourteen days, the consequence of the absence of his third soul in the divine presence. The ministerial office among the Khonds thus assumed, may be laid aside at pleasure.

The ministers of religion are of two classes,—one is devoted exclusively to the vocation, and the other follows also a secular calling. The former contend for exclusive prerogatives, which, however, are rarely recognised, except in the instance of a human sacrifice; at which a principal and fully instructed priest alone can officiate; and in the worship of the god of war, which must be performed by his own priest.

The priest or Janni who devotes himself exclusively to the religious service of his order, can possess no property, nor money, nor even look at a woman. That he may appear as diverse from other men as possible, he must live in a hut, in the most degraded condition. He must not wash, except with spittle, nor leave his abode, except when sent for. Occasionally he may stray from his habitation to a neighbouring palm-tree, where, after drawing off and imbibing the inebriating juice, he may be found drunk at its foot. He is not distinguished for decency in his apparel, and when abroad carries in his hand a broken axe or bow. He is sottish in appearance, but nevertheless witty enough in all that relates to his office. He consumes with special gusto the grilled skin of the feet of sacrificed buffalos, and the heads of sacrificed fowls. When a deer is cut up, half of the skin, with an ear on it, and possibly the hairy skimmings of the pot may be assigned him.

The second class of priests live as other men. They eat apart from laymen, but may drink with them. They may receive as perquisites a portion of the offerings they have presented, and possibly gifts at harvest, if a fruitful season affords evidence of their influence with the gods. They occupy their appropriate places at public and private festivals.

Matters connected with all public ceremonies of religion are under the control of the chief, who takes his measures after due consultation with the priest. If the ceremony prove inefficacious the chief is blamed, and he in his turn blames the priest. The priest 'recriminating on the chief, may attribute the failure to the chief's infidelity in not providing a better buffalo, or to the improper demeanour of the chief's family, or to the want of faith in the worshippers. Frequently, however, the affair ends in the infliction by public decree of a summary fine upon the chief, from whose homestead they abstract a pig or sheep, which they forthwith consume at a common feast.

It is the duty of a priest, in case of sickness, to decide whether the event is an infliction from Dinga, from the displeasure of some deity, or from the magical devices of an enemy. The Janni seats himself by the sick person, takes rice, and dividing it into small heaps, dedicates each to some particular deity. He then hangs up a sickle balanced with a silk thread, places a few grains of rice upon each end of it, and calls upon all the gods by name. If the sickle is slightly agitated as a particular name is pronounced, that proves that he has come and rested on the heap dedicated to him. The priest lays down the sickle, naming the god, and counts the grains of rice in the heap dedicated to that divinity: if the number is odd the deity is offended, but if even he is pleased. In the former case the priest is thereupon filled with the divinity, shakes his head wildly, and, with dishevelled hair, pours forth a torrent of incoherent words. The patient humbly inquires the cause of the divine displeasure, what laws he has broken, what rites neglected, and what the required atonement for his offences. The general influence of the Khond priesthood is said not to be great.

THE WORSHIP OF BOORA PENNU, THE GOD OF LIGHT.

The principal ceremony connected with the worship of the Supreme takes place about the time of the rice harvest,—it is called Salo kallo, from Salo, a cattle pen, and Kallo, spirituous liquor, which being prepared in a cattle pen the place gives its name to the feast. To the tribal feasts representatives are sent from every village to that of the chief of the tribe. An authorized priest conducts the ceremony, which is continued through five days. During that period every one eats freely of fermented rice, which produces an intoxicating effect; wild dances, accompanied by the most stunning music, are kept up day and night; and every kind of unrestrained licentious enjoyment is indulged in.

The story of the creation of the world and of man is recited. Although in the worship of Boora Pennu a sacrifice is not absolutely requisite, that of a hog, as the most valuable victim, is offered. It is hung up in the cattle pen by the hind legs, and when stabbed in the neck its blood is diffused over the ground. The priest then prays to Boora to confer every needed good, while individuals implore that which they may severally desiderate.

At another festival to Boora Pennu, called the dragging festival, a buffalo that has been consecrated from its birth as a victim, and permitted to range at pleasure in any pasture till five or six years old, is brought out; several ropes are attached to its neck and its hind legs, which are seized by about fifty men, who permit the animal to rush about till it is brought up to the foot of the tree where it is slaughtered. The priest declares that its exhaustion is the result of miraculous agency.

The priest recites a legend accounting for the origin of the festival, which it is unnecessary here to introduce.

There is another religious ceremony, called the Jakri festival, at which prayers are offered up to Boora Pennu, and a buffalo sacrificed at the foot of the sacrificial tree; while every form of wild festivity, eating, drinking, frantic dancing and loud music, is kept up for at least two days.

At the commencement of the ploughing season special prayer is offered to Boora and all other gods, accompanied by an offering to Boora of a fowl, rice, and spirituous liquor. The following prayer is uttered on the occasion:—"O, Boora Pennu! and O, Tari Pennu, and all other gods! (here naming them). You, O, Boora Pennu, created us, giving us the attribute of hunger; thence corn food was necessary to us, and thence were necessary producing fields. You gave us every seed and ordered us to use bullocks, and to make ploughs, and to plough. Had we not received this art we might still indeed have existed upon the natural fruits of the jungle and the plain, but, in our destitution, we could not have performed your worship. Do you, remembering this,—the connexion betwixt our wealth and your honour,—grant the prayers which we now offer. In the morning we rise before the light to our labour, carrying the seed. Save us from the tiger, and the snake, and from every stumbling-block. Let the seed appear earth to the eating birds, and stones to the eating animals of the earth. Let the grain spring up suddenly like a dry stream that is swelled in a night. Let the earth yield to our ploughshares as wax melts before hot iron. Let the baked clod melt like hail-stones. Let the ploughs spring through the furrows with force, like the recoil of a bent tree. Let there be such a return from our seed, that so much shall fall and be neglected in the fields, and so much on the roads in carrying it home, that, when we shall go out next year to sow, the paths of the field shall look like a young corn-field. From the first times we have lived by your favour. Let us continue to receive it.

Remember that the increase of our produce is the increase of your worship, and that its diminution would be the diminution of your rites."

THE WORSHIP OF TARI PENNU, BERA PENNU, THE EARTH GODDESS.

In tho worship paid to Tari Pennu by her sect, the chief rite is human sacrifice. It is celebrated as a public oblation by tribes, branches of tribes or villages, both at social festivals held periodically, and when special occasions demand extraordinary propitiation. And besides these social offerings, the rite is performed by individuals to avert the wrath of Tari from themselves and their families.

The time is so arranged that each head of a family is enabled to obtain a shred of flesh for his fields about the time his chief crop is laid down. All associated with the sacrificing tribe hold their land on the express terms of contributing to the religious burdens, and they are therefore bound to contribute to the expenses incident to those sacrifices.

The occasions requiring common offerings of a special character are unusual mortality by disease, or by tigers; or should many die in childbirth, or should the flocks and herds suffer largely from disease, or from wild beasts; or should the greater crops threaten to fail; while the occurrence of any marked calamity to the families of the chiefs, whose fortunes are regarded as the principal index to the disposition of Tari towards their tribes, is held to be a token of wrath that cannot be too speedily averted.

Individuals make the great oblation when signal calamities fall upon themselves, or upon their families. If, for example, a child watching its father's flock be carried off by a tiger supposed to be Tari, the priest is called, they dash vessels of water over him, seat him in his wet garments, and set a cup of water before him. He dips his fingers thrice into the water, smells them, sneezes, becomes inspired, and begins to make utterances in the name of the divinity by whose presence he is filled. If he then declare a sacrifice expedient, the father vows to offer it, and must fulfil this purpose within the year.

Victims are called "Meriah" by the Oriyas; and by the Khonds they are denominated "Tokki," or "Keddi." Persons of any age, or race, or sex, are accepted as victims,—except Brahmans, who, as invested with the sacerdotal string, are already dedicated to God.

The victims to Tari must be *purchased*, or born of purchased victims. The principle is that the victim must be either naturally, or by purchase, the property of the person who offers it.

The victims are procured by persons, Panwas, who are attached to Khond villages for the discharge of this and other peculiar offices. The Panwas purchase the victims without difficulty, or kidnap them in the low-country, from the lower classes of Hindus. Sometimes they are procured to order, and on other occasions on speculation; and they moreover sell their own offspring; and children, of whom they are the guardians. In time of famine, the Khonds themselves sell their children, and consider the designation as beneficial to mankind, and as leading on the part of the victim to final happiness as the most honourable end. On one occasion, it is related that a Panwa reproached a parent for selling his child because he wished to marry her; and he was so enraged that he spat in the man's face. Some bystanders consoled the father of the child by saying, "Your child has died that all the world may live, and the earth goddess herself will wipe that spittle from your face."

The victim is brought blindfolded to the village, and is placed in the custody of the chief, in fetters if grown up, or at liberty if a child. As a consecrated person he is welcomed at every threshold. Victims may grow up and form an attachment for the wife or daughter of a Khond; this is grateful to the parties as a special favour. To a Meriah youth a wife, herself a victim, may be given, and a portion of land, with a farming stock assigned. Though the offspring may sometimes be spared, if needs be, the whole household may be devoted to death. The escape of victims is rare. They are treated with so much kindness—almost to veneration—that they are under no temptation to flee, and the less so, because among many the apprehension of immolation is not strong. If he escaped, the other tribes would not afford him an asylum; he must be given up to the tribe to whom he belongs. Besides, they are taught that should they escape they will perish by disease, whereas immolation leads to certain paradise.

In prospect of a sacrifice, at a space of ten or twelve days from the event, the hair of the victim, hitherto unshorn, is cut off in token of his dedication. Those villagers who intend taking a part in the ceremony, on hearing of the day appointed for the solemnity, perform a preparatory ceremony, called "Bringa." All wash their clothes, and, in company with the priest, they leave the village, when he invokes all the gods, and addresses Tari as follows:—

"Oh, Tari Pennu,—you may have thought that we forgot your commands after sacrificing such an one (naming the last victim), but we forgot you not. We shall now leave our houses in your service, regardless of our enemies, of the good or ill-will of the gods beyond our boundaries, of danger from those who, by magical arts, become Mleepa tigers, and of danger to our women from other men. We shall go forth on your service. Do you save us from suffering evil while engaged in it. We go to perform your rites; and if anything shall befal us, men will hereafter distrust you, and say, you care not for your votaries. We are not satisfied with our wealth; but what we do possess we owe to you, and for the future we hope for the fulfilment of our desires. We intend to go on such a day to such a village, to bring human flesh for you. We trust to attain our desires through this service. Forget not the oblation."

The benefit sought by the sacrifice being universal, all may attend. Generally a large concourse of people of both sexes is present. The ceremony lasts three days, and is characterised by the wildest proceedings and the grossest excess. The first day and night are spent in drunken feasting, and frantic dances, under the inspiration, as is believed, of the goddess. On the second morning the victim who has been kept fasting from the commencement of the ceremony, is washed, attired in a new garment, and led forth from the village with music and dancing. They proceed to a deep shady grove, called the Meriah Grove, through which flows the Meriah stream. This is a consecrated spot, supposed to be haunted, and its trees are never cut. The victim is bound by the priest to a post. He is anointed with oil, clarified butter, and turmeric, and adorned with flowers. He is reverenced as divine. The greatest wish is evinced among the frantic crowd for the least relic connected with him; a little of the turmeric paste, or a drop of his spittle is regarded as of special virtue, especially by women. The feasting and dancing are continued. Upon the third morning, the victim is refreshed with a little milk or palm sago. About noon they consummate the orgies, amid the shouts and music of the frantic assembly.

The victim may not be bound, nor is he to show any resistance, and therefore in some instances his legs and arms are broken, or, which is the more common and humane course, he is stupefied with opium.

After all the preparations are completed, the religious ceremony proceeds, some parts of which are conducted in a semi-dramatic form by those who are clever in the art of acting. The following account is abridged from the one furnished by Captain S. Charters Macpherson.

After addressing Tari, and all the other divinities, the priest recites the following invocation:—

"O, Tari Pennu! when we omitted to gratify you with your desired food, you forgot kindness to us. We possess but little and uncertain wealth. Increase it, and we shall be able often to repeat this rite. We do not excuse our fault. Do you forgive it, and prevent it in future by giving us increased wealth. We here present to you your food. Let our houses be so filled with the noise of children, that our voices cannot be heard by those without. Let our cattle be so numerous, that neither fish, frog, nor worm may live in the drinking ponds beneath their trampling feet. Let our cattle so crowd our pastures, that no vacant spot shall be visible to those who look at them from afar. Let our folds be so filled with the soil of our sheep, that we may dig in them as deep as a man's height without meeting a stone. Let our swine so abound, that our home fields shall need no ploughs but their rooting snouts. Let our poultry be so numerous, as to hide the thatch of our houses. Let the stones at our fountains be worn hollow by the multitude of our brass vessels. Let our children but have it for a tradition, that in the days of their forefathers there were tigers and snakes. Let us have but one care, the yearly enlargement of our houses to store our increasing wealth. Then we shall multiply your rites. We know that this is your desire. Give us increase of wealth, and we will give you increase of worship."

At this point individuals supplicate personal favours. One asks a good husband; another a good wife; another that his war instruments may be effective.

The priest then proceeds with the recitation of legends relating to the origin of the worship now being performed: this has already been given in a former part of this chapter. The legend goes on with a description of the first sacrifice, as ordered by Tari, and describes the circumstances under which it was presented amid assembled multitudes. The semi-dramatic character of this part of the ceremony is so peculiar in itself, and serves so fully the purposes of illustration as regards the religious sentiments of the Khonds, that it may not be withheld, not that it is possible to give more than a brief view of the whole.

The victim wept, and reviled, and uttered curses. The people rejoiced; but those who had brought up the child and the priest were grieved. "The world rejoices," said they, "but we are filled with despair;" demanding why the rite was instituted. Then Tari, through the priest, said, "Away with this grief. Your answer is this: when the victim complains, say to him, Blame not us, but your parents who sold you. The earth goddess requires a sacrifice. It is requisite for the world. The tiger, the snake, fever, these afflict us; you can suffer no evil. You, when you have given repose to the world, will become a god."

The victim answers, "Have you no enemies; no vile and useless child; no debtor to another tribe, who obliges you to sell your lands to pay his debts; no coward, who deserts his comrades in battle?"

The priest replies: "You misapprehend our principles. We did not kidnap you when gathering sticks in the jungle, nor when at play. They to whom you refer can never become gods. They are only fit to perish by epilepsy, falling in the fire, by ulcers or other dreadful diseases. Such sacrifices are valueless. To obtain you we have toiled fearless of the tiger and the snake. We stinted ourselves to advantage your parents, and gave them our brazen vessels. They gave you to us as freely as one gives light from a fire; if any, blame them."

The victim: "Did I share the price? Did I consent to the transaction? No one remembers his mother's womb, nor the taste of his mother's milk; you I regarded as my parents. I received delicacies from all. When other children suffered, they grieved; but when I suffered, all grieved. When did you conceive this fraud, this wickedness to destroy me? You, O my father; and you,—and you,—and you, O my fathers! do not destroy me."

The chief of the village in which the victim was kept, or his representative, now interposes, briefly refers to the divine origin of the rite, adding, "Oh, child, we must destroy you! Forgive us. You will become a god."

The victim pleads his ignorance of these traditions and the intentions of those with whom he has lived; and then refers to the acts of his life, to the trees he has planted, to the house he has helped to build. He points to the tobacco they are chewing, as the fruit of his labour, and to the flocks he has tended, that still look at him with affection.

The chief replies: "You will soon be deified, and we shall be benefited by your fate. We may not argue the matter; but do you not remember that when your father came to claim the price, and you snatched up a brass vessel, we said, 'That is your father's;' and you threw it at him, and ran away amongst the sheep? You remember your hair being cut? Did not the Janni bring the divining sickle, when many were sick, and say that the goddess demanded a victim?"

Some of the bystanders may here say, "I should have told you"—"and I"—"and I;" when others add, "I thought—I thought of the just price we paid for him, and of the loss if he escaped. You might have known."

The victim: "True; but your aged mothers, your wives, and your beautiful children, my brothers and sisters, assured me that you were humane, and would never destroy so useful and beautiful a child as I. They said, 'They will rather sell their lands and buy a substitute.' This I believed, and continued with you."

The chief: "We cannot satisfy you. Ask your father, who is present. I satisfied him with my favourite cattle, my valuable brass vessels, and my sheep, and with silken and woollen cloths and axes. A bow and arrows, not four days old, I gave to his fancy. Your parents, forgetting your beauty, forgetting the pleasure of cherishing you, turned their hearts to my cattle, and my brass vessels, and gave you away. Upbraid *them*. Heap imprecations upon them. We will curse them with you, imprecating upon them—that all their children may be similarly sacrificed. That they may lose within the year the price for which they sold you. That they may have a miserable and forlorn old age, lingering childless and unfed. That when they die in their empty house, there may be no one to inform the village for two days, so that when they shall be carried out to be burned, all shall hold their nostrils. That their own souls may afterwards animate victims given to hardhearted men who will not even answer their death plaints consolingly. Curse them thus, and we will curse them with you.'"

The victim will now turn to the priest, saying: "And why did you conceal my fate? When I dwelt with the chief like a flower, were you blind, or dumb, or how were you possessed, that you never said, 'Why do you cherish so lovingly this child—this child who must die for the world?' Then had I known my doom and leapt from a precipice and died. Your reason for concealment, living as you do, apart from men, is, that you thought of yourself. 'I am great. The whole world attends on my ministrations.' But, world, look upon him! What miscreant eyes! What a villanous head, with hair like a sumbully-tree! And see how enraged he is! What a jabber he makes! What a body he has got, starved upon worship which depends upon men's griefs! A body anointed with spittle for oil! Look, O world! Look and tell! See how he comes at me leaping like a toad!"

The Janni replies: "Child, why speak thus? I am the friend of the gods; the first in their sight. Listen to me. I did not persuade your father or your mother to sell you. I did not desire the chiefs to sell their fields to acquire your price. Your parents sold you. These chiefs bought you. They consulted me inquiring, 'How can this child become blessed?' The hour is not yet over. When it is past, how grateful will you be to me! You, as a god, will gratefully approve and honour me."

The victim: "My father begat me; the chiefs bought me, my life is devoted, and all will profit by my death. But you, O Janni! who make nothing of my sufferings, take to yourself all the virtue of my sacrifice. You shall, however, in no respect profit by it."

The Janni: "The Deity created the world, and everything that lives; and I am his minister and representative. God made you, the chief bought you, and I sacrifice you. The virtue of your death is not yours but mine; but it will be attributed to you through me."

The victim : "My curse be upon the man who, while he did not share in my price, is first at my death. Let the world ever be upon one side, while he is upon the other. Let him, destitute, and without stored food, hope to live only through the distresses of others. Let him be the poorest wretch alive. Let his wife and children think him foul. I am dying. I call upon all, upon those who bought me, on those whose food I have eaten, on those who are strangers here, on all who will now share my flesh—let all curse the Janni to the gods!"

The Janni: "Dying creature, do you contend with me? I shall not allow you a place among the gods."

The victim: "In dying I shall become a god, then will you know whom you will serve. Now do your will on me."

The place of sacrifice having been ascertained the previous night, by persons sent to probe the ground in the dark, who mark the first deep chink as that indicated by the goddess: there a short post is inserted; around it four larger posts are usually set up, and the victim is placed in the midst. The priest, assisted by two of the elders of the village, inserts the victim within the rift of a branch of a tree cut for the purpose, fitting it in some districts over the chest, in some on the neck. Cords are then twisted around the open extremity of the branch, which is, as far as possible, closed by force. The priest then slightly wounds the victim with his axe, whereupon the crowd falls on the victim, stripping the flesh from the bones, but leaving untouched the head and intestines.

The remains may not be touched by the profane or by an animal, and therefore they are watched through the night. On the following morning the priest and chiefs consume them along with a whole sheep, on a funeral pyre, when the ashes are scattered over the fields, and laid as paste over the houses and granaries. To consummate the sacrifice the father of the victim, or the party who sold him, is presented with a bullock in final satisfaction of all demands. Then a bullock is sacrificed for a feast, and the following prayer is offered up, after an invocation of all the gods :—

"O Tari Pennu! You have afflicted us greatly; have brought death to our children and our bullocks, and failure to our corn ; have afflicted us in every way. But we do not complain of this. It is your desire only to compel us to perform your due rites, and then to raise up and enrich us. We were anciently enriched by this rite; all around are great from it, therefore by our cattle, our flocks, our pigs, and our grain, we procured a victim and offered a sacrifice. Do you now enrich us. Let our herds be so numerous that they cannot be housed ; let children so abound that the care of them shall overcome the parents—as shall be seen by their burned hands; let our heads ever strike against brass pots innumerable hanging from our roofs ; let the rats form their nests of shreds of scarlet cloth and silk ; let all the kites in the country be seen in the trees of our village, from beasts being killed there every day. We are ignorant of what it is good to ask for. You know what is good for us. Give it to us."

The bullock sacrificed is then cut to pieces and distributed. Those who have come from distant villages for the purpose, return home immediately, when they find the village priest and all the inhabitants observing a strict fast, ready to receive them. The flesh is now exposed on leaves, conveyed and placed on a handful of grass in the presence of all. The heads of families, accompanied by the priest, go for their portion of the flesh. He divides the portion into two, and then again one of these into as many pieces as there are families. The priest now addresses the propitiated deity as follows :—

"O Tari Pennu! Our village offered such a person as a sacrifice, and divided the flesh among all the people in honour of the gods. Now such a village has offered such a one, and has sent us flesh for you. Be not displeased with the quantity, we could only give them as much. If you give us wealth we will repeat the rite." The priest then seats himself on the ground, scrapes a hole in it, and deposits one of the two portions of the flesh therein while his back is turned towards it, so that he cannot see his own act. Each man adds earth, and the priest pours water on it. The heads of families then fold their portions of flesh in leaves, and raise a shout of exultation. A sort of battle now takes place. Then each man buries his portion of the flesh in his favourite field in the manner the priest performed the act. After burying the flesh all return home and feast, sometimes in common, and sometimes the families apart. In some districts silence is observed for three days,—no house is swept, and no fire may be given, nor wood cut, nor a guest received. Upon the fourth day the people reassemble at the place of sacrifice, and slaughter and feast on a buffalo. A year after a hog is slaughtered in sacrifice, and the following formulary used :—"O Tari Pennu, up to this time we have been engaged in your worship, which we commenced a year ago. Now the rites are completed. Let us receive the benefit."

In some districts the victim is destroyed by fire. A low stage is erected in a sloping manner like a roof, upon which the victim is placed, his limbs wound round with cords so as to confine him without preventing his struggles. Fires are lighted, and hot brands are applied so as to make the victim roll up and down on the slopes of the stage. The efficiency of this rite, especially if for rain, will be proportioned to the tears the sufferer sheds. The victim is cut to pieces on the following day.

In the paper communicated to the Royal Asiatic Society, by the gentleman who has been already named, much interesting information is given respecting the worship paid to the first class of inferior deities, as the god of rain, the god of increase, the god of the chase, and of war, &c. The rites appertaining to the second class of inferior divinities are also stated. As it would swell this little volume beyond the prescribed limits, were any attempt made to detail the ceremonies incident to these varied objects of Khond worship, the points selected and stated at considerable length must suffice.

FEMALE INFANTICIDE.

It might be imagined that in the details of the Meriah sacrifice we had exhausted the sad catalogue of atrocities practised under the name of religion; but such is not the case, there being still other scenes of horror to be unfolded among the hill tribes of India. The horrifying practice of female infanticide exists not only among the Khonds, but among several other aboriginal tribes, and also among the Rajputs, a class who arrogate to themselves the most extraordinary claims to high origin. To preserve the natural sequence of the subject, in regard to the tribes it may be best to present, in the first instance, some account of the infanticide of the Khonds.

This inhuman practice seems to have existed on the hills among the aborigines from time immemorial; generally the life of no female child is spared except when a woman's first child is a female, or when the head of a tribe or the branch of a tribe desires to form connexions by intermarriage. The practice is not confined to the sectarists of Tari, whose horrible rites have just passed under review, but among the milder sect of Boora Pennu. It is said that villages containing a hundred houses may be seen without a single female child.

The usage is defended by the Khonds on grounds of social expediency; it is also sanctioned and encouraged by their religious doctrines. Captain Macpherson, writing on this subject and giving some account of the origin of the practice, says,—"The influence and privileges of women are exceedingly great among the Khonds, and are I believe, greatest amongst the tribes which practise infanticide. Their opinions have great weight in all public and private affairs; and their direct agency is often considered essential in the former. Thus the presence of the sisters and daughters of a tribe is indispensable at its battles to afford aid and encouragement; and the intervention of its wives, who are neutral between the tribes of their fathers and those of their husbands, is necessary to make peace. The Khond women frequently settle difficult questions between their tribes and the Rajahs, through the ladies of these, with whom they are always in communication; while these ladies. it, may be observed, are employed on critical occasions as irresistible instruments to sway the Khond chiefs."

"But the ascendency of Khond women in these tribes is completed by their extraordinary matrimonial privileges; with respect to which, however, it is to be borne in mind that intermarriage between persons of the same tribe, however large or scattered, is considered incestuous and punishable with death."

So far is constancy to a husband from being required in a wife, that her pretensions do not, at least, suffer diminution in the eyes of either sex when fines are levied on her convicted lovers; while on the other hand, infidelity on the part of a married man is held to be highly dishonourable, and is often punished by deprivation of many social privileges. A wife moreover may quit her husband at any time, except within a year of her marriage, or when she expects offspring, or within a year after the birth of a child, and she may then return to her father's house, or contract a new marriage; while no man who is without a wife may, without entailing disgrace on himself and his tribe, refuse to receive any woman who may choose to enter his house and establish herself as its mistress."

The usages of the Khonds are peculiar as regards marriage engagements, in other respects besides those already stated. The bridegroom gives for his bride a large consideration in cattle and money. The amount is in part at least contributed by the tribe, and paid over to the bride's father, who again distributes it amongst the families of his own branch of the tribe. If she quits her husband he may reclaim what he has paid. The father must return the property he has received for his daughter, and consequently calls upon those among whom he has distributed it to return the money or cattle. These usages it may be easily imagined are exceedingly inconvenient, lead to dissension and disputes, and to sanguinary conflicts among the tribes. Under these circumstances the Khonds are wont to say,—"To any man but a rich and powerful chief who desires to form connexions, and is able to make large and sudden restitutions, and to his tribe, a married daughter is a curse. By the death of our female infants before they see the light, the lives of men without number are saved, and we live in comparative peace."

The practice of infanticide is common to both the religious sects of the Khonds. Those who do not immolate human victims admit the propriety of this usage, and consequently female infanticide is universal. They allege that when Boora Pennu gave his final directions for the regulation of human affairs he said,—"Behold from making one feminine being, what have I and the whole world suffered. You are at liberty to bring up only as many women as you can manage."

As before stated, the Khonds entertain singular notions about the constitution and condition of the soul. Each child born in a tribe is the re-appearance of a person attached originally to that tribe; the child is sent by Dinga for purposes of moral rule, and its condition as a soul under the full sanctions of the system is dependent on the ceremony of naming the child on the seventh day after its birth. Should an infant die before it is named, it does not re-enter the circle of tribal spirits, but returns to the mass of spirit which the Supreme ruler has set apart for each generation of mankind. By the destruction of a female infant therefore, the addition of a new female soul is averted, and the chance of getting a new male infant is gained, or at any rate the evil is got rid of for the present.

The Khonds have another incentive to continue the practice of female infanticide. They hold that in proportion as the mass of spirit assigned for the production of souls is devoted to the male sex will be its vigour and its endowments, both physical and mental.

Under this combination of supposed advantages the Khonds have strong inducements to continue the practice under consideration. This is very clearly stated by Captain Macpherson:—"The first prayer of every Khond being for money and highly endowed male children, the belief that the mental quality of these may be raised by the destruction of the female infants, is no slight incentive to the practice, superadded to the motives afforded by the belief that the number of the males may be increased by it, that it is expressly permitted by Boora, and that it averts much of the strife and bloodshed arising from the capricious dissolution of marriage ties by women."

The religious belief and practice of that portion of the aborigines which has now passed under review are in many respects as curious as they are horrifying. Although from our ignorance of the condition, social and religious, of the different tribes that occupy other tracts of the alpine regions of India, it is impossible to affirm aught that is definitive, or to say that their superstitions are accordant with what we have ascertained from actual observation and inquiry; yet the presumption is, that a great degree of homogeneity exists among the tribes who have a common origin, and whose external circumstances are in no way essentially different. What an appalling consideration it is, that in our own possessions, in a country so highly civilized, such cruel rites as those detailed should exist! That up and down the interior and elevated tracts, in the interminable forests, on the slopes of those hilly regions, and in the interjacent valleys of its swelling mountains millions of immortal beings should be found in such a state of social and religious degradation! This part of our work may well be concluded by a quotation from the paper from which so much has been abstracted for the matter of this chapter. Captain Macpherson says:—

"The religion of the Khonds, then, is a distinct theism, with a subordinate demonology; and the sum of its chief doctrines is briefly as follows:

"The Supreme being and sole source of good, who is styled the god of light, created for himself a consort, who became the earth goddess, and the source of evil, and thereafter he created the earth, with all it contains, and man. The earth goddess, prompted by jealousy of the love borne to man by his Creator, rebelled against the god of light, and introduced moral and physical evil into the world. The god of light arrested the action of physical evil, while he left man perfectly free to receive or to reject moral evil, defined to be 'disobedience towards God and strife amongst men.' A few of mankind entirely rejected moral evil, the remainder received it. The former portion were immediately deified; the latter were condemned to endure every form of physical suffering, with death, deprivation of the immediate care of the Creator, and the deepest moral degradation. Meanwhile the god of light and his rebel consort contended for superiority, until the elements of good and evil became thoroughly commingled in man and throughout nature.

"Up to this point the Khonds hold the same general belief, but from it they divide into two sects directly opposed upon the question of the issue of the contest between the two antagonist powers.

"One sect holds that the god of light completely conquered the earth goddess, and employs her—still the active principle of evil—as the instrument of his moral rule. That he resolved to provide a partial remedy for the consequences of the introduction of evil, by enabling man to attain to a state of moderate enjoyment upon earth, and to partial restoration to communion with his Creator after death: and that, to effect this purpose he created three classes of subordinate deities, and assigned to them the office; first, of instructing man in the arts of life, and regulating the powers of nature for his use, upon the condition of his paying to them due worship; secondly, of administering a system of retributive justice, through subjection to which, and through the practice of virtue during successive lives upon earth, the soul of man might attain to beatification.

"The other sect hold, upon the other hand, that the earth goddess remains unconquered; that the god of light could not, in opposition to her will, carry out his purpose with respect to man's temporal lot; and that man, therefore, owes his elevation from the state of physical suffering into which he fell through the reception of evil, to the direct exercise of her power to confer blessings, or to her permitting him to receive the good which flows from the god of light, through the inferior gods, to all who worship them. With respect to man's destiny after death, they believe that the god of light carried out his purpose. And they believe that the worship of the earth goddess by human sacrifice is the indispensable condition on which these blessings have been granted, and their continuance may be hoped for; the virtue of the rite availing not only for those who practise it, but for all mankind."

The horrible practice of female infanticide is not less appalling in some other parts of India, although it is perpetrated on other principles. Some years ago it was stated that in Kattiwar, a thousand, and in Kuch, two thousand female infants annually perished, and that among a population not amounting to more than 125,000 souls. Thus in a small territory the amazing total of ninety thousand infants meet a cruel end in a single generation!

In 1835 Mr. Williams, the political agent in Rajasthan,

brought to light the most astounding facts on this subject. It was broadly stated in some of the accounts published some years ago in Calcutta, that in Malwa and Rajasthan, including Joudpore, Jaipur and Jaissalmir, thousands annually perished. Care was taken to form an estimate in order to ascertain the extent of the crime, and the following statistics were made. In one tribe, sons 118, daughters 16; in another, sons 240, daughters 98; in a third, sons 131, daughters 61; in a fourth, sons 14, daughters 4; in a fifth, sons 39, daughters 7. When it is recollected that in India as in Europe the number of the sexes born is nearly equal, it may easily be inferred how fearful was the destruction of females from the practice of infanticide in the provinces under review. The crime is common not only in Rajasthan, but also among the Sikhs, in Bhopal, and the inhabitants of Bundi, Jaipur, Udaipur, and Jabalpur. The Minas, a wild mountain tribe, admit that the usage is common among them. An accurate census of eleven villages showed that where the aggregate of boys under twelve years of age was 369, the number of girls of that age was only 87. In other returns the proportion of boys to girls is 44 to 4; 58 to 4; and in another village no girls at all, the inhabitants freely "confessing that they had destroyed every girl born in their village." Mr. Williams well observes: "The above details must satisfy every one that female infanticide is carried on to a frightful extent throughout Malwa and Rajputana." This is not the only testimony; Captain, after Sir Henry Pottinger, says, "I quite concur with Mr. Williams that infanticide is carried on to an extent of which we have hardly a complete notion in India."

The question starts up,—how and by whom is this horrid deed done? This inquiry has been answered by various authorities from Sir John Shore downwards. Starvation or the withholding of nature's aliment; strangling; the juice of the madár plant; the poison extracted from the tobacco plant; the juice of the poppy; and other violent means.

Slaves are employed by the wealthy to destroy their offspring. Sometimes a hole is dug, filled with milk, and the infant dropped into it. On other occasions a pill of opium is prepared by the father. Sometimes the helpless babe is left to expire lying on the ground. Often the umbilical cord is drawn over the mouth and respiration is thus prevented. The mother is commonly the executioner of her own child. She becomes the vile conspirator against that life that has been confided to her, "puts opium to the nipple, which the babe inhaling with its milk, it expires. Professing to open the fount of life to her own infant, she cruelly and deliberately impregnates it with the elements of death."

Another question arises,—What are the motives, the reason, the end, of this cruel practice? How, that the annals of humanity were thus, on system, stained with such acts of atrocity? Was it cruelty? There is no reason for such a conclusion. We may not enter on the abstract question as to what we are to understand by the word cruelty. Does the fearful practice arise from, or is it perpetuated from, a total destitution of maternal affection? Competent judges say, "No." Facts may be adduced to show that the maternal instinct in the females of Rajputana is what we find it elsewhere. There, even there, the fond mother, as her bowels yearn over the destiny of her offspring, can exclaim, "For Shri Krishna's sake, spare the innocent babe; Oh, pollute not the sacred day by the commission of so black a sin!" Her allusion to a particular day had reference to the day as specially sacred to the divinity Krishna. What, then, is the cause? Is it some gross perversion of human fancy called superstition or religious prejudice? The Rajputs plead not this in extenuation of their foul conduct. The wild tribes, the Minas, do. Space will not permit our going into an induction of particulars on this melancholy subject, and it must suffice to state, on the unanimous testimony of European and native authorities, that the real cause resolves itself into two peculiarities connected with the state of Rajputana civilization. One is the difficulty of procuring suitable matches for their daughters if permitted to attain adolescence, coupled with the disgrace attaching to the presence in a family of grown up unmarried daughters. The other peculiarity referred to is the difficulty of defraying the marriage expenses on a scale commensurate with the usages of the tribe. They regard other tribes as unworthy to receive their daughters in marriage; and they therefore prefer putting them to death to the prospects of dishonour attaching to the unmarried state. Inability to advance the requisite sum for the marriage ceremony operates as widely. They account it better to perpetrate the horrid crime of infanticide than to wound aristocratic pride by abating aught of the nuptial profusion: that were to admit a decline of fortune, a lapse into a lower condition. The whole question, then, although apparently so difficult of solution, resolves itself into the simple elemental principle, PRIDE. "Whenever and wherever there is no reasonable prospect of obtaining suitable marriages for daughters, or of defraying the customary nuptial expenses, there and then, must the life of the female infant be considered as forfeited." The name of the race, Rajputs, literally, the sons of kings, conveys the reason, the only reason, for the practice we have stated. Family descent is the matter on which they above all things pride themselves. To be inalienably and for ever identified with illustrious pedigrees, originating in solar and lunar dynasties, is the great object that absorbs all other considerations. Rather than brook the fancied disgrace of uniting with inferior tribes, or celebrating a marriage with other than princely profusion, it were better to consign their daughters to the regions of forgetfulness.

Even among the Hindus, infants are sometimes abandoned, under the impression that they are subject to demoniacal influence. If an infant refuse its food, and appear to decline in health, the inference is drawn that some malignant demon has taken possession of it. Such are frequently destroyed in the northern districts of Bengal, by being exposed on the tree where the demon is supposed to dwell. The mother deposits her infant in a basket and hangs it on the tree, leaving it to perish by starvation, or by birds, or beasts of prey.

THE EXPOSURE OF THE SICK ON THE BANKS OF THE GANGES.

This cruel practice may deserve a brief notice. The Hindus worship the river Ganges, and believe that a dying man brought to expire within its sight ascends to a higher blessedness than if he died under other circumstances. The following extract, from a Hindu essayist, will place the practice in its true light:—

"Whenever," says he, "the disease of a native patient arrives at such a stage, as, according to the judgment of the natives, renders any further attempt of his recovery fruitless, the first thing that is suggested to his friends and relatives, as a matter of duty, is to carry him to the banks of the river, or to use the homely phrase of the natives, 'To give him to Ganga.' Here we must observe, that in the minds of the orthodox Hindus, the carrying of their sick to the river, is at all times and in all circumstances, reckoned as a higher and stronger duty, than the seeking of means for their recovery. Their reasoning on this head, is indeed very simple. 'Life and death,' say they, 'are in the hands of the gods; but the carrying of the sick to the river lies entirely in our own hands, therefore we must first do our duty, let the doom of the sick be as the gods may determine.' Such being the state of the minds of the natives, the scene which next follows is highly affecting. No sooner do the native practitioners pronounce the case of a Hindu patient to be hopeless, than all the members of his family, assisted by their neighbours, begin, with all haste and precaution, to make preparations for taking him to the river; which consist in bringing that wretched imitation of a couch, called the khat for the dead, and a number of torches, if it be night, in sending for the old and experienced persons, and in giving a general notice throughout the neighbourhood. In the meantime the friends of the sick watch with great diligence and anxiety over the progress of his disease; but, alas, not because they care so much for his death, as for his dying at home. When the necessary preparations are made, a piece of cloth, which is the worst and the dirtiest in the patient's bed, is spread over the couch on which he is to be carried, and then he himself is laid upon it. Now is presented the most moving part of the scene. All the relatives of the dying sick, the females in particular, who of course are not allowed to go out of the doors, gather round his couch, beat their breasts and foreheads; some go to clasp their dying friend with their arms; others, in the height of grief, fall flat on the ground; while all raise a cry, the shrillest that can ever be imagined. From the midst of this most distressing scene, the sick is brought out, not without much exertion, and carried to the river, the bearers and attendants throughout the way repeating loudly the names of the gods and goddesses arranged for the purpose in a certain order. When they arrive at the banks of the river, they step down the ghat, and lay their burden close to the waters of the Ganges; then they ask

him to cast a look on her wide expanse, and cause him to say, that he is come to see the mother Ganges. He is then brought upon the ghat, where either a low, damp, and miserable hut, or, as is in some places the case, a decent building, but crowded with a multitude of the dying sick, and filled with all manner of dirt and nuisance, receives him. Here he is brought down from the khat and laid on a miserable bed on the floor, surrounded on all sides with beings like himself, whose shrieks and groanings disturb his repose at every moment. A few minutes before his death, he is again brought down on the brink of the river, where, half immersed in water, he gives up the ghost."

Some most heartrending recitals have been made regarding the usage of the Hindus under notice. The habit of choking the dying patients with the water and mud of the Ganges is undoubtedly practised; and hundreds and thousands, who might have recovered, have thus been destroyed. It is estimated that a thousand per diem die on the Ganges; of whom, no doubt, many are immolated at its shrine.

Should a person conveyed to the river in prospect of death recover, he is rejected as an alien of his mother's children, and ever after treated as an outcast.

The following prayer addressed to the Ganges, from a popular religious poem, may serve to show the extraordinary importance which the Hindus ascribe to the sacred stream:

"O, mother Ganges, I now bow down at thy feet; have mercy upon thy servant. O, who can describe thy virtues, since they are past the comprehension of the powers of man! The supreme divinity, Brahma, can alone describe some of thy qualities. Were the greatest of sinners, the perpetrator of endless sins, to pronounce the word Ganga, he, being delivered from all his sins, shall be translated to the blissful abode of the celestials. Thou alone art properly called the 'source of happiness,' and the 'saviour of men.' Infinite sources of salvation are at thy command. In whatever state a man may die, he is saved, as is proved in the case of the deliverance of the sons of Ságar, who had been reduced to ashes by the curse of a sage. It is only children that say that it is necessary to be in a state of consciousness. He who performs ablutions on thy banks not only saves himself but also saves his ancestors, the ancestors of his mother and the ancestors of his wife. Where but in thy bosom do still-born children find their place of repose? Thou art material, thou art immaterial! Thou art simple, thou art compound! Thou art the eternal source of all."

CHAPTER XVI.

BUDDHISM.—CAVE TEMPLES OF ELEPHANTA AND SALSETTE.—ROCK TEMPLES OF ELLORA.—THE JAINS.—THE PARSIS.—THE JEWS.—THE MOHAMMEDANS.

The reference occasionally made in this little work to Buddhism seems to demand some notice of its doctrines. The former prevalence of this system in the Indian peninsula; its present existence and influence in India, in the adjacent countries of Birmah, China, and Ceylon; as well as the antiquities connected with it, and which must be briefly described, seem to require some account of its principles. The devices on ancient coins found in India; the discovery, in places wide apart, of Buddhistic relics and symbols; the extraordinary excavations and their sculptures and inscriptions in various parts of India and Ceylon, and the blending of Brahmanical with Buddhistic imagery in some of the ancient cave temples, sufficiently attest the power this system once obtained. At one period it struggled hard with Brahmanism for dominion. Although it may not be conceded that Buddhism was anterior to Brahmanism, or that it ever occupied in India a pre-eminent position, it was at one epoch co-extensive with it, and for a time rose to superiority. It appears to have extended as far north as the Caucasian range. Some of the most illustrious monarchs of India were numbered among its disciples,—monarchs who made treaties with Antiochus the Great, and who successfully opposed the Greeks of Bactria. It seems at one time to have occupied a place side by side with Brahmanism and Mithraism in the worship of the Hindu Scythians. India gave its Buddhism to China: it conveyed the Buddhistic faith into that country not long after the birth of Christ; and it is now the religion of three hundred and seventy-four millions of our fellow-men in that vast empire. It is also the religion of Thibet, Tartary, Birmah, Siam, Japan, and south and central Ceylon. Upwards of five hundred millions of the human family are at this moment the adherents of Buddhism and Brahmanism, a fact too significant to allow the philanthropist to pass over the inquiry into their principles. Under these impressions it is deemed right to occupy a page or two with a few remarks on this widely extended system of religion.

It is probable that both the systems of Brahma and of Buddha had a common origin, the former having the precedence in the order of time. The extravagant pantheism of the Brahmanical schools of philosophy seems to have created a reaction in certain minds, which resulted in the Buddhistic theory. The pantheist taught that there is only one sole, self-existing being—God; that all things are God. The revulsion of mind from this extraordinary doctrine produced the denial of the existence of a supreme Intelligence, and the persuasion that no such being as God exists at all. Thus pantheism was met by the opposite extreme of atheism. The Brahmanical theory resolves all things into spirit, to the exclusion of matter, whose existence he denies; and the Buddhistic theory resolves all things into matter, to the exclusion of spirit, whose being it ignores.

There are strong reasons for concluding that the Egyptian, Chaldean, Sabæan and Indian systems, in which the sun occupies so prominent a place as an object of adoration, had a common origin.

About the commencement of the Christian era, a fierce struggle was maintained between the followers of Brahmanism and Buddhism, that ended in the entire expulsion of the latter from India: the precise date of this event has not yet been ascertained.

The Budha at present revered was born at Pataliputra or the modern Patna, on the Ganges, B.C. 623; attained the perfection which raised him to the deified position of Budha, B.C. 588; and died at the age of eighty, B.C. 543. The Buddhistic system teaches that every individual born into the world may become Budha, as being equally eligible for the attainment of the highest intellectual perfection, and consequent final beatitude, which consists in the extinction or cessation of being. Budha is not worshipped as a deity, or a still existent or active agent of benevolence and power; he is venerated as a remembrancer, an exemplar, the effulgence of whose purity is to serve as a guide and incentive to the future struggles and aspirations of mankind. The sole superiority which his doctrines admit is that of goodness and wisdom; and Budha himself, having attained to this perfection by the immaculate righteousness of his actions, the absolute subjugation of his passions, and the unerring accuracy of his unlimited knowledge, became entitled to the homage of all, and was required to render it to none.

This system interweaves with itself the doctrine of the metempsychosis; it teaches a series of existences, but denies that the present body or soul had ever a prior existence. The present existence is the effect of previous being, as a tree is of an antecedent seed or tree: it is not the tree from which the originating seed or tree came—desire produces the future existence. The past being terminates; the supervening existence arises from the cherished passion of that which has ceased to be. The metaphor of a lamp, as well as that of a tree is employed to illustrate this dogma. One lamp is employed to light another, but the lighted lamp is not the one from which the light was derived. Final beatitude, or the escape of the soul from existence, is not absorption into the Supreme Essence,—that is denied to exist at all,—but a complete and final cessation of being: hence Buddhism differs from Brahmanism.

As to the visible universe, that is the self-originated result of procession from eternal matter, this eternal matter is naturally subject at remote intervals to decay and formation;

but this and the organization of animal life, are bùt the results of spontaneity and procession, not the products of will and design on the part of an all-powerful Creator.

Such are the leading principles of this system as regards the condition of things animate and inanimate. The notions of the Buddhists on geography and astronomy, the existence of superior and inferior worlds, the existence of supernals and infernals, and places of temporary enjoyment and misery, are much the same as those of the Hindus.

These notices of the Buddhistic religion, although very short, will suffice in relation to the object of their introduction, which is that of elucidating some of the peculiarities found among the antiquities of India. They may also be useful to some who may wish to understand the peculiarities of religious belief existing among eastern tribes. In my intercourse with intelligent friends in England, the question has often been raised as to the difference which exists between the systems of the Brahmanists and the Buddhists; the preceding paragraphs may serve to convey to any into whose hands this little volume may come, the information which some may desiderate.

In this chapter it is proposed to give a brief account of some of the most remarkable antiquities; but the notices will be short, and made in subservience to the main object pursued, that of casting light on the opinions, observances, and religious establishments of the Hindus. In many parts of India and Ceylon there are numerous places sacred to the objects of religion, and for which a deep veneration is cherished by the people. Some of these hallowed spots are the natural features of the country, as mountains, rivers, waterfalls, promontories, and other objects, which have become famous by some real or supposed event connected with them in the legendary stories of Hindu literature. The lofty Himalayas, the Ganges, Adam's Peak, Ramisseram, Cape Comorin, and other places, are regarded with intense interest by all earnest Hindus who are conversant with the stories recorded in the popular literature, and they are consequently visited by pilgrims from every part of the country.

Besides these, and similar objects, there are monuments of art that attest the zeal and munificence of those who originated them: such are the extensive excavations, the cavern temples and monasteries, and the rock or monolithic temples, in the provinces of Bombay and on the eastern coast. To some of these interesting objects it is now proposed to direct attention; and, in the first place, I shall endeavour to describe briefly the wonderful caves in the Presidency of Bombay, some of which I had the opportunity of visiting previous to my departure from India. The antiquities of the class under review are so numerous and extensive, that it were impossible to do more in this brief survey than make a few references to their number and character; the chief may be enumerated, and one or two selected for more particular description.

The most remarkable cavern and rock temples are at Karli, Ajantá, Nasik, Ellora, Salsette, Elephanta, and Mahavalipuram. The architecture of the caves is monumental in its character, possessing much of the colossal grandeur and vastness of the Egyptian style, with which it harmonizes in its general outline and design. In the absence of any distinct base, and in the exhibition of double capitals peculiar to Egypt, and in the sculptured figure of a devotee or saint instead of Isis, on the capitals, the Indian cave pillars are similar to those of Egypt. When I visited the excavations of Egypt after my departure from India, I could have imagined myself again at Salsette, had not the subjacent valley of the Nile served to dispel the illusion: I refer more particularly to the minor excavations at Beni Hassan and Tel-el-Amana. It may be remarked that in the excavations of Egypt there is a lightness and beauty that create a cheerful feeling rarely felt in viewing similar monuments in India. The cave of Elephanta seems pervaded with a sentimental gloom that is not dissipated by a near inspection of its sculptures: these harmonize best with the worst features of Puranic story. Its shrines, the tri-faced figure of the Hindu Triad, the colossal guards, the groups of preternatural personages, the symbol of the Saiva worship, are all alike fitted to overawe the votaries of Hinduism, and to secure their reverence and prostration. The expression given to the features in Egyptian sculpture is generally extremely agreeable. There is a calm repose, a stillness and an air of tranquillity, that contrasts to great advantage with the stern, the malign and demon forms so prominent in the groups of Indian sculpture.

In the caves of Western India the personages represented in the sculptures are connected with the simple forms and manifestations of Budha, and the complex and elaborate objects of the Brahmanical Pantheon. The Buddhistic excavations are diverse from the Brahmanical in having numerous cells and apartments, with stone seats extending around their walls, showing that they were dedicated to the use of a monastic fraternity, and the education of disciples who had retired from the scenes of secular life for purposes of seclusion and religious discipline. In some of their habits and institutions the Buddhistic ascetics appear to have resembled the ancient anchorets of Egypt, who dwelt in the rocks on the borders of the Lybian desert. The Buddhistic further differ from the Brahmanical in being associated too with tombs constructed with great care, and, in some instances, with incredible labour, for the burial of their saints. In some of these mausolea various relics, as gold and silver boxes, coins, pearls, and precious stones, have been discovered. Some of the coins are of a highly important character, casting light on periods of history connected with central Asia, that have not hitherto been susceptible of study in any other way.

In many of the caves there are inscriptions, some of them long, in a peculiar character, which it has been ascertained was in use in many parts of India several centuries anterior to the Christian era. In the magnificent and extensive monuments at Ajanta, there are numerous frescoes, which in character and artistic skill harmonize well with those found in the grottos of Egypt. The subjects of these paintings are diversified: persons are represented as variously employed, some bearing burdens, some conversing together; ladies writing or drawing on tablets, in apartments on whose walls musical instruments are hung; some are promenading under parasols, and others are seated under canopies. Female figures, having their tresses adorned with fillets of flowers, and apparently intended to represent the natives of the south of India, adorn some of the caves. The caves of Ajanta are in the face of lofty and precipitous rocks in sequestered ravines, which are, where nature admits of it, clothed with verdure; and they are enlivened by a cascade seventy or eighty feet high, whose foaming waters leap down the ravine in a noisy torrent.

The wonderful monuments at Ellora we can only refer to; they are so numerous and so elaborate in workmanship that volumes might be written in describing them. The Monolithic temple called Kailas, the paradise of Siva, must, however, be specially pointed out. This monument is a pagoda or tower one hundred feet high, standing in a spacious area four hundred feet deep. This immense block of stone is formed into a magnificent temple with various apartments, and decorated within and without with endlessly varied mythological figures, some of which, as elephants, tigers, divinities, &c., are of colossal dimensions. There is another architectural monument called Tin-tal, or three-storied, having as many apartments one above the other, and designed to represent the three worlds already noticed: the worlds are heaven, earth, and hell.

At Mahavalipuram, called by navigators the Seven Pagodas, on the eastern coast of India, about thirty miles south of Madras, there are some extraordinary monuments, of the same general character as those just described. Some are excavations in the solid rock, and others are monolithic. In one of the excavations, dedicated to Siva, there is a gigantic figure of Vishnu, sleeping on the serpent Shesha; and, at the opposite end of the apartment, is a figure of Parvati, mounted on a lion. She is represented as at Ellora destroying Maheswar; a similar piece is found in Egyptian temples, and represents Horus sleeping on a lion. The two are considered by archæologists as designed to represent the same mythological sentiment. By the serpent couch of Vishnu in the Indian cave three figures stand apparently in an attitude of grief and meditation. On one of the rocks a spirited scene, in well-executed bas-relief, represents the deity Krishna attending the herds of Ananda; in which there is a colossal figure of that divinity, surrounded by the shepherdesses, who are attired as the women of Southern India at the present day. One group represents a man playing on a flute for the amusement of an admiring auditory crowding around him. This is executed in a very spirited manner, and with great taste.

It is supposed by some that Mahavalipuram is mentioned by Ptolemy as an emporium of eastern commerce at a period prior to the Christian era; he calls the place Mahamaliappur. Tradition states that there was once a large city here, that has been submerged by some convulsion of nature. Most likely the city has been destroyed by the encroachment of the sea, which on this coast in some places is known to be advancing on the land.[1]

When I passed through Bombay, on my way to England, I visited the beautiful island of Elephanta, in the harbour of that port. The island lies seven miles east of the city of Bombay. This little insular place is famed for its cavern temple. The island derives its name from a colossal statue of an elephant, that was erected as an ornament in the way

[1] More than twenty years ago I wrote an account of this place, which appeared in the "Calcutta Christian Observer," along with some lithographic prints from original drawings sketched on the spot by a Missionary friend, the Rev. Thomas Hodson.

Day & Son Lith^rs to the Queen.

CAVE OF ELEPHANTA.

leading from the landing-place to the temple. When I visited Elephanta there was an artist, engaged by the Honourable East India Company, who was making accurate drawings of the sculptures that have given so much celebrity to the excavations of the island. I was informed that orders had been issued by the Court of Directors to the local authorities to preserve from further mutilation these and other valuable relics of antiquity, and also to take such steps as may be found necessary for collecting archæological information relating to the history and mythology of the country. Abbas Pacha in Egypt has taken similar precautions relative to the antiquities of the Nile; he has ordered the Grand Temple, at Karnak, in Eastern Thebes, to be cleared out; and I was informed that he had made arrangements for the preparation of a complete work on the ancient monuments of Egypt.

The caves of Elephanta are hewn out of the solid rock. The area of the principal apartment is about 130 feet square. In front of the principal entrance, which, being to the north, is, for the most part, sheltered from the sun, a good view is obtained of the sea and the country lying beyond it; besides this portal there are two openings at the sides, which are available for ventilation and light. The rock which forms the roof is supported by twenty-six pillars and sixteen pilasters. There are several small apartments or chapels connected with the chief area; in one of these chapels is a figure of the Saiva symbol, serving to show that the cave was dedicated to that divinity. The pillars supporting the roof, as well as those that form the principal entrance, have suffered from age; these latter, which are somewhat of the Egyptian style, must have been peculiarly elegant when entire.

On entering this cave temple, the first object that strikes the visitor is a colossal figure, composed of three heads united in one bust, as may be seen in the accompanying representation: it is thirteen feet high. This imposing piece of sculpture represents the Hindu Triad, Brahma, Vishnu, and Siva.

On the right and left of this bust are two human figures, which appear to occupy the place of attendants or guards. In different parts of the temple, on the walls, are groups of figures in bold relief, illustrating some particular event in the history of the god Siva. In one of the groups he is depicted in a hermaphrodite form, having one breast, which is undoubtedly intended to represent the mystic doctrine, already noticed, of a female energy. In the same group Siva is represented holding a trident, which is the symbol of his dominion over the three worlds. The four-faced Brahma appears in this group, attended by his swans; the swan is the vehicle on which he rides. Kartikèsha and Ganèsha also appear in this tabular and historic piece. Surmounting the whole, a company of nymphs or celestial choristers is sculptured, who appear attendant on their lord. In another compartment Siva is represented as the avenger and destroyer; here he wields a sword, and the victim of his wrath trembles before him. The serpent is introduced into this group; and the divinity is sculptured as wearing a string of human skulls round his neck. The ornaments on the walls, the presence of the Linga as a shrine, and, indeed, all connected with the cave, show it to be the work of a people who were devoted to the Saiva worship.

As previously intimated, I visited Salsette, about twenty miles from Bombay. Leaving the public road at Vihar, I passed through a thick jungle for about four miles before I reached the celebrated excavations for which this island is distinguished. On my way to Salsette I passed by the railway several times.

The excavations at Salsette are formed on the sides of hills in the precipitous rocks, and generally consist of a series of stories one higher than the other, and connected by flights of steps cut in the sides of the rocks. Some of these ascents are in almost impracticable places, and require the visitor to proceed on his way with caution; were he to lose his balance he might be precipitated and destroyed. Some of the numerous apartments in these excavations are spacious and well executed. Connected with those that were used for the resident recluses are well formed cisterns for the reception of the rain-water, which, as may be seen, was conducted into them by grooves or conduits cut in the rocks. There are several deep pits built up with burnt brick, which appear to have been used for the burial of the dead.

The largest cave of this mountain is a curious vaulted excavation of the form of a Christian church, having a nave and aisles. The apsis is occupied by a deghob or mausoleum; it is cylindrical in the shaft, and surmounted by a cupola. On the right and left of the portico are two colossal figures of Budha, perhaps twenty feet high. On the columns of this portico there are two long inscriptions. A Chinese traveller, about the year A.D. 406, mentions a cavern temple of five stories and numerous cells in this region, which are supposed to be these excavations; they are evidently Buddhistic.

In some places we find the beetling rocks, or natural recesses in mountainous regions, converted into temples or monasteries; this mode obviated the immense labour necessary in excavations. One of this description I visited in the Island of Ceylon, in 1843; it is situated at Dambool, about forty-five miles from Kandy, on the Trincomalie road. The rock in which this famous cavern temple is found is a mass of gneiss, about five hundred feet high. The recess is a deep cavity, which has been built up at the front with considerable pretensions to architectural effect. The interior is profusely decorated with paintings and highly-coloured devices; it also contains a recumbent statue of Budha, forty-seven feet in length, of good proportions. From the size of this figure some idea may be formed of the extent and magnificence of the apartment; the largest apartment in this temple is one hundred and ninety feet long by ninety feet wide, and forty-five feet high. With reference to the colossal statues so often met with among Buddhistic antiquities, I may mention one in the Mysore, about seven miles from Chenroypatanam. This statue is a monolith, and has been formed by cutting away the rock and leaving the figure as it now stands in all the proportions of a human being. This statue, which is twenty-six feet between the shoulders, is seventy feet and seven inches high. In its immediate neighbourhood there is a beautiful waterfall of eight hundred perpendicular feet, whose stream issues in a river that is navigable for nearly twenty miles from the sea.

Even from these very brief notices of the works of art, the inference is forced upon us, that the people who produced them must have been numerous, powerful, and highly civilized. And since the two religious sections, the Brahminists and the Buddhists, occupy great prominence in these ancient monuments, it follows that the systems must at one time have been in an ascendent position. Nothing can exceed Kailas, the temple of Mahádeb at Ellora;—as far as possible this is represented in a lithograph prepared by Messrs. Day & Son, and prefixed to the chapter on the fine arts of the Hindus;[1]—all that is splendid and ornamental in architecture above ground is here produced in the interior of the mountain. In the solid granite of these rocky precipices we have repeated in sculptured relief the personages and the deeds of Hindu mythology amidst peristyles, chapels, pilasters, porticos, on walls, columns, obelisks and in colossal statues. Nothing can be conceived more imposing than a row of huge elephants introduced to sustain the superincumbent weight of this extraordinary place. Some idea may be formed of the magnitude of this unique specimen of sacred art, when it is known that the vestibule of Kailas is eighty-eight feet deep by one hundred and thirty-eight feet in breadth. This vestibule introduces the spectator into the temple itself, which measures one hundred and forty-two feet in length. The pyramidal and monolithic temple already noticed is one of the most striking objects of this wonderful assemblage of ancient monuments; the variety, richness, and skill, displayed in its decorations surpass descrip-

[1] Page 127.

tion; and, with the magnificent pagodas of the south, may be regarded as proving the eminence the Hindus once attained in architecture.

The question of chronology naturally occurs to the mind when such monuments as those we have been describing are under review. Whilst very opposite opinions have been expressed, it would be hazardous for any one, unless indeed on very certain data, to make any positive assertion regarding the time of their origin. Some archæologists are disposed to ascribe them to an age extremely remote, whilst others contend for a comparatively modern date. That some of them, perhaps most of them, belong to periods anterior to the Christian era, can hardly be doubted. Be that as it may, they are the works of an extraordinary and highly civilized people, and indicate the religious influence which an all-powerful priesthood had over them. Powerful indeed must have been the effect on the mind of the ancient Hindus, of a system that was enforced by so much that was imposing in the creations of literary genius as presented in the epic writers, and in its mythology thus pictorially exhibited in the splendid works of art always before them; and these were rendered trebly more impressive, because associated with the religious rites, ceremonies, and festivities of their oft-recurring and attractive commemorations. Combined, as the system always has been, in their literature, their decorated sanctuaries, their festivals and their daily ceremonial, and upheld by numerous learned and zealous priests, it is easy to see that the religion of India must exert a magic and plastic influence over its votaries.

THE JAINS.

As reference is occasionally made in works on India to the heterodox sect known by the name of Jains, it may not be out of place to give some account of these sectarists. At one time they were very popular in some parts of India, and they are still numerous in the north-western provinces.

One of their temples at Bombay is a structure of considerable preténsion. They have an extensive and independent literature, including works on various subjects of science and philosophy, and also numerous Puranas.

"The leading tenets of the *Jains*, and those which chiefly distinguish them from the rest of the *Hindus*, are well known; they are, first, the denial of the divine origin and infallible authority of the *Vedas;* secondly, the reverence of certain holy mortals, who acquired by practices of self-denial and mortification, a station superior to that of the gods; and thirdly, extreme and even ludicrous tenderness for animal life.[1]

"The disregard of the authority of the *Vedas* is common to the *Jains* and the *Bauddhas*, and involves a neglect of the rites which they prescribe: in fact, it is in a great degree from those rites that an inference unfavourable to the sanctity of the *Vedas* is drawn; and not to speak of the sacrifices of animals which the *Vedas* occasionally enjoin, the *Homa*, or burnt-offering, which forms a part of every ceremonial in those works, is an abomination; as insects crawling amongst the fuel, bred by the fermented butter, or falling into the flame, cannot fail to be destroyed by every oblation. As far, however, as the doctrines they teach are conformable to *Jain* tenets, the *Vedas* are admitted and quoted as authority.

"The veneration and worship of mortals is also common to the *Jains* and *Bauddhas*, but the former have expanded and methodised the notions of the latter. The *Bauddhas*, although they admit an endless number of earthly *Budhas* to have existed, and specify more than a century of names, confine their reverence to a comparatively small number—to seven. The *Jains* extend this number to twenty-four for a given period, and enumerate, by name, the twenty-four of their past age, or *Avasarpini*, the twenty-four of the present, and

[1] At Bombay I visited an hospital established for the reception of old and infirm animals, which is kept up at a great expense from the motives here noticed.

the twenty-four of the age to come. The statues of these, either all or in part, are assembled in their temples, sometimes of colossal dimensions, and usually of black or white marble. The objects held in highest esteem in *Hindustan* are PARSWANÁTH and MAHÁVIRA, the twenty-third and twenty-fourth *Jinas* of the present era, who seem to have superseded all their predecessors.

"The generic names of a *Jaina* saint express the ideas entertained of his character by his votaries. He is *Jagat-prabhu*, lord of the world; *Kshinakermmá*, free from bodily or ceremonial acts; *Sarvajna*, omniscient; *Adhiswara*, supreme lord; *Devádideva*, god of gods; and similar epithets of obvious purport; whilst others are of a more specific character, as *Tirthakára* or *Tirthankara*, *Kevali*, *Arhat*, and *Jina*. The first implies one who has crossed over, (*Tiryate anena*,) that is, the world compared to the ocean; *Kevali*, is the possessor of *Kevala*, or spiritual nature, free from its investing sources of error; *Arhat* is one entitled to the homage of gods and men; and *Jina* is the victor over all human passions and infirmities.

"Besides these epithets, founded on attributes of a generic character, there are other characteristics common to all the *Jinas*, of a more specific nature. These are termed *Atisayas*, or superhuman attributes, and are altogether thirty-six; four of them, or rather four classes, regard the person of a *Jina*, such as the beauty of his form, the fragrance of his body, the white colour of his blood, the curling of his hair, its non-increase, and that of the beard and nails, his exemption from all natural impurities, from hunger and thirst, from infirmity and decay; these properties are considered to be born with him. He can collect around him millions of beings, gods, men, and animals, in a comparatively small space; his voice is audible to a great distance; and his language, which is *Arddha Màgadhi*, is intelligible to animals, men, and gods: the back of his head is surrounded with a halo of light, brighter than the disk of the sun, and for an immense interval around him, wherever he moves, there is neither sickness nor enmity, storm nor dearth, neither plague portents nor war."

THE PARSIS.

An immigrant population of Parsis exists in India, of which the bulk is settled in Bombay. It is estimated that the Parsi population of that great centre of political and commercial activity amounts to nearly one hundred thousand. They are fire worshippers, and at Bombay they maintain their religious rites with great zeal. Their mode of disposing of the dead is very singular. In the suburbs of Bombay they have several large circular enclosures, erected probably thirty feet high, and about fifty feet in diameter, within which are arranged three concentric platforms, provided with slight depressions on their surface, in which the dead, shrouded in cloth, are deposited. The outer circle is for males, the next for females, and the innermost for children of both sexes. In the centre of the enclosure is a deep pit for the reception of the remains as they may be washed off the platforms by the rain. This enclosure is open to the heavens, and therefore the dead are exposed both to the elements and the birds of prey, of which large numbers are present in the surrounding trees. The vulture, not being indigenous in that part of India, was imported for the purpose of consuming the dead. I was informed by a gentleman, who kindly accompanied me to the locality under notice, that the dead are delivered up to the custody of a particular class of Parsis, whose business it is to attend to all the rites of sepulture.

The Parsis are an active and energetic race, and sometimes not inaptly called the Anglo-Saxons of India. In commerce and in practical science they are distinguished above the Hindus, by their greater energy and perseverance.

THE JEWS.

The Jews are found in Calcutta and Bombay, where they have synagogues that I have attended. The Rabbi who was in Calcutta when I was resident there, was a native of Bagdad, and a most agreeable person. He frequently came to my house to read Hebrew with me, and he gave me a copy of the first printed edition of the Syriac New Testament.

On the western coast of India, at Cochin, there is an ancient colony of Jews, consisting of two classes, the white and the black. They settled on the coast of India, according to their own account, shortly after the destruction of Jerusalem. Dr. Buchanan obtained from them a very valuable copy of the Pentateuch in the Samaritan character. The white Jews have received an infusion of new blood, from time to time, from Persia and Arabia, and therefore they retain their national characteristics. Probably the colony emigrated at a very remote period from the countries just named, for commercial objects, and settled as did the members of the so-called Syrian Church.

The black Jews of Cochin, who have sometimes been regarded as descendants of the ten tribes, are no doubt converts to Judaism from the natives of the western coast of India. This is the account given of them by the white Jews themselves, who have so far imbibed the caste-feeling of the country that they regard their darker brethren as a separate and inferior caste, refusing to intermarry or even to associate with them, and compel them to have a separate low-caste synagogue of their own. The black Jews are, however, strongly attached to their religious rites.

THE MOHAMMEDANS.

The Mohammedan population of India amounts to about ten or twelve millions of souls, and is scattered abroad throughout the land in varied proportion to the Hindus. They are generally inaccessible, hard-hearted, contemptuous, ignorant, and proud: they are peculiarly intolerant and bigoted, and therefore they have been called by some the Roman Catholics of the East.

CHAPTER XVII.

CHRISTIANITY IN INDIA.—ST. THOMAS.—PANTÆNUS.—COSMAS.—ALFRED THE GREAT'S EMBASSY TO INDIA.—THE PORTUGUESE, THEIR VIOLENT PROCEEDINGS. — XAVIER. — ROMISH PERSECUTION OF THE SYRIAN CHURCH.—THE MISSION OF THE JESUITS AT MADURA.—PROCEEDINGS OF THE DUTCH.

AMONG the strangers at Jerusalem, especially among the "Parthians," who felt the impulses of the day of Pentecost, we may, without any great licence, imagine, that there were some, who, destined to open the way for the introduction of the Gospel into "the regions beyond," were at that time fitted to extend the objects of that event even to the borders of India. That Christianity was planted in the south of India at a very early period, admits of no doubt; but there is no historical evidence to show by whom it was conveyed. The legend which states that St. Thomas and St. Barnabas preached the Gospel in South India and Ceylon rests on no valid grounds, although it has been received with a good degree of confidence by some eminent men even in the Reformed Church.

Eusebius states that in the division of the Gentile world among the Apostles of our Lord, Parthia, that part of Central Asia bounded by the river Indus, was assigned to St. Thomas. Origen, who wrote in the third century, says expressly that St. Thomas published the Gospel in Parthia, Media, Caramania and Bactriana. The last-named kingdom bordered on the territory of Indo-Scythia, and that of the Massagetæ, through which the Indus flowed. Though St. Thomas himself may not have crossed into India Proper, it is probable that he received his title of Apostle of India, from the proximity of his field of labour to that country. In the absence of historic data we are left to conjecture the means first employed by Providence for conveying the message of mercy to the interesting country of which this volume treats. To set the subject in as clear a light as possible, I will here introduce all the information relating to it that I have been able to gather.

Beginning then with credible history, we find that St. Mark, who in the early part of his mission travelled with Paul and Barnabas, settled in Egypt and founded the Church of Alexandria. At that time there resided in that emporium of Eastern commerce numerous strangers from Arabia, Persia, Media, and Parthia, some of whom, like the Apostle himself, had probably witnessed the events of Pentecost and felt its power. It is not improbable that some of these, in the pursuit of commercial objects, were in the habit of travelling to India, and in some cases remaining there at least for a time, as is the case with the Arabians and Abyssinians at the present day; and of necessity, if earnest men, they would not only observe the usages of their religion, but speak of the wonderful events so recently witnessed at Jerusalem. Socotra, an island midway between Egypt and India, also received the Gospel at a very early period, and no doubt from those who were in the habit of trafficking with that insulated spot. There is enough in the Acts of the Apostles to show that in the early ages of the Church, as now, Providence used various methods for the diffusion of the truth. The pilgrim from the queen of Ethiopia, the man of Macedonia, are examples in point. The strangers scattered abroad by the early persecution of the Church, conveyed the glad tidings of salvation, and because the hand of the Lord was with them, they so spake that many believed. It were inconsistent with the history of the Church not to believe that those days of the right hand of the Most High furnished many bright examples of men, who, animated with divine love, went forth, possibly as far as to India, to preach among the Gentiles the unsearchable riches of Christ. We know that many did obey the command of our Lord, and that through them the word sounded forth to the ends of the earth: the testimony of Eusebius on this point is explicit. Thus far, however, as regards India we are left solely to inference.

We have more satisfactory evidence as regards the early church in India about the year 200. Then we are informed that Demetrius, the Bishop of Alexandria, received a message from certain persons in India, earnestly requesting him to send some one to instruct them in the doctrines of Christ. Whether those who had gone thither for commercial or other purposes made the request, or whether the natives themselves, who might have heard something of Christianity, and were desirous to know more of its teaching, sent to the Bishop, is not apparent. The constant communication kept up between the two countries rendered the transmission of the message easy. Pantænus, a Stoic philosopher, who had embraced Christianity, and at that time presided over a school at Alexandria, on hearing of the requisition from India, offered to undertake the mission. He went, remained some time, how long does not appear, and returning to Egypt, afterwards resumed his former occupation. Though some doubts have been thrown on the mission of Pantænus as to the country to which he went, it being alleged by some that he went no further than Arabia or Abyssinia, there is circumstantial evidence that India was the scene of his labours: for his pupil, Clemens Alexandrinus, alluding to the inhabitants of that country, describes the ascetics, the Brahmans, and speaks also of Budha: it is probable that he had his information from his teacher, Pantænus.

After the establishment of Christianity as the religion of the Byzantine empire under Constantine, at the Council of Nice, held by order of the Emperor in the year 325, one of the assembled prelates, named Johannes, subscribed as Metropolitan of Persia and of the Great India. At that time an active trade was carried on between western countries and India, through Persia. This would lead to the residence of Persians in the emporia of commerce in India and Ceylon: over these no doubt the bishop in question presided.

We now pass on to the next notice of the Indian Church which is found in history. In the sixth century Cosmas, in the reign of Justinian, wrote a work, entitled, Christian Topography, for the purpose of vindicating the Cosmography of the Old Testament, from what he believed to be the heresies of the Ptolemaic System. This writer, surnamed Indicopleustes, the Indian Voyager, was a merchant of Alexandria, then the emporium of eastern trade both for Rome and Constantinople. The accuracy of his geographical description of the western coast of India, and of the commerce carried on with that country both by the Red Sea and the Persian Gulf, is unquestionable. His testimony is as follows: "There is," says he, "in the island of Taprobane (Ceylon), in the furthermost India, in the Indian Sea, a Christian Church, with an episcopal form of discipline, priests, and deacons, and a liturgy. In Malabar (the western coast of India), where pepper grows, there are Christians, with a bishop, who comes from Persia." At the time Cosmas visited them these Christians are said to have been Nestorians in belief. This further serves to show that they were subject to the Primate of Persia, who held the Nestorian creed. It may be remarked that the Syrian Christians, as they are generally called, on the western coast of India, are not now Nestorians, but Jacobites. They changed their tenets when the Patriarch of Seleucia adopted the Jacobite notions. The testimony of Cosmas regarding the existence of the Church in India and Ceylon is most explicit, and harmonizes with the statements coming from other sources, as already given.

It will be in place to notice that Alfred the Great, apparently under the impression that St. Thomas planted the Church in India, in accordance with the custom of his times, sent an embassy to visit his shrine: Swithelm, or Sighelm, the Bishop of Sherburn, was selected for this mission. It is not improbable that the sagacious Saxon, in sending this embassy, had reference to the advantages to be derived from commercial intercourse with the East.

History affords evidence that the Christians on the western coast of India at one time had become sufficiently numerous and powerful to assert their independence of their heathen rulers, and for a brief period had an independent government. They, however, afterwards lost their political influence, and became subject to the Hindu Rajas of Travancore.

It is matter of regret that no evidence exists of the extension of this ancient branch of the Church: it would appear that, with the exception of the branch in Ceylon referred to by Cosmas, and which, in all probability, consisted of Persian merchants, no other community of Christians existed. The branch in Ceylon was most likely settled at the commercial emporium at Mantot, near the pearl fishery in the Bay of Condatchy. It may be remarked that, after Cosmas, no writer makes any allusion to the existence of Christianity in Ceylon. It may be inferred that the Church he referred to was composed of foreigners who were located on the coast for commercial objects, similarly circumstanced to the English merchants who visited India in the seventeenth century, and for whose spiritual benefit clergy, as we shall find, were sent from Great Britain. On the rise of the Mohammedan power in India, and the changes induced thereby, it is probable that the old emporia of trade were broken up, and consequent thereupon the local church alluded to was dissolved. Two Mohammedan travellers who visited Ceylon in the ninth century; Marco Polo, the Venetian traveller, who made his way to Ceylon at the close of the thirteenth century; and an adventurous Moor, who visited the island in 1324, are equally silent on the subject of Christianity. This is the more remarkable, since mention is made of the prevailing systems, Brahmanism and Buddhism. It is, therefore, fair to conclude that the early Church was planted only on the western coast of India, where, from the first traditional notices of it, the light of truth has flickered in a dark place; being, as it would seem, almost withdrawn, in accordance with the law of Christian privilege so obviously ordained of Heaven,—that when the Church ceases to extend itself, by concealing, from whatever cause or motive, the heaven-derived light, or by neglecting to hold forth the word of life, it shall forfeit, at least in part, the privileges conferred upon it. The history of this Church, therefore, like others in the East, becomes premonitory to those who have the light, to see to it that they walk in its beams, and strive to let that light so shine before men, that they may be led to rejoice in its cheering rays, and to glorify God.

The early church on the western coast of India is generally known as the Syrian Church, because in its faith and in the form of its ecclesiastical government it resembled that Church. Looking at its polity, doctrine, and character, and attentively tracing, as far as we are able, its history, it is pleasing to find it preserving the general features of its primitive origin. Doubtless, it partook, as it still does, of the alloy which too early corrupted the Church in every part of the world. Its polity was that of the primitive Church. It had, we are informed, its bishops, its presbyters, its deacons, and its liturgy. The existence of a church thus constituted, in so remote a part of the world, and founded at a period so near that of the Apostles, may be regarded as affording an argument in favour of the episcopal form of government. It would be difficult to define the doctrinal belief of the members of the Indian Church; it may, nevertheless, be affirmed that they combined at different periods the views of the Nestorians and the Jacobites, with whom they were connected. There is too much reason to conclude that as in Syria, so in India, "the simplicity of the gospel was fashioned and painted with the colours of Syriac theology."

The Nestorian and Jacobite sects, during the seventh century, were propagated thoughout the eastern world. Under the reign of the Caliphs, first the Nestorian, and afterwards the Jacobite Church was diffused from the Mediterranean Sea to China, and the members together were computed to surpass those of the Greek and Latin communion. The Nestorian hierarchy consisted at one time of twenty-five Metropolitans or Archbishops. Hundreds of thousands were attached to the Nestorian communion.

In a former part of this work, the successes of the Portuguese navigators are recorded, and their discovery of the passage to the eastern seas, by way of the Cape of Good Hope, is mentioned. That event, which happened in 1498, was the beginning of a new epoch in the annals of commerce and of conquest. Some of the details relating to the early progress of the Portuguese are of the most astounding character. Their entrance into India; their conquests; and the efforts made under their authority, to spread the doctrines and practices of the Romish Church, require now to be stated in elucidation of our subject. The fierce, remorseless and unpitying conduct which marked the proceedings of the Portuguese on their arrival, is almost beyond belief. To give an instance, by way of example, from the pen of the Jesuit Lafitan, who furnishes an account of Vasco de Gama's second visit to the western coast of India in 1502: he says, "On reaching the Malabar coast, he fell in with the *Meris*, a large ship, which the Sultan of Egypt sent every year to Hindostan, from which it brought back a rich cargo on his account. The ship also carried many passengers, whom devotion led to visit the Mohammedan tomb at Mecca. On overtaking her, Vasco gave way a little too much to the movement of his hatred against the Moors, and that too in a manner unworthy of a gentleman: for not content with plundering the vessel, which offered no resistance, and taking out of her in the first place twenty children, whom he destined to become monks in the monastery of our Lady, at Belem, he tried to sink the vessel, in order to drown all that remained on board, to the number of nearly three hundred persons. But not being able to succeed, he was obliged to attack her by open force and set her on fire."

In one of his disputes with the Zamorin of Calicut, Vasco de Gama picked up fifty harmless fishermen, who were peaceably engaged in their daily occupation, ignorant and unconscious of danger; and when the Zamorin refused to comply with certain terms which Vasco de Gama proposed, he hung up the whole of these poor innocent creatures in sight of the town, and cutting off their feet and hands, floated them ashore with the tide on a raft. In some instances, we are informed, children were torn from the bosoms of their parents, and their brains dashed out against the walls. Such were the incidents connected with the early conquests of the Portuguese in India. Their history, as regards India, is one of the most gloomy records of European chroniclers. Their proceedings at subsequent periods in the north of India, were not less disgraceful to humanity. "Invincible in fight, fierce, cruel, and remorseless, insolent and overbearing in their demeanour, tyrannical and exacting beyond all Hindu or Mohammedan precedent, with hearts set on gold, and hands stained with blood; such was the aspect in which the European followers of Jesus first showed themselves to the natives of Hindostan."

The second fleet to India bore five Franciscan missionaries, designed to preach the Gospel to the Hindus. King Emanuel signalized his zeal, and although greatly at fault in his views of the methods for promoting it, was nevertheless zealous for his faith. The Bishop of Visen publicly consecrated the standard; and a hat blessed by the Pope was placed on the head of Cabral, by the king himself. The object of the expedition was to obtain from the Zamorin, the native ruler on the western coast of India, permission to preach the Gospel freely in his dominions. Cabral was directed, in case of failure, "to do him all the harm he could in every possible way." This cruel and unprincipled despotism on the part of

Portugal, was eventually expiated by the loss of all her possessions in India and Ceylon.

The ecclesiastics commenced their operations among the members of the Syrian Church. This secluded and apostolic branch of the Church, that had for centuries enjoyed immunity from the extravagant and intolerant claims of Rome, was made the first victim of priestly rapacity. Hindu and Mohammedan rulers had for centuries tolerated the peaceable followers of Christ, and protected them in the enjoyment of their religious privileges, whereas the Romanists accounted it a pious deed to destroy by fire and sword all who refused conformity to their prescriptions. We shall see, in the few notices now to be given, how the history of the Romish Church in India illustrates the spirit of the Papacy. The account to be presented shall be compressed into as brief a space as possible.

On the arrival of Cabral at Cochin, the Syrian Christians sent a deputation on board the ship to beseech him to take them under his protection, and presented him with an ornamented staff, the sceptre of their own deceased king. They seemed not to have entertained any idea of a Christianity different in tone and spirit from what they had learnt in the Gospel, and entertained no suspicion that they were proffering submission to a power that ere long would treat them with intolerance and cruelty. They were received courteously, and dismissed with fair promises. The Portuguese rapidly advanced in their conquests, and very soon they possessed themselves of the principal places on the western coast of India; the island of Ceylon was soon added to their dominions, and several towns on the eastern coast of the peninsula. The Friars sent out did not, it would appear, for several years do anything to promote the conversion of the Hindus. This supineness is severely animadverted upon by Philip the Fourth of Spain.

In 1542 Francis Xavier, one of the earliest disciples of Ignatius Loyola, arrived at Goa, and with unexampled zeal and devotedness entered on the work of an evangelist. The Bishop of Goa received him courteously and promised him his favour. Knowing that the work he had undertaken depended for its success on the promised gift of the Holy Spirit, Xavier determined to seek that comprehensive blessing; and that he might in the outset obtain it, he shut himself up in one of the churches, and spent his first night in India in prayer to God. He found the state of the Portuguese at Goa deplorably wicked, and set about their reformation. In this effort he was in some degree successful. Being requested to take charge of a college established at Goa for the education of native youth speaking several languages, according to the provinces from which they came, he refused, but induced its transfer to the Society of the Jesuits, and called it the College of St. Paul. Xavier paid special attention to the wants of the poor, and the protection of the destitute.

In prosecution of his direct evangelistic labours among the natives, Xavier begun by visiting a low class known as Paruvars, on the coast near Cape Comorin. They were rescued from the oppressive yoke of the Mohammedans by the Portuguese, and embraced the religion of their benefactors. Xavier was ignorant of their language, having been in the country only four or five months; and he therefore obtained a translation of certain formulæ, and having committed these to memory, he went round with a bell, collected the people, men, women, and children, repeated as well as he could the words he had deposited in his memory, baptized them, bade them teach others, and took his departure for another village. On the Sunday he assembled those willing to hear, and expounded to them the Creed, repeating it, and the Lord's Prayer. After the Creed he taught the Ten Commandments. He spent fifteen months among thirty villages, and taught this dependent people. He formed several congregations, and built several small churches, appointing the best of the converts to the office of Catechists, and had them provided for out of the public treasury. He attempted to gain access to the Brahmans, but finding them impracticable, he left them and confined his labours to the Paruvars. On his return to Goa, he took several youths, and placed them in the College of St. Paul. In one of his letters to a friend he says: "I am wholly ignorant of the language of the people, and they understand as little of mine; and I have no interpreter. All I can do is to baptize children, and serve the sick." This is certainly a singular admission. How is it to be accounted for that he did not at once acquire the language of the people among whom he took up his abode? The ability to communicate the word of truth was accounted so indispensable to the first preachers of the Gospel, that miraculous power was exerted to communicate the gift of tongues; and yet this devoted man was content to confine himself to the performance of the rite of baptism and duties to the sick. It may be presumed that Xavier relied on the *opus operatum* in his proceedings.

Subsequently Xavier left Goa and went down to Travancore; and as the Portuguese had requested the Raja to allow it, he preached there; and such was his success that he baptized in one month ten thousand persons. Knowing that Xavier laboured under the auspices of the paramount power of the Portuguese, and the authority of the Archbishop of Goa, no one acquainted with the character and position of the non-caste and oppressed poor among whom Xavier laboured, can wonder at the progress he made in the wholesale business of conversion. Such is the obsequiousness of the lower orders to power, and the pliancy with which they ever accommodate themselves to the wishes of those whom it may be their interest to conciliate, that it is easy to understand how the clergy under the influence of the Portuguese succeeded as they did with the illiterate natives of Southern India and Ceylon. Knowing what we do of the unscrupulous character of the Portuguese government existing at that time in India, and its fierce and cruel proceedings, it may be safely inferred that in some instances the lower classes were encouraged by their heathen rulers to offer themselves for baptism, and the recital of the Christian formulæ to be committed to memory: they were a sort of offering to the terrible Moloch of a dreaded power.

It may not be out of place to advert to a similar success achieved by a modern missionary, among some ignorant tribes of demonolators in the island of Ceylon. In his progress through the jungles, where these wretched semi-barbarians roam, in company with a civilian, this zealous man baptized some scores of these foresters, with whom he could only communicate by means of an interpreter in a sort of *patois* Singhalese. There and then, however, these poor simple beings were made the subjects of the sacred rite of baptism, about which they knew as little as the wild animals around them: the defence was, that they were baptized as children in order to instruction. The case was similar to that of Xavier. In both, the simple subjects of the rite, when required by a beneficent foreigner, wearing the garb of a priest, and one in immediate intercourse with imperial personages, to submit to an aspersion of pure water, could not object. Why should they? Such an element as water, accompanying the voice of a living benefactor, could never subserve the purposes of malediction: some benevolent result, some ulterior benefit, would follow the rite,—whether sacred or civil was not a matter of much moment.

But in the case of Xavier's converts, there was something more than mere passivity; there was a substantive benefit. In his letter to the Archbishop of Goa, John III., under date 1546, says—"His Majesty lays down the principle that Pagans may be brought over to our religion, not only by the hopes of eternal salvation, but by temporal interest and preferment;" and he therefore directs that, on professing Christianity, they were "to be provided with places in the customs, to be exempted from impressment for the navy, and sustained by the distribution of rice out of the public revenue." But as these benefits could not reach the thousands baptized, we are left to account for the multitudinous conversions after all. This is easy: the head men, the inferior officers, in order to gain their own ends the more certainly, would evince their zeal in bringing under the rod those within their influence; these would be led to conform, under the impression that the auspices of government would be secured to hamlets, villages, and indeed whole communities; and no doubt it was so. The jargon committed to memory, and recited on Sundays, would be regarded with a confidence proportioned to its unintelligibleness: it was indeed in harmony with the initiatory teaching of Brahmanical priests, whose divine sentences, the sacred *mantras*, those magic incantations whose potent influence can move even divinities—it was a comparatively easy Shibboleth, and it procured positive good. To my own mind, the success of Xavier has never been a matter of surprise since I became acquainted with the facts and circumstances of his history, his political auspices, and the character and position of those among whom his success was achieved.

In regard to those who were nominally associated with the communion of the Church, it must be remembered that their embracing a new faith did not necessarily imply the abjuring of any imperfect system of demonism they had received from their ancestors. The reception of Christianity imposed no restraints, it involved no sacrifices; on the contrary, it procured benefits, and gave to those who had no caste distinction a position, even placing them under the protection of the foreign and invincible power that had been planted on their shores. Such is the facility of the mind to believe in systems apparently contradictory with equal allowance, that even now Hindus of caste and station sometimes propitiate the shrines of Romish saints, and there present votive offerings. On alluding to this strange anomaly in conversation with a learned Hindu of high caste on one occasion, he replied sarcastically and sceptically by quoting the native proverb—"If a deal of husks be eaten, one grain may turn up." He meant that possibly some of the shrines might belong to a true divinity; insinuating both by the proverb and its application that such modes of religious observance were nevertheless comparable only to husks.

The views expressed in the preceding paragraphs on the character of Xavier's success, although they may impinge on the wisdom of his proceedings, and on the theory of belief he entertained, are not intended to reflect on his character; he was undoubtedly a man of intense devotion and of untiring zeal. Had his yearning pity, his burning charity, been associated with correct apprehensions of the Gospel, his labours might have produced really beneficial and permanent results. The following testimony from a Jesuit missionary of thirty years' experience in the very scene of Xavier's labours, gives the most correct opinion on the subject of his character and labours. His words are:—"One of the first missionaries was St. Francis Xavier, a Spanish Jesuit of the greatest merit, and animated with a truly apostolic zeal, and still known under the appellation of the Apostle of India. He traversed several provinces of India, and is said to have made many thousand converts, at a period when the prejudices of the natives against the Christian religion were far from reaching the height they have since attained. Xavier soon discovered in the manners and prejudices of the natives an insurmountable bar to the progress of Christianity among them, as appears from the printed letters, still extant, which he wrote to Ignatius Loyola, his superior. At last Francis Xavier, entirely disheartened by the invincible obstacles he everywhere met in his apostolic career, and by the impossibility of making real converts, left the country in disgust, after a stay in it of only two or three years."

Xavier wrote letters to Europe, and appealed to the zeal and sympathy of Christendom in behalf of the realms of Paganism; but no effect followed but that of intense admiration of his zeal. He visited Ceylon, and tried to induce the government to take up arms against the Raja of Jaffna, who persecuted the converts at Manar. He afterwards made a voyage to the islands of Malacca and Java; and on another occasion to Japan. In 1549 he proceeded to Japan again, and died on the 2d December, 1552, at the island of Sancian, within sight of China. His body was conveyed to Goa, where it was placed in a coffin enchased with silver and precious stones, and enshrined in a monument of exquisite art.

Though such devout men as Francis Xavier are connected with a system, some of whose tenets are subversive of the essential doctrines of Christianity, yet their spirits rise above their system; and their disinterested zeal, their fervent devotion, their simple faith in the Lord Jesus, and their love for mankind, command our admiration. Xavier laboured with unexampled zeal and with equal sincerity, but the effects of his labours, however imposing the array of numbers as to converts, were nominal and superficial. His proceedings, as well as those of the Dutch Reformed Church, whose efforts will hereafter be noticed, were directed to the object of a conformity to certain external things easily complied with; no truth being brought to bear on the heart through the Gospel, coming, not in word only, but in demonstration of the Spirit and with power, it would have been wonderful, indeed at variance with the history of early Christianity, if any saving effects had followed. The connexion of his teaching, as well as that of the Dutch clergy in Ceylon, with government, to say the least, jeopardized the interests of vital Christianity. In the present day the case is far otherwise: under the wise and tolerant rule of Great Britain, the rights of private judgment are respected, and all are permitted the full enjoyment of any opinion and religious practices that are not at variance with social order and public freedom. Religious opinions are no bar to secular employment with the British statesmen of India, nor do they affect promotion. The teachers of Christianity among the Hindus are in the safest position as regards the exertion of legitimate influence, when the government allows them to pursue their duties unfettered and unaided by its interference. When the truth of God, harmonizing with all the scientific deductions of human reason, is brought to bear on the mind, it cannot be doubted that, with the promised blessing of God, prayerfully sought, every obstacle will give way, and the desiderated results will be realized.

More space has been given to the history of Francis Xavier than it really deserves, in relation to the brief sketches it is intended to give of such matters in this volume; but as misconception exists in many minds relative to the character of the success that attended his labours, it was thought the best to enter somewhat at length into his missionary history.

It is now proposed to follow the course of events connected with the Portuguese period of Christianity in India. In the year 1560, the Inquisition, by order of John III. of Portugal, was erected at Goa, and the diabolical scenes incident to that horrid tribunal were soon introduced. For a full recital of the cruelties perpetrated under its sanction, it must suffice to refer to Dr. Buchanan's "Christian Researches," and to Hough's "Christianity in India." The most heartrending cruelties were inflicted upon hapless victims in the dark abodes of that inhuman institution. No regard was paid to age, or to sex, or to rank, but torture, without distinction, was alike administered to all that fell under the ban of the Holy Office. The records of the awful cruelties excite mingled feelings of indignation and pity. Oh, how different from that gracious economy that proceeded from the infinite clemency of the world's Redeemer! It is gratifying to know that the growing power of the British in India led to the entire abolition of this vile and detestable institution in 1816.

It might not be expected that the Church of Rome would tolerate the independent jurisdiction of the Syrian Church of Southern India; though it had from almost apostolic times enjoyed the utmost immunity and freedom in its tranquil and distant seclusion. In 1545 the first attempts were made by the Friars of St. Francis to bring the Syrian Christians into the communion of the Church of Rome. A brother of this order, of the name of Vincent, described as a great servant of God, was in the first instance deputed by the Bishop of Goa to inquire into the state of the Syrian Church, and to induce them to acknowledge the Papal supremacy. At first they welcomed him as a Christian minister, charged with an errand of good will towards them; but they soon discovered that instead of attending to their improvement, and affording them the protection they expected, his principal object was to make them proselytes to a faith of which they had not, up to that time, even heard; and to bring them into subjection to a church whose authority they had never acknowledged. After this discovery, Vincent perceived that they paid no further regard to his exhortations, and as he was distant from the seat of the Portuguese power, he had not the means of coercion. He determined to try other measures. He founded a college, educated Syrian youths who were invested with orders, but the people would not recognize them; they shut the doors of their churches against the Portuguese and against their own sons. Failing of his object, he tried conciliatory measures, such as the adoption of the Syriac language and the permission to the students to retain their costume; this did not succeed. The priests in orders refused to preach against their ancient prelates, and even mentioned the Patriarch of Babylon in their prayers.

The Jesuits were not, however, to be foiled: they were animated by a strong feeling against everything that opposed them, and the more so perhaps, because the events now passing under our notice were concurrent with those of the Reformation in the West. Perceiving then that the presence of the Syrian bishop was unfavourable to their designs, they formed a plot for sending him to Rome. He was eventually summoned to Goa by the bishop, and sent to Portugal. He there promised, in the spirit of dissimulation, it is apprehended, to cleanse his church from error, and to do his utmost to bring it over to the Church of Rome. He was permitted to return. During his absence the Patriarch of Babylon, at the request of the church in India, went and consecrated another bishop. The Jesuits tried to intercept him, but he eluded them by travelling in disguise, arrived at his destination, and was received with demonstrations of joy. The former bishop arrived from Portugal, and though regarded as a time-server, he was permitted to go to the south, in the hope, that by schism among themselves the Syrian community might be overcome. He acted the part of a traitor, as indeed he had already done, and sought the interference of the Archbishop of Goa against the newly consecrated Syrian bishop. The Raja of Travancore consented to allow the Portuguese troops to enter his dominions, seize the new bishop, and convey him to Goa, whence he was transported to Rome. The ship was driven into a port in the Mozambique channel, where he effected his escape, and proceeded to Mosul, where he was by new credentials confirmed in his position as Bishop of Malabar. Having no prospect of success without the auspices of the Pope, he resolved to go to Rome and obtain the sanction of his holiness. He there renounced the Syrian faith, anathematized his ancient creed, and engaged to bring over his people to the Romish Church. He acted as perfidiously as his predecessor had done. He was made Archbishop of Anga Male, and returned. During this interval the bishop in charge had thrown off the mask, and was maintaining doctrines he was said to have abjured. He was reported to the Bishop of Goa, seized and sent to Rome, where he died, how or when is not recorded.

On the arrival of the bishop from Rome, he was not, as he expected, allowed to proceed to the south, but under various pretences detained at Goa. He however made his escape, and found his way to his own country, where he was received with great delight by the people. Orders were issued for his apprehension. He was not secured by force, but eventually being cited to attend a council at Goa, he went. He was required again to abjure his Syrian creed, and make profession of his faith in that of Rome. He returned to Malabar. He resumed ancient practices, however, and paid no attention to his promises. He wrote to the Patriarch to explain why he had attended the Council, and stated that he did so from fear of the Portuguese, who were over his head as a hammer is over an anvil; and that when before the Council he delivered a confession of faith which none of the Latin bishops was able to contradict. He requests an assistant, and the Patriarch sends a young man of the name of Mar Simeon. The stranger seeks by winning the affections of the people to supersede his aged colleague, and great commotion ensues. The Portuguese are appealed to, who secure the junior and sent him to Rome and Portugal; he died in Portugal. The senior was summoned to attend another council at Goa, whereupon he not only refused to obey, but openly avowed his adherence to his ancient faith.

When the account of these events reached Rome, Don Alexis de Menezes was about to leave Italy as the newly-appointed Archbishop of Goa. Accordingly Pope Clement VIII. addressed to him the brief he issued on the occasion. His Holiness expressed his views on the Nestorian heresy, commanded the books to be examined, corrected and purged; and he ordered strict inquisition to be made into the conduct of the bishop whose defection led to these measures; and no bishop from Babylon was to enter Malabar. Thus armed as a crusader against an unoffending and ancient Church, the new archbishop entered on his allotted task without loss of time. Bishops and priests from Babylon attempted in vain to enter Malabar. The archbishop strove to persuade the vicar-general to throw up his commission, and offered him various inducements to join the Church of Rome; but he, being a man of principle and devotion, refused: he died soon after. The bishop himself also died, leaving his testimony in favour of the Syrian Church.

The archbishop hereupon nominated a Jesuit of the name of Francis Roz to the vacant post, but aware how the appointment would disparage them in the eyes of the Syrian Church, the Council of Goa hesitated to confirm the nomination.

Before his death the late bishop had confided the government of the Church to his archdeacon, George, a man held in great estimation by the people. The council devised a commission to be composed of the archdeacon, the Jesuit Roz, and the rector of the Jesuits' college. The archdeacon demurred, and was permitted the sole charge. They press him to subscribe a confession of faith, which he refused, boldly stating that he had no more to do with the apostolical Church of St. Thomas than the Apostle had to do with the Church of Rome: the people supported him. He eventually subscribes a confession, but repudiates the authority of the Church of Rome. The archbishop determined to proceed in person to the scene of action, and then after a long continued series of persecutions, the Syrian Church was subjugated by the Church of Rome.

The proceedings of the archbishop were of the most nefarious character. To effect his purpose he convened a synod, that there might be an appearance of legality in his proceedings; but its freedom was destroyed. By promising the Portuguese advantages of a commercial character, should he succeed, he secured their concurrence: by threats, promises, or bribes, he induced the most influential of the Hindu Rajas and their officers to promote his object: by intimidating the archdeacon, by ordaining a number of clergy, caressing those already in orders, and with presents conciliating the chief of the laity, he prepared them to listen to decrees which eventually placed the Syrian Church under papal jurisdiction, and thus destroyed its primitive character and independence.

The Syrian Church, however, feeling the oppression of the Roman yoke, determined to throw it off. The Jesuits had prohibited the marriage of their priests, seized all their churches, suspended images in them, and by bribing unprincipled priests, they thus treated a people once free as slaves. The Syrian Church sent repeated complaints to Rome, but obtained no redress. At length they elected an archdeacon, a relative of the late one, and placed themselves under his care until they could obtain a bishop from their Patriarch. Just at this time the Dutch deprived the Portuguese of all their possessions in Ceylon, and on the Continent greatly abridged their power. Under these circumstances the Syrian Church was encouraged. The Patriarch at Mosul sent a bishop, a man of the name of Attala. He set out and arrived at Meliapore, was seized by the Jesuits and sent to Goa. The Syrian Christians resolved to take up arms and rescue their bishop; but eventually returned without effecting their object. They hold a solemn convention, and swear on the Gospel to yield spiritual obedience to none but their newly-appointed archdeacon. Twelve priests consecrate him, and a council is appointed to aid him in the management of his diocese. Attala was condemned by the Inquisition at Goa, and put to a cruel death. Certain Carmelites were now sent by the Pope: their arrival awakened the jealousy of the Franciscans, they therefore obtained passports from the Dutch Commodore, who was then carrying on an offensive war against the Portuguese all along the coast. The Carmelites meet the archdeacon, but the conference is fruitless; the Syrian Church had taken its measures. The Portuguese aided the archbishop, and the archdeacon is obliged to flee, when his effects were brought out and burnt before the Church; the archbishop expressed regret that he could not add the owner to the flames.

The Dutch then took Quilon and Cranganore, besieged Cochin, and took that. The Dutch, by authority, banished every European ecclesiastic; they stated that the Dutch East India Company had found the Jesuits inimical to their government,—the Jesuits at Jaffna in Ceylon having conspired against them. The Carmelite bishop being obliged to leave the coast, consecrated a native, under the title of the bishop of Megara—he was the first native Indian bishop. The Syrian Church was thus Romanized. The accompanying engraving represents a bishop of the Syrian Church on the western coast, and also a priest. After that period the history of the Syrian Christians is but very imperfectly traced. In

1732 the missionaries of the Society for Promoting Christian Knowledge at Madras, mention Syrian priests as coming from Malabar to the shrine of St. Thomas. The Danish missionaries are visited the following year by a Syrian priest, who refused to eat with the Christians at Tranquebar, lest he should lose caste!

In 1725 the Committee of the Society for Promoting Christian Knowledge wrote to their missionaries, suggesting that they inquire into the state of the Syrian Christians, and if possible, associate their priests with themselves in the work of evangelizing the heathens. The missionaries expressed the opinion that it was neither desirable nor practicable; and the Syrian Christians were of the same sentiments. The prejudices of caste are as inveterate among them as among the heathen. The missionaries ascertained, that although the Syrian Church had been emancipated from the tyranny of Rome, it had not abandoned her superstitions.

On the present state and condition of the Syrian Church the records of the Church Missionary Society afford all needed information. That society took up the work of its evangelization many years ago with great zeal, and adopted plans for effecting this object of the most extensive and efficient character. The Church Missionary Society aimed in the first instance to stimulate to activity the slumbering church in this region. The missionaries preached in the Syrian churches, and even superintended the education of its clergy. It was hoped that in this way the Syrian Church would reform itself. This plan failed, and it was determined to make a difference between the living and the dead, by inviting those desirous of receiving evangelical truth, to open and avowed association with the Church of England.

The Syrian Church is now under the authority of the Patriarch of Antioch. "In some respects," says a clergyman of the Church of England, who recently visited them, "their practice, if not their theory, is preferable to that of the Church of Rome. They are not opposed to the circulation and study of the Bible in the vernacular, and they profess to regard it as the highest standard of appeal. They are opposed to image-worship; they permit their clergy to marry; and they show a commendable degree of respect for the Lord's day. They are also apparently more open to conviction than the Romanists. On the other hand, there is less union, order, and discipline among them; and, at present, with a large staff of governors, they are without government. Instead of one bishop they have at present five, each of whom regards the other four as intruders. When there were three of them, the Patriarch of Antioch sent out a bishop to supersede the three, and transmit to him his annats, which had been stopped; but instead of doing this he applied himself diligently to the work of making money, without rendering any report to the Patriarch. Another bishop was then sent to call the former to account, but he also has forgotten the poor Patriarch's wants, and flown upon the spoil. The

Travancore government, being unable to determine which of the five bishops ought to be recognised, has hitherto refused to recognise any of them, and without its recognition and sanction they cannot exercise legal jurisdiction or reform abuses. In consequence of this state of things, every priest does that which is right in his own eyes, and every bishop ordains by wholesale as many as are able to pay him his fees; and hence in some of the churches the number of the officiating priests is so great, and each of them is so hungry when it comes to his turn to officiate for a few days, that the poor sheep are in danger of being not only fleeced, but skinned.

"At Cottayam we visited one of the Syrian churches, which is built in something of the style we call Lombard. The interior was close and dark, and smelt strongly of bats. Corresponding to our organ-loft there is a gallery, which is intended as a place of residence for unmarried priests. The nave was quite unadorned, the chancel better lighted than the nave, and gaudily painted. A peculiarity of all these churches is, that the chancel-roof is higher than that of the nave, instead of being lower, as it is with us. At the entrance of the chancel, and opposite the altar, a lamp is kept burning day and night. I did not inquire of the Syrians why they lighted a lamp in their church in the daytime, but it seemed an apt emblem of their preference of the light of their own inventions to the light of 'the Sun of righteousness.'"

The preceding hasty review of the history of Christianity in India and Ceylon would be very imperfect without some brief notices of the proceedings of the Jesuits in Madura, which, in Southern India, was one of their most distinguished scenes of labour and success. It is generally admitted "that the Jesuits have been most energetic and laborious missionaries; sincere in their convictions, whether they were right or wrong; persevering for centuries in pursuit of their object, and for that object enduring privations, persecutions, even death itself, with a courage and constancy beyond all praise." The account I am about to furnish is abridged from a full article on their mission in Madura, and contains no quotation except from the Jesuits themselves or some Roman Catholic author. The territorial limits of the Jesuit mission in Southern India was originally confined to the peninsula, being triangular, with Cape Comorin for its vertex, the Coleroon river for its base, and for its sides the western Ghauts and the eastern sea. It was known as the kingdom of Madura. The shores of the Gulf of Manar, stretching from Cape Comorin to Adam's Bridge, and usually called the Pearl Fishery Coast, were the scene of the labours of St. Francis Xavier. About one hundred and fifty years ago, as we are told, this area was distinguished by the moral features of paradise. Miracles, we are assured, were numerous; rivalry and strife unknown; hundreds of thousands were added to the Church; and the converts lived and died in all the fervour of their first love, and with the purity of the angels of heaven. The Church possessed unparalleled blessings and equal success. Dr. Wiseman, in a very beautiful description of the Church of Rome in her missionary capacity, declares that, "no clamour or boast is heard within her; but she perseveres in the calm fulfilment of her eternal destiny, as unconscious of any extraordinary effort as are the celestial bodies in wheeling round their endless orbits, and scattering rays of brilliant light through the immeasurable distances of space." We may try his criteria at Madura.

Xavier landed in 1545. Nine years later, the historian Bercastel informs his readers that the number of converts on the Pearl Fishery Coast alone amounted to upwards of 500,000,—"all fervent, and desiring nothing more than to become martyrs of their faith." The Jesuits of Madura condemned his policy as ineffectual; it differed essentially from that of Robert de Nobili, the founder of the Madura Mission, who entered the country about fifty years later. This remarkable man, to whom reference has been made in another chapter, under the appellation Tatwabódhakar, was the nephew of Cardinal Bellarmine and the grand-nephew of Pope Marcellus II. The system of conversion he commenced in 1606 was carried on for a period of one hundred and fifty years by his successors.

The first distinct notice of this mission is contained in a letter from Father Martin, and dated Balasore, Bengal, 30th January, 1699, expressing delight that, being ordered to Pondicherry, he should be at the door, as it were, of the famous mission of Madura, which he wished to enter. He says, speaking of his endeavours to gain the needed qualification for his work: "As soon as I arrived in this fine kingdom, I applied myself seriously to the study of the Bengali language. At the end of five months I found myself sufficiently far advanced to be able to disguise myself and to enter into a famous Brahmanical university." Leaving the marvellous and the questionable in mental and moral science found in this averment, let us listen to his testimony regarding the Madura Mission. He says: "We shall be there, my dear father, at the door of the Madura Mission, the finest, in my opinion, in the world. There are seven Jesuits there, nearly all Portuguese, who labour indefatigably with incredible success and with incredible hardships. You will easily understand why I feel so strongly attracted thither, when I tell you that the mission is reckoned to have more than a hundred and fifty thousand Christians, and that every day a very great number is added to it; the least that each missionary baptizes is a thousand a year. Father Bouchet, who has laboured there for ten or twelve years, writes, that for his own part he has baptized two thousand in the course of this last year, and that he has administered the initiatory sacrament to three hundred in a single day: so that his arm fell down from weakness and fatigue. Besides, says he, these Christians are not like those in other parts of India; we baptize them only after strong proofs of their sincerity, and after three or four months' instruction. After they once become Christians they live like the angels, and the Church of Madura seems like a true image of the primitive church. This father protests further, that he has sometimes listened to the confessions of several villagers without finding among them a single individual guilty of a mortal sin. Let it not be imagined, adds he, that ignorance or shame hinders them from opening their consciences to this sacred tribunal; they approach it as well instructed as the clergy themselves, and with all the candour and simplicity of novices."

The testimony of Father Barbier, in 1720, is to the same effect. "Among the hundreds, says he, whom I confess, scarcely shall I find eight who have fallen into any considerable fault. All edify me infinitely by their scrupulous exactness in fulfilling the duties of religion, by the eagerness with which they listen to the word of God, and by the patience with which they endure afflictions and maladies. It seems to me that I look upon a revival of the fervour of the early ages."

Father Trembloy says, "Yes, the Christians of India adore our God in spirit and in truth; their worship is pure, without any mixture. Their aversion to idolatry is carried even to scrupulousness."

We are next informed of the power of the Christians over demons, who, it would appear, possessed almost all Hindus. Father Bouchet says: "It is a fact, which no one in India doubts, and in regard to which the evidence does not admit of a doubt, that the devils utter oracles, and that these wicked spirits seize upon the priests who invoke them, or indiscriminately on any of those who are present, and take part in these spectacles." They are represented as appearing to catechumens under hideous forms, and conveying them away by force. He further affirms, "At Áúr I myself have been an eyewitness how Christians of every age, of both sexes, and every rank in life drive away devils, by a single invocation of the name of Jesus Christ, by the sign of the cross, by holy water, and by other holy practices." "Thus," says he, "it is that our neophytes have a sovereign contempt for the devils, over whom their quality of Christians alone gives them so great authority."

Father Bernard de Sa holds a colloquy with a demon, which surprised the idolaters. He demanded, "Where are the gods whom the Hindus adore?" the answer was, "They are in hell, where they suffer horrible torments." "What becomes of their worshippers?" "They go to hell, where they burn in fire with the gods they have worshipped."

The Lutherans suffer from these demons we are told. Father Calmette says, that when a Lutheran convert and his wife, in Tanjore, were witnessing the exorcism of a heathen, the devil left him and entered the female heretic. The exorcist asked the reason of this, when the devil said that she was his property as much as the other person he had just left. The terrified husband went at once to a Roman Catholic Church, asked pardon of God, and taking up a little earth, moistened it with his tears, and laid it on the head of his wife, who was instantly dispossessed. They are led to remark in one letter, "It is said among the missionaries, that the devil is the best catechist in the mission." Travelling along one night, Father Trembloy tells us that he and four Christians that were with him, came upon a tiger, and being terrified, they exclaimed, "Santa Maria," when the animal moved "out of the path and showed, so to speak, by his posture and the grinding of his teeth, how sorry he was to let such a fine prey escape." And so Father Martin tells us, that when heathens and Christians are journeying together, the animal devours the former without doing any harm to the faithful. At Cotar miracles are wrought before a large cross continually. Water burns instead of oil in the lamps before the shrine of the church. Miracles are continued at St. Thomas, near Madras; here he is said to have suffered martyrdom, but Rufinus and Socrates say he was martyred at Edessa, in Syria. A Hindu vows to pay eight fanams to a certain shrine at Cotar, if his child be cured of blindness. The sight is restored, and he proceeds to the place and presents only five, whereupon blindness at once comes on his son again. He pays the arrears, and rubbing a little oil on the eyes of his son from one of the lamps, his sight is restored. A covetous heathen, who put into a lottery, obtained repeated success by propitiating the shrine of St. Xavier with money.

The angelic neophytes of Madura pay special deference to the saints, and are rewarded. Father Bouchet says, "Those whom they invoke most frequently are their guardian angels, —their patron; St. Joseph, St. John the Baptist, St. Michael (the protector of our mission) St. Peter, St. Paul, St. Thomas (the Apostle of these countries), St. Ignatius, and St. Xavier."

A Christian Pariar, condemned to death for killing a cow, is released from bonds by praying to St. Xavier, and escapes from his sleeping guards. It was a common practice to wear on the person medals of the Virgin and saints, as a preservation from danger, and especially from evil spirits.

We cannot, for want of space, multiply evidence on the subject of these gross myths; let us just glance at the principles upon which the Madura mission was founded.

Father Robert-de-Nobili, knowing that the natives entertained strong prejudice against Europeans, and believing that it was invincible, studied hard to acquire the language and a knowledge of the customs and usages of the people, aided by a Brahman whom he won over to his plan. He then entered Madura as a Brahman, having with him a forged document to attest his superior order. He produced his written scroll, and made oath that he was a Brahman. He next assumed the garb of a religious order—that of the Sanyasis, and conformed in all things to Brahmanical usage, wore a tiger skin, carried a sacred staff, and smeared his person with purifying cow-dung. Thus did all his associates deny that they were Europeans, and professed to be teachers of the *law* of God. Father de Bourges says, "Our whole attention is given to the concealing from the people that we are what the people call Feringees (Franks); the slightest suspicion of this on their part would impose an insurmountable obstacle to the propagation of the Gospel." A Heathen convert on the coast, who objects to receive baptism from a European, is sent to Madura that he may receive the rite from the Sanyasis.

This infamous system had for its object the conversion of the Brahmans, and the fraud thus practised was accompanied with every species of deception and conformity to heathen usage; the whole system was no more than a paganized Christianity devised by wicked and crafty men. It was first proscribed at Goa, but without effect; then by Pope Gregory XV. in 1623. Clement XI. sends an apostolic Visitor in 1702; he examines the evidence adduced on all hands relative to the proceedings at Madura, and by various devices obtained correct information on the real state of things. They are commanded to discontinue heathen usages and superstitions; his decrees are sent to Rome; the Jesuits send deputies, and endeavour to contravene the legate, and ward off the consequences of the mission. One of these returned, and stated, and protested in the church at Pondichery, that the Pope had assured him that the decree was not binding, calling to witness the body and blood of Jesus Christ. The Pope transmits a brief to say that the statement is "*false, and without the slightest foundation.*" They however continued their course despite of brief after brief. Benedict XIII. interfered; Clement XII. examined the question; Benedict XIV. went into the case fully, and shortly issued a brief, which terminated the fraud.

When it was discovered that the Madura missionaries were Europeans the heathen were disgusted; the thousands that had adhered to them abandoned them; and twenty years later the remaining Christians are described as living in the lowest state of ignorance and superstition. Abbé Dubois says, after twenty-five years' experience among them,—"I would hardly dare to affirm that I have anywhere met a sincere and undisguised Christian." Such was the rise, progress, and decay of the Jesuits' Madura Mission.

After the decay of Portuguese power in India and Ceylon, and the ascendency of the Dutch, the Romanists were almost wholly dependent on the college at Goa for a supply of priests; and consequently their religious establishments, for many years, were not maintained with much efficiency. Within the last twenty years, however, there has been a great change. Most of the large stations are now supplied with European priests, and a regular communication is kept up with Rome. The various orders of the priesthood are maintained, colleges are established, the printing-press is active, and Romanism wears altogether another aspect from that I witnessed on my arrival in 1826. In some instances, schism has resulted from the intervention of the Italian priests. Those who formerly occupied the posts as priests from Goa, have in several instances refused to vacate their charge, and the people in part have joined them. Where they have prevailed, the European priests have been obliged to form a new establishment.

Having gone through the history of the Syrian Church, including the general proceedings of the Romanists, I shall here introduce some notices of the character of the Hollanders, as evangelizers. These superseded the Portuguese in political power, and were not less zealous to take their place in the work of conversion. The auspices under which the Dutch advanced in the work of conquest in the eastern sea, were highly favourable to the stability and extension of their power. The decline of the Portuguese was rapid. We have seen enough in the preceding paragraphs to show that their policy had been characterized by most unscrupulous acts of perfidy and aggression. "Their merchants were pre-eminent for rapacity and deceit; and in their demeanour towards the natives of all ranks and religions, they had excited an unusual feeling of disgust and impatience by their personal insolence and tyrannical assumption."

The Dutch, as they obtained a footing in their colonial possessions, uniformly introduced the reformed Church of

Holland as the established religion. They lost no opportunity of depressing the adherents of the Papacy, and showed great indignation against the symbols of its worship, paying no deference to the most revered objects of superstition. The intrigues of the Jesuits were possibly more or less injurious to the Romanists; be that as it may, it is a matter of history that the Dutch were less tolerant of them than of the Brahmanists and Buddhists. In 1658, a law was promulgated which made it a capital crime to conceal a Romish priest. The Romanists were forbidden to educate their children, and Hindus were prohibited the external observance of their religious rites. In the peninsula of Jaffna, the Dutch took possession of the Roman Catholic churches, and they attached schools to each; the Dutch minister visited them periodically, and baptized the children. In 1685, their records state, that in that peninsula alone, there were 185,000 native Christians. Among the Singhalese, where the same alacrity was not manifested, a proclamation was made to accelerate the work; and it was thereby made known, that only baptized persons, should aspire to offices under government,—they eventually numbered among the Singhalese, 340,000 baptized persons. Under such impulses, even Brahmans accepted the rite of baptism; retaining, nevertheless, their own views, and adhering to their own ceremonial. They judged that it was equally just for them to avail themselves of temporalities in this way, as it was for government to confer them on such conditions. Attendance at school was made *compulsory*. We need not be surprised that a chaplain at Galle, writes,—"Idolatry is on the increase, so much so, as to render me doubtful of the propriety of baptizing the children of the natives, lest that which is holy be given unto dogs."

The Dutch laws made baptism essential to legal registration. How such a rule would operate on an unenlightened people might easily be anticipated—among the ignorant, servile, and time-serving, its enforcement was easy. An anecdote is told of a native in Malwana, who being ill when away from home, and anxious to have the due registration secured for his child before his death, sent for his brother, and requested his kind aid in the matter. The brother, with the wonted facility of his race, to evade a difficulty, instead of carrying the child all the way to Colombo for baptism, borrowed one in the town, and had it baptized in the name of the absent child who was at home: in this way the same infant has frequently been baptized several times. And in a way equally exceptionable, I have reason to believe, converts have in some cases been again and again baptized by the same minister; being presented by a mercenary catechist on special days, to swell the number of candidates, and induce the belief that the work of conversion was steadily advancing! One so zealous and successful could but be well reported, and eventually as certainly benefited by promotion: *efficient* labourers are always in demand.

The Romanists flourished notwithstanding the persecution to which they were subject by the Dutch. A distinguished priest, despite the ordinances of the government, travelled through the country, and preached to the people. He was regarded with great veneration; and his name is revered almost as much as that of Xavier. They maintained their ground; and to this day, are exceedingly numerous in every part of Ceylon, as well as in the maritime provinces of India. We have not space to pursue this subject further. Sufficient has been advanced to prepare the mind to anticipate the results which followed the withdrawal of the compulsory system of the Dutch. When the English enfranchised the native mind, it asserted openly its rights; and the natural phases of heathenism appeared in an open and undisguised light. The hundreds of thousands of baptized heathens were lost, and resolved into the original and ancestral systems of heathenism:—

"They melted from the field, as snow,
When streams are swollen, and south winds blow,
Dissolves in silent dew."

In the absence of efficacious truth, proclaimed and applied by earnest men able to deal with the mind in the vernaculars, it were wonderful if caste, and Hinduism, or Buddhism should give way. On a cool, shrewd and acute people like the Brahmanised portion of Ceylon, the attempt to force on their acceptance any form of religion, would produce a strong revulsion. Compulsory methods would only impress them the more with an idea of the inherent weakness of the system that required such violence; and with the conviction that its promoters were either ignorant fanatics, or sinister agents of a political expediency. Among the Hindus and Buddhists, with whom dialectics form so large a portion of religious teaching, no progress can be made apart from well-attested, divinely-authenticated, and self-evidencing truth.

I am personally acquainted with Hindus who were baptized under the Dutch régime, and even held office as Christian teachers. One old gentleman of this class I remember very well, who was present on one occasion at a public Christian service, wearing his sectarial marks as a Saiva, and looking exceedingly venerable, being more than eighty years of age. On the morning in question there was to be a baptism of four or five youths of highly respectable families, and the excitement was therefore greater than usual. When the young men came forward, the old gentleman rose with an air of dignity, which his tall person and years well sustained, and said that he would suggest the propriety of a little delay in the administration of the holy rite, as in his judgment the youths were too dependent on heathen relations to permit their free action, and under such circumstances they might possibly contravene the rules of Christianity by marrying heathen wives, &c. He also hinted that the youths had been unduly influenced in the course of their education by their teachers, and that their desire to become Christians was the result of undue persuasion. I was well aware how the whole matter stood, as the school in which they were instructed was under my own superintendence; however, as the early history of the old gentleman himself was a monitory evidence of the need of caution in administering the ordinance, I resolved to postpone the baptism.

This led to a conversation between the old gentleman and a native minister who was present. The latter defended the propriety of using all legitimate influence by way of inducing intelligent Hindus to become Christians. To strengthen his argument he had recourse to various illustrations and similes, and among others he alluded to the artificial means used for ripening certain kinds of fruit, such as plantains, by exposing them to the action of smoke and warmth, &c.; and jack-fruit, by slightly bruising the rind. As these means promoted maturity in fruit, so instruction and persuasion might mature the moral purpose; this was his strain of argument with the shrewd gentleman, who listened with great attention, as did a large company of respectable Hindus who were seated around. The old gentleman rose to reply, and evidenced by the confidence of his expression his advantage in the argument, and said, "If the gardener will allow her to take her course, Nature will ripen the fruit without either smoke or stripes; time, the sun and the elements, will complete the process. In like manner, if you will allow these youths to think for themselves, they will eventually adopt the course most in accordance with the nature of things."

Many of the Dutch ministers were men of great eminence, and equally distinguished for talent, erudition and piety; these no doubt felt that the political influence exerted to promote Christianity was attended with serious evils.

Among the descendants of Europeans there were some bright examples of religious consistency. I knew a devoted old lady of the name of Schraader, who for many years, in a large town in the northern province, was the sole instructress of a considerable community. She was in the habit of assembling the people in her own house for divine worship, when she read the Scriptures and conducted Divine Service in the Portuguese language. She translated several religious books from Dutch into Tamil and Portuguese, and circulated them in manuscript written with her own hand. She also composed in Portuguese a metrical history of the chief parts of the Bible. After the age of fifty-five she acquired English, and translated a volume of hymns out of that language into Portuguese. She died about four years ago at the advanced age of eighty-five. Highly intellectual, elegant in manners, and eminently distinguished for sweetness of disposition, this pious and devoted woman was one of the most influential persons in her neighbourhood. For many years she conducted a school, and was well qualified to teach Dutch, Portuguese, and Tamil. Doubtless this sainted matron secured the commendation of that Saviour, of whose love she was wont to discourse with so much sweetness. There was a dignity in her manner, a solemnity and a cheerfulness, that combined to make her a most remarkable person. Her form, her expression of countenance, her faltering accents of religious wonder and delight have often cheered my mind; and she lives in my memory as a monument of the singular providence of God in the peculiar and bereaved circumstances of a small Christian community, who were in her provided with a light that shone in a dark place, till the day of enlarged and more diffusive light dawned, under the increased and multiplied means of instruction eventually provided.

CHAPTER XVIII.

CHRISTIANITY IN INDIA (*continued*). — DANISH MISSION AT TRANQUEBAR. — ZIEGENBALG AND HIS COLLEAGUES. — TRANSLATION OF THE SCRIPTURES INTO THE TAMIL LANGUAGE.—EVANGELISTIC AND PASTORAL LABOUR.—MISSION AIDED BY THE SOCIETY FOR THE PROPAGATION OF THE GOSPEL.—LETTER OF GEORGE THE FIRST.—ARCHBISHOP TENISON'S LETTER.—PROGRESS AND DECAY OF THE MISSION.

In the history just sketched of the progress of European commerce, conquest, and the religious proceedings of the Portuguese and the Dutch in India, we see nothing that bears the true evangelical stamp with reference to the conversion of the Hindus to the faith of Christ. The Portuguese introduced a system, we dare not call it Christianity, that was distinguishable from that of the Hindus by little else than a foreign terminology, and the greater amount of pride, injustice, and cruelty, by which it was promoted. The Dutch created an imposing monument of unprincipled conformity to an unknown system, which vanished on the withdrawal of the power by which it was upheld. The English, disregarding altogether the dying myriads with whom commercial enterprise and conquest brought them into contact, even denying, as we shall see, in the high places of the Church, the obligation to propagate the Gospel among them, but very inadequately provided for the external maintenance of religion even among their own servants. The honour of enlightened and consistent conduct in the matter of attempting India's evangelization was reserved for the Danes. A few remarks may suffice to show how this was brought about.

The increased traffic with India by the Dutch and English

led to the formation of a company at Copenhagen. The first vessel from Denmark arrived on the Coromandel coast in 1616. For the protection and convenience of an increasing trade, the Danes procured by purchase a small territory from the Raja of Tanjore, and built the town of Tranquebar. For many years no efforts were made for the conversion of the natives. At length, however, this object was suggested to Frederick IV., King of Denmark, who, with becoming zeal, resolved on the attempt to evangelize his Hindu subjects. This noble act was but one of many that might be referred to, originating at the commencement of last century, in proof of an awakened state of religious feeling in the Reformed Church. Then Schmidt of Holland encountered the African savage, and gained him over to Christ; then Egede of Norway, and David of Moravia, and many others, braved the inhospitable climes of Greenland and Labrador,

> "To plant successfully sweet Sharon's rose
> On icy plains, and in eternal snows."

Eliot and Brainerd, whose happy experience and devoted zeal operated so magically on our own revered Martyn, went forth among the wild American Indians, fearing no evil. The acute and philosophic Berkley, with his laudable scheme for converting the savage Americans by a college to be founded in the isles of Bermuda, may be mentioned in this connexion. He employs the following eloquent terms to set forth his noble project :—"A benefaction of this kind seems to enlarge the very being of man, extending it to distant places and to future times; inasmuch as unseen countries and after ages may feel the effects of his bounty, while he himself reaps the reward in the society of all those who, having turned many to righteousness, shine as stars for ever and ever." In the present chapter it is intended to narrate the events connected with the first efforts made by a reviving Protestantism to attack the gigantic fortress of Hindu superstition. The narrative is given in detail because it illustrates the principles of the men employed, and shows how their conduct was in character with their relation to the Head of the Church and the solemn objects of their mission.

In 1705 Dr. Lutkins, one of the Danish king's chaplains, suggested to him the propriety of attempting the conversion of his Hindu subjects in the territory of Tranquebar. His Majesty at once applied to Professor Francke, of Halle; and two young men, Ziegenbalg and Plutscho, were selected for the embassy. They were chosen as persons distinguished for piety, sound judgment, amiability of disposition, and who had also the requisite talent and acquirements for such an important and trying service. His Majesty provided for their maintenance out of the public treasury. For the further consolidation of missionary plans, the Danish monarch, in 1714, set up a Missionary College at Copenhagen, consisting of some of the leading ecclesiastics and councillors of state. Special instructions were issued by the King to the College or incorporated Society, in which "every member was solemnly exhorted to think it his duty, after hearty prayers put up for the purpose, to lay to heart a work of so great concern, and to employ what gifts Providence had bestowed upon him for so Christian a design—viz. that the Gospel of Christ be preached to the Gentiles, and thereby many souls be brought over to Jesus Christ." The College, thus prompted by royal counsel, was careful to aid the labourers employed, and also to augment the number, whilst they were attentive to promote the temporal and spiritual interests of those brought into the fold of Christ abroad. "Happy omen for Denmark, when its reigning monarch, regarding himself simply as a member and citizen in the Church and commonwealth of the Redeemer, felt the sacredness of the obligation to do what in him lay to advance the great ends of the redemptive economy, and honour and support those who were appointed its heralds and ambassadors to the realms of heathenism!"

The 29th November, 1705, was the day on which Ziegenbalg and his colleague set out on their mission to India. The incidents and events on the voyage are delineated by the missionaries with graphic simplicity. On the 9th of July, 1706, they arrived at the place of their destination. Being on their station, and in the scene of action, they express their views respecting their great work. They resolve to use every means, in dependence on divine aid, spiritually to enlighten the understandings of men, to exalt and magnify the Lord Jesus in their souls, and by the grace of God, to convey such a lively knowledge of the Gospel as might render the heathen obedient to the faith, and thereby save them from everlasting ruin. How strikingly and advantageously does this contrast with the proceedings of the Romanists and Hollanders! They begin with no preconceived and ill-adapted plan; but, relying on the instrumentality of the Word and the promised aid of the Holy Spirit, they enter on the work of heralding the message they had received from the Lord Jesus. Being fired with holy zeal, these apostolic men would have hastened at once to deliver the message, but the language was required. They had arrived in a country where they met an utter destitution of all aids to the enterprise in which they were engaged. They had no grammars and dictionaries, except those of the natives, which of course, as being wholly in the native or Tamil language, and in the high or poetic dialect, were as unsuited to them as would have been a grammar of the Chinese. There was no Bible, although the Romanists had preceded them two centuries. As the Portuguese language was used among descendants of Europeans, and to some extent among the natives of the Danish settlement, they resolved to acquire that as easier, and as a readier way to their main object. Soon, however, they discovered that the *patois* Portuguese could never be made the vehicle for conveying instruction to the Hindus, and, therefore, resolved on the study of Tamil. Ziegenbalg made rapid proficiency, and soon composed a grammar, from which I learnt the rudiments of the language nearly a hundred and twenty years after it was published. He next compiled a dictionary.

Among other difficulties that impeded their progress they name the prejudices produced in the native mind by "the abominably wicked lives of the Christians." "They," the natives, "look upon Christians as the very dregs of the world, the vilest and most corrupted people under the sun, and the general bane of mankind." They frequently asked whether the Christians led as wicked lives in Europe as they did in the East Indies. Under these circumstances the judicious missionaries sought, by instruction and prayer, to improve the Europeans, and their efforts were not unattended with good.

They speak of the state and proceedings of the Romish Church at Tranquebar, and confirm the statements elsewhere made respecting the corrupt proceedings of the priests. They describe a procession of neophytes, who were led to baptism with music and banners, sprinkled in multitudes, and being led back, had small coin thrown among them. The Danish Mission, whilst protesting against such wholesale baptisms of ignorant men and women, were careful to make it known that they sought conversion as the result of enlightened and free choice. In these proceedings the Danish missionaries are worthy examples of all who are called to labour among the Hindus. It is now, as then, of the utmost importance that the missionaries of the Reformed Church, "by raising high and conspicuous the standard of Protestantism, substituting openness, candour, and kindness, for concealment, guile, and violence; the spirit of inquiry for the stupor of apathy—knowledge for ignorance—mental freedom for blind acquiescence—the distinct and independent individuality of man for his irresponsible absorption into the general mass—the right of private judgment for the obligation of passive obedience, should seek to render the contrast between Protestantism and Romanism as striking to the shrewd common sense of the heathens, as if they were severed by an impassable gulf."

These forerunners of Protestant missions soon found, as they advanced in their work, that the Hindu system of religion, its metaphysics and mythology, and the power of its priesthood, had to be met in their progress as being sent "for the defence and confirmation of the Gospel." Consistently with their high vocation, they procured the sacred books of the Hindus, as far as they could, and endeavoured to acquire information on those subjects that were found to preoccupy the minds of those they sought to enlighten and save.

Zeigenbalg describes the Hindus as a "wily sagacious people, that need to be managed with a great deal of wisdom, circumspection, and discretion—a quick and understanding people, who require good reasons and arguments for everything." They used every means for securing the enlightenment of those they laboured amongst. Thus they "preached" and they "taught" in public on stated occasions, in private, and "from house to house." A volume of the friendly conferences they had with the natives was published at an early period of the mission. In India sermons alone will not meet the case of the native churches. The people must be catechised. The truth must be instilled and fixed by a careful attention to the state of the mind and the progress of truth in its enlightenment. However correct and valuable symbols, standards, and formularies are in their place, they do not reach the mind of a native in its ordinary condition.

The honoured men whose labours we are now considering, were not unmindful of the main business, that of supplying the native church with the precious book, the Bible. Zeigenbalg entertained a profound sense of the importance of this work, and speaks of it as calculated to exert a mighty influence "in establishing the religion of Christ on a firm foundation." His difficulties were immense. Though he brought to the work a well prepared mind, richly stored with the requisites of matured scholarship, the language into which he had to turn the divine word, was then for the first time to be used as a vehicle of inspired truth. Few, apart from actual experience, can estimate the extreme difficulty felt in the selection of words for Christian teaching in a language used for ages as the exponent of false philosophy and pagan superstition. The work was however completed. In 1714 the version of the New Testament was printed; and the Old, including the Apocrypha, was put forth in the years 1725—28. More than thirty books in Tamil, and upwards of twenty in Portuguese, issued from the first mission press at Tranquebar. They established a boarding-school with special reference to the careful education and training of a select number of native youths. They also entertained strong impressions as to the necessity for a higher course of training for the preparation of missionary agents.

The Danish missionaries built a church at Tranquebar. In 1713 they numbered two hundred and forty-five converts, chiefly of the lowest order of natives and the Portuguese. Though the Bible affirms that not many mighty, not many noble, not many wise, are called, yet it is true that the first convert from Hinduism among the natives of the south, was a young man of royal extraction; and another was one of the most learned men in the country. The missionaries set up a paper manufactory. To relieve converts who had lost all as the consequence of embracing Christianity, they also began various manufactories to enable them to earn an honest livelihood.

It is impossible to read the records of the first mission of the Reformed Church in India, without deep admiration of the apostolic zeal and practical good sense of its first agents. In the true sense, they became all things to all men, that they might gain some. In this they persisted, and with the varied measures the principle necessitated they persevered; they adopted such means as they found from experience would best subserve the one grand design, that of converting men from error to truth, from sin to holiness. Referring

Christian missions to their main scope, object, and design, and comparing the proceedings and spirit of the Danish missionaries with Apostolic models and evangelical acquirements, we judge that all men who take their measures from the living Word, must accord to them the highest praise.

The records of their proceedings when published in Europe were not passed over as idle stories, but treated with the respect and deference to which they were entitled. The wisest and best men of the day gave heed to the things they made known, and whilst they cherished a warm sympathy with the devoted men engaged in the noble enterprise, they showed their beneficence and aided the work.

George the First of England was led to take the deepest interest in the Danish Mission; yea, and to enter into direct personal correspondence with the Missionaries. No act in the life of that British monarch does more credit to his head and heart than the penning of these Royal Missionary letters. On a visit to England Ziegenbalg was introduced to the King, George the First, and to the Prince and Princess of Wales, who received him courteously, entered upon the subject of the conversion of the Hindus with much warmth of feeling, and assured him of their patronage. He received similar assurances from the Archbishop of Canterbury, and the Bishop of London; and every one of these distinguished personages afterwards redeemed the pledges they had so kindly given In a word, his visit to England answered all his expectations; it proved both serviceable to his Mission, and honourable to himself.

The publication of the Missionaries' correspondence in Germany was productive of sympathy, and therefore the Rev. Mr. Boehm, Chaplain of Prince George of Denmark, the consort of Queen Anne, published in 1709 an English translation of several letters which he had received from the Missionaries, dedicating his work to the Archbishop of Canterbury, President, and to the other members of the Society for the Propagation of the Gospel in Foreign Parts, which was, as is well known, established by Royal Charter in 1701. Shortly after the publication of the letter in question, the venerable Society resolved to render some assistance to the undertaking in behalf of the Hindus, and sent the Missionaries a grant of twenty pounds and a case of books, accompanying the first-fruits of British beneficence in behalf of the conversion of India, with letters of encouragement. It must indeed be matter of sincerest gratification to every right-minded person to recognise, in the directors of the noble Society just then organized in England, such sentiments as we read in the following extract from one of their letters to India :—

"May the Lord bless you, whom He hath counted worthy to sow the first seed in a work, which, in time, may grow to a tree, in whose branches the birds of the air may build their nests. Your confidence in your work may gather strength, from the evidence you already have of the power of God in carrying it on thus far. For though yet but small, still it is as a grain of mustard-seed, which, by its indwelling vitality and strength, makes itself known by touching the hearts of men. Love and humility must be the two pillars whereon to raise your edifice, if it is to have an immovable foundation which no turbulence of storms or waves shall be able to overthrow. Upon many a one has the door, once opened, been shut again, because he has not kept it open with a holy fear, humility, and love. If we do not shut it upon ourselves, the promise remains, 'No one shall close it.' We may go forth boldly, but it must be in the name of Christ: we may go on, but it must be in his strength. When all who profess the name of Christ throughout the world, shall hold together as members of one body, in holy love, they will show forth great strength, and exercise a mighty, though secret influence over the heathen, who then cannot but see, hear, and feel, that there is a power residing in us to which they are strangers."

Ziegenbalg visits Madras. He is kindly entertained and refreshed by the English. He afterwards purchases a garden with the funds received from England, in the neighbourhood of Tranquebar. In 1710 a second abstract of their proceedings was published in England, and excited greater interest in their undertaking. The Society for Promoting Christian Knowledge now undertakes the business of supply, but yet the funds collected were placed in the hands of Archbishop Tenison and Mr. John Chamberlayne, the President and Secretary of the Society for the Propagation of the Gospel. "Nothing could be more gratifying than the liberality of the English, who distinguished themselves on this occasion. People of all ranks, nobility and clergy, ladies and gentlemen, citizens and merchants, contributed to a large amount, some without wishing it to be known."

Part of the money contributed at this time was expended in the purchase of a printing-press, type, printing-ink, books, and a set of mathematical instruments. An edition of the Portuguese New Testament was printed in London for the Tranquebar Mission. The Secretary of the Society for Promoting Christian Knowledge wrote to the Rev. Mr. Lewis, the English Chaplain at Madras, and inquired into the state of religion on the coast. In his reply he says that they "ought and must be encouraged in the first attempt of Protestants to diffuse the truth in India." "We must not," says he, "put out the smoking flax; it would give our adversaries, the Papists, who boast so much of their congregations, too much cause to triumph over us." In 1716 another Chaplain, the Rev. Mr. Stevenson, who had visited Tranquebar and where he spent several days, speaks in a highly commendatory manner of the labours of the Missionaries in the Tamil and Portuguese languages. He observes with reference to the practice of catechising, "The children are greater proficients in true Christian knowledge than those of an advanced age among us."

The mission, at the request of the Governor and Chaplain of Fort St. George, who rendered aid towards the desiderated object, was extended to Madras in 1717. Ziegenbalg and his colleague sent a report of their mission about this time to George the First. His Majesty transmitted the following gracious reply :—

George, by the grace of God, King of Great Britain, &c., to the Reverend and Learned Bartholomew Ziegenbalg, and John Ernest Grundler, Missionaries at Tranquebar.

"Reverend and Beloved,—Your letters, dated the 20th of January of the present year, were most welcome to us; not only because the work undertaken by you, of converting the heathen to the Christian faith, doth, by the grace of God, prosper, but also because that in this our kingdom such a laudable zeal for the promotion of the Gospel prevails.

"We pray that you may be endued with health and strength of body, that you may long continue to fulfil your ministry with good success; of which, as we shall be rejoiced to hear, so you will always find us ready to succour you in whatever may tend to promote your work and to excite your zeal. We assure you of the continuance of our royal favour.

"GEORGE R.

"Given at our Palace of Hampton Court, the 23d of August, A.D. 1717, in the fourth year of our reign."

Need we remark that such a letter from the first of the House of Brunswick, called by Divine Providence to rule over the British empire, argued well for that Protestant faith which he was exalted to defend? The following letter from the Archbishop of Canterbury was written and transmitted to the honoured men who were labouring to plant the Gospel in India :—

To Bartholomew Ziegenbalg and John Ernest Grundler, Preachers of the Christian Faith on the Coast of Coromandel.

"As often as I behold your letters, Reverend Brethren, addressed to the venerable Society instituted for the Promotion of the Gospel, whose chief honour and ornament ye are; and as often as I contemplate the light of the gospel, either first now rising on the Indian nations, or after the intermission of some ages revived, and as it were restored to its inheritance, I am constrained to magnify that singular goodness of God in visiting nations so remote, and to account you, my brethren, highly honoured, whose ministry it hath pleased Him to employ in this pious work, to the glory of His name, and the salvation of so many millions of souls.

"Let others indulge in a ministry, if not idle, certainly less laborious, among Christians at home; let them enjoy in the bosom of the Church, titles and honours, obtained without labour or without danger; your praise it will be (a praise of endless duration on earth, and followed by a just recompense in heaven) to have laboured in the vineyard which yourselves have planted, and to have declared the name of Christ where it was not known before; and through much peril and difficulty to have converted to the faith those among whom ye afterward fulfilled your ministry. Your province, therefore, brethren, your office I place before all dignities in the church. Let others be pontiffs, patriarchs, or popes; let them glitter in purple, in scarlet, or in gold; let them seek the admiration of the wondering multitude, and receive obeisance on the bended knee: ye have acquired a better name than they, and a more sacred fame; and when that day shall arrive when the Chief Shepherd shall give to every man according to his work, a great reward shall be adjudged to you. Admitted into the glorious society of the Prophets, Evangelists, and Apostles, ye, with them, shall shine like the sun among the lesser stars for ever and ever.

"Since then so great honour is given unto you by all competent judges on earth, and since so great reward is laid up for you in heaven, go forth with alacrity to that work to which the Holy Ghost hath called you. God hath already given unto you an illustrative pledge of His favour, an increase not to be expected without the aid of His grace. Ye have begun happily, proceed with spirit. He who hath carried you safely through the dangers of the seas to such a remote country, and hath given you favour in the eyes of those whose countenance ye most desired; He who hath so liberally and unexpectedly ministered to your wants, and who doth now daily add numbers to your church; He will continue to prosper your endeavours, and will subdue unto Himself, by your means, the *whole continent* of *Oriental India.*"

"O happy men! who standing before the tribunal of Christ, shall exhibit so many nations converted to His faith by your preaching. Happy men! to whom it shall be given to say before the assembly of the whole human race, 'Behold us, O Lord, and the children whom Thou hast given us.' Happy men! that being justified by the Saviour, shall receive in that day the reward of your labours, and also shall hear that glorious encomium, 'Well done, good and faithful servants, enter ye into the joy of your Lord.'

"May Almighty God graciously favour you and your labours in all things. May He send to your aid fellow-labourers, such and as many as ye will. May He increase the bounds of your churches. May He open the hearts of those to whom ye preach the Gospel of Christ, that hearing you, they may receive life-giving faith. May He protect you and yours from all evils and dangers. And when ye arrive (may it be late) at the end of your course, may the same God, who hath called you to this same work of the Gospel, and hath preserved you in it, grant to you the reward of your labour, and an incorruptible crown of glory!

"These are the fervent wishes and prayers of, Venerable Brethren,

"Your most faithful Fellow-servant in Christ,

"GULIELMUS CANT.

"From our Palace at Lambeth,
"January 7th, 1719."

The honoured Ziegenbalg entered into rest before this paternal epistle reached its destination. He died Feb. 23d, 1719, in the thirty-sixth year of his age. His remains were interred in the first church he built, amid the sobs of his friends and his native flock. Besides a small mural tablet recording his name, age, &c., no monument has been raised to his memory; but his name stands inscribed on the records of ecclesiastical history in India. His labours, especially those bestowed on the translation of the Sacred Scriptures, embalm his memory with odours sweeter far than any spices that were ever compounded for the dead.

The Head of the Church, notwithstanding the removal of the labourers whom He had sent into the field, still continued the work, and gradually extended it to various parts of the country. Cuddalore, Madras, Tanjore, Trichinopoly, Negapatam, Tinnevelly, were added to the sphere of their labours, and during the last century upwards of fifty missionaries arrived in India, in connexion with the Tranquebar mission. Ziegenbalg, Swartz, and Gericke, are names familiar to all who are acquainted with the records of missions. Dr. Schultze was the first Telugu scholar and translator of the Bible into that language. Dr. Kohlhoff was the colleague of Swartz, and succeeded him. Dr. Rotler was a man of science. Fabricius possessed superior powers; he revised the Tamil Bible, and published a volume of hymns in Tamil, which is deservedly popular among the native Christians of the present day.

Dr. John, of Tranquebar, was the first missonary who commenced an English school. Drs. Kohlhoff, Cæmmerer, and Rotler, I had the pleasure of knowing. The others had fallen asleep before I went out. Many of these distinguished men laboured for very long periods,—Rotler, I think, was in the country sixty-four years. Kiernander, who removed from Cuddalore, in 1758, to Calcutta, founded the mission in that city; and built the first Christian church in 1770, called Beth Tephillah, the house of prayer. He laboured more than half a century in the country. The missions, as they branched out, were conducted on the same plan as the one first commenced at Tranquebar. The Missionaries employed the same means that Protestants do at the present day. The preaching of the word was the primary business, and that in the vernacular language. They made extended tours for the purpose of making known the truths of the Gospel. They founded regular congregations, and statedly ministered to them. They catechised those under their pastoral care, and in this way, by a skilful and familiar system of interrogation, ascertained what their flocks knew, and imparted instruction accordingly. They translated the Bible, and wrote other religious books; thus laying the foundation of a native literature. Their educational plans were extensive and efficient. Some of their converts, under their training, became sufficiently matured in knowledge and grace to enter the ministry, and took their place as the precursors of what all must desire to see as the only ground of hope for a self-propagating Christianity—an indigenous ministry. The baptized converts amounted to upwards of fifty thousand. Had the cause been supported with the same efficiency under which it was commenced, and had labourers of the same spirit been continued in undiminished succession, the Church of Christ would ere this have been planted in the greater part of Southern India. Towards the end of last century the missionaries entered the field few in number, and far between, and eventually the supply was entirely cut off. In 1816, only three missionaries remained in connexion with the once flourishing field, and two of these were supported by English funds. Many of the native Christians, as sheep having no shepherd, fell away, and were scattered. Others were absorbed in the growing ranks of other missionary institutions.

CHAPTER XIX.

CHRISTIANITY IN INDIA (CONTINUED).—ANGLO-INDIAN GOVERNMENT MEASURES.—INADEQUACY OF RELIGIOUS INSTRUCTION IN INDIA.—THE ZEAL OF SOME OF THE ENGLISH CHAPLAINS: BUCHANAN, BROWN, MARTYN, CORRIE, THOMASON, KERR.—INDIAN EPISCOPATE.—BISHOP'S COLLEGE.—MISSIONS OF THE CHURCH.

AMID much that is traditional, vague, and uncertain in regard to the question of early Christianity in India, there is sufficient to assure us of its existence there at a period comparatively near that of the Apostles. It is, however, evident that the influence it exerted was but partial and local, confined almost wholly to those foreign residents whose commercial pursuits had led them thither for secular purposes. There is no proof that its adherents, whether foreign or native, or both, used any means to extend into the "regions beyond" the western coast, where it was first planted, the gospel of the grace of God. This absence of benevolent aggressiveness on the part of the early Church in India is, to my own mind, a strong proof that its action and influence were almost, if not wholly, confined to the commercial residents who, as agents of Alexandrian, Parsi, and other foreign merchants, were temporarily or permanently located in the emporia of trade. Lacking the native vigour and expansiveness of genuine Christianity, the Church made no effort to extend itself, and it was equally feeble in resisting the aggressions of Rome, as the details already furnished clearly show. But the proceedings of the Romanists are not thereby justified; their artifice, intrigue, fraud, and violence, must evoke feelings of the strongest indignation; whilst the prostration of the original institutions and primitive economy of the Indo-Syrian Church will excite painful regret. The timid, selfish, fraudulent, and unprincipled proceedings of some of the Syrian ecclesiastics must have produced a withering effect on the members of the Syrian Church. There seems no reason to believe that the state of Christian feeling and practice among the Syrian Christians was very different, when the Portuguese arrived on the coast, from that now existing, and which has been described by one whose testimony has been already introduced into these pages.

The deeds of violence and of blood connected with the efforts of Portugal to convert the people of Southern India are but ill compensated by the zeal and activity of the sincere but mistaken Xavier. Bloody massacres, cruel persecutions, imprisonments, and, indeed, all the horrors of the inquisition of Goa, are but a poor substitute for the word of truth, the Gospel of salvation, of which in their proceedings we read nothing. Consecrated banners, blessed hats, crucifixes, images of the saints, a transferred Hindu paraphernalia of idolatry, are substituted for the Bible. It would appear that the Portuguese, far from improving as they became better acquainted with their new possessions, became worse and worse. One of their own governors, in 1545, says, "I dare not govern India by men who are so changed from truth and honour." "The Portuguese entered India with the sword in one hand and the crucifix in the other; finding much gold, they laid aside the crucifix to fill their pockets." They are said to have "wallowed in wealth and wantonness." Who can look at the proceedings of the Jesuits at Madura and elsewhere without a feeling of surprise, as he witnesses the incredible spectacle of wholesale fraud adopted there for introducing Christianity? Italian priests attired, or almost naked rather, like Hindu ascetics, conforming to pagan usages, foisting a book on the natives under the name of a Hindu ordinance, denying that they were Europeans, could hardly be imagined, were not the narrative of their proceedings authenticated by the most unquestionable authority. These facts, so prominent in the history of Christianity in India, grievously mar its pages.

Nor is the period during which the Dutch bore sway, and exerted themselves for the advancement of Presbyterianism, more satisfactory. Dishonesty, cruelty, and intolerance, combined with the sinister motives their policy involved, were not much better fitted for this end than the pitiless cruelty and unblushing fraud of their predecessors. The Dutch, as did the Portuguese, numbered their converts by hundreds of thousands; but subsequent occurrences afforded abundant evidence that they were apocryphal and nominal, not real believers. Neither cruelty, nor fraud, nor appeals to self-interest, could lay the foundation of genuine Christianity.

The Mission from Denmark begins a new epoch in the history of Christianity in India. The proceedings of its agents stand in delightful contrast to those of the Portuguese and of the Dutch. As commanded by our Lord, they preached the glad tidings, and commended themselves and their doctrines to the judgments and consciences of those whose salvation they sought to promote.

Although the establishment of British power in India was not made subservient to the diffusion of the truth among the Hindus, or even of the liberty of British Christians to use efforts for its propagation, yet the supreme government has gradually removed the obstacles which local authority created; and eventually, as we have seen, the local government, by a *lex loci*, removed every cause that might be construed into an abridgment of the rights of private judgment. We shall see, as we advance, that the annals of Christianity assume an improved character. The efforts to convert the Hindus to the faith of Christ will be found, within the new and more auspicious period, of a very different nature from some of those we have been compelled to narrate. The unadorned influence of the Gospel, the efficacy of truth unaided by the favour and uninfluenced by the power of secular rulers, have been the instruments, the only means that have been tried since Britain cast her ægis over the millions of India. The Bible is the instrument on which alone the modern missionary can depend. Its truths are expounded and applied, its evidences are adduced, and its sanctions unfolded, as the authorized means of enlightening the understanding and awakening the conscience. The judgment and the heart are cultivated; and therefore the fruit realized, though not great in quantity, is satisfactory in quality.

It is now proposed to furnish a succinct statement of the progress of Christianity in India since the English became masters of the country. The subject may be considered under various aspects, as connected with the several objects that have been pursued, and the means adopted by different parties. It will be the aim to present some of the more interesting facts connected with the advancement of Christianity under the paramount power of the English.

Following the track of English progress in India, it seems most natural to narrate the events that have arisen out of government measures in relation to the Church of England. This will lead us to the labours of the Chaplains, and the founding of the Indian Episcopate. The latter fact will connect itself with the establishment of the Bishop's Missionary College. Having glanced at the events connected with this branch of the subject, we shall briefly delineate the commencement and progress of Protestant Missions, and their present state and prospects.

The East India Company was incorporated December 13th, 1600, and their first fleet sailed on the 2d of May, 1601. No provisions were made by the Legislature for the instruction and conversion of the natives with whom they traded. This is not to be wondered at in the first instance. The practical character of the English stands opposed to mere theories and schemes that have no promise of utility. Commerce, not conversion, was the object of the Hon. East India Company's charter, and to its extension and permanency all efforts were directed.

Cromwell is said to have entertained the intention to include, in his "great design" for promoting Protestantism, the territories in India. He seems to have admitted it to be "the duty of the State to provide religious ordinances and instruction for its subjects." The views and intentions of government were lost sight of amid the strife and confusion that ensued, and till the reign of William and Mary nothing was attempted. Five years after the accession of William and Mary, in 1694, the learned Dr. Prideaux, Dean of Norwich, drew up a paper entitled, An Account of the English Settlement in the East Indies, together with some Proposals for the Propagation of Christianity in those parts of the World. In that paper the writer ascribes the superior prosperity of the Dutch to their greater solicitude to promote the honour of God. He writes under the felt persuasion that extending conquests and power bring along with them increased responsibility. To redeem the English from the reproach attaching to them, and to secure the blessing of Almighty God, he proposed a comprehensive scheme for the promotion of education in India, the providing of English seamen and the military with instruction and the means of grace, as well as some proposals for the establishment of missionary stations. He also suggested that a seminary should be established in England to train persons for Eastern missions, into which students brought from India might be introduced. He moreover suggested that when Christianity should be sufficiently established in India to authorize the appointment of a bishop, the seminary might be removed thither.

By an act of the Legislature in the reign of William III., it was enjoined that in every garrison and superior factory in India, one minister should be provided for the decent maintenance of divine worship; and, moreover, it was made incumbent on such ministers as should be sent to reside in India, to apply themselves to learn the native languages of the country, the better to enable them to instruct the Hindus who should be servants of the Company or of their agents, in the Protestant religion.

"These injunctions of the British Legislature were not followed by corresponding exertions to discharge the obligation so distinctly acknowledged. For many years, the English residents were very inadequately supplied with chaplains; and those gentlemen were never *required* to do more than attend to their official duties to their own countrymen."

"But, though the British authorities were thus indifferent about the religion of their heathen subjects, they did not interfere with the Romish missionaries, but left them at liberty, with the single exception of the Jesuits, to prosecute the work of conversion. Indeed they favoured them with more than bare toleration; for about the close of the seventeenth century, they took some pains to procure a religious teacher for the numerous Romanists within the Madras presidency. A Capuchin missionary, named Father Euphrem, touching at Fort St. George, on his way to their mission at Pegu, was invited by the English to remain there, and take charge of the members of his church within the Company's territories. Assured of protection and assistance in the exercise of his functions, he acceded to the proposal, and, under the auspices of the English governor, founded a Capuchin establishment at Madras, which exists to the present day.

"This missionary had not entered long on the duties of his office before he received substantial proof that his confidence in the English was not misplaced. On one occasion, when preaching upon the honour that belonged unto God, he exposed the idolatry of the Romish practice of giving greater honour to the Virgin Mary, and carefully explained the difference between the homage due to God, as Creator, and the respect to be paid to the memory of the Virgin, who, he said, was a mere creature. This was heard by some Portuguese, who had come from St. Thomé; and, being 'as superstitious as the heathen,' says the *Romish* author, they were much offended at his so depreciating 'the Queen of Heaven,' and reported the heretical sentiment that he had uttered to the Inquisition at Goa. The inquisitors, who were Jesuits, sent immediate orders to have him apprehended, and transported to Goa. But it was no easy matter to execute these orders while he was under British protection: they therefore resolved upon a stratagem to draw him away from Madras. A feigned disturbance was raised at St. Thomé, which Father Euphrem was sent for to appease; but he had no sooner arrived than he was seized by the officers of the Inquisition, and carried to Goa as a criminal, bound hand and foot. Arriving there at night, he was hurried at once from ship-board, and immediately thrown into one of the dungeons, without going through even the form of a judicial process. The English, at Madras, no sooner heard of this tyrannical proceeding, than their indignation was roused, and they resolved without delay to break the prisoner's bonds and restore him to liberty. For this purpose they sent a vessel to Goa, with eight or ten resolute men on board, who, immediately on their arrival there, presented themselves at the gate of the Inquisition, with their weapons concealed under their clothes, and pretended that they were come peaceably, merely wishing to pay a visit to the court. Having gained admittance, two of them secured the gate, and the rest rushed forward, sword in hand, and threatened the inquisitors with instant death if they did not open the prison doors, and set Father Euphrem at liberty. The father was soon restored to them, when they carried him off in triumph, the sentinels keeping the gate till he was safe on board. They then followed, and the vessel sailed for Madras, where they arrived in safety, and reinstated the Father in his mission, rejoiced at having escaped out of the hand of 'his tormentors,' and filled with gratitude to his generous deliverers."

It would appear that the legislators of 1701, in making provision for the instruction and comfort of our own countrymen, were not altogether unmindful of the spiritual interests of the Hindus. Under any circumstances it would be imagined that men who are moved by the Holy Ghost to enter on the responsible office of the ministry, would seek to save all that in the course of Providence might be brought within their influence, and the more so when the original document from the Christian legislature of this country makes specific provision for the extension of religious instruction among them. Truth however obliges the confession that, notwithstanding the considerate provision for the publication of the truth to the Hindus, hundreds of chaplains have gone to that country who never troubled themselves about the native languages, and who made no attempt to make known a Saviour's love to the native inhabitants. There are, however, some noble exceptions to this general apathy, which shall shortly be adduced.

The Government has never done anything beyond what we have named in furtherance of the Gospel among the natives. The voluntary efforts of its chaplains, occasionally made, are the only State interference in the work of enlightening the millions of India. Indeed, some of the leading men belonging to the Honourable East India Company have denied that the chaplains, supported as they are by the State, have any right to obtrude on the natives of India the teachings of Christianity.

Howsoever unfounded the fears some have cherished in regard to any attempt on the part of government to instruct the subjects of its rule in British India, it may be conceived that many right-minded and conscientious men have opposed such a course from the best of motives; yet no such excuse can be found for the utter inadequacy of the religious instruction which was provided for the Christian subjects scattered throughout the vast territories of the British dominions in India. That the absence of all religious instruction and the ordinances of public worship, in the early periods of our connexion with the country, led to a gross degeneracy of manners, cannot be doubted. Living among the heathen without the restraints of pastoral oversight, those who once listened to the voice of conscience, and paid some attention to the outward observances of religion, were easily led by the seductions of vice into dissolute and licentious habits. In the early period of our rule it was only here and there that a chaplain was to be found. There were no altars raised to God, even where a chaplain chanced to be, he was consequently obliged to conduct divine service at the drum head, in a riding-school or court-house, or some such place.

Even as late as the year 1798 one of the chaplains in India writes: "It is certain that neither the number nor the choice of the clergymen the Court of Directors have appointed to Bengal, have been in proportion to the number of their servants, nor the importance of the object in view; whether you regard keeping up the appearance of religion among Europeans, or disseminating its principles among the Hindus. On this establishment their full complement of chaplains is only nine; their actual number seldom exceeds five or six. Two of these always being fixed at the Presidency, all the other European stations, dispersed over a tract of country much more extensive than Great Britain, are committed to the charge of the other three or four individuals. In consequence of this, the presence of a clergyman is seldom seen, or even expected, to solemnise the usual ceremonies of marriages, baptisms, or funerals. Prayers are sometimes read at the stations where a chaplain happens to reside; but I have seldom heard of any sermon delivered, except by his Majesty's chaplains, and these at Calcutta. Hence it must happen that many persons must have left England at an early age, and resided in India perhaps for twenty or thirty years, without once having heard divine service, till their return."

On undoubted testimony, we learn that the sanctity of the sabbath was almost universally violated. Where a chaplain might be stationed it was not universally the rule to conduct public worship; it not unfrequently happened that the commanding officer set his face against it. Claudius Buchanan was for some years chaplain at Barrackpore without once enjoying the privilege of summoning the people to worship. The violation of the sabbath was so glaring and general that the Court of Directors protested against it. Their document is dated 25th of May, 1798. The following may suffice as a specimen :—"We cannot avoid mentioning," say they, "the information that we have received that at the military stations it is no uncommon thing for the solemnity of the day to be broken in upon by horse-racing, whilst divine worship (for which the sabbath is especially enjoined and set apart) is never performed at any of these stations, though chaplains are allotted to them. And we have now before us a printed horse-racing account, by which it appears that not less than eight matches were run at Chinsurah, and that on a Sunday." In the same letter the decent observance of the sabbath is strictly enjoined; and the chaplains are directed to attend to their sacred duties on pain of dismissal from the service. The preparation and transmission of such a document reflects no little honour on the men from whom it emanated. It implies, however, great laxity on the part of those who at that period filled the sacred office in India.

Although the first stone of St. Mary's Church at Madras was laid as early as the year 1680, no sacred edifice was raised in Bengal till 1770, when the old, or Mission Church was built, and followed by St. John's, the old Cathedral, in 1787. The letter from which an extract has been made had a most beneficial effect. The improvement which has steadily advanced began under Lord Cornwallis, and was encouraged alike by Sir John Shore and the Marquis of Wellesley. In 1806 the Rev. Daniel, afterwards Bishop, Corrie, wrote: "The state of society is much altered for the better within these few years. The Marquis Wellesley openly patronized religion: he on every occasion made moral character a *sine quâ non* to his patronage, and sought for men of character from every quarter to fill offices of trust. He avowedly encouraged and contributed to the translation of the Scriptures into the native languages; and wherever he went paid a strict regard to divine worship on the Sunday." Sir John Shore observed to a clergyman in a conversation, alluding to the change that had taken place for the better, "You have full churches, and the most serious attentive audiences I ever saw; and in company I never hear an offensive expression. I believe there is nothing like it in any part of the world."

The change had been effected by the instrumentality of those holy men, the Rev. David Brown and the Rev. Claudius Buchanan, whose heart-stirring appeals God had abundantly blessed; and these were the more effectual because of the preparatory work of the Rev. Mr. Kiernander, who had long laboured in the field they afterwards entered.

The Rev. David Brown arrived in Calcutta on the 8th of June, 1786. Though he went out to India for the purpose of taking charge of the Military Orphan Asylum, he eventually relinquished that appointment, at a considerable pecuniary sacrifice, and took charge of the congregation at the old church, the Beth Tephillah, built by Kiernander. Brown was a man of devoted piety, eminently endued with the spirit of power, of love, and of a sound mind. For a period of twenty-five years he continued at his post; and during that long space he was absent from Calcutta only once, and then merely for a short excursion on the river. On the Sunday he officiated twice in the old, or Mission Church, once at St. John's, and once in the Fort: at one period he had a school in his own house. His visits to the hospital and jail were unremitted; as an agent of the Bible Society, and the Missions of the Church, he was indefatigable, and his labours were amply compensated by the wonderful blessing that attended them. His church was crowded, hundreds statedly received the holy communion, and the tone of society proved that the effects of his labours were more than those apparent in external improvement. Various societies sprang up under his eye, which exist in unimpaired efficiency to the present day. Speaking of his zeal in promoting the cause of the Bible Society, which was at that time engaged in providing the word of life for the millions of India, his biographer says:—"He made it the dream of his night, and the thought of his day, to devise every kind of plan for prosecuting this important, and, as it proved, this closing purpose of his life.' Nearly twenty years after the death of this honoured man, when the present Bishop of Madras had charge, I was in the habit of occasional attendance at the church in which he ministered, and can bear my testimony to the peculiarly devout character of the congregation assembling there at that time. The mantle of the revered Brown fell on the shoulders of a succession of men worthy to wear it.

Among these, Claudius Buchanan stands first in the order of time; indeed he was associated with Brown, not only in the ministerial duties of Calcutta, but as Vice-Provost and Classical Professor of the College of Fort William, of which the Rev. D. Brown was Provost. The early history of this distinguished man is romantic. In the course of a gracious providence his ardent and enterprising spirit was arrested by the powerful ministry of Mr. Newton, of St. Mary Woolnoth, and yielded to God and the service of the Church. After he had graduated at Cambridge he was appointed to the ecclesiastical establishment in Bengal. His learning and piety were combined with comprehensive thoughts for the propagation of Christian truth in India. Although his schemes have not succeeded as he would have desired, there is no doubt that the objects he contemplated have been gradually and successfully pursued. He entertained the hope of making the college of which he was a professor instrumental in the translation of the sacred Scriptures into the oriental languages. The undertaking was commenced under the most noble the Marquis Wellesley, the great patron of useful learning, and aided by learned pundits from the provinces, who as they became acquainted with the Divine Book they aided to translate, confessed their admiration of its heavenly doctrines, holy precepts, and divine eloquence. There was at that time a fair prospect of preparing for the diversified nations of India correct and duly authorized versions of the Holy Scriptures. Dr. Buchanan's hopes were however blighted. Remarking on his disappointment he says, "Our hope of evangelizing Asia was once founded on the College of Fort William. But a rude hand hath already touched it, and, unless the Imperial Parliament interpose, it will soon be said of this great and useful institution which enlightened a hemisphere of the globe, *Fuit Ilium et ingens gloria.*" Its name, however, will remain, for its record is in many languages; and the good it hath done will never die, for it hath taught many the way to heaven. Had the college of Fort William been cherished at home with the same ardour with which it was opposed, it might in the period of ten years have produced translations of the Scriptures into all the languages, from the borders of the Caspian to the sea of Japan."

Dr. Buchanan's views, with respect to an ecclesiastical establishment for India, were akin to his projects for the preparation of the living oracles,—they were comprehensive. Had the same spirit he cherished in regard to this subject actuated all who followed him, and given tone and vigour to his measures he was so powerful an agent in producing, far greater advancement would, ere this, have marked the progress of our ecclesiastical institutions in India. He, with others, among whom the philanthropic Wilberforce holds a prominent place, contributed largely to the removal of those restrictions on missionary efforts, which was effected at the renewal of the Honourable East India Company's charter in 1813. Missionaries were thenceforth permitted to reside in the territories of the East India Company, in the prosecution of those benevolent objects on the success of which Dr. Buchanan, in common with all enlightened men, judged our permanent possession of India to depend. But whilst Dr. Buchanan, in common with enlightened statesmen, saw the connexion subsisting between the extension of Christian teaching and the permanence of social institutions, he advocated the propagation of the Gospel among the Hindus, not on that account merely, but because he believed it to be the only instrument appointed by God for the enlightenment and salvation of men. The charity that prompted his activities was the fruit of the Spirit, the constraining love of Christ. Under the influence of this grace, he prosecuted his duties and finished his course with joy.

The next chaplain of the East India Company, whose praise is in all the churches, on account of his devoted zeal in the cause of Christian missions, is the ever to be remembered and honoured Henry Martyn. Invested with the office of chaplain, he zealously discharged the duties of that appointment for the benefit of his countrymen who sojourned in India; but he never forgot the correlative obligation lying upon him to promote to the utmost of his power the advancement of Messiah's Kingdom among the Hindus and Mohammedans, his fellow-subjects. He was a man equally distinguished for his talent and academic attainments as for the fervency of his zeal. On his arrival in India he commenced preparations for the work of a missionary, by the diligent study of oriental languages. Though he had but feeble health, he was unremitting in his efforts; and whenever his duties as a chaplain would permit, he engaged in evangelistic duties among the natives. His literary remains attest his toils, embalm his memory, and are the lasting monuments of his zeal. He translated the New Tastament into Persian and into Urdu, and a part of the Old Testament into the latter language; and he superintended the translation of the New Testament into Arabic. His biographer justly remarks, "He doubtless forsook all for Christ; he loved not his life unto death. He followed the steps of Zeigenbalg in the old world, and of Brainerd in the new; and whilst he walks with them in white, for he is worthy, he speaks by his example to us who are still on our warfare and pilgrimage upon earth." Time and space do not permit a larger notice of this extraordinary man—the worthy exemplar of modern missionaries. Possessed of high intellectual endowments, and bound by social ties the most endearing, he had the strongest motives for remaining at home; but the aspirations of his soul extended to the regions beyond, where Christ had not been named; and to those he hastened with all the ardour of his apostolic zeal. Seeing the moral victories promised to the faithful over ignorance and superstition, he paid the cost at which their sublime rewards may be won, he relinquished his friends and country, encountered the perils and privations, and endured the toils incident to ardent pursuit, not counting his life dear unto himself, that he might finish his course with joy and the ministry he had received of the Lord Jesus.

The next chaplain, whose name illustrates the annals of the church in India, is the devout and discreet Corrie. So rapidly did they succeed each other in their entrance into the field, that we find the three revered men, Brown, Martyn, and Corrie, located together under the same roof, comforting and sustaining each other in their apostolic career. The Rev. Daniel Corrie has justly been styled "the model of a colonial chaplain." I had the happiness of knowing him when he filled the office of archdeacon in Calcutta. He frequently called on me, and greatly did I admire his mild, affectionate, and paternal disposition; his friendly and condescending manners could not fail to win the confidence of those who were favoured with his acquaintance. He was universally esteemed and greatly revered by all who knew him. "Corrie, though not so brilliant as Martyn, had the advantage of superior steadiness." He was in many respects a rare man. Corrie was charged with the onerous duties of chaplain, but he found time for the acquisition of native languages, for the translation of religious books, for the superintendence of native schools, and for various other benevolent labours incident to the position of a Christian minister dwelling among the heathen. He translated Sellon's "Abridgement of the Scriptures," the Prayer Book, and Homilies. He also wrote a compendious school-book, containing a valuable sketch of ancient history for Hindu youth. This work I introduced into several Anglo-Tamil schools under my care, and found it, as a work based on Scripture history, invaluable. He was the soul of all the operations carried on by the Church Missionary Society. He laboured as chaplain at Chunar, Cawnpore, Agra, Benares, and Calcutta. During the period of archidiaconal position in the metropolis of British India, he was indefatigable in his efforts to promote the interests of sound education and true religion. Combining in his character, even after he became archdeacon, the twofold relations of chaplain and missionary, he was foremost in promoting missions, establishing schools, building churches, and in the furtherance of every good work. I well remember the venerable form of this sainted man at the examinations of public schools in the city of Calcutta. His appointment to the highest office in the church, abated not his zeal. On one occasion he writes, "I long to see more life among us, steady, lively apprehensions of the nature of things divine, above all created good. When shall it be? I have certainly seen a great extension of good in this place. May those who are following behold a hundredfold increase." He lived under the practical influence of these lofty aspirations.

The Rev. Mr. Thomason was another chaplain whose character was very much what Bishop Corrie's was. In the midst of his labours in that capacity he translated the Old Testament into Urdu, and revised the Arabic New Testament. During the sixteen years he was attached to the Old Church in Calcutta, he was the zealous promoter of the Bible Society and of the missions of the Church of England. His ministrations were eminently blessed; his public labours were very effective, and his pastoral duties were performed with incalculable good to his flock. He kept up a constant intercourse with families and individuals, and thus extended the weight of his devout example among all ranks of society.

The Rev. Mr. Fisher, another chaplain at Meerut, besides attending to the duties of his office, founded a Native Church, and exerted himself to diffuse among the heathen the knowledge of Christ. I had the pleasure of knowing him. We are now on the eve of the present time, and must forbear to speak of the successors of the illustrious men whose names we have recounted.

From the early notices we have of the state of religion in the Presidencies of Madras and Bombay, it would appear that English society was, for the most part, more distinguished for its pursuit of wealth, than by zeal for the propagation of true religion. The severe rebuke of the eloquent Burke seems to have been well merited. He observes of the English who visited India, "They rolled wave after wave on the shores of India, with appetites ever increasing for food ever decreasing."

Madras has the honour of being first to raise the standard of the cross in India. Under the government of Streynsham Master the church of St. Mary, in Fort St. George, was erected, its first stone being laid on the 28th of October, 1680. This house was raised to the honour of God without any aid or countenance of the Company. For more than a century no marked occurrences are recorded connected with the progress of religion among the Europeans of Madras. In 1792, a young Irish clergyman of the name of Kerr, who had gone to Bombay, was led, by unexpected events, to settle at Madras, and after some time was appointed to the office of chaplain. He was put in charge of the Male Orphan Asylum, where he established a school of industry.

In 1796 he built a chapel in Black Town, for the convenience of the East Indians and other Protestant inhabitants; and very soon a brighter day began to dawn on Madras. Eventually he became the senior chaplain on the Madras establishment, which appointment opened his way to greater freedom and usefulness. To check the downward tendencies of infidelity, which prevailed to a great extent in the Presidency, he commenced the publication of a series of religious tracts or sermons, suited to the existing state of things, and they were circulated throughout India and Ceylon. These publications were eminently useful in exciting attention to questions of vital religion. He urged the necessity for more chaplains on the attention of Government. He was brought into collision with the governor and commander-in-chief, for refusing to allow, at their request, a young clergyman of disreputable character to preach in his pulpit. He submitted a plan for promoting the increased efficiency of the ecclesiastical establishment, and obtained greater influence with the authorities. About this time the native troops at Vellore mutinied, and massacred several of their officers and many of the European troops. Although it was proved, by the most incontestible evidence, that the atrocious doings at Vellore were instigated by the family of Tippoo, the chieftain to whom our arms were opposed, it was alleged that the mutiny was prompted by the efforts made to convert the native troops to Christianity. The Court of Directors inquired if there were any truth in the report. In his reply, the Commander-in-Chief, General Hay McDowall, triumphantly confutes the slanderous report, and says, "It may occasion some degree of surprise that the people of this country should be brought to believe, that those who apparently conduct themselves with so much apathy in respect to what concerns religious worship, should have formed any serious scheme for converting whole nations of different castes and persuasions to the Christian faith. None but the weakest and most superstitious could have been deluded by so improbable a tale; and accordingly we find the rumour alluded to was by no means general, and, except at Hyderabad, it had made little or no impression."

In the same document, the commander-in-chief urges on the Government the necessity for a greater provision for the religious instruction of the Company's servants, both civil and military. In 1807 Dr. Kerr was so enfeebled that he entertained serious thoughts of returning to Europe. The letter he then received from Dr. Buchanan may best serve to set the value of his services in a true light. Dr. Buchanan, deprecating the step, writes—"You are the representative and sole supporter of the Christian religion in the Peninsula—I say, public supporter, for other labourers are under your general direction. I pray that, while the battle lasts, you may be enabled to hold up both hands, like Moses when he fought against Amalek. Our armour in this contest is certainly *spiritual;* and if we try a mail of any other temper, we shall be certainly foiled. Other people must teach *your* children, and you must teach children *six feet* high."

Dr. Kerr died the next year, and was interred in the Black Town Chapel. His career was distinguished by great activity, and his plans for promoting religion were of the most judicious and comprehensive character. He was an accomplished scholar and an edifying preacher. His generous and disinterested disposition was associated with agreeable manners and a great knowledge of the world.

The Bombay Presidency was not exempt from the general dearth of religious feeling in the early part of our Indian ecclesiastical history. In 1714, when the Rev. Mr. Cobbe arrived there as chaplain, he found the congregation in an upper room. He very soon proposed the erection of a church, and raised a subscription amounting to the sum of 42,402rs. He succeeded in the attempt, and built a church, the present cathedral. A charity school was soon established. It appears, however, that no marked results followed these institutions; at the end of last century religion is represented as being in a very low state. In 1812 Sir Evan Nepean arrived as governor; he was a man remarkable for his attention to his religious duties. He scrupulously attended church twice on the Lord's-day, and this example had a good effect on society at large: the number of the chaplains was increased chiefly as the consequence of his earnest appeals.

We may now proceed to a brief narration of the political events which ushered in a new era with respect to the propagation of Christianity in India. Sufficient evidence has been adduced to show the extreme inadequacy of the provision made by the British Government even for the instruction of its own servants; and we shall not, therefore, be surprised to be informed that they were unwilling to advance the cause of Christianity among their Hindu and Mohammedan subjects.

In 1793 certain clauses were prepared in a bill then depending before Parliament for the renewal of the Company's charter, to the effect that Christian men might be allowed to proceed to India for the purpose of propagating our most holy faith. These were peremptorily negatived; and what is more remarkable, a learned prelate actually deprecated "any attempt to interfere with the religion, the laws, and local customs of the people of India;" alleging that, "as Christians there was no obligation upon us, were it possible, which he denied, to attempt the conversion of the natives of India; and that the command of our Saviour to his apostles to preach the Gospel to all nations did not, as he conceived, apply to us." He might as well have asserted that the promise of perpetuated presence on the part of the Saviour did not apply to us.

In 1813, when again the discussions came on for the renewal of the charter, as may be imagined, great opposition was made to the proposals for the establishment of the Indian episcopate then brought forward. Scores of pamphlets were written against such a proceeding, as being fraught with the most imminent danger to our Indian possessions. The battle was fought, and among the foremost in the conflict was the immortal Wilberforce; the victory was complete. It was enacted that branches of the Christian establishment of Great Britain should be extended to India for the benefit of its European residents, and that Christian missionaries should be freely permitted to go out and labour among the natives, for the diffusion of the blessed Gospel of grace and salvation. What was the issue? It had been loudly acclaimed, from the Ganges to the Thames, that the arrival of a bishop and missionaries in India would be the signal for wide-spread confusion and ruin. In November, 1814, Bishop Middleton landed in the metropolis of British India: he was everywhere welcomed by all ranks and classes. On his first visitation to Madras, the Nawab affectionately embraced him; throughout his extended tour he was acknowledged with the greatest respect. The Raja of Tanjore sent his minister to the Christian bishop, invited him to the palace, where, descending from his throne, he embraced him with affection, and expressed the gratification with which he saw the chief of our religious establishment in his country and in his court. There was no alarm, no symptom of irritation; native princes, priests, and gentry, as well as all classes and castes, received the bishop in all places with every mark of reverence, far greater than any of his brethren could find in their own native land. No one acquainted with the Hindus could have expected any other result from the tour of a dignitary of the Church through the provinces of India. I have no hesitation in saying that the Hindu is far likelier to be conciliated in our favour by our consistency in the zealous maintenance of our holy faith, than by our neglect of its most obvious sanctions, provided he is left in the full possession of the rights of private judgment.

The first Indian Bishop, Middleton, who landed in Calcutta on the 28th of November, 1814, preached the next Christmas-day his first sermon before a congregation of 1,300 persons, and administered the holy communion to 160 communicants, including the judges and members of council.

The state of the new diocese was then deplorably low. There were at that time in Bengal thirty-two clergymen, in Madras twelve, and in Bombay five; but as many of these were disabled by sickness or absent, there were only in Bengal eight, in Madras six, and at Bombay one—in all, fifteen. At the end of December, Bishop Middleton set out from Calcutta on his first visitation.

About the year 1820, probably at the end of 1819, the bishop began to form his plans for the establishment of a Mission College at Calcutta. The Archbishop of Canterbury had in the year 1818, as President of the Society for the

Propagation of the Gospel, made a vigorous movement in favour of Indian Missions, by proposing to place 5,000*l.* at the disposal of the Bishop of Calcutta to enable him to carry out the objects of the institution; good hope being entertained of the result, now that the affairs of the society were to be placed under proper diocesan control. The bishop's biographer says that the intelligence of these proceedings was as the breath of life to the bishop. He determined to commence the undertaking, and sketched out for transmission to the Society for the Propagation of the Gospel his plans for founding a college. Its objects were stated as follows:—

1. For instructing native and other Christian youths in the doctrines and discipline of the Church, in order to their becoming preachers, catechists, and schoolmasters.

2. For teaching the elements of useful knowledge, and the English language, to Mussulmans and Hindus, having no object in such attainments beyond secular advantages.

3. For translating the Scriptures, the Liturgy, and moral and religious tracts.

4. For the reception of English missionaries, to be sent out by the Society, on their first arrival in India.

The first stone was laid on the 15th of October 1820, with all due and impressive solemnity. The elegant and appropriate structure was completed; and, under the guidance of its first principal, Dr. Mill, it was ere long brought into operation. Bishop's College, of which a beautiful drawing by Messrs. Day & Son ornaments this volume, stands on the right bank of the river Hooghly, to the north of the Honourable Company's Botanical Gardens, and is about three miles below Calcutta, the metropolis of British India. There is in the appearance of the noble group something peculiarly imposing, conveying an appropriate idea of academical tranquillity, which at once leads the mind across intervening seas and lands to the seats of learning in Europe. From its situation, it is one of the first public buildings the foreigner beholds as he approaches the City of Palaces; and it is a happy circumstance that it is so well fitted to produce and leave a favourable impression in regard to the provision the national church has made for its extension in that vast country. The design of Bishop's College is one of the most important that can be entertained, and if it be carried out, must eventually effect the most beneficial results among the millions of India, and probably the adjacent countries. "The institution was designed to be strictly collegiate, in constitution, in discipline, and in character; its objects are said to be the education of Christian youths in sacred knowledge, in sound learning, in the principal languages used in the country, and in habits of piety and devotion to their calling, that they might be qualified to preach among the heathen. The attention of the learned persons connected with it was to be directed to the making accurate versions of the Scriptures, of the Liturgy, and of other godly books; it was to endeavour to disseminate useful knowledge by means of schools, under teachers well educated for the purpose, and it was to aim at consolidating, so far as might be, into one system, and directing into one course of sentiment and action, the endeavours which are here made to advance the Christian religion." Such are stated to be the noble objects it was intended to pursue. "Bishop's College was intended to be emphatically and pre-eminently a missionary institution. The principals and professors were to be men actuated by a fervent missionary spirit, and from their personal and experimental acquaintance with missions among the heathen, their history, nature, and the materials required for carrying them on to a successful issue, together with the difficulties connected with them; from their rich and varied stores of knowledge and experience, they were to impart to the students under their care an amount of missionary instruction, which would enable them to go forth no novices in their profession, strong in faith, in sound doctrine—the doctrines of the Protestant creed and formularies of the Anglican Church, derived from, and based on, the Holy Scriptures, as the one rule of faith and practice. Humble in demeanour, zealous in spirit, energetic, yet prudent in action; to labour in the portion of God's vineyard allotted to them, and to earn the illustrious name, and the high reward of evangelizers of the heathen."

These designs are not less grand than beneficial, and, could they be fully carried out, the extension of Christianity throughout India would be rapid and satisfactory. Considered as a "central point, a well replenished repository, of enlightened, active missionary enterprise," nothing is more desirable than such an institution as Bishop Middleton contemplated. Its bearing on the agency from home, and that which is indigenous, should be equally beneficial; and such it would be, if energy and charity had their legitimate action. The absolute need there is for such a local institution, fitted to qualify an indigenous agency for the work of Christian Missions, cannot be too strongly urged. Can the teeming population of India be provided with Christian teachers from Europe? Can the Church at home supply the men? Does it possess the disposition to support them sufficiently long to secure the creation of a self-supporting Church? Are not the expenses incurred by Missionary Societies in sending out, year by year, many whom the climate disables and compels to retrace their steps, frequently more than would be incurred in training men on the spot? And is it not obvious that natives habituated to the climate, and who possess an intimate knowledge of the vernacular languages, and the manners, customs, feelings, sentiments, and prejudices of the people, can labour with peculiar effect in disseminating the truth throughout those wide realms of paganism? Only one reply can be given to the last of these questions; and therefore every possible effort should be made for giving to Bishop's College greater efficiency and extent of operation. It has sent out some admirable men, but the number within its walls was for many years exceedingly small. The limited character of its operations was a matter of deep regret to that excellent prelate,

Bishop Turner. He greatly desired to extend its influence, by placing it on the basis intended by its founder. Bishop Turner wished to make the expensive agency, and other available means, applicable to the instruction in useful knowledge of all classes of the community, of pupils of every religious persuasion throughout the provinces of India, whom he would have admitted, requiring as a *sine quâ non*, conformity to the Christian usages of the institution, and consequent abstinence from those of their respective classes, whether Hindu, Mohammedan, or Romish. The bishop died in a little more than a month after he gave me a full account of the plan he was then drawing up for transmission to England. He felt that Bishop's College was too limited in its operation, and that possessed as it was of so many advantages, it was desirable to make it subservient to the diffusion throughout the country of a superior education in the English language.

It is to be devoutly wished that the Bishop's Missionary College should fully answer the design of the distinguished founder. If a succession of men endued with apostolic zeal, well acquainted with the working of Christian Missions among the natives of the country, can be secured; who, assuming the parental character, will identify themselves with the students, and give to the training more of a home education, so as to impress their own sentiments upon the youth committed to their care and tuition; and if in addition to a competent knowledge of the original languages of the Bible, care be taken to give the students a knowledge of the learned Sanscrit, and an adequate acquaintance with the religious systems they will have to oppose and refute, there will be reason to believe that this well-devised institution will answer the end designed by its benevolent founders and supporters.

Then indeed might the splendid visions of the exemplary Middleton, the first Anglican prelate, be realized; then that "noble fabric gracing the banks of the Ganges, with its imposing Gothic structure,—with learned and religious men at the head of the seminary, a goodly number of students, Native and European, being educated for the various departments of the Missionary work; the worship of God solemnly conducted in the College chapel, in accordance with the rubric and usage of the Reformed Church of England; the press of the institution in full operation, sending forth its translations of the Scriptures, Liturgy, and other godly books in the vernacular tongues, for distribution among the myriads of India, who are perishing for lack of knowledge; the Missionary hospitably received on his arrival in a strange country, instructed by the resident professors in the languages, religious systems, moral habits and prejudices of the Hindu and Mussulman population, among whom his after labours should be carried on; surrounding schools crowded with the rising generation, all anxious to acquire European learning, and 'trained up in the nurture and admonition of the Lord,' one student after another leaving the seminary, well prepared for propagating the Gospel of Jesus Christ among theists and idolaters,—and ready to spend and be spent in promoting the temporal and spiritual interests of his fellow men; the contiguous congregations of native Christians, the simple church and the village school,—all this, and far more than this, emanating from, or in connexion with, Bishop's College may be realized."

Such were the objects the profound Middleton contemplated. "These were the glowing thoughts which," to quote the words of his biographer, "were among the brightest, perhaps the very brightest, of Middleton's existence; thoughts which cost him many a laborious day and many a sleepless night; they were glorious visions, which oftentimes made his pulse beat high with hope, and furnished his powers with an excitement that kept them in vigorous and salutary action."

The Danish Mission at Tranquebar, almost from its commencement, received pecuniary aid from the Society for the

Propagation of the Gospel. The funds raised in England were collected by the Society for Promoting Christian Knowledge, but managed, at least for some time, by the President and Secretary of the Society for the Propagation of the Gospel. Eventually the Society for Promoting Christian Knowledge took the sole charge. Some account of the manner in which these important institutions furthered the early Missions of India, and the narrative of their formal transfer to the Incorporated Society for the Propagation of the Gospel, cannot be out of place here, as it is desirable to show how the Anglican Church has evinced its sympathies with the openings of Providence for the conversion of India to the faith of Christ. Desirous of making the best provision for its Missions in British India, the Committee of the Society for Promoting Christian Knowledge in 1824 referred to the Standing Committee to consider the expediency of transferring the management and superintendence of the Mission to the Incorporated Society for the Propagation of the Gospel in Foreign Parts. On the recommendation of that Committee the transfer was proposed to the Society for the Propagation of the Gospel, and they undertook the trust confided to them. It was therefore unanimously resolved by the Board, that the management and superintendence of the Society's Mission in Southern India be transferred to the Society for the Propagation of the Gospel in Foreign Parts.

The reasons for the adoption of this measure are thus stated to the public in the Report of the Society for Promoting Christian Knowledge for the year 1825:—

"The object of the Society, from its commencement to the present day, has been the promotion of Christian knowledge throughout the world, and the conversion of heathen nations has always been a principal instrument for this purpose. But it appears from the earliest proceedings of the Society, that its constitution was not considered fit for the establishment of extensive Missions. To meet this difficulty its principal members obtained a charter of incorporation under the title of the

Society for the Propagation of the Gospel in Foreign Parts, and pursued that branch of their original designs under the character of a separate institution.

"Subsequently, the Danish Mission College at Copenhagen established a Mission, for which the Society received and transmitted benefactions. The Mission gradually extended to Vepery, Tanjore, Trichinopoly, Tinnevelly, Cuddalore, and Ramnad. And this Society's connexion with it became more and more intimate, until eventually several of the missionaries were adopted as missionaries of the Society, and the Mission Stations at Vepery, Tanjore, Trichinopoly, and Tinnevelly, were made over to it by the Danish College. Such was the origin of the Society's Indian Mission." The undertaking was blessed with no ordinary measure of success. The missionaries who have been employed are famous throughout the Christian world. "But still the establishment of this Mission was an experiment upon a comparatively small scale; and the Society did not feel itself enabled, even by success, to extend its care to the whole of Hindustan, although it resolved not to relinquish the work in which it had been engaged. The Society perceived and regretted the impossibility of doing more, while no public countenance was given to Christianity, and even the European inhabitants of Asia were most inadequately provided with religious instruction. Under these circumstances nothing remained but to persevere in the limited task which had been undertaken, and be ready to improve the first opportunity of promoting Christian knowledge upon a larger scale. By the erection of the see of Calcutta, such opportunity was at length afforded. Soon after the arrival of Bishop Middleton in the East, the establishment of committees, under his Lordship's sanction, placed the Society in direct communication with every part of India; the Society's Mission in Southern India was enlarged, and the missionary operations under the patronage of the Society were extended. The Missions originally commenced by the Danish missionaries have thus been formally placed under the direction of a society expressly recognised by the State, and governed by the highest authorities in the Church. A chartered body, with a perpetual succession of *ex-officio* members, gives a pledge for continued good management which no voluntary association can offer." The Diocesan Committees at the Presidencies in British India, composed of lay and clerical members, take the charge of the Missions in their several provinces, direct their proceedings, appoint the agents, audit the accounts, and authenticate the local reports of the different operations being carried forward.

LAHOR

RE.

CHAPTER XX.

CHRISTIANITY IN INDIA (*continued*).—SOCIETY FOR PROPAGATING THE GOSPEL.—CHURCH MISSIONARY SOCIETY.—KINDRED INSTITUTIONS.—PROGRESS OF ENGLISH EDUCATION AND WESTERN SCIENCE.—CLAIMS OF INDIA AS A MISSION FIELD.—INVITING PROSPECTS.—THE GLORY AWAITING BRITAIN.

In the preceding chapters we have seen how the early Mission of the Danes was aided by the liberality of the two great English Societies; and how at length the institutions, for many years supported by the Society for Promoting Christian Knowledge, were formally transferred to the venerable Society for the Propagation of the Gospel in Foreign Parts. It has been shown how the first Missions of the Danes were favoured by the presence of the British power, and consequently how they extended their operations beyond the limited territory of Tranquebar, where they were first planted. The evangelic tree springing from a right and vigorous seed, like the beautiful emblem of the Church, the self-propagating and shady banyan,—

> "Spread her arms
> Branching so broad and long, that in the ground
> The bended twigs take root, and daughters grow
> About the mother tree."

The central station at Tranquebar excepted, all the important branches from the parent stem, have long been watched and watered by the British Church. The widely-extended sphere of missionary action in Southern India, including Madras, Tanjore, Madura, Tinnevelly, and some other parts of the Carnatic, is now under the immediate control and superintendence of the Diocesan Committee, of which the Right Reverend the Bishop of Madras is the president. In the Presidency of Bengal the Missions are also under the care of a Diocesan Committee. The appointment of these Committees affords the utmost security for the right management of the Society's Missions. Their oversight affords a guarantee to the public in India and also in England for the proper application of the resources of the Mission; and a local court of appeal in all matters both secular and sacred is thereby provided. These committees of management stand between the Parent Committee in London and the agents it contributes to sustain, without denying the right of appeal from the local to the central board. The fact that the funds expended are partly local and partly home contributions, and the fact that the agents likewise are partly local and partly home selected, render it expedient that there be a responsible and sufficiently accredited board within the sphere of the Church's missionary operations.

The following extract from the last report made up to December 1853, will show the present state of the Society's Mission in the Diocese of Madras. The Committee say,—

"It will be seen that thirty ordained missionaries are connected with the Society in this diocese, of whom four are Natives; eleven European and East Indian catechists; ten European and East Indian schoolmasters; two Native catechists; and 297 General Native agents, *i.e.* catechists, readers and schoolmasters, appointed by the Reverend missionaries themselves in the several districts, and whose pay varies from rupees 3½ to 15 per mensem. The return of schools will show that 185 schools are maintained by the Society (of which twenty-two are boarding-schools) containing 5,543 children under Christian instruction. Finally it will be seen that exclusive of evangelistic efforts there are twenty-two Missionary Districts occupied by the Society, comprising 233 villages, and containing 15,167 members of congregations (of whom 3,412 are communicants) and 5,050 catechumens."

In order to prepare suitable agents for the service of the Mission, several institutions are maintained in efficient operation in the diocese of Madras; of these

THE MISSION SEMINARY,

at Madras, is under the charge of the Rev. A. R. Symonds, A.M., who, as Secretary of the Diocesan Committee, undertakes the duty of principal. In the fundamental rules of this institution it is stated that it shall be purely of a missionary character and object; its sole design being to prepare for employment in the Missions of the Society such young men as may enjoy its advantages. Both Native and European students are admitted, who reside with the principal, sit at the same table, and, as much as possible, are identified with himself and family. There are several exhibitions connected with this seminary, and also a Prize Fund, whose annual proceeds are awarded for the best Tamil essay on a given theological subject: this prize is open to the competition of all students in this and other institutions throughout the diocese. This Missionary Seminary is conducted with great efficiency by its present able and indefatigable principal.

NATIVE MISSION SEMINARIES AT VADIARPURAM, AND SAWYERPURAM, IN THE PROVINCES OF TANJORE AND TINNEVELLY,

are also conducted with great efficiency, and contain about two hundred youth. From these institutions valuable agents, from time to time, go out into the service of the Mission as Catechists, Scripture Readers and Schoolmasters. About three years ago I visited these institutions, and was much gratified by the manifest vigour with which they are conducted.

ENGLISH SCHOOLS

have been begun in various places where openings were presented. These schools are valuable as bringing superior Native youth belonging to the wealthy and influential classes under the immediate supervision of the European missionary; and as affording the opportunity of selecting suitable candidates of a better class and more advanced in knowledge for the higher seminaries.

The improvement of the missionary agency in this diocese has for some time been an object of special consideration. In Tinnevelly and Tanjore each missionary regularly convenes his agents for the purpose of giving them systematic instruction. Every year an examination is held upon subjects announced in the previous year, essays are read, prizes are awarded, and promotions in the service are made with reference to ascertained proficiency.

THE VEPERY GRAMMAR SCHOOL,

is worthy of distinct and special notice as one of the most efficient institutions in Madras; its staff of teachers is large and effective. Since the present head-master, W. S. Wright, Esq., of Trinity College, took charge of this institution, its numbers have been quadrupled, and marked progress has been made in the general discipline of the school and the proficiency of the pupils. The written and oral examinations are of the most careful and satisfactory character. Some time ago a gentleman arrived from England who has introduced into the school the art of singing on the Hullah system with signal success. He has a large class in the Vepery school itself, and also a branch class at St. Thomé, the station lying south of Fort St. George. As most of the youth in this school are Europeans, their improvement and advancement in intellectual and moral culture must have a very beneficial influence on the European society of the Presidency, and a consequent effect for good on the surrounding Hindu and Mohammedan population.

Some months ago I had the opportunity of witnessing the general working of the Missions in Southern India during a tour of more than twelve hundred miles, and am able, from personal observation, to speak in the highest terms of their general progress. In visiting the Missions of the two Church Societies in the south of India, I was much struck with the prominence they both give to the Sacred Scriptures: they appeared to me to be pre-eminently Bible Missions. Great activity characterises the well devised and comprehensive plans in operation,—and equally marked success. The Missions are being extended gradually into the regions of heathenism. The members of the Church are becoming

ELHI.

more and more intelligent, and a spirit of liberality, indicated in pecuniary contribution to the local funds of the Church, is a gratifying feature, and peculiarly encouraging as affording ground for hope that the cause of Christ will ere long become more or less self-supporting.

The Mission in this diocese has, in consequence of its improved efficiency, grown in public confidence, and shares more largely its benefactions. The Jubilee celebration was one of the most satisfactory demonstrations ever witnessed in Madras. The sermons were listened to by full congregations, and good collections were made in aid of the funds of the Society. The General Meeting in the public Banqueting Hall was a most impressive spectacle. The Bishop of the diocese, after the Jubilee Prayers had been offered, opened the proceedings in a fervid and luminous speech, and his lordship was followed by other friends appointed to take part in the proceedings, whose eloquent addresses riveted the attention of the delighted auditory. It was an evening that will long be remembered by those who were privileged to be present; and to the friends of the Society afforded the best proof that could be desired of the place the Society's agents at Madras occupy in public estimation. It seems to be the object of the Diocesan Committee at Madras, as far as possible, to improve the Native agency, and thereby to give it greater efficiency. By this means the European missionaries take a more presiding position, and are more at liberty to extend the work among the heathen.

The Diocesan Committee in the Bengal Presidency has about ten stations under its management, and about as many missionaries, under whose care there are baptized and unbaptized persons numbering nearly three thousand, besides about fifty Scripture-readers and catechists.

The Society has just commenced a Mission in the north-western province of India, at the imperial city of Delhi. The following extract from the Society's Annual Report for 1853 will place this important object in its true light. The Committee say,—

"A much greater undertaking was the establishment of a mission, on a well-considered plan, at Delhi. To the importance of this city as a missionary station, the attention of the Society had long been directed by many zealous members of the Church, who proved the sincerity of their zeal by the contributions which they raised; but chiefly by the admirable chaplain of the station, the Rev. M. J. Jennings. At this time the local contributions amount to between two and three thousand pounds; and the Society has resolved to appropriate the whole of the interest of 8,000*l.*, the portion of the Jubilee Fund dedicated to Indian objects, to the establishment of a well-considered Mission at Delhi. The Mission is directed to the twofold object of preaching to the native Hindus and Mahometans, and offering opportunities of instruction in Christian doctrine to such pupils of the Government School, and others, as may be willing to avail themselves of it.

"Already there have been a few instances of remarkable conversion among the more educated classes at Dehli; and the Society heartily prays that Almighty God will vouchsafe to bless this new attempt to propagate the Gospel of His Son in that ancient and benighted city.

"The missionaries who have been appointed to take in hand this arduous but promising work, are the Rev. J. Stuart Jackson, M.A. Fellow of Caius College, Cambridge, and his friend the Rev. A. R. Hubbard, B.A., of the same College."

The importance of this once imperial city as a missionary station may easily be seen by reference to its position on the map. It was once the capital of one of the most powerful of the Hindu sovereigns; and under the rule of the Mohammedans it was one of the most splendid cities of Asia. The accompanying engraving represents the fort and palace as seen from the river. The ruins of this ancient city extend over an area of nearly twenty square miles. There is a beautiful minaret a few miles from the city two hundred and forty-two feet high. The city is rapidly improving, and, as a mart of commerce, it occupies a most important relation to the adjacent provinces. Delhi contains 250,000 inhabitants. It is about 900 miles from Calcutta, and not far from 1,400 from Madras.

The Bishop's Missionary College in Calcutta is the institution on which the Mission of the Incorporated Church Society depends for agents in Bengal and North India. As we have already seen, that noble institution was originally designed to provide for the whole of India in all that relates to

Missions, education and Christian literature. But owing to circumstances, the comprehensiveness of the scheme has been greatly abridged, and since the Church Missions of Southern India and Ceylon have established efficient local means for the training of agents, and the promotion of Christian and general education, Bishop's College occupies a place similar to them. That there may be equality in the distribution of the Church's resources, in regard to the promotion of Christianity in India, by means of collegiate and professorial arrangements, it seems necessary that the institutions in the South and in Ceylon should be more adequately provided for. The increase of educational institutions is a legitimate subject for gratulation, and no doubt the College of St. Thomas in Ceylon and the Mission seminaries in Southern India, will produce most beneficial results; it is nevertheless a matter of regret that the Bishop's Missionary College should, especially in view of its expensive and effective staff, be abridged in usefulness. Its statutes have recently been revised, and they permit Native scholars, paying a moderate fee, to graduate, under circumstances that must prove highly favourable to their acquirements and future prosperity. If it be made efficient, and approve itself to the judgment of the Indian community, there can be no doubt that Bishop's College may take a high place among the educational institutions of India.

THE CHURCH MISSIONARY SOCIETY.

This efficient institution has long exerted a most beneficial influence on the progress of Christianity in India. As early as the year 1807 it made considerable grants for missionary purposes, and as the jealousy of the Honourable East India Government gave way, it gradually extended its operations, which now far exceed those of any other missionary society. Its mission was begun in Madras in 1814, and extended to Tinnevelly in 1820. In 1815 it commenced its labours in Bengal. In the movements of the Church Missionary Society the revered Corrie took a lead, and he has been consequently styled the Parent of the Society's missions in Bengal. Miss

Cook, afterwards Mrs. Wilson, whom I had the pleasure of knowing, was mainly aided by this Society. Her efforts for the promotion of female education were of the greatest value. After she became a missionary's wife, she continued her labours with unabated zeal, and, on some occasions, accompanied her husband when he went round his neighbourhood preaching the Gospel out of doors. On his departure for England, she remained behind at her post, and never saw him again, as he died on his voyage. On my way to England I met this devoted woman, at Malta; she is now endeavouring to exert her influence in connexion with the Protestant College in that island.

The Church Mission was afterwards extended to Goruckpore, to Agra, to Burdwan, to Meerut, to Bombay, to Karachi, to Nasik, to Krishnaghur, to Benares, and now at length to Amritzar in the Punjab.

The following summaries will show the extent of the Society's agency and success in the Presidencies of India:—

BOMBAY MISSION.

Stations, 5; European Missionaries, 10; Native Missionaries, 2; European Lay-Teachers, 2; East India and Native Teachers, 24; Communicants, 57; Schools, 33; Scholars, 2,177.

BENGAL AND NORTH INDIA MISSION.

Stations, 23; European Missionaries, 36; European Lay-Teachers, 5; Native and Country-born Teachers, 305; Attendants on Public Worship, 6,871; Communicants, 1,085; Schools, 109; Scholars, 7,068.

MADRAS AND SOUTH INDIA MISSION.

Stations, 21 European Missionaries, 28; Native and East Indian Missionaries, 13; European Laymen, 5; European Female Teachers, 5; East-Indian and Native Teachers, 669; Communicants 4,800; Schools, 378; Scholars, 10,878.

The educational institutions of the Church Missionary Society are of a high order. The English institution called the *Money Institution*, at Bombay, contains 400 pupils. On my way to England I spent some time in examining the working of this valuable school, and was greatly delighted with its evident efficiency. The site chosen is well suited for the purpose.

There is an excellent training institution at Palamcottah, in Tinnevelly, designed for the education of native Christian teachers, that is admirably conducted. I had the pleasure of visiting this institution about three years ago, and was greatly pleased with its order and healthy appearance.

The accompanying engraving may represent a native teacher with a Christian youth seated beside him, and a Hindu youth with his sectarial marks, standing on his left.

The Society has entered upon the new territory in the Punjab, whose capital, Lahore, is represented in the accompanying engraving; they have taken up Amritsar as a station, which is properly the capital of the Sikh nation. It is a most sacred place, as its name imports, which signifies *the fount of immortality*. The openings for the promulgation of the Gospel in this lately acquired region seem to be of the most encouraging character. One of the Company's chaplains says, "I believe no such opening has ever before existed in India."

From Peshawar an urgent request has been sent to the Church Missionary Society. A meeting was recently held there, presided over by the chief magistrate of the district. Major Edwards, the gallant hero of Multan, who in his speech gave expression to the noblest Christian sentiments. An address was agreed upon to be sent to the Parent Society, and it was accompanied with a promise of 3,000*l*. In the address the following passage occurs:—"As residents in a heathen land, with every error rampant around us, we would desire to encourage you to renewed exertions in your great and noble office. The way is plain,—'Go forward,' and your work will prosper. Our prayer is that our universities and seats of learning may be stirred up to the appreciation of the great openings on every side, and of their duty to engage personally in the work of evangelizing the Natives; and also that the rich may be made willing to give liberally of their wealth, to maintain those who may be sent by them to heathen lands, that thus the knowledge of salvation through Christ may be proclaimed to all, to the praise and glory of God."

A glance at the map will suffice to show how widely distributed the agents of the Church Missionary Society are, and the vast extent of the field they occupy. The actual results as evinced in the number of conversions are, like those of other societies, confessedly small. This, however, is accounted for from the extreme difficulty of the work in which the agents are engaged, and the care observed in the admission of candidates to baptism. The missionaries of the Church Missionary Society are careful to admit none into the

ST. PAUL'S, CALCUTTA.

ALCUTTA.

communion of the Church of Christ but those in whose minds they are persuaded a work of grace has been commenced.

Besides the two missions of the Incorporated and Church Missionary Societies, there are kindred institutions actively engaged in India, and in direct communication with the bishops; such are the Church Building Society, the Additional Clergy Society. These are exceedingly active, and are contributing largely to the advancement of the Church in India.

In connexion with the Church Missions, and the progress of religion among the regular chaplains of the Honourable East India Company, great efforts have been made in promoting the erection of churches. Foremost in point of magnitude stands the cathedral church of St. Paul, recently raised to the honour of God in the metropolis of British India. This sacred edifice, of which a beautiful engraving ornaments this volume, is designated by the present Right Reverend the Metropolitan a Cathedral Missionary Establishment. The entire length of the building is two hundred and forty-eight feet, and the height of the tower and spire two hundred and six. Throughout India and Ceylon numerous churches have been erected within the last ten or fifteen years, some of which are equal in point of architectural style to the average of the sacred edifices that are so rapidly rising throughout England. An attempt to describe those I have seen, would occupy too much of our space, and therefore this general reference to the fact must suffice.

However much reason for humiliation there may be in the obvious inadequacy of the agency the Church of England has at work for the conversion of India, there is, nevertheless, room for devoutest thanksgiving on account of the improved state of things since the arrival of Bishop Middleton, in the year 1814. Comparing the present with that period, there is ground for the exclamation, "What hath God wrought?" With reference to the progress of religious principle in India, a living prelate some time ago remarked that it was "almost incredible. The character of the clergy has been raised; a mild Episcopal Church discipline has been effectually established; the disposition of our Indian rulers towards Christianity has been rendered more favourable; the moral and religious conduct of the servants of the Honourable Company has become purer; the institution of holy matrimony more honoured; the Lord's day better sanctified; the number of chaplains and missionaries increased ten-fold; churches multiplied perhaps twenty-fold; the general esteem of the pious and consistent ministers and missionaries of Christ is higher; the attendance on public worship more numerous and punctual; and the reverence for the old established and Scriptural Liturgy, offices and usages of our Protestant Church, as laid down by our first Reformers, more enlightened and influential."

The efforts of the last century for the conversion of India, begun by the Danish missionaries, aided, in the first instance, by the Society for the Propagation of the Gospel in Foreign Parts, and extended by the Society for Promoting Christian Knowledge, were the exclusive means directed to the great object. The Germans and the Danes were the only agents employed up to the end of the century. But from the commencement of the present century various Missionary Societies in England, in Germany, and in America, as well as the Church of Scotland, have sent their representatives into the field of Indian Missions. Upwards of twenty Protestant Missionary Institutions are prosecuting their respective labours with different degrees of efficiency, and with varied sentiments as to the relative prominence that ought to be given to peculiar modes of Missionary effort. The Missions of the Scottish Societies are most efficient.

Between twenty and thirty mission presses are in active operation. The Bible has been translated into numerous languages; the Liturgy of the English Church is in daily use in various tongues, and the foundation of a healthy Christian literature is laid in numerous works on subjects of useful knowledge. Many valuable tracts in refutation of Hinduism, Mohammedanism, and Romanism have been published in the different languages in which the missionaries are making known the gospel of Christ, and they are widely circulated throughout the various provinces of India and Ceylon. There are not wanting proofs of persons, who have had no intercourse with a living teacher, being brought to a knowledge of the truth by the reading of the sacred Scriptures and religious tracts; thus encouraging the efforts made to diffuse the silent messengers wherever there may be a hope that they will be entertained.

Vernacular schools and boarding schools of a superior order for both sexes have been established, and their value in promoting the evangelization of the Hindus has been abundantly attested. The number of Hindu females under instruction in the various mission schools cannot be much under twenty thousand. Almost every station has now female schools in operation; and the prejudices of the native mind, though

exceedingly strong, are in some degree being overcome. The engraving here inserted is an exact picture of a school-house belonging to one of the stations of the Church Missionary Society.

The Church Missionary Society and the American Missions not only support ordinary station boarding schools, for the education of a select number of native females, but also schools of a superior and normal character, for the training of native schoolmistresses. One of this class of seminaries, belonging to the Church Missionary Society, I visited in Tinnevelly, that is conducted with great efficiency. In the ordinary schools, which are, for the most part, conducted in the vernacular languages, the rudiments of a plain and useful education are imparted, and generally the children make very commendable progress. I have frequently examined ordinary day schools, and found the acquirements of girls of from seven to ten years of age surprisingly great, especially in matters relating to the sacred Scriptures. There is a peculiar aptitude in Hindu youth to acquire knowledge, and a precocity that renders the work of tuition very agreeable. The accompanying group may serve the purpose of illustration on the subject under notice: it is singularly correct.

Education has been so uniformly adopted as a part of mission work for many years, that the knowledge of the Gospel is very extensively diffused through those districts that have enjoyed the benefit of religious instruction. The preparatory work in this way must be regarded as of great extent and value. In such neighbourhoods few are found who have not some knowledge of the leading principles of Christianity; and many possess an acquaintance with revealed truth that is most surprising.

Districts remote from missionary stations are visited periodically, as the seasons may favour, either by European missionaries or their assistants. In Bengal, the Missionary Union is wont to form a plan of itinerant labour for the cold season, which includes the most important and populous

parts of the province. On those occasions the missionaries generally go forth two and two together, visiting the villages and towns, preaching in the Bazars, and distributing tracts to all who may be able to read. This is a most interesting and important work, and it has frequently led to inquiry into the claims of Christianity, that have resulted in conversion. I have known persons visited on such tours who, on coming into the station, have called at the Mission House to pay their respects and ask for Christian books.

The character of the Native Church is an interesting point, upon which a word may not be out of place. It needs not to be stated that, as in other countries, so in India, the visible Church is composed of persons of varied character, of some of whom it can only be said that they have a name to live. But as a general rule, it may be affirmed that the members of the Native Church in India are equal to those of any other country, and many of them are animated with the spirit of the Gospel as much as the earnest and devout in Christian lands. They generally entertain correct views of the value of the means of grace, and cherish a deep veneration for the word of God. Many evince their liberality by contributing systematically towards the support of local objects; and where regular pastoral oversight is exercised, the Native Church wears the aspect of a vital and healthy institution. In many places it may be said, in the fullest sense, that the Church is planted; its ordinances are administered; believers are built up on their most holy faith; and as they pass through the valley of the shadow of death, experience the support which belongs to those who have sought and found refuge under the wings of the God of Israel. The Sabbath services are often seasons of great refreshment. The intelligence and decorum observable in the assemblies of God's house, the fervid responses made to the solemn service, the devout attention paid to the exposition of the word, indicate a condition of mind that mere human teaching cannot effect.

The efficiency of the Christian agency employed in the Indian Church greatly tends to its advancement. The remarks made on the character of the Hindus would imply a correspondent superiority in all that relates to their ability. The various grades of labourers, the teachers of the young, the

Scripture Readers, the Catechists, the Native Clergy, are all in their several stations distinguished for their willingness, their gentleness, their kindness and efficiency. Some of the native ministers who are now engaged in India are equally distinguished for ability, fidelity, and zeal.

The harmony subsisting between the agents of the different Missionary Institutions is a remarkable fact in the history of Indian Missions. I have attended a monthly meeting for prayer in Calcutta where there were present the Archdeacon, a Chaplain of the Hon. East India Company, a Missionary belonging to each of the Church Societies, and others connected respectively with the Kirk of Scotland, with the Baptist, the Wesleyan, and the London Missionary Societies: these men found no difficulty in reciprocating kindly feelings, none in common counsel on questions affecting the progress of Messiah's kingdom, and none in united prayer for the promised gift of the Holy Spirit.

In looking at India as a sphere for Christian enterprise and benevolence, there are numerous interesting points to which attention should be paid. Some of them may be enumerated as inducements to increased effort.

The demand for education and books in the English language is an important fact as bearing on the progress of Christianity in India. At the seats of government, and in other large towns, the value of English as a medium of intercourse and communication with the civil governors, in the courts of law, and in the halls of commerce, may easily be imagined; and hence the importance of seizing the occasion for making the study of this language subservient to the dissemination of truth, as well sacred as scientific. The desire for English has the effect of bringing into immediate and daily contact with the Missionary and his agents, the most influential portions of society, since, as a general rule, the wealthy and superior ranks aspire to offices of trust, and, as capitalists, engage in mercantile pursuits. To both classes the English language as a medium of communication is of great advantage. Tens of thousands are at the present moment enrolled on the lists of the English seminaries, and in the ordinary routine of study, except in the schools of the Hon. East India Company, make use of books in which there will be found a large infusion of Christian truth; and they are also carefully instructed in the Bible. This course has been pursued with greater or less efficiency for more than twenty years in the presidencies of British India; and it is rapidly enlarging and extending itself throughout the provinces. The natural consequence is the production of a new class of native society—an Anglo-Indo class, in origin, connexion, association, and sympathy one with the whole nation, and, for the most part, in rank and influence its very flower. This portion of the community is still Hindu, but Anglicised; and it is rapidly increasing in numbers and influence. The Committee of Public Instruction, in one of their reports in Bengal, say, "The study of English, to which many circumstances induce the natives to give the preference, is daily spreading." Some years ago, from the report of the Calcutta School Book Society we learnt that in one year, whilst 31,649 English books had been circulated within the year, only sixteen Sanskrit had been sold.

It is, I conceive, impossible to exaggerate the importance of these facts, and especially as to their influence for good or for evil on the Hindu mind. This will become more apparent when it is known that English education, apart from religious instruction, is subversive of Hinduism. This announcement may be made consistent by a few words of explanation. The literature and science of the Hindus, as we have seen, being incorporated with their religion, if you destroy the former, which abounds with palpable errors, by the introduction of the true science of Europe, the foundation of the latter must be overthrown. The editor of a public paper in Calcutta says, in relation to government education, from which Christianity is wholly excluded,—"No missionary ever taught us to forsake the religion of our fathers; it was government that did us this service." Another says, himself too the editor of an English paper:—"Has not the Hindu College been the fountain of a new race of men amongst us? Have all the efforts of the missionaries given a tithe of that shock to the superstitions of the people, which has been given by the Hindu College? This at once shows that the means they pursue to overturn the ancient reign of idolatry is not calculated to ensure success, and ought to be abandoned for another which promises better success." Though we are not ready to adopt the conclusions the educated native forms of other means of enlightenment, we cannot reject his testimony as to the efficacy of those that detached him and others from their ancestral faith.

It is a most interesting fact, that in almost every part of India—I mean its chief cities—the spread of the English language and literature is rapidly altering the phases of the Hindu mind, giving it a sceptical infidel cast that may be fraught with serious consequences as respects the subjects of it, and ominous in relation to the stability of our power. Whilst the result of twenty-five years in government education may well serve to suggest to considerate minds the consequences to the State of its continuance, it may no less serve to impress the Christian missionary, and his supporters at home, with the importance of an instrument so potent as English education is found to be, and of the necessity there is, that whilst engaged in pulling down one system, care be used to construct a better. No one acquainted with the history of the human mind can avoid seeing how important it is that, in the cities of India, where these movements are taking place, the agents of the Church should be earnestly set to exert a plastic power on this newly forming mass of Hindu mind. Nor can it escape observation that minds of a peculiar order are required for this work. Seeing that the English language is in demand, and may be made so much of as an instrument in relation to a class, the wealthy and influential, not otherwise easily reached, for awakening, arresting, and affecting the intellectual powers, and in moulding and directing them, how imperative does it seem that this leverage should be employed by the Church.

The following well-expressed sentiments, from the pen of a gentleman, himself many years resident in India, are worthy of the most serious consideration :—

"At Calcutta, and in the great cities of Bengal, the Government have founded colleges and seminaries to instruct natives in European knowledge, and to fit them for the very responsible and high offices in the public service to which they are now eligible. But the knowledge so imparted is not confined to the few who draw the higher prizes in the lottery of Indian official life, nor even to the larger number who hope, by fitness, to open the way to selection for office ; it will have imparted its tone to all who come within the scope of its operations and of its results; and it is accordingly acknowledged that the native mind is awakened and inquisitive on matters to which it was formerly utterly indifferent. The truths of science and the philosophy of real history cannot consist in the same mind with Pauranic fables, and the abominations of mythology and idolatry ; but it is too well known that they may consist with the profession of benevolent atheism, or still more with the seductive and self-applauding discoveries of natural religion. It is to the native mind in this advanced state of cultivation that it becomes important that Christianity should be presented with its saving truths, in the effulgence of Divine light."

This will appear the more urgent when it is known that these English schools are the proper ground from which the future students in theology are to be selected. Trained in one of these English seminaries, the Hindu youth gains possession of the key of all needed knowledge secular and sacred; he has thereby access to the spacious temple of truth, and may explore all of value in literature and science, and supply his own mind, whence, as from a fountain, through his own vernacular, he can pour forth the full stream of knowledge into the minds of his less favoured countrymen.

The progress actually made by the extension of education, chiefly by means of Government institutions, has created a necessity for greater energy and activity on the part of the Church. The presence in European firms of educated Hindu capitalists, the position such have acquired in responsible situations connected with the offices of Government, and the gradual enlightenment and intelligence arising from greater intercourse with Europeans, may well assure us that a progress is being made that ought to be accompanied with a corresponding effort to improve and exalt the character. This work belongs to the Church of Christ.

The supreme Government has done much for the improvement of India, and it continues its noiseless efforts to secure the gradual amelioration of its condition.

"It has not hitherto been deemed safe, nor would it be desirable, that the rulers of India should appear as the promoters of conversion, lest the unenlightened masses, misinterpreting their intentions, should suspect them of a design to use the power which they are known to possess, for the forcible subversion of the systems in which the natives have been born and hitherto protected. But it is fair to remark, that the Indian Governments are more favourable to the prosecution of that work by religious societies and bodies than they were; and they have themselves done important service to the cause of truth, by the removal of many disabilities under which the native Christians formerly laboured. Religious profession is no longer a bar to public employment, and legislative provision is made to prevent alienation of property becoming a legal consequence of departure from the rules of caste, or the adoption of another creed."

Some of the measures of Government are of the most beneficent and humane character. The cruel and inhuman rite of *Sati*, by which the Hindu widow was encouraged to immolate herself on the funeral pyre of her deceased husband, has been abolished by an Act of the Legislature. Hindu mothers are prohibited from casting their innocent offspring into the jaws of devouring alligators. Infanticide, though not yet exterminated, has been greatly mitigated, and continued efforts are being made for its entire abolition. Human sacrifices systematically offered among the hill tribes, the Khonds, have been prohibited to the extent of British influence, and means adopted for the rescue and training of the unhappy victims that were drawn unto death and ready to be slain. Thuggee has been put down, and an institution established at Jubbulpore for training the families of Thugs to various useful employments. Slavery has been wholly abolished throughout the Honourable East India Company's territories, and in the island of Ceylon. The bonds which connected the Government with the administration of the heathen temples have been severed.

These facts are cheering. The reformation they secure has been the achievement of the last thirty years. They afford the evidence how much may be done by enlightened legislation for the moral and religious improvement of the people, and also the ground of hope that the acts of Government will not be withheld when they can be made subservient to the amelioration of its subjects.

It is evident that, notwithstanding the obstacles in the way, great advancement has been made. In estimating the progress Christianity has made in India, we must look beyond the statistics. The actual progress is much greater than the apparent. Where truth conveying grace has issued in conversion and attachment to the visible Church, we have the name enrolled: in India more than a hundred thousand souls are thus registered in the records of the Native Church. But the Gospel has exerted its influence far beyond this numerical limit. The intellectual suffrages, the assent and persuasion of the mind in favour of Christianity, are well-nigh coextensive with the educational training in the superior Mission schools. A large proportion of the educated are free to confess their persuasion of the truth of Christianity. The Hindus in vast numbers have learned that their system is full of errors; that the *science* of their Shastras is worthless and contemptible; that their idol worship is an insult to the Supreme Spirit; that the characters ascribed to their gods in the sacred books are full of vice and crime; that the Shastras themselves are full of inconsistencies; that their worship is unworthy of reasonable beings; and their priesthood sinister and frequently ignorant. Many now attach a value to Hindu aphorisms that they have collected from diffused evangelic truth. They conceive of the Divine Being more worthily; His moral attributes are more fully appreciated. Thousands have an assured persuasion that Hinduism must decay and perish. Contributions to temples are in many places withheld, from the prevalence of scepticism. The attendance at festivals is not, in many places at least, so numerous as formerly, though the population may have increased very greatly. The oracles of Brahmanism are not consulted with the same universal reverence and confidence. The views and sentiments of the people, where the Gospel has been preached regularly, are greatly altered; they understand and admit the claims of religion as it affects the moral sense. Truth has done much among the people to develop a conscience. These are matters of deepest importance as regards the prospects of Christianity in India.

The lower castes thrust aside the Brahmans from place and power, and among them wealth and learning, and consequently influence, are vastly on the increase. Thousands now approve of female education; and the ladies in Hindu families in Calcutta, and to a much greater extent in Bombay, are receiving private tuition. A numerous body is now coming forward in society, possessing far more enlightened notions than their fathers did; men who contemn the sacred books as idle and fictitious, and who regard the adherents of such as ignorant bigots. The contrast between the old and the new school shows how great the progress of enlightenment is. The truths of the Bible are heard with greater allowance. Cases are rare where tracts are snatched, rolled up, and, as missiles, aimed at the missionary's head. Numerous persons read

Christian books. I know cases of select companies of Hindus meeting together, week after week, on the Sabbath day, for the purpose of reading the Scriptures and discussing their sublime doctrines. Facts, irreffragable and numerous, attest the change that is silently coming over the public mind. The word is not lost: like good seed, it will spring up and put forth, first the blade, then the ear, after that the full corn in the ear. When that word shall be applied by the Holy Ghost sent down from heaven, the little one shall become a thousand, and the small one a great nation. The signs of the times are cheering.

Yet little, comparatively, has been achieved. Hinduism still stands like a mighty fortress. Although the present state of Christian missions in India affords ground for encouragement, and for the assured hope of their final and universal triumph, yet this volume may serve to show that the Gospel has to encounter the most formidable opposition. The obstacles are immense: licentiousness, superstition, sophistry, refined and abstruse speculation, are alike arrayed against it. Its novelty stands in striking contrast to the time-worn and immemorial systems of the Hindus. Christianity, destitute of all external patronage or prestige, and supported only by its own intrinsic excellence, has to assail and displace systems sung by poets, venerated by sages, honoured by successive dynasties of illustrious kings, and recommended by the adhesion of ancestral observance. The lisping foreigner has to oppose the subtle, the acute, the sophisticated priests and their devoted adherents. His message proclaims holiness, and denounces the vices and cherished licentiousness of the Hindu votary. Under these circumstances, we may expect that Christianity will be slow in its progress. The very slowness of its progress is at once a proof of the fidelity of the missionaries in enforcing the sanctions of the Bible and of its own truthfulness. To appreciate the claims of Christianity, implies an effort at once intellectual and moral, and requires a powerful motive. In the full view of those claims, and under the strongest influences that truth and grace may be supposed to exert in the Hindu mind, the surrender of the heart, the renunciation of the old paths, the violent separation from the associations and bonds of family, and the severance of the ties and usages of caste, the utter self-abnegation of all that is social, civil, and religious, and the encountering of the shame and dishonour incident to the abandonment of his ancestral system by the Hindu, may well be regarded as almost impossible. Impossible it would be but for the supervening grace of the new-creating Spirit. It belongs not to human nature to escape easily from an elaborate, complex, and comprehensive system of religion like that of the Hindus, a system which exerts its influence on all the acts and habits of life from the very dawn of reason. "Pass over to the isles of Chittim and see; and send unto Kedar, and consider diligently, and see if there be such a thing: Hath a nation changed their gods?" Here inspiration itself testifies to the extreme difficulty of conversion from an ancestral system.

But notwithstanding the difficulties, it is evident that, as a Mission field, India has many features of attraction. The facilities for the proclamation of the Gospel are as great there as in England, and access to the higher classes by means of English education is easy, whilst the effects of such education, as numberless instances prove, are of the most encouraging kind. Everything invites to action. The field is attractive, too, because of the character of the people and the nature of the work. The Missionary on his arrival in India, it is true, finds himself in a new world. He has to engage in the study of new languages; but they are worth studying. He has to acquire facility of utterance, which will enable him to discuss difficult points of controversy with acute and learned men. The theories of religion, and the psychological peculiarities, and the mythology of the Hindus, form new and interesting subjects of study. The manners and customs, the prejudices and superstitions, the rites and ceremonies, are all so many new and exciting objects of attention. The apathy and indifference of the masses, the steady resistance of the native mind to the teachings of Christianity, the slowness of the progress truth makes, and the incessant toil incident to an undertaking so great as the enlightenment and conversion of such a people as the Hindus, may perhaps deter some from entering on such an enterprise. But the magnanimous will judge differently. The circumstances of the Missionary among the inhabitants of India are such as are best fitted to call into exercise the highest susceptibilities of the educated Christian mind.

The motives that might be supposed capable of moving to action the enlightened and zealous in the Church of Christ, are numerous and most cogent; and there is just cause for surprise on the one hand that so few are disposed to engage in such a glorious undertaking, and on the other, that so little is contributed by the wealthy to promote the extension of Christ's kingdom among our Hindu fellow-subjects. The indifference of many arises, it may be, from the want of due information regarding the moral wants of our fellow-men; and others are unconcerned because they have not been taught to identify themselves in sympathy and effort with the kingdom of Christ. The final cause of extended empire, as regards the British nation, is by many never considered, except as it bears on national aggrandisement, and the increase of wealth and luxury. But the wise, the good, the devout, cannot surely be ignorant of our responsibilities to God, and of the duty we owe to Him and his Church. England is bound by many considerations to attempt the conversion, the intellectual and moral emancipation, of her Pagan subjects: some of these considerations may be stated.

England has herself been freed by missionary effort from the darkness of Pagan superstition, and delivered, too, from the despotism of Papal Rome. Possessed as she is of the pure word of God, is she not bound, as a witnessing Church, to preach the Gospel as "a testimony to all nations?" Can she monopolise without jeopardy the precious light of heaven, or put that light under a bushel? "To him that hath shall be given, and from him that hath not shall be taken away that which he seemeth to have." England is unspeakably indebted to God. Hers is the Church, the altar, the sacrifice, the calm refuge from the cares and distractions of the world. How is she to repay Him for all these favours? Surely by extending them to the dark and destitute nations who, in His providence, have been placed under her rule. The members of the Church are stewards, and it is required in these that they be found faithful. Manifold grace, powers of doing good, at home and abroad, to the souls and bodies of men, involve solemn responsibility. Those who possess wealth and influence are designed of God as channels of good and clouds of blessing to others; and such cannot withhold help and be blameless. "Freely ye have received, freely give." "The Lord giveth liberally, and upbraideth not;" let them be "followers of God as dear children." The members of Christ's mystical body ought to show a spirit of liberality and a cheerful beneficence. He that showeth mercy is to do so with cheerfulness.

The position of the British Church is such as never fell to the lot of any people,—its privileges are unequalled, its means of doing good are almost boundless. Throughout the empire there is one universal cry, directed especially to England, "Come over and help us." The brief sketch given in this little volume may suffice, it is thought, to show how urgent are the claims of India. How much there is to attract and encourage the benevolent! Let the eye rest on that vast realm of heathenism, and, if possible, take in the extent and magnificence of the empire which Britain has there reared. How much wealth and influence are derived from that vast territory! Everything in India may serve as an incentive to Christian enterprise. There is an assemblage of rare objects at once calculated to impel to action the zealous labourer and the privileged supporter of such labours.

The Government is becoming more and more impressed with the importance of India, and its leading members are ready to help forward, as far as may consist with their responsibility, the efforts which the Church may make for its evangelization. The rulers of that important part of our empire have a solemn responsibility; and their acts are, for the most part, accordant with their position. Hitherto the proceedings of the British Government have served to impress the Hindu most favourably; and the suffrages its moderation has won are its best guarantee for continued peace and order. It is most satisfactory to know that, generally, the Hindus consider their subjection to Britain one of the greatest blessings which Providence has conferred upon them. In its stable, paternal, and beneficent rule, the Hindu feels alike secure from any invasion of his civil, social, or religious rites. The work of India's evangelization belongs to the Church of Christ, and every facility and encouragement for its prosecution is presented in the circumstances of its inhabitants. To Christendom at large the undertaking is inviting. Germany and the United States admit the claims of India, and send forth their agents for its enlightenment and improvement; but it must be admitted that England is specially charged with the weighty responsibility which its conversion involves. Would that the members of the Church of England had a more impressive sense of duty in regard to this most important undertaking!

The peculiar interest attaching to India has been more or less set forth in this work, and may be compendiously presented in the following passage from the pen of one whose head and heart are alike devoted to promote its intellectual and moral improvement. The points of interest the eloquent appeal offers for consideration are as varied as they are important. "If," says he, "the events of civil and military history be worthy objects of entertainment or pursuit—where shall we find these more abundantly furnished, than in the actions of that amazing series of conquerors that has passed over the stage of India, from the days of Alexander down to the present hour? If poetry and romance and chivalry,—are there not ample stores of poetic effusion and romantic legend in the Mahabharat and Ramayana—the great epics of India—that might not be disclaimed as unworthy by any of the older nations of Europe? and are the records of any state more crowded with the recital of daring adventures and deeds of heroism, than the annals of Rajasthan? If ethnography and philology,—where can we find more original languages, or varying dialects? more especially, where can we find the match of the Sanskrit; perhaps the most copious, and certainly the most elaborately refined, of all languages, living or dead? If antiquities,—are there not monumental remains and cavern-temples, scarcely less stupendous than those of Egypt; and ancient sculptures, which, if inferior in "majesty and expression"—in richness and variety of ornamental tracery, almost rival those of Greece? If the beautiful and sublime in scenery,—where can the pencil of the artist find loveliness more exquisite than among the streams and dells and woody declivities of Malabar or Kashmír? or grandeur more overawing than among the unfathomed depths and unscaled heights of the Himalaya? If natural history,—where is the mineral kingdom more exquisitely rich—the vegetable or animal more variegated, gorgeous, or gigantic? If the intellectual or moral history of man,—are there not curious remains of pure and mixed science, and masses of subtile speculation and fantastic philosophies, and infinitely varied and unparalleled developments of every principle of action that has characterised fallen, degraded humanity? If an outlet for the exercise of philanthropy,—what field on the surface of the globe can be compared to Hindustan, stretching from the Indus to the Ganges, and from the awful defiles of Affghanistan to Cape Comorin, in point of *magnitude and accessibility combined*, and *peculiarity* of claims on *British* Christians?"

Let the British Christian consider his privileges and his

duties, in connexion with the facilities now presented in India, and other parts of the empire, for extending Messiah's kingdom, and he cannot long remain unmoved; he must find himself impelled to action. The magnitude of the undertaking is confessed, the difficulty is equally apparent as regards India, but the enterprise is certain in its results. The promise of God cannot fail; and what can equal the transcendent glory of the object contemplated? The emancipation of the nations of India from the intellectual and moral bondage of ages may well stimulate the energies and the activities of all who are acquainted with the designs of infinite love in the provisions of the Gospel. This subject might be pursued indefinitely, and every aspect under which it might be placed would serve to render it more and more impressive.

The following eloquent passage from a writer in the Calcutta Review may appropriately close our work: he says,—

"For Britain our prayer is, that ere she drop the most potent sceptre ever wielded over Indian realms, she may be enabled to take up the language, not of boastfulness, but of gratitude to the God of Providence for the successful discharge of her delegated trust and say:—I found India one wide and universal scene of anarchy and misrule; I left it one peaceful and consolidated empire;—I found its people ground down by the most frightful oppression, its industry paralysed, and person and property exposed to the assaults of lawless violence and the invasion of every ruffian plunderer; I left its people exempt from the multitudinous exactions of covetousness and wrong, its industry revived and augmented in productiveness a hundredfold, person and property secure, from the improvement of individual, domestic, and social morals, and the uniform administration of equitable law;—I found India lying prostrate beneath the yoke of blinding ignorance and brutifying superstition; I left her joyfully recovered from the double yoke,—revived by the kindling beams of fairest science, and the revelations of Heaven's own illumining truth; I found India the chosen habitation of the most horrid cruelties that ever polluted the earth, or disgraced the family of man; I left her as the most favoured domain and dwelling-place of righteousness, benevolence, and peace:—

"Be these thy trophies, Queen of many isles!
On these high heaven shall shed indulgent smiles.
First, by thy guardian voice to India led,
Shall Truth divine her tearless victory spread.
Wide and more wide, the heaven-born light shall stream,
New realms from thee shall catch the blissful theme;
Unwonted warmth the soften'd savage feel,
Strange chiefs admire, and turban'd warriors kneel;
The prostrate East submit her jewell'd pride,
And swarthy kings adore the crucified!
Yes, it shall come! E'en now my eyes behold,
In distant view, the wish'd-for age unfold.
Lo, o'er the shadowy days that roll between,
A wand'ring gleam foretells th' ascending scene!
Oh! doom'd victorious from thy wounds to rise,
Dejected India, lift thy downcast eyes,
And mark the hour, whose faithful steps for thee,
Through time's press'd ranks, bring on the Jubilee!"

APPENDIX.

CASTE.

THE QUESTION OF CASTE AS AFFECTING THE PROPAGATION OF THE GOSPEL AMONG THE HINDUS.

CASTE distinctions were permitted in the Syrian and Romish Churches from the beginning. The Dutch allowed its usages unrestrained observance. The Danish Mission at Tranquebar fostered it by using two cups at the Lord's Supper, and the venerable Schwartz, Gerricke, and others, tolerated it in various ways.

The evil as affecting the character and progress of Christianity was first assailed by the Rev. Messrs. Haubroe, Shreyvogel, and Rhenius, about thirty years ago.

In 1824 events arose which more or less impinged on the prejudices of the observers of caste, and an appeal was made by them to the Diocesan Committee at Madras, but without any satisfactory effect. The aggrieved then wrote to Bishop Heber. His lordship replied. The letter which his lordship then wrote was followed by certain articles of inquiry on the question of caste. These documents are here inserted for the information of those who take an interest in the conversion of India.

BISHOP HEBER'S LETTER TO THE REV. MR. SCHREYVOGEL.

Chillumbrum, 21st March, 1826.

REV. AND DEAR SIR,—I wrote yesterday to Dr. ——, to express my regret at not being able to visit you at ——. Since that time having again looked over your letter to me, as well as that which you sent on the subject of distinctions of caste, and of other customs yet remaining among the native Christians, which you reprobate as heathenish and improper, I have been led to wish for some explanation of those customs, and of your reasons for objecting to them, of which the latter, as expressed in those papers, (to deal freely with you) do not seem to me satisfactory. With regard to the distinctions of caste, as yet maintained by professing Christians, it appears that they are manifested;

(*a*) in desiring separate seats in church, (*b*) in going up at different times to receive the holy communion, (*c*) in insisting on their children having different sides of the school, (*d*) in refusing to eat, drink, or associate with those of a different caste.

Now it is desirable to know whether these are insisted on as religious, or as merely civil distinctions; whether as arising from a greater supposed purity and blessedness in the Sudras over the Pariars, or whether they are not badges of nobility and ancient pedigree, such as those which in Spain, even among the poorest classes, divide the old Spaniards and Castilians from persons of mixed blood,—and in the United States of North America entirely exclude negroes and mulattos, however free and wealthy, from familiar intercourse with the whites; also, whether the Christians of high caste adhere to these distinctions as supposing that there is any real value in them, or merely out of fear to lose the society and respect of their neighbours and relations? If these questions are answered in the affirmative, (as they have been very solemnly by the Rev. ——, in answer to my repeated inquiries,) I confess that I do not think the evil so great as to be insufferable, or to justify the ministers of Christ in repelling from the communion those who adhere to them,—though it may be that the spirit of pride, (from which they flow) should, by gentle means, be corrected as far as possible. We all know that in Europe persons of noble birth or great fortune claim and possess precedence in our churches, and I have already observed that the whites take the same priority to themselves in America. But there is no reason for this but custom, inasmuch as a gentleman and a beggar are as much equals in God's sight as a Sudra and a Pariar. The reason why a Christian gentleman conforms to these rules is, because by acting differently he would lose influence with those of his own degree in society, and a Sudra may say the same thing, and does say it. It seems, then, to me, that these distinctions of castes in church may still be allowed to continue, provided due care is taken to teach our congregations that they are all naturally equal.

With regard to their private meals and social intercourse, it seems to me, that we have still less business to interfere, "For meat and drink destroy not him for whom Christ died." In the schools, indeed, and among the children,—taking places, &c. must be arranged, as it appears to me, without regard to caste, but even here caution should be observed to disgust no man needlessly.

I perceive you object very strongly to certain ceremonies usual in marriages, such as going in procession through the streets, with music, erecting a pandal, &c. On what grounds of reason or Scripture do you object to these? Are they idolatrous? Are they necessarily or usually attended with uncleanness or indecency? In what respect do they essentially differ from those ancient ceremonies which are known on the like occasions to have been practised among the Jews, to which both the prophets and our Saviour make repeated allusions, without ever naming them, and which, judging from analogy, must have been practised at that very marriage of Cana, which our Lord sanctioned by His presence?

Again, it appears that one of your principal causes of complaint against the —— has been, that they would not sanction the sentence of excommunication pronounced against a person who had dancing girls in his house, and another who had acted some theatrical part. Now here, too, I much want information. Were the dances indecent in themselves? Were the performers persons of notoriously indecent character, prostitutes or servants of some heathen temple? Or did you object to the dancing itself as unchristian and a fit ground for excommunication? In like manner, was the acting on a public stage and for money? Was the drama indecent or immoral? Or was it (as from the little which I yet know of Indian customs, I am led to suspect) one of those masqued fooleries in which the common people of Germany and England often indulge at Christmas and harvest home; and which, though they may sometimes be abused, are not regarded as in themselves criminal, or worthy of ecclesiastical censure?

My reasons for asking information on these subjects will be plain, when I mention, that the question of caste, and of such practices as these, has been referred to my consideration both by the Christians and missionaries of Vepery; and that in order to gain more light on the subject, a select Committee of the Society for Promoting Christian Knowledge has been at my desire appointed. In the mean time, I am most anxious to learn from every quarter, especially from a Christian minister of your experience and high character, the real truth of the case. God forbid that we should encourage or suffer any of our converts to go on in practices either antichristian or immoral, but (I will speak plainly with you, as one brother in Christ should with another) I have also some fears that recent missionaries have been more scrupulous in these matters than need requires, and than was thought fit by Swartz and his companions. God forbid that we should wink at sin,—but God forbid also that we should make the narrow gate of life narrower than Christ has made it, or deal less favourably with the prejudices of this people, than St. Paul and the primitive Church dealt with the almost similar prejudices of the Jewish converts.

It has occurred to me, that if either you or ——, (to whom pray offer my best wishes and respects) could find time on Easter Monday to come over to meet me at Tanjore,—my doubts might be the better cleared one way or the other, and other matters might be discussed in a few words, of much advantage to the cause of Missions in this country.

I remain,
Rev. and dear Sir,
Your faithful and obedient Servant,
(Signed) REGINALD CALCUTTA.

BISHOP HEBER'S ARTICLES OF INQUIRY ON THE QUESTION OF CASTE.

I. *General.*

1. Is the distinction of castes observed among the Christians of your Mission?

2. If not, has the neglect of it been recently introduced? or has it been always so since the first establishment of the Mission?

3. Be pleased to distinguish accurately,—1. Such observances of caste among Native Christians as are purely civil; 2. Such as are purely heathenish and idolatrous; 3. Such as are of a mixed nature.

4. Do such observances arise from supposing a greater degree of inherent purity or blessedness in the higher classes above the lower? —or are they simply insisted on, as badges of nobility and ancient privilege?

5. Do Christians of high caste, who adhere to them, attach any real value to them *per se?* or do they retain them only as a means of influence among their heathen neighbours and relations, and from a fear of losing their respect in society?

6. Do the heathens regard those Christian converts who adhere to their former distinctions of caste with any greater respect than they do those who violate them? and to what extent is any such respect carried? and for what purposes is it really valuable?

7. Is the profession of Christianity, as it is a new law and condition of life, considered by the heathens in the light of a caste, conveying to the converts new privileges of a social as well as of a religious nature?

8. If your own experience does not enable you to answer the last question fully, can you throw any light on it from the analogy of converts to Mohammedanism from Hinduism? Are such converts, though they abandon their former caste entirely, looked upon as transferred to a new caste, in itself respectable and privileged?

II.—*Church.*

1. Are separate places appropriated in your churches to the several castes? Is a separate chalice and paten ever suffered for separate castes

in the administration of the Lord's Supper? Do they go up at different times to the holy table?

2. Do you consider such appropriation desirable or necessary? Does it seem to rest on the same grounds of the proper gradation in the different orders of society, in the point of wealth or official station, as obtains throughout Christendom? or does it rather lead to confound those natural distinctions of rank and order, introducing others more inconvenient and mischievous?

III.—*School.*

1. Is any objection evinced by native Christians to send their children for instruction to a school which is open to all castes? or do they express a wish to have a different school for the higher and lower castes?

2. Supposing the native Christians of all castes are willing to send their children to one common school, do the parents of higher caste show any objection to their children mingling in the same class at school with children of lower caste, and taking places with them?

3. Do the children of Christian converts observe any holidays but those which are of Christian origin? And if so, be pleased to enumerate them, and to state their nature;—and also whether observances of these holidays affect the attendance of the children at school.

IV.—*Social Intercourse.*

1. Supposing Natives of different castes to become converts to Christianity, do they object to eat and drink together of the same provisions? and if the objection is made, is it on the side of the higher or lower caste?

2. Are any distinctions observed among Christian converts in contracting and forming marriages? And if so, are those distinctions merely of their trade and calling, or of a religious nature?

3. In addition to the ceremonies of the Church in solemnizing marriages, do the Christian converts observe any other ceremonies? And if so, enumerate them, stating whether they are observed in the procession to or from church, or in the domestic festivities consequent on the marriage.

4. Are there any such observances in the case of funerals, either at the time of the service, or at any subsequent period?

V.

Be pleased to add such other points of information on the subject as you consider important in order to a clear judgment of the question.

Rev. and dear Sir,—The special Committee of the Madras District Committee of the Society for Promoting Christian Knowledge, appointed by the late Bishop Heber for the purpose of collecting information on the subject of caste in the native churches of the south, beg to forward to you the accompanying articles of inquiry. and earnestly request your attention to the important subject. In order to ensure distinctness as much as possible in the valuable materials which they thus hope to collect, they will be obliged to you to return answer to each question as concisely as possible, and to favour them, under the last number, with such further information for the guidance of their judgment as the preceding articles may not embrace.

I have the pleasure to enclose a copy of Bishop Heber's letter, addressed to one of your body, when the subject was proposed to his lordship, and upon which the Committee have endeavoured to ground their present inquiries.

I remain,
Rev. and dear Sir,
Your faithful Servant,
(Signed) Thomas Robinson,
President M. D. C.

Madras, 27th October, 1828.

STATEMENTS RELATIVE TO THE ARTICLES OF INQUIRY ON THE QUESTION OF CASTE, BY THE TANJORE MISSIONARIES.

I.—*General.*

1 and 2. The distinction of caste, though not in its full extent, has been observed among the Christians of Tanjore since the establishment of this Mission by the late Rev. Mr. Schwartz, soon after the year 1762. Mr. Schwartz in permitting, with some restrictions, a custom apparently so opposite and prejudicial to the spirit of the Gospel, to remain in the new congregations, was guided by his own discretion as well as by the example of the Tranquebar missionaries before him; and that both they and himself were actuated herein by motives of prudence and caution, is plain from several of their letters still extant.

In the course of administration of the Mission affairs since the death of Mr. Schwartz, myself and several of my colleagues successively have endeavoured to act with similar caution and forbearance, at the same time seizing every opportunity to soften the mutual prejudices arising from distinction of caste, and to bring our Christians by degrees into closer union with each other as brethren of one Lord and Master,

Christ. And we have had the satisfaction to observe, that distinction of caste has, until of late, been seldom the object of controversy among Christians, and has gradually lost a great deal of its importance.

3. It is usually thought that distinction of caste originated from, and was founded upon, the Brahmanical system, and was one of the chief auxiliaries in its support and defence. The latter may be true as far as it relates to heathens, but is certainly not the case in reference to Christians; for they, by embracing Christianity, renounce all idolatrous practices connected with the religion of Brahmans, and particularly with the observance of caste. But as for the distinction of the several castes itself, it is by no means certain that it originated from the Brahmanical system. The more probable opinion—of course not among Brahmans, but among intelligent Natives of other castes—is that the several castes existed distinct one from another, long before the Brahmans came to this country; that it was merely of a civil or political nature, and that the Brahmans only blended it with their idolatry, by persuading the original inhabitants of this country to believe that the four principal castes of mankind, viz. Brahman, Kshatriya (Chattriar), Vaisya, and Sudra, owed their origin to Brahma, who produced the first class from his head, the second from his shoulders, the third from his thigh, and the fourth from his feet, and distinguished each of them by a higher or lower degree of moral purity and blessedness in this world as well as in a future state. As nearly all the historical documents relative to former ages were destroyed by the Brahmans on their arrival in this part of India, it is difficult to discern the small remains of truth among the vast mass of imposture. Otherwise it might most likely be discovered that the abject state in which some of the lower castes are at present, originated from political causes, as conquests, conspiracies, treasons, &c. One instance of this nature is, indeed, handed down by tradition and recorded by Brahmanical writers, viz. that the Kamaller, a higher-caste than that of Pariars, on account of a conspiracy raised by them, were deprived of several privileges, which even Pariars enjoy, as riding a white horse, using a white umbrella, and going in a pálki, &c.

If, therefore, the Brahmanical story concerning the origin of caste be false, heathens, who embrace Christianity, return back, in point of caste, from error to original truth; they make caste again, what it had been before, a civil distinction. And supposing even the Brahmanical account to be correct, then, too, such of the heathens as become Christians and renounce everything connected with the superstition and idolatry of the Brahmanical system, can of necessity retain nothing in the distinction of caste but what is merely of a civil nature; none of their observances in this respect can, properly speaking, be of an idolatrous or even mixed nature, as among heathens, nor have such ever been permitted to be practised in their Mission, for the same reason.

4. The higher classes, at least the more intelligent and better informed individuals among the Christians, do not, in the observance of such distinction, act from a supposition that they are morally better than those of a lower class, or entitled to greater spiritual privileges; but they insist on it merely as a badge of superior rank in society, as an ancient civil prerogative.

5. They do not adhere to such distinction, because they attach any real value to it *per se*, but because by neglecting it they would give offence to high and low among heathens and Christians, lose not only their respect in society, but likewise all their influence among their heathen neighbours and relations.

6. The more bigoted heathens consider every Christian convert, of whatever caste he may be, as degraded, and in former times he was in their opinion, undeserving of the rights of social intercourse; but one who violates or entirely gives up his caste, is treated as an outcast. Every heathen will avoid him more carefully than he would even Pariars, Pallers, or Sackliars.

At present high caste Christians meet with more respect from heathens than formerly, owing partly to their own personal character and conduct, partly to the high stations to which some of them have been advanced. And though the circumstance does not immediately contribute to the furtherance of the Gospel, yet it serves greatly to make Christianity in general more and more respected among the neighbouring heathens. In regard to Native priests and high caste catechists, this respect is of still greater importance. They gain easier admittance among respectable natives of high caste, and meet with more frequent and favourable opportunities to converse with them freely on religious subjects, privileges which no Pariar can look for. This respect, however, and all the advantages derived from it, is forfeited for ever, as soon as they violate the observance of caste; Native priests and catechists will thereby render themselves entirely useless to the Mission.

7 and 8. The heathens, who consider the different castes among themselves as religious distinctions, connected with greater or less privileges, look undoubtedly also upon the profession of Christianity as such a distinction, but as one of the very lowest degree, and which degrades below all the castes of Hinduism. As for new privileges of a social as well as of a religious nature, they can scarcely be said to allow it any, for in their estimate the loss of those privileges which Christian converts enjoyed while heathens, can never be compensated by anything. If they respect, therefore, in some measure, Christians of high

caste, as stated above, it is merely on account of superior personal qualities, rank, and conduct; but upon the Christian religion itself they will always look as unworthy of comparison with their own.

They would treat Mahommedanism with no less contempt, had not the respect which they at present show to it been formerly forced from them by the sword, and did not Mahommedans still form so numerous and powerful a body in the Indian community.

II.—*Church.*

1. At church the Christians of the high caste, both men and women, sit on the right, and those of the low caste on the left, side of the pulpit, but without any intermediate space between them.

There has never been used a separate chalice and paten for separate castes in the administration of the Lord's Supper. But they go up at different times to the holy table.

2. The appropriation of separate places to the several castes (chiefly two, high and low castes) though not desirable, will be necessary as long as the distinction of caste itself remains; for any interference in this respect would at present be looked upon by all of them as an encroachment upon their civil rights. It rests on their own estimate of a proper gradation in the different orders of society, and as both sit according to their rank and station on their respective sides—though they are not so very anxious about it—the natural steps of rank and order are always conspicuous.

III.—*School.*

1. No objection has ever been made by Native Christians to send their children for instruction to the Mission schools, because they are open to all castes; nor have they at any time expressed a wish to have different schools for the higher or lower castes. It ought to be remarked particularly that the teachers are very often of the low caste; but this, too, has never been objected to.

2. The children of one class sit indiscriminately, and take their places only according to their attainments and diligence in their respective lessons. This order has always been willingly submitted to by parents of high caste children.

3. Children of Christian converts do not observe, nor would they be permitted, if they wished to do so, any holidays but those which are of Christian origin. There are four principal heathenish festivals, connected with more or less outward show, which children are fond to look at; but this is merely curiosity, and is never allowed to interfere with their attendance in the school. The festivals are the following:—

a. *Pongal* (middle of January). The heathens worship the sun as the author of all good, by boiling rice, offering it to the sun, and then worshipping it. The next day they repeat the same offering to cattle as a secondary source of good, and pay them also divine adoration.

b. *Kaumen*, or *Karnadahanam* (beginning of March). This they celebrate in honour of Siva, who burnt and consumed *Manmada* by the eye of his forehead.

c. *Dusara* (middle of October). The heathens perform religious ceremonies to Sarasvati, the goddess of Wisdom; during this festival they perform the Aitha Pujá, *i.e.*, they wash the particular implements of their respective trades and worship them.

d. *Diparaly* (beginning of November). This festival is celebrated in commemoration of the death of a Rauchuden (giant), Naragasuren by name, who in ancient times had committed a great deal of mischief in the world. The people rejoice, visit, and congratulate each other.

IV.—*Social Intercourse.*

1. Converts of Christianity from different castes will, in separate places, eat and drink of the same provisions, if they be prepared by a high caste person, but not, if prepared by one of the low caste. The objection is always made on the side of the higher caste, not by Sudras only, but by all successively, who have or think to have one caste below them. Thus the Sudra will not eat the meal of a Kammalen, the Kammalen not that of a Parian, the Parian not that of a Pallen, the Pallen not that of a Sacklien, &c., and the two latter, thinking themselves higher or cleverer than the Pariar, will not eat anything prepared by them. But all will eat what is prepared by a Sudra.

2. No marriage is contracted between parties belonging to two different castes. This custom is strictly observed, not from a religious view of distinction of caste, but principally with the intention of preserving their family interests undivided, and of keeping up their particular trade and calling.

3. The ceremonies in solemnizing marriages are the following:—According to the custom of the country, the nearest relations of the bride and bridegroom erect a pandal in or near the house, as neat as their circumstances will enable them, in order to accommodate their relations and friends. There the *Parisam* (dowry) is given to the bride before the people assembled; from thence they proceed to church, sometimes singing divine hymns, accompanied by soft music. After the marriage ceremony is over, they return home in the same manner as they came, join in prayer, distribute betel and nut to every one, and then separate. The following day they give an entertainment to the relations, and carry the bride and bridegroom, accompanied by music, in procession to visit their friends at their houses.

4. At funerals they observe the following customs:—After the corpse has been buried, the relations bathe. The chief mourner shuts himself up at home for about a week or ten days; he then receives the condolence of his friends, and gives them an entertainment; he puts on a new turban given him by one of the nearest relations, and thus the mourning ends.

V.

Distinction of caste in its full extent, as it prevails among heathens, is certainly a great hindrance to the propagation of Christianity; for it is so closely interwoven with the Brahmanical system, that while it receives from thence its principal strength, it again becomes one powerful bulwark of Brahmanical imposition; and in its nature and tendency it opposes the very first principles of the Gospel, humility and love.

That such a barrier, therefore, should be abolished, must be the wish of every one who is desirous of the success of the Gospel in this country. The experience, however, of more than a century has proved that it is not at once and by force that this obstacle is to be removed, but by gentle means and by degrees. Compulsion, as in many other cases, would particularly here greatly increase the evil. Difficulties in bringing Gentiles within the pale of Christianity, already great, would become nearly insurmountable, while the Christian congregations already collected would fall a prey to confusion and contention.

A great point is gained when, through the influence of the Gospel, distinction of caste becomes divested of all its reference to, and connexion with idolatry, and is thus reduced to its original shape as a civil distinction in the community. And what more may be done, in order to overcome some remaining prejudices, to which particularly new converts are liable, by a cautious and conciliating proceeding, Mr. Schwartz and other excellent missionaries have sufficiently shown by their example. Christians who have been carefully instructed, and who have been imbibing the spirit of the Gospel, will, though different in caste, always consider and esteem each other as members of one body in Christ, and, as joint-heirs with him, they will exercise the Christian law of love, and never refuse their assistance, if they have it in their power, to one, because he belongs to a lower caste.

That the high caste Christians do not intermarry nor eat with those of the low caste, is owing to the different occupation and way of living peculiar to the several castes. The labours in the field, the employment of undertaker, and all the other mean occupations necessary in a community, are according to the ancient *Mammul* (custom) exclusively the duty of low caste people, whether heathen or Christian; nor would they allow any one of another caste to intrude on their trade. This, of course, has a great influence on their way of living.

To oblige, therefore, a man of a higher caste and accustomed to a genteeler way of living, to eat with them, is doing force to common delicacy and to the natural feelings of sense, and may be sometimes of serious consequences to bodily health. Some of the ancient missionaries once persuaded a Siva convert (who, according to the custom of his caste, lived only on vegetable food) to eat meat, in order to show that he did not abstain from it on account of superstition and pride. He complied, but nearly died by making the trial!

There is every reason to hope that the more Native Christians grow in the knowledge and practice of the truth, the weaker will become their prejudices of every kind; they will more and more approach each other, and by degrees become accustomed to put little or no value on their distinction of caste: but if compulsion of any kind be resorted to, in order to abolish their distinction, the majority will immediately consider it as a privilege in danger, and attach an importance to it which it never had before. Jealousy will engender discord, and social intercourse, such as it has been, will cease. In short, a breach will be made which it will be difficult, if possible, to fill up again.

The death of Bishop Heber, and the short tenure of office held by his successors, Bishops James and Turner, prevented any further official action until the present Metropolitan was appointed to the diocese. He entered upon the consideration of the subject promptly, comprehended the whole bearing of the question, and decided that as caste, in the way in which it was observed by the Protestant Christians of the south of India, differed not from the Hindu institution, which is demonstrably at variance with the history of creation itself, he resolved that "the distinction of caste must be abandoned decidedly, immediately, and finally." His lordship's decision appears in the following circular:—

BISHOP WILSON'S CIRCULAR.

To the Rev. Brethren the Missionaries in the Diocese of Calcutta, and the flocks gathered by their labours or entrusted to their care.

Palace, Calcutta, July 5th, 1833.

REV. AND DEAR BRETHREN,—Having heard that some usages of an unfavourable nature prevail in certain of the Native churches, and more particularly in the southern parts of the Peninsula, I am led by the obligations of my sacred office to deliver to you this my paternal opinion and advice. My honoured and revered predecessors in this See, now with God, laboured to abate the inconveniences to which I allude; and I am much relieved in discharging my own share in this duty by the memorials of their previous admonitions, which I have had the opportunity of consulting. Their abstinence from any official interference ought to have commended their advice to your cheerful acquiescence, and to have superseded the necessity of my now entering upon the subject. But as their forbearance and kindness have failed to produce the desired effect, you will not be surprised if I feel compelled, as the Pastor and Bishop of Souls, under Christ our Lord, in this Diocese, to prescribe to you what seems to me essential to the preservation of the purity of the Christian faith amongst you.

The unfavourable usages to which I refer, arise, as I understand, from the distinctions of castes. These castes are still retained; customs in the public worship of Almighty God, and even in the approach to the altar of the Lord, are derived from them; the refusal of acts of common humanity often follows,—processions at marriages and other rites of heathenism are at times preserved; marks on the countenance are sometimes borne; envy, hatred, pride, alienation of heart, are too much engendered; the discipline and subjection of the flock to its shepherd are frequently violated; combinations to oppose the lawful and devout directions of the Missionaries are formed—in short, under the name of Christianity, half of the evils of paganism are retained.

These various instances of the effect of the one false principle, the retention of caste, might be multiplied. They differ no doubt in different places; in some stations they are slight and few, in others numerous and dangerous,—many native congregations are, as I trust, free from them altogether, many have nearly accomplished their removal. I speak, therefore, only generally, as the reports have reached me. I throw no blame on individuals, whether ministers or people; it is to the system that my present remarks apply, and it is in love I proceed to give my decision.

The distinction of castes then must be abandoned, decidedly, immediately, finally; and those who profess to belong to Christ, must give this proof of their having really put off concerning the former conversation the old, and having put on the new man in Christ Jesus. The Gospel recognises no distinctions, such as those of caste, imposed by a heathen usage, bearing in some respects a supposed religious obligation, condemning those in the lower ranks to perpetual abasement, placing an immovable barrier against all general advance and improvement in society, cutting asunder the bonds of human fellowship on the one hand, and preventing those of Christian love on the other—such distinctions, I say, the Gospel does not recognise; on the contrary, it teaches us that God "hath made of one blood all the nations" of men; it teaches us that "whilst the princes of the Gentiles exercise dominion over them, and they that are great, exercise authority upon them, it must not be so amongst the followers of Christ, but that whosoever will be great amongst them, is to be their minister, and whosoever will be chief among them, is to be their servant, even as the Son of Man came not to be ministered unto, but to minister, and to give his life a ransom for many.

The decision of the apostle is, accordingly, most express. "There is neither Jew nor Greek, there is neither bond nor free, there is neither male nor female, for we are all one in Christ Jesus." For if the strong separation between the holy nation and the Gentiles, which was imposed by God himself, and had subsisted from the first legation of Moses, was abolished, and the wall of division dug down, and all the world placed on one common footing under the Gospel, how much more are heathen subdivisions, arising from the darkness of an unconverted and idolatrous state, and connected in so many ways with the memorials of polytheism, to be abolished.

Yet more conclusive, if possible, is the holy apostle's language in another epistle :—"Seeing ye have put off the old man with his deeds, and have put on the new man, which is renewed in knowledge after the image of Him that created him, where (in which transition, when this mighty change has taken place) there is neither Greek nor Jew, circumcision nor uncircumcision, barbarian, Scythian, bond nor free, but Christ is all, and in all." So overwhelming is the flood by which all petty distinctions of nation, caste, privilege, rank, climate, position in civilization are effaced, and one grand distinction substituted, that between those who are renewed after the image of God, and those who remain in the state of fallen nature.

Imagine only the blessed apostle to visit your churches. Suppose him to follow you in your distinctions of caste, to go with you to the table of the Lord, to observe your domestic and social alienations, to see your funeral and marriage ceremonies, to notice these and other mummeries of heathenism hanging upon you and infecting even what you hold of Christianity, to hear your contemptuous language towards those of inferior castes to yourselves,—to witness your insubordination to your pastors and your divisions and disorders. Imagine the holy apostle, or the blessed and divine Saviour himself, to be personally present and to mark all this commixture of gentile abominations with the doctrine of the Gospel, what would they say? Would not the apostle repeat his language to the Corinthians, "Therefore come out from among them, and be ye separate, and touch not the unclean thing; and I will receive you, and be a Father unto you, and ye shall be my sons and daughters, saith the Lord Almighty?" And would not the adorable Redeemer say again, what he pronounced when on earth, "He that loveth father and mother more than me, is not worthy of me; and he that loveth son or daughter more than me, is not worthy of me; and he that taketh not his cross and followeth after me, is not worthy of me."

There are two objections, dearly beloved, which may be raised against this statement. The one, that St. Paul became all things to all men, "that by all means he might save some." The other, that civil distinctions are recognised in the New Testament and prevail in all Christian nations.

To the first I answer that the apostle did indeed, for a time, tolerate the Jewish prejudices in favour of the Mosaical law, which had been itself of divine institution, and was not wholly abolished till the destruction of Jerusalem and the dissolution of the Jewish polity; but that this lends no support to a distinction, heathenish in its origin, and inconsistent with the equal privileges to which all are under the gospel admitted. A divine law introductory to Christianity, though at length superseded by it,—and a cruel institution, which sprung at first from idolatry, and is opposed to the whole spirit of Christianity, are totally different things. Nor are we to forget that even during the brief period that the Jewish law was permitted to retain any force, the apostle denounced in the strongest manner and directed the whole Epistle to the Galatians against the fatal error of trusting to it before God. All the mildness and gentleness of the apostle, therefore, we desire to imitate in the wise and gradual instruction of the new convert; but an inveterate evil, spread through large bodies of professed Christians, and going on to evaporate the whole force of the gospel, we must carefully eradicate.

The other objection is answered in a word. The civil distinctions of rank amongst Christians form no hindrance to the intercourse and offices of charity: there is no impassable barrier. The first noble in the land will enter the abode and administer to the wants of the poorest cottager. There is nothing to hinder any one from rising, by industry and good conduct, to the loftiest elevations of society. The shades and gradations of rank are shifting perpetually. Birth condemns no class of men from generation to generation to inevitable contempt, debasement, and servitude. The grace of Christ, charity, the church, the public worship of God, the holy communion, various circumstances of life and occasions of emergency, unite all as in one common fold, under one common Shepherd. The rich and the poor under the gospel meet together, the Lord is the Maker of them all. Distinctions in civil society the gospel acknowledges and retains only when they are the natural result of difference of talents, industry, piety, station, and success.

The decision, therefore, remains untouched by these objections, in the necessity of making which I am confirmed by two circumstances the one, that in Bengal no distinction of castes is known amongst the converts—it is renounced in the very first instance; the other, that apostasies to heathenism have been of late but too frequent in the congregations where the distinction is permitted to remain.

In the practical execution, however, of the present award, dear Brethren, much wisdom and charity, united with firmness, will be requisite.

1. The catechumens preparing for baptism must be informed by you of the Bishop's decision, and must be gently and tenderly advised to submit to it. Of course the minister informs the bishop or archdeacon a week previously to the intended baptism of each convert, agreeably to the directions given by my honoured predecessor in his charge delivered at Madras in November 1830, and this will afford opportunity for each particular case being well considered.

2. The children of native Christians will, in the next place, not be admitted to the holy communion without this renunciation of caste,—their previous education being directed duly to this amongst other duties of the Christian religion, no material difficulties will, as I trust, arise here.

3. With respect to the adult Christians already admitted to the holy communion, I should recommend that their prejudices and habits be so far consulted as not to insist on an open direct renunciation of caste. The execution of the award, in the case of all new converts and communicants, will speedily wear out the practice.

4. In the meantime it may suffice that overt acts, which spring from the distinction of castes, be at once and finally discontinued in the church—whether places in the church be concerned, or the manner of approach to the Lord's table, or processions in marriages, or marks on the forehead made with paint or other mixtures, or differences of food or dress—whatever be the overt acts, they must, in the church, and so far as the influence of ministers goes, be at once abandoned.

5. Subjection, in all lawful things, to the ministers and pastors set over them must further accompany this obedience to the gospel. The resistance to due discipline, the tumults, the slanders, the spirit of insubordination, the discontent, of which I hear such painful tidings, must be renounced, and the temper of evangelical piety and obedience, according to the word of Christ, must be cultivated.

6. The only effectual means, dear Brethren, missionaries and pastors of the native congregations, of restoring the simplicity and purity of the gospel, is to preach and live yourselves more fully according to the grace of the New Testament. The union of spiritual doctrine with holy consistency of conduct, is the secret of all revivals of the decayed piety of churches. You will observe that when the apostles depress and condemn inferior and petty distinctions and grounds of separation,

they do it by exalting the gigantic blessings of salvation, by declaring "that they who have been baptized into Jesus Christ, have put on Christ," by asserting "that if any man be in Christ, he is a new creature," by pronouncing that "Christ is all and in all" to those who believe in his name.

7. Let us do the same. The holiness of God's law, the evil of sin, the fall of man, his responsibility, his helplessness, his state of condemnation before God—these are the topics which prepare for the gospel of Christ. Repentance is thus wrought by the grace of the Holy Spirit in the heart. Then the glory of Christ begins to break out upon the awakened and contrite soul. The sun shines not with more clearness, when the whole heaven is illuminated and gilded with his beams, than the Sun of Righteousness pours his bright light upon the unveiled mind. This leads to pardon, justification, acceptance, adoption, peace of conscience, hope of heaven. Then regeneration and progressive sanctification have their due course. Holiness is the fruit of faith, and follows after justification. The inhabitation of the Spirit consecrates every Christian a temple of God. Good works, in all the branches of newness of life, are thus produced, even as the rich fruit by the tree, enabling us to discern its real nature and value. Prayer, the worship of God, the divine authority of the Sabbath, the sacraments, the apostolical order and discipline of the church, the obedience due to pastors, the general duties springing from the communion of saints, with preparations for death, judgment, and eternity, close the main topics of evangelical doctrine.

8. When these are enforced with the tenderness and boldness which become the minister of Christ, when they are accompanied with private visits, exhortations and prayers, and are bound upon the conscience by the consistent walk of him who delivers them, the blessing of the Holy Spirit gives efficacy to the instructions. Men are awakened, born anew, roused, brought from the darkness of heathenism into the light of the Gospel, and from the power of Satan unto God. They burst the thraldom of a natural state. Friends, family ties, privileges, caste distinctions fall like Dagon before the truth, of which the ark of old was the symbol; the convert rejoices "to count all things but loss for the excellency of the knowledge of Christ Jesus his Lord." He crucifies the whole body of sin: he "presents his body a living sacrifice," holy, acceptable to God, which is his reasonable service."

In this way, beloved Brethren, will the God of all grace recover your decayed churches. Thus will the power of godliness revisit you. Thus will apostasies cease, and the weak be confirmed and built up on their most holy faith.

Full of love to you all is the heart which dictates these lines—I long to be able myself to visit you, and see the effects of this my paternal letter upon you. Think me not harsh, severe, too rigid. God knows the tenderness with which I would direct you, as a nurse cherisheth her children. It is that very tenderness which induces me to grieve you for a moment, that you may attain everlasting consolation. Faithless is the shepherd who sees the wolf coming, and fleeth and leaveth the sheep. So would be the bishop who hearing of the enemy of souls ravaging amongst you, if he shunned, from a false delicacy, to warn you of the danger. Rather, brethren, both ministers and people, I trust that my God will give an entrance to His word, by however weak and unworthy an instrument, into your hearts. Rather, I trust, you will "suffer the word of exhortation." Rather, I hope, you will be ready, before you read these lines, to put away from you these practices which weaken your strength, and dishonour the holy name wherewith you are called. Yes, let each one say, It is the voice of the good Shepherd that we hear, we will follow the call,—we will rejoice to renounce for Christ's sake our dearest objects of affection, we will offer our heart upon the altar, we will give up ourselves without reserve, not only in these instances, but in every other, to Him who hath lived and died and revived, that "He might be Lord both of the dead and living."

To the grace of this adorable Saviour I commend you, and am,

Your faithful Brother,

(Signed) DANIEL CALCUTTA.

This Circular was read in the churches of Tanjore. It was received by the native Christians with great displeasure, and they showed their views by seceding in a body.

On the erection of the See of Madras the matter as regards that Presidency was transferred to the new Bishop. It does not appear that Bishop Corrie did more than write conciliatory letters to those who chose to appeal to his sympathies or authority. The ever to be revered Corrie entertained the views of caste which Bishop Wilson had circulated.

Bishop Spencer dealt cautiously with the matter, yet announced the determination not to admit to orders any who refused to associate in the ordinary rites of hospitality with the Christian brotherhood.

Commissioners were appointed in 1845 to inquire into the state of caste feeling and practice in the Vepery congregation, which on inquiry addressed the following letter to Bishop Spencer. It is a well considered, able, and satisfactory document.

REPORT OF THE MADRAS COMMISSIONERS.

To the Right Reverend the Lord Bishop of Madras.

May it please your Lordship,

1. Having, as your lordship's commissioners, inquired as fully as lay in our power into the matter submitted to us in your Lordship's letter, dated July 21, 1845, we have the honour to submit to your Lordship the result of our examination of various individuals connected with the Vepery mission, and to add the following notes on the subject.

2. The matter proposed for inquiry is twofold.

3. First, the "sense" in which caste is held by the native Christians of the Vepery mission; and

4. Second, the "extent" to which they hold it.

5. First, as regards the "sense" in which caste is held by the native Christians, we are of opinion, from the examination of the various witnesses who have appeared before us, that it differs in no respect from that in which it is held by the heathen natives around them. The principles of it are the same in both, and the practices arising out of it are precisely similar; and although it appears that some of their customs, of a public ceremonial nature, have, of late years, been gradually relinquished, those which are still retained tend, in our opinion, to point to this identity of the principle from which they spring.

6. Caste, an institution peculiar, we believe, in the present day to the natives of India, appears, as amongst the ancient Egyptians,[1] Medes,[2] Persians,[3] Athenians,[4] and Peruvians,[5] (if we are right in supposing the classifications of those nations to have been analogous to Hindu caste,) to have originated in priestcraft and superstition, in ages of intellectual darkness. Whatever may have been its political advantages, and whatever the ambitious aims of its inventors, nothing but a subjection to a truly slavish superstition could have induced the lower ranks especially to submit, for so many generations, and under so many insulting provocations, to so debasing and despotic a tyranny. The distinctions are, unquestionably, religious distinctions, originating in, and maintained by, the operation of Hindu idolatry. The tyranny of the institution is such, as to be perfectly unaccountable on any other supposition, and it is freely acknowledged to owe its dominion

[1] Herodotus, lib. ii. cap. 164.
[2] Ib. lib. i. cap. 101.
[3] Malcolm's History of Persia, i. 205.
[4] Plato's Timæus.
[5] Carli, Lettres sur l'Amérique, Letter 13, as quoted by Mill.

to this cause by the Hindus themselves. It was long since observed by Europeans, that "the influence of priestcraft over superstition is nowhere so visible as in India. All the commerces of life have a strict analogy with the ceremonies of religion."[1] The laws of Manu, and Halhed's Gentoo code, supply complete foundation for all that might be said of the close connexion existing between caste and the idolatrous superstitions of the Hindus. It is by no means analogous, as is sometimes erroneously supposed, to the distinction of ranks amongst Europeans: it is clearly a religious as well as a social distinction; and under no circumstances, in our opinion, can caste exist, without some bond, however imperceptible to ordinary observation, which connects it with the national superstitions.

7. But it may be objected, that however true this may be when predicated of caste amongst the heathen Hindus, a doubt may arise as to this 'sense' of it, as prevalent amongst the native Christians. In charity, we will avoid the positive assertion of their habitual consciousness of its genuine character; but the facts elicited, even in this inquiry, do not admit of our acquitting them of being perfectly sensible of its utter incompatibility with the very principles of Christian morals. This conviction is evinced by Pariars and caste-men alike; they seem to be well aware of its heathen origin, and are not blind to its unchristian character. Amongst them, as amongst the heathen Hindus, caste is lost by defilement, and retained by purity, as those qualities are conceived of, not by the Christian, but by the Hindu religion. Contact with an outcast or Pariar, admission of such a person into their houses, eating food with him, or eating food prepared by his hands: these and similar sources of defilement, as amongst the heathen Hindus, constitute pollution, and subject the parties affected to loss of caste. In one instance, it appears that a Christian native of the Telugu Indra caste was considered to have finally lost caste by assuming, not the European costume generally, but the hat in particular, the lining of which is formed of leather, the skin of a dead animal, a thing unclean in the superstitions of the Hindus. The intercourse still kept up between native Christians and heathens of the same caste, while both alike shun all familiarity with Christian and heathen Pariars, seems to afford additional evidence of the identity of the tie which still binds them together. If, therefore, caste is a superstitious distinction with the one, and we cannot doubt it, then may we reasonably suspect it to be the same with the other. It is one of the evils of heathenism, which has unwarily and most unfortunately been allowed to accompany the native convert in his passage to Christianity.

[1] Orme on the Government, &c. of Indostan.

8. That superstitious influences should retain a secret hold on the mind, after all open subjection to the gross idolatries from which they spring has been professedly disavowed and discarded, is by no means inconsistent with the infirmities of human nature. The converts at Corinth, in the days of St. Paul, were, probably, more intellectually endowed and equally civilized with our Hindu converts at present. The general character of the Greek nation forbids the supposition, that the immediate neighbours of the Athenians were inferior in such respects to the natives of Hindustan. Yet we know that their lingering dread of their national gods caused the holy Apostle much solicitude, and gave occasion for his reproving those stronger-minded persons, who inconsiderately exposed their weaker brethren to the temptations connected with it. Now is it impossible that similar remains of idolatrous superstition may secretly influence the native Hindu Christians in their retention of caste, with all its idolatrously-conceived ceremonial pollutions and perverted notions of purity? May we not apprehend that a more searching inquiry by the missionaries themselves might, perchance, elicit much to confirm the suspicion that a secret dread, perhaps a modified secret worship, of their false national gods may still lurk amongst the professedly Christian observers of caste?

9. With regard to the second branch of this inquiry, the 'extent' to which caste is held by the native Christians of the Vepery mission, we regret to say, that in every instance the parties who appeared before us, Pariars and Tamulians, seemed to be in some sense or some degree tinctured with it. However deeply the former were sensible of its degrading influence, when operating against them, they were all conscious of precisely similar feelings and practices, arising apparently from similar principles, towards those unfortunates, who, in the scale of Hindu castes, are lower than themselves. The adherence of these prejudices, even to the Pariar Christians, is a remarkable evidence of the nature and extent of the evil. But its mode of operation in separating the nearest and dearest relations, even against the will of the parties themselves; its unseemly contempt of what is due to the ministers of Christ; its creation of artificial barriers against the communion in Christian charity between the members of the church; its unhallowed intrusion into the temple, and even to the table of the Lord; all and each mark it as one of those spirits of antichrist, which, we think, God's ministers cannot tolerate without sin, cannot encourage without impiety.

10. Under these convictions, we cannot but believe that those worthy men, who, like Schwartz and Gerické, at the outset of our Protestant missions to the Hindus, unwarily submitted to the continu-

ance of caste among their converts, were deceived as to its necessary character. Had it appeared to them as we view it now, it seems impossible that they should for one moment have permitted any false ideas of expediency to have betrayed them into so fatal a step as its open acknowledgment. In their day, our acquaintance with the science, religion, languages, customs, and national character of the Hindus, was comparatively in its infancy. They were themselves men of holy simplicity, and of the most zealous Christian charity; of that charity which, under no suspicion of imposition or of duplicity, "thinketh no evil," "beareth all things, believeth all things, hopeth all things, endureth all things." We venerate those pious men too well, to believe them capable of consciously tolerating idolatrous practices amongst their converts. Had they viewed caste as we view it, no temporizing policy would have withheld them from urging its downfall. They knew that the convert who was not prepared to give up all for Christ, was not worthy of Him.

11. In conclusion, we desire to record our deep concern at the lamentable fate of young Christian widows. We fear this is in some degree connected, indirectly perhaps, with caste prejudices. Left in utter desolation, without protectors or advisers, frequently at an age which we should deem that of simplest childhood, they are allowed to grow up in a humiliating sense of degradation. Debarred by the criminal customs of their people from all hope of honourable marriage, and without adequate restraints of a moral or religious nature, they too often become unhappy victims of irregular indulgence of passion. Even if innocent of this, they are scarcely free from the imputation of guilt; and under the most favourable circumstances, they are in danger of becoming objects of suspicion, contempt, and obloquy. Any immediate remedy for this evil seems scarcely to be hoped for; but we do entertain a strong trust, that the total abolition of caste might in time favourably affect the unhappy prejudices of the native converts on this important subject.

12. We are aware that this examination may appear to have elicited fewer striking or novel revelations of the evils of caste, than might have been anticipated by persons unacquainted with the native character. Such persons can have little notion of the wariness and astuteness with which the natives evade unpalatable inquiry into their practices and prejudices. It was often only by repeating the same question in various forms, and admonishing them against deceit, that definite answers were finally obtained; and in one instance, we were obliged to relinquish our examination in absolute despair. Enough, however, we think, has been here recorded to warrant our impression of the real character and extent of this evil, and to suggest the

propriety of the general adoption by our Church Societies of some definite plan for resolutely discountenancing or suppressing the continuance of it.

We have the honour to be, my Lord Bishop,
Your Lordship's faithful servants,
(Signed) G. W. MAHON,
" A. R. SYMONDS.

Fort St. George, Madras,
October 29, 1845.

THE following declaration was first drawn up and signed by the Clergy at the Presidency in the year 1848; and having since received the signatures of the Lord Bishop and the Clergy generally, is republished as the united testimony of the ministry of the Church of England:—

WE, the undersigned Bishop and Clergy of the Diocese and Archdeaconry of Madras, having observed with great pain the disabilities to which our native Christian Brethren are subject amongst their countrymen through the Heathen institute of Caste, as well as the unprecedented obstacles to the progress of the Gospel springing from the same source, and perceiving that the disabilities alluded to arise more from relinquishing caste than from renouncing idolatry, deeply deplore and reprobate this system of tyranny, grounded upon a totally false standard of rank, irrespective of virtue, learning, or station.

We desire further to express our extreme concern that such an evil, tending to perpetuate one of the most mischievous features of a false religion, should have found any place in the Christian church: and we are of opinion that the exclusive distinctions of caste, however divested of the idea of ceremonial defilement, are inconsistent with the spirit of the Gospel, which teaches that we are the Body of Christ, and members in particular.

[Here followed the names of the Bishop and his Clergy.]

NOTE.—I most fully concur in this excellent address; the precise purport of which I endeavoured in 1834, both by word of mouth and by repeated letters, to enforce. In the diocese of Calcutta the first thing a Catechumen does is to reject caste *in toto*.

D. CALCUTTA,
Metropolitan.

Madras,
2d February, 1849.

So far as the authority of the Bishops of the Episcopal Church in India, and the general expression of opinion on the part of its ministers, are concerned, the question of caste may now be regarded as settled.

I may remark that many of the missionaries require the members of their churches to sit down together at what they call a *Love Feast*, where all partake of plain food, be it prepared by whomsoever it may.

MISSIONARY TESTIMONIAL.

The following papers will be read with pleasure as evincing the grateful position which missionary labour among the Hindus may secure:—

EXTRACT FROM THE COLOMBO OBSERVER.

Testimonial to the Rev. P. Percival.

About eighteen months ago, at a meeting of the Native pupils and friends of this much respected missionary, a committee was appointed to take the necessary steps for making a public acknowledgment of the many and various benefits that have resulted to the Tamil community, from his arduous labours in this province. The Committee having accomplished the object for which they were nominated, invited the Rev. gentleman to a public meeting, in St. Paul's school-room, on Thursday, the 15th inst., for the purpose of presenting to him the testimonial which had been entrusted to them. A large number of respectable Natives, with a few Europeans—the personal friends of Mr. Percival, and especially invited by the Committee—were present on the occasion.

Peter Parinpanayaga Modaliar, the chairman of the Committee, having been elected to preside over the business of the evening, briefly explained the object of the meeting; and then called upon H. F. Mutukistna, Esq., the Deputy Queen's Advocate, one of Mr. Percival's late pupils, who read the Committee's address to Mr. Percival, and presented the Testimonial, a purse of seventy-five guineas.

The following is the address, together with Mr. Percival's reply:—

ADDRESS.

Jaffna, May 15, 1851.

Reverend Sir,—As the Committee appointed for the purpose a year and a half ago, at a general meeting in Wannarponne of your Native pupils and friends, we have the honour, on the eve of your departure for a season to your own land, to request your acceptance of the accompanying expression, unworthy and inadequate though it may appear, of our grateful appreciation of your untiring and well-directed labours in this province during seventeen years.

We gladly embrace the present opportunity to acknowledge our obligations to the Missionary Institutions of England and America, whose reverend agents have visited North Ceylon. The name of the venerable society which you have so efficiently represented, will ever be associated with the most pleasing recollections of our hearts.

You will always be remembered by us with peculiar affection and esteem. The monuments around us, of your architectural taste and toil, will be equally regarded as appropriate memorials of your multiform enterprise and zeal.

Before your arrival from Bengal, in the year 1834, both the Natives and the European descendants of the town and neighbourhood of Jaffna, were almost entirely dependent for the means of instruction on the Batticotta Seminary, and educational establishments still more remote. At the risk of health, at a sacrifice of comfort, and to some extent of substance, and under circumstances of considerable discouragement, you cheerfully and fully met the crying exigency. Your practical supervision of the department thus seasonably extended in connexion with the Jaffna Mission has proved incalculably beneficial. Many who have been your pupils, are now in the employment of Government or in the service of the Christian Church, holding situations of trust and responsibility in various parts of the island. The eminent skill with which you conducted the intellectual training of those under your care, your earnest and benevolent efforts to improve their position in society, and the deep interest you have continued to manifest in their moral and temporal welfare, have made an indelible impression on our minds.

We regard you as the principal instrument through whom we have enjoyed the educational privileges extended to us by the Colonial Government. We attribute much to your ready co-operation in various measures for the happiness and elevation of the Native community originated by the able and generous agent of this province. You share with him the honour of having organized the Jaffna Friend-in-Need Society, and founded the General Hospital and Dispensary.

You have done credit to our language, and our country has been greatly benefited by your literary labours. Several of your publications are peculiarly adapted to the Hindu mind. Youths in their studies, Christians before their family altars, and the worshippers in Protestant temples, have been materially aided by some of the books you have published. You have furnished us with valuable tracts, composed for our use admirable religious songs, and described to us, according to your Scriptures, "the rise and progress of religion in the soul." We especially congratulate you on the successful completion, in the face of many obstacles, of your laborious revision of the Tamil Bible. It is highly gratifying to us that this new translation has the general approval of your Missionary brethren, we believe without exception, in the Tamil districts of India and Ceylon. We are greatly delighted to be told, by those competent to assure us, of its faithfulness to the Hebrew and Greek originals. And to its simplicity, perspicuity, and idiomatic purity, we are happy ourselves to bear explicit testimony. But we do not, in this address, attempt anything like an enumeration of your many services as a public man. These cannot be overestimated; for we know and feel, that they are intimately and inseparably connected with the great social and religious improvement which, especially during the past twelve years, has taken place in this Province, and we also rejoice to know that the results of your efforts, through the medium of the Tamil press especially, extend far beyond the shores of our own isle.

It is our well-grounded conviction that your engagements were never perfunctorily fulfilled. Your labours have seemed to be invariably directed to specific objects. These have been often original, and always worthy. It is evident that you regard numerical results as of far less importance than right principles and vigorous action. We have never detected in your proceedings anything unbecomingly sectarian. In short, we have been often impressed with the singleness of your aims, the propriety of your decisions, and the remarkable judiciousness of your plans.

It has been to us a source of surprise, and still more of thankfulness, that, amid all your toils, you have enjoyed, apparently, uninterrupted health. We pray that this inestimable blessing may be continued to you by the God whom you serve. May the Providence that separates us, we trust only for a time, guide you in all your ways, prosper your exertions, and spare you for many years to the Tamil population of India and Ceylon. We hope to welcome you back, dear Sir, to the scene of your former labours. But whatever your future circumstances, be always assured of our gratitude, veneration, and love.

With deep emotion, we now bid you farewell,

PETER PARINPANAYAGA, Modr.
A. SINNATAMBY, *alias* F. BROWN.
S. WAYTILINGAM.
C. MOOTATAMBY.
S. MERWIN.
S. MCKINSTRY.
C. ARUNASALAM, THEOPHILUS LESSEY.
C. VERAVAGOE ODEAR.
V. SOLOMON.
RICHARD WATSON.
PHILIP JOSEPH.

REPLY.

Gentlemen,—The position you have assigned me this evening, as you may easily imagine, yields me unmingled pleasure; and the object for which you have invited me hither combines with numerous facts and circumstances to enhance that pleasure, and to create in my breast the most grateful joy. Not the least of these is the fact, that for so long a period such a measure of health has been vouchsafed to me. To the Author of all good I would therefore, in the first place, offer my devout thanksgivings. I feel grateful that He has permitted me to engage in the enterprise of Christian Missions, and thankful for the auspices under which He has graciously continued my services to the present hour.

I am grateful also to the Society under whose patronage I have laboured among you, for the very prompt and liberal support which they have given to those measures that were considered necessary to promote the welfare of the community among whom I have toiled. To the Colonial Government I acknowledge myself under the greatest obligations for pecuniary aid rendered at different times for various objects, and also to the Central School Commission for that assistance which now for several years has given greater extension to our educational plans. To the public at large, both European and Native, I would offer my sincere thanks for the aid they have afforded to promote the various interests of the Central and Branch Stations. To the members of the different Missions I am indebted for much fraternal co-operation in various schemes of good that, without their friendly aid, must have languished, if not utterly failed. To the Bible and Tract Societies, in common with all Missionary Agents, I am greatly indebted for patronage and pecuniary aid, that have given effect to labours which otherwise must have been left in embryo. In meeting you on this occasion, I feel constrained thus publicly to acknowledge my indebtedness for numerous helps that are inseparably identified with my course of public service, and any good that may have been achieved.

Nor can I omit in this connexion to express my admiration of the kind consideration which the ladies, both European and Native, have evinced towards my family now absent in England. Many of those whose names are attached to the tribute of respect intended for Mrs. Percival, were for many years under my eye as pupils. The advantages thus derived are now felt in various relations of life, and not a few are diffusing a charm in the family circle and in society. To these, who live in my warmest affections, and to the ladies generally who are connected with the generous conduct under review, I offer my unfeigned thanks in behalf of Mrs. Percival. The address and the handsome tribute[1] of affection confided to me, I hope to present in person, in the course of a few months, when a reply will be forwarded to the friends who have united their efforts to acknowledge the services Mrs. Percival rendered to the School under our joint superintendence.

The presence, on this interesting occasion, of so numerous and respectable an assembly, affords me high satisfaction, evincing, as it does, the state, and in some degree the extent, of public sympathy in the objects of Christian Missions—objects of far higher moment than the presentation of any tribute of respect to a single individual. I regard this convention of my native friends, and the objects that have brought them together, with lively interest. This manifestation of kindly feeling, as it witnesses to the *past*, brings before me in a pleasing point of view those who in by-gone days were the objects of my solicitude and the recipients of instruction;—it also reveals, on the part of these, the *present* state of grateful minds, authorizing the belief that my plans of labour were well designed, and effectual to the ends contemplated in their formation;—and in the tangible form in which personal respect has been embodied, a testimony is secured that will in *future* days reflect credit on all concerned. The principle that has prompted your combined effort to identify your grateful feelings with benefits received, is most cheering to my own mind; and your spontaneous and generous effort cannot fail to encourage those self-denying friends in England whose Christian zeal and beneficence have originated, sustained, and perpetuated the means of their communication. Your kind consideration of me as the messenger of the distant Churches of Britain, your appreciation of my imperfect efforts to advance your welfare, the honour you confer on me this evening, and the munificent manner in which you have embodied your regards, I most cordially acknowledge, and through you, Gentlemen, as their representatives, I beg to offer to the Committee and friends my best thanks.

Your expressions of affection and esteem are highly gratifying to me; and I am happy to assure you that your best feelings in this regard are most entirely reciprocated. Many of those connected with the tribute presented this evening, some of whom are deprived by distance of the pleasure of being present with us, I have long known, and, because of highly commendable traits of character, esteemed; and it is, therefore, a happiness to me to be assured of the continuance of a friendship I so greatly value.

Although no particular form has been enjoined on me for giving visibility and perpetuity to your valued tribute, it is nevertheless my intention to procure such a memento as may serve to evidence the bond of kindly feeling that unites me with my esteemed and beloved

[1] A purse of forty guineas.

friends at Jaffna. Of this you may hear at some future time, if we are spared.

Your reference to my labours among you is of such a nature as precludes remark, except as it may be conveyed in the expression of deep regret that a work so momentous as that in which I have been engaged, so divine in its appointment, so everlasting in its consequences, and calling for such an entire consecration of the whole man, should have been performed with so little vigour, so little affiance in God, such manifold imperfections, and with so small a felt apprehension of the never-failing succours of an ever-present and omniscient Master. Whilst humbly acknowledging my own unfaithfulness and my utter unworthiness, I would give expression to the readiness of a willing heart to devote myself anew to the service of the Church. As to any beneficial effect that may have followed my labours, I would ascribe that to the Giver of all good things; and as for the acceptance of my person, so for the acceptance of my services, and for any reward with which Divine mercy may be pleased to crown them, I would trust in the alone merits of the Redeemer's sacrifice. "Not unto us, not unto us, O Lord, but unto thy name be all the praise."

The reference you make to the intellectual and moral improvement that has been going on for some years around us, may allow of a few observations on the general advancement of knowledge in the Province. The progress, so evident to all, who have been for any length of time conversant with the history of this part of the Island, is not ascribable to the effort of any single individual, but is the common product of all that has been done by those who are gone and those who still are in the field, and therefore in adverting to that, I shall not be thought guilty of egotism. It is indeed cheering to witness the position the Native mind has attained; and the numerical extent to which the advantages of intellectual culture have been carried is not less marked, than are the instances of a few of the more successful, whose acquirements entitle them to high consideration in the community of which they are distinguished members. The obvious advancement is however seriously disparaged by shortcomings equally palpable, and which, in the mind of the true philanthropist, must create apprehensions of a painful nature. The benefactors of the people of this Province have to mourn over a numerous, and it is feared an increasing, class, who are content to rest in the acquisition of mere knowledge, and its consequent temporal advantages. Knowledge is pursued by the majority as the instrument of secular aggrandizement: but few are seen pushing forward under its guidance into the fields of intellectual and moral excellence, where a richer harvest, of a far more enduring fruit, might be gathered. Under these circumstances, therefore, whilst we congratulate the Native inhabitants at large on the advancement they have actually made in education, conducted in the English language as well as the vernacular tongue, we are constrained to warn the class alluded to, lest they should eventually have to lament over the folly of a conduct that cannot fail to end in disappointment.

It may be assumed that few places of equal population and physical extent, either in this island or on the continent of India, could convene a Native assembly like the present, at once so numerous and so far advanced as regards the advantages which a superior English education confers. Such is your privilege. We congratulate you on this account, but must not omit to remind you of the grave responsibilities of your position. The views of truth you have acquired involve duties, personal and relative, that must be discharged, or your elevation is gained only as the prelude of a fall, that, in the certain retributions of Heaven, will assuredly succeed to slighted mercies. Permit me to commend to your most serious consideration the question of religious truth as one of supreme importance. The ministers of Christ, whose labours have conferred so much upon you, cannot, dare not, omit to press on your acceptance the precious boon of Christianity. Remember the religious truth that has been communicated to your minds, and meditate on its solemn sanctions. "If Christianity be true," it has been well said, "it is tremendously true." Christianity, as presented to you in the truth and beauty of its own heaven-originated purity in the sacred volume, we press on your attention as a matter of personal concernment. It is this superadded to secular knowledge that alone can give it value. Christianity in its vitality and power is the legitimate end of pursuit; this gives to all other advantages grace and beauty, and imparts the finish to the human character.

Some of my native friends, I rejoice to know, have put on Christ. Be you faithful. Let your light shine. Hold forth the word of life, that, however I may have to mourn over others, in respect of you at least "I may rejoice in the day of Christ that I have not run in vain, neither laboured in vain." "Let your conversation be as becometh the Gospel of Christ; that whether I come to see you, or else be absent, I may hear of your affairs, that ye stand fast in one spirit, striving together for the faith of the Gospel." "I commend you to God, and to the word of his grace, which is able to build you up, and to give you an inheritance among them that are sanctified."

Your reference to the eminent individual who is charged with the affairs of Government in this Province, affords me the opportunity of congratulating you on the high political advantages you enjoy under the sway of Her Britannic Majesty. If equal laws, due administration of justice, security of person and property, and freedom from the fear of foreign aggression, be political privileges, then assuredly they are yours. Under the fostering hand of British rule you enjoy an amount of temporal good unknown to your ancestors. Your religious prejudices are tolerated, and you enjoy in the fullest sense the right of private judgment. Among you, public tranquillity and individual rights are never violated by official tyranny; and national works and public institutions have for some years been rapidly multiplying among you.

In your Address you advert to the future: you express the hope that when in England your interests will be remembered and advocated by me. Be assured that your confidence shall not be disappointed. There are several matters of interest connected with the diffusion of knowledge among you, and the advancement of society in Jaffna, which for some time have occupied my own mind and those of others also; and on which I shall not fail to bestow continued attention. This is not the time nor place for details on the point to which I advert. You may, however, indulge the assurance, that whether iu this country or in England, I shall not, whenever opportunity shall offer, omit to advocate your cause, and plead on your behalf. It is my hope institutions may be organized among you whose scope shall be commensurate with your largest desires, and whose well-considered plans and efficient operation shall provide for all your wants.

You express a hope for my return to the scene of my labours. What my destination may be I cannot now say. Be it what it may, I cherish the hope that my lot will be cast with the people of my choice, and that whilst health and ability to labour are vouchsafed, it will be my highest pleasure to promote to the utmost the spiritual and temporal welfare of the inhabitants of this country.

In conclusion, permit me again to tender my grateful acknowledgments for the honour you have this evening conferred upon me, and with the sincerest feelings of regard to bid you all an affectionate

FAREWELL.

The Meeting was further addressed by Mr. Advocate Mutukistna, Rev. L. Spaulding, Rev. B. C. Meigs, A. Ambalavarner, Esq., Messrs. N. Niles, G. Hallock, and S. Manicavasager. An excellent address in Tamil, from the inhabitants of Cattavelly, was presented to Mr. Percival in the course of the evening by Mr. John White, who had been deputed to read it at the Meeting.